Trauma and the Body

The Norton Series on Interpersonal Neurobiology
Daniel J. Siegel, M.D., Series Editor

The field of mental health is in a tremendously exciting period of growth and conceptual reorganization. Independent findings from a variety of scientific endeavors are converging in an interdisciplinary view of the mind and mental well-being. An "interpersonal neurobiology" of human development enables us to understand that the structure and function of the mind and brain are shaped by experiences, especially those involving emotional relationships.

The Norton Series on Interpersonal Neurobiology will provide cutting-edge, multidisciplinary views that further our understanding of the complex neurobiology of the human mind. By drawing on a wide range of traditionally-independent fields of research—such as neurobiology, genetics, memory, attachment, complex systems, anthropology, and evolutionary psychology—these texts will offer mental health professionals a review and synthesis of scientific findings often inaccessible to clinicians. These books aim to advance our understanding of human experience by finding the unity of knowledge, or "consilience," that emerges with the translation of findings from numerous domains of study into a common language and conceptual framework. The series will integrate the best of modern science with the healing art of psychotherapy.

A NORTON PROFESSIONAL BOOK

Trauma and the Body

A Sensorimotor Approach to Psychotherapy

Pat Ogden, Kekuni Minton, and Clare Pain

Series Editor's Foreword by *Daniel J. Siegel, M.D.*

Foreword by *Bessel van der Kolk, M.D.*

W. W. Norton & Company
New York • London

For information about permission to reproduce selections from this book, write to
Permissions, W. W. Norton & Company, Inc., 500 Fifth Avenue, New York, NY 10110

Composition and book design by: MidAtlantic Books & Journals
Manufacturing by: RR Donnelley-Harrisonburg
Production Manager: Leeann Graham

Library of Congress Cataloging-in-Publication Data

Ogden, Pat.
    Trauma and the body : a sensorimotor approach to psychotherapy / by Pat Ogden,
Kekuni Minton, and Clare Pain.
        p. cm.
    "A Norton Professional book."
    Includes bibliographical references and index.
    ISBN 0-393-70457-2
    1. Mind and body therapies. 2. Psychic trauma—Treatment. 3. Self. 4. Body
language. 5. Body, Human—Psychological aspects. 6. Sensorimotor integration.
I. Minton, Kekuni. II. Pain, Clare. III. Title.

RC489.M53 0353 2006
616.89′1—dc22

                                                                    2005049533

ISBN 13: 978-0-393-70457-0
ISBN 10: 0-393-70457-2

W. W. Norton & Company, Inc., 500 Fifth Avenue, New York, N.Y. 10110
www.wwnorton.com
W. W. Norton & Company Ltd., Castle House, 75/76 Wells St., London W1T 3QT
    5 6 7 8 9 0

In memory of
Martha Barth Ogden,
1904–2001

Contents

Acknowledgments

THIS BOOK WAS INFLUENCED AND SHAPED by many individuals who supported our writing, inspired our thinking, acted as sounding boards, and mentored us over three decades of professional development. We are indebted to the Board of Advisors of the Sensorimotor Psychotherapy Institute, many of whom regularly contribute to the development and scientific understanding of our work: David Baldwin, Emilie Conrad, Ron Kurtz, Ruth Lanius, Reo Leslie, Ian Macnaughton, Peter Melchior, Melissa Miller, Martha Stark, Clare Pain, Allan Schore, Ellert Nijenhuis, Kathy Steele, Onno Van der Hart, and Bessel van der Kolk.

In particular, Bessel van der Kolk has strongly influenced our work, and we extend to him our heartfelt appreciation for countless discussions, feedback, inspiration, and unwavering support in furthering our understanding of neuroscience and of sensorimotor theory and technique. Additionally, we are most grateful for the practical, clear theories about dissociation and action systems developed by Onno van der Hart, Kathy Steele, and Ellert Nijenhuis, and the dynamic collaboration we have enjoyed with them, which has changed the way we think about trauma and how we work with clients. We also want to thank Allan Schore, who set aside time and effort to help us understand the interface between neurological development and clinical practice, and whose work has had a profound effect on how we understand psychotherapy. And we are grateful for Ruth Lanius's confidence in this work and in its relevance for even the most traumatized individual, and her contributions to this book, including her clarity about the possible implications of current neuroscience research for trauma treatment.

We also wish to acknowledge colleagues who have influenced our thinking over the years: Jon Allen, Betty Cannon, Rich Chefetz, Marylene Cloitre, Christine Courtois, Charles Figley, Judith Herman, Ilan Kutz, Sue Kutz, Ulrich Lanius, Rudolpho Llinas, Karlen Lyons-Ruth, Sandy McFarlane, Laurie

Pearlman, Steven Porges, Pat Sable, Allen Scheflin, Judith Schore, Arieh Shalev, Dan Siegel, Marion Solomon, and David Spiegel.

Many of the somatically-oriented theories and interventions described in this book are common to body psychotherapy. The one pioneer in this field who deserves an enormous thank-you is Ron Kurtz, who for 30-plus years has been our mentor and primary inspiration in somatic psychology and whose ideas and interventions are foundational to sensorimotor psychotherapy. We are also grateful to many others in this and related fields: Susan Aposhyan, Paul Joel, Marianne Bentzon, Bill Bowen, Christine Caldwell, Emilie Conrad, Fred Donaldson, Annie Duggan, Peter Levine, Richard Strozzi Heckler, Emmett Hutchins, Jim Kepner, Aubrey Lande, Ian Macnaughton, Lisbeth Marcher, Al Pesso, Thomas Pope, Marjorie Rand, Bert Shaw, Kevin Smith, Betta van der Kolk, and Halko Weiss. And our deep appreciation goes to Peter Melchior, who died before this book was published, for hours of brainstorming about the structure and movement of the body and for helping design the somatic resources map (in Chapter 10) during a long summer afternoon several years back.

So many people contributed directly to the writing of this book. We thank Christine Caldwell and Charles Figley, who were the first to encourage us to write, and Dan Siegel, who prompted us to submit a proposal to Norton and so generously helped us to fine-tune our terminology just before press. David Baldwin, Lana Epstein, Julian Ford, Mary Sue Moore, and Steven Porges reviewed specific chapters, and we are most appreciative of their help. We are indebted to Bonnie Mark Goldstein for giving so much valuable time, energy, and skill to this project, seeing it through to the very end. Kathy Steele deserves a special thank-you for freely offering us encouragement, expert advice, and editing par excellence when the going got rough; as does Onno van der Hart for his generous and steadfast support in the form of concept development, superb editorial help with each chapter down to the eleventh hour, and emotional encouragement. And last, this book is a better book because of Janina Fisher's exceptional editing skills combined with her grasp of sensorimotor psychotherapy theory and technique, and we extend our gratitude to her for being our "fourth author"— reviewing, rewriting troublesome sections, and adding her input to every chapter of this book.

The founding trainers of Sensorimotor Psychotherapy Institute, Christina Dickinson and Dan Thomas, joined more recently by senior trainers Deirdre Fay and Janina Fisher, have participated in countless brainstorming sessions, and we thank them for their continuing collaboration, wisdom, emotional support, and dedication to teaching this work. We are grateful to Jennifer Fox who so competently and cheerfully kept the Sensorimotor Psychotherapy Institute going when Pat was immersed in writing, and Jennifer Ryder who went the extra mile to complete the references. And we are most appreciative of the people at Norton: Deborah Malmud, Andrea Costella, Michael McGandy, Casey Ruble, and Margaret Ryan for their patience and helpful advice along the way.

On a more personal note, Pat would like to thank Susan Aposhyan, the late Paul Joel, Susan Melchior, Ria Moran, and Kali Rosenblum for their unflagging emotional support over the years of writing this book. Heartfelt appreciation goes to the children of all ages in her extended family for their laughter and patience: Darci Hill; her godchildren, Jovanna Stepan, Allison Joel, and Quinsen Joel; and, most especially, her son, Brennan Arnold, for his steadfast emotional and practical support. Kekuni would like to thank his family, Terrell Smith Minton and Kealoha Malie Minton, for their incredible patience and support in the writing of this book. Clare would like to thank her family and friends, especially Judy, Bill, Christine, and Josh for their sanity and humor.

Lastly, we express heartfelt appreciation to our students and clients who have challenged us, inspired us, and ultimately taught us most of what we know about psychotherapy.

Series Editor's Foreword

Daniel J. Siegel, M. D.

AN INTERPERSONAL NEUROBIOLOGY PERSPECTIVE draws on a broad range of disciplines to create an integrated picture of human experience and the development of well-being. Using parallel findings from various fields of science, clinical practice, and the expressive and contemplative arts, this consilient approach to understanding "being human" attempts to weave a wide vision of our subjective experience. By bringing together often disparate ways of knowing, the aim of this endeavor is to expand our view of the mind and promote well-being in individuals, couples, families, communities, and our larger society.

Trauma has a huge impact on all aspects of our human civilization and individual lives. Yet, the reality of trauma is often overlooked in societal approaches to public policy, education, and the resources offered for the promotion of mental health. How can the pain of trauma be so often missed? When we write books or formulate approaches to an issue, we are often filled with concepts and words that distance us from the experiential reality of the topic at hand. Often we think in words, creating abstract ideas framed by linguistic packets of information, such as these you are reading right now. Such word-based theoretical frameworks are important in pulling us out of the immediacy of moment-to-moment experience, allowing us to gain a perspective on the larger picture than what direct sensation by itself allows. The benefit of this experiential distance is to give us a clearer vision of the whole by creating a wide perspective of a broad entity. But abstract ideas symbolized by words can also make it difficult for us to sense the "lived" details of our human experience. Such experiential knowing is often created best through direct sensation. Without the balance of the non-linguistic world of images, feelings, and sensations, the seduction of words and ideas can keep us from direct experience in our daily lives and professional work. On a societal level, such an imbalance can keep us in a state of denial. In a psychotherapeutic setting, focusing primarily on word-based thinking and narratives can keep therapy at a surface level and trauma may remain unresolved. An overemphasis on logical, linguistic, linear, and literal thinking may tilt the balance of our minds away from the important sensorimotor, holistic, autobiographical, stress-reducing, image-based self-regulatory functions of our non-verbal neural modes of processing. Linking these two very different but important ways of knowing is the essence of creating balance in our lives and in our understanding of complex human experiences such as trauma.

The central idea of interpersonal neurobiology is that integration is at the heart of well-being. Integration is the linking of differentiated elements into a functional whole. With an integrated system, our lives become flexible, adaptive, coherent, energized, and stable. Without this integration, the flow of our minds moves toward rigidity or chaos. In this way, trauma can be seen to fundamentally impair integration within an individual, dyad, family, or community. Posttraumatic states are filled with experiences of rigidity or chaos that continue the devastation of trauma long past the initial overwhelming events. By integrating many domains of our experience within a receptive form of awareness, we develop a more connected and harmonious flow in our lives. Such linkages include implicit with explicit memory, left- with right-hemisphere modes of processing, and mindful awareness with bodily sensation. Our minds have an innate movement toward integration and healing that may often be blocked after trauma. Releasing this drive toward well-being is a central goal of psychotherapy that enables the creation of integrated states that establish adaptive self-regulation. The therapist can utilize the view that neural integration, a coherent mind, and empathic relationships form three sides of a triangle of mental health that can be seen as the focus of healing in the process of psychotherapy.

Within an interpersonal neurobiology view of therapy, as we "sift" the mind, we attempt to integrate the sensations, images, feelings, and thoughts that comprise the flow of energy and information that defines our mental lives. Sensations include the non-verbal textures created by the body that involve the state of the muscles in our limbs and face, our internal organs, impulses to act, and actual movements. Sifting the mind with curiosity, openness, acceptance, and love—the "coal" that warms the heart of change—enables us to integrate these many elements of our mind in new ways that permit healing to emerge. As we focus on these many domains of the mind, the empathic communication within psychotherapy enables new states of coherence to develop as neural integration—the physiological linkage of the widely distributed neural patterns in the brain and body-proper—evolves and new forms of healthy, adaptive self-regulation are established.

In *Trauma and the Body*, Pat Ogden and her colleagues offer us deep experiential insights that can awaken our minds to the wisdom of the body. By turning toward the body with mindful awareness of here-and-now sensory experience, the pathways to integration are opened and healing becomes possible. This receptive awareness involves an accepting, loving, non-judgmental attention that may be the essence of how the mind can move from chaos and rigidity in non-integrated states to the coherent functioning that emerges with integration. Mindful awareness of the body enables the individual to move directly into previously warded-off states of activation, which left the body out of the experience of mental life following acute or chronic traumatization.

With beautifully articulated applications of neurobiology extensively referencing state-of-the art scientific literature, the authors create an exquisite theoretical framework in the first half of the book. This framework sets the stage for the "whole forest" view that emphasizes why clinicians should intellectually and linguistically understand the central importance of the non-intellectual, non-linguistic neural and interpersonal processing of the individual. The mind, often unaware of these sensory and motoric states of the body, can finally achieve the integration that adaptations to trauma had blocked for so long.

The second half of the book offers a phase-oriented description of the "how-to" behind the practical aspects of these important therapeutic interactions. A sensorimotor approach to psychotherapy is more than just using the body as another frame of reference for rationalizing good psychotherapy. Rather, turning to the sensations, impulses, and movements of the body enables the therapist to open the crucial world of the non-verbal for direct processing within mindful awareness that is useful for a range of psychotherapeutic approaches.

Focusing on the body for the achievement of mental well-being is an approach spanning thousands of years of practice in the contemplative traditions. Somehow, in modern times, we have forgotten the hard-earned wisdom of these ancient traditions. Modern neural science clearly points to the central role of the body in the creation of emotion and meaning. Though some interpretations of neuroscience think of the "single skulled brain" as the source of all that is mental, this restricted view misses the scientifically established reality that most brains live in a body and are part of a social world of other brains. The brain is hard-wired to connect to other minds, to create images of others' intentional states, affective expressions, and bodily states of arousal that, through our mirror neuron system's fundamental capacity to create emotional resonance, serve as the gateway of empathy. In this way, we see that the mind is both relational and embodied. The authors of this wise text pay careful attention to the scientific reality of the embodied and relational mind in understanding the impact of trauma and in delineating a pathway toward healing. The interactions between therapist and client/patient seen through the light of this attachment-informed, somatic, and sensory-focused work enables clinicians of all persuasions to understand practical approaches to psychological growth and development in a new and useful light. While this perspective is based on extensive clinical practice, its theoretical framework is consistent with science. Bringing a sensorimotor focus to therapy pushes the envelope of our understanding of the interface between subjective experience and "objective" research findings into a wonderfully new realm: The authors have taken on the important challenge of putting words to a world without words. It is my pleasure to introduce you to their important contribution to understanding the relational and embodied mind in The Norton Series on Interpersonal Neurobiology. Let it bathe all the dimensions of your mind, and let us know your experience.

Foreword

Bessel A. van der Kolk, M.D.

THE DRAMATIC ADVANCES IN NEUROSCIENCE over the past decade have led to important new insights into how mind and brain process traumatic experiences. The work of neuroscientists such as Antonio Damasio, Joseph LeDoux, Jaak Panksepp, Steve Porges, Rodolfo Llinas, and Richie Davidson has shown that living creatures more or less automatically respond to incoming sensory information with relatively stable action patterns: predictable behaviors that can be elicited over and over again when they are presented with similar input. The function of the "mind"—that extraordinary human capacity to observe, know, and predict—is to inhibit, organize, and modulate those automatic responses, thereby helping us manage and preserve our relationships with our fellow human beings, on whom we so desperately depend for meaning, company, affirmation, protection, and connection.

However, the mind, although able to organize our feelings and impulses, does not seem to be particularly well equipped to entirely abolish unacceptable emotions, thoughts, and impulses. In fact, it seems to be geared more toward creating a rationale for troublesome behavior (e.g., "it's for your own good" or "to create a better world") than toward eliminating it. As a consequence, people seem to be condemned to accommodating their "irrational" longings and unacceptable feelings of fear, anger, helplessness, lust, and despair without ever being able to completely master them.

Fundamentally, life is about making our way in the world, and how we do that depends on the hard-wiring of our brains. This hard-wiring is derived from the evolutionary legacy that we more or less share with all living creatures, combined with the imprints of our own personal early experiences.

The basic blueprint of our map of the world and the way we move through it consists of connections between the arousal system of the brain (the reptilian brain) and the interpretive system in the mammalian brain (the limbic system). These connections organize how all animals, including humans, organize their responses to sensory stimuli—and these responses, first and foremost, concern movement.

Neuroscience research has come a long way in helping to clarify why the same stimulus that pleases some people, irritates others. Emotional responses occur not by conscious choice but by disposition: limbic brain structures such as the amygdala tag incoming sensory stimuli to determine their emotional significance. The interpretation by these subcortical brain structures is based largely on prior experience, which determines our disposition to approach or avoid whatever we encounter. Moreover, it is becoming more and more apparent that *response* refers to an action we are *impelled* to take—that is, how we are *physically* inclined to move after receiving any particular stimulus. Neuroscience has confirmed earlier observations by scientists such as Darwin and William James that *physical, bodily* feelings form the substrate of the emotional states that shape the quality of our decision-making efforts and the solutions we create to deal with particular dilemmas. These physical feelings in turn, propel the human organism to take certain actions: as Roger Sperry, who won the Nobel Prize for medicine in 1981, said, "The brain is an organ of and for movement: The brain is the organ that moves the muscles. It does many other things, but all of them are secondary to making our bodies move" (1952, p. 298). Sperry claimed that even perception is secondary to movement: "In so far as an organism perceives a given object, it is prepared to respond to it. . . . The presence or absence of adaptive reaction potentialities, ready to discharge into motor patterns, makes the difference between perceiving and not perceiving" (1952, pp. 299–300).

The neuroscientist Rodolfo Llinas summarized the relationship between action and the brain as follows: In order to make its way in the world any actively moving creature must be able to predict what is to come and find its way where it needs to go. Prediction occurs by the formation of a sensorimotor image, based on hearing, vision, or touch, which contextualizes the external world and compares it with the existing the internal map. "The . . . comparison of internal and external worlds [results in] appropriate action: a movement is made" (Llinas, 2001, p. 38). People experience the combinations of sensations and an urge for physical activation as an emotion.

Both Charles Darwin (1872) and Ivan Pavlov (1928) clearly understood that the goal of emotions is to bring about physical movement: to help the organism get out of harm's way, in the case of negative emotions, and to move it in the direction of the source of the stimulus in the case of positive ones. Darwin, in particular, pointed out that human beings are not any different from animals in this regard. Emotions activate the organism to respond in prescribed ways, such as defending oneself, preparing to fight, turning one's back on someone, or approaching someone for greater intimacy and care. In short, emotions serve as guides for action.

Nina Bull, Jaak Panksepp, Antonio Damasio, and others have demonstrated that each particular emotional state automatically activates distinct action tendencies: a programmed sequence of actions. When people process incoming perceptions, they interpret the new information by comparing it with prior experience. On the basis of this comparison the organism predicts the outcome of various possible actions and organizes a physical response to the incoming stimulus. As Damasio said, "Physical actions are creating the context for mental actions; bottom-up processes are affecting upper level processes. [This is] the feeling of what is happening" (1999, p. 27). Damasio (1999) further explained:

> It makes good housekeeping sense that [the brain] structures governing attention and structures processing emotion should be in the vicinity of one another. Moreover, it also makes good housekeeping sense that all of these structures should be in the vicinity of those which regulate and signal body state. This is because the consequences of having emotion and attention are entirely related to the fundamental business of managing life within the organism, while, on the other hand, it is not possible to manage life and maintain homeostatic balance without data on the current state of the organism's body proper. (p. 28)

What makes people unique in the animal kingdom is their flexibility: their capacity to make choices about how they respond to their environment. This flexibility is the result of the property of the human neocortex to integrate a large variety of different pieces of information, to attach meaning to both the incoming input and the physical urges (tendencies) that these evoke, and to apply logical thought to calculate the long-term effect of any particular action. This allows people to continually discover new ways of dealing with incoming information and to modify their responses on the basis of the lessons they have learned in a much more complex way than the conditioning we see in dogs and other animals.

However, this capacity to respond in a flexible manner emerges only slowly over the course of human development and is easily disrupted. Small children have little control over their crying and clinging when they feel abandoned, nor do they have much control over expressing their excitement when they are delighted. Even adults are prone to engage in automatic behaviors when they are stirred by intense emotions. They are likely to execute whatever "action tendency" is associated with any particular emotion: confrontation and inhibition with anger; physical paralysis with fear, physical collapse in response to helplessness; an inexorable impulse to move toward sources of joy, such as running toward people we love, followed by an urge to embrace them, and so on. Since at least 1889 (Janet) it has been noted that traumatized individuals are prone to respond to reminders of the past by automatically engaging in physical actions that must have been appropriate at the time of the trauma but that are now irrelevant. As Janet noted: "Traumatized patients are continuing the action, or rather the attempt at action, which began when the thing happened and they exhaust themselves in these everlasting recommencements" (1919/1925, p. 663).

The current discoveries in the neurosciences about the automatic activation of hormonal secretions, emotional states, and physical reactions in response to sensory input have once again confronted psychology with a reality that was first emphatically articulated by Freud: that most human actions and motivations are based on processes that are not under conscious control. The implications of these discoveries are particularly relevant for understanding and treating traumatized individuals. Realizing that they are prone to activate automatic trauma-related hormonal secretions and physical action patterns clarifies why they would tend to respond to certain triggers with irrational—that is, subcortically initiated—responses that are irrelevant and even harmful in the context of present demands: They may blow up in response to minor provocations, freeze when frustrated, and become helpless in the face of trivial challenges. Without a historical context to understand the somatic and motoric carryover from the past, their emotions appear out of place and their actions bizarre. These symptoms of an uncompleted past tend to become a source of shame and embarrassment to those who experience them.

One of the most robust findings of the neuroimaging studies of traumatized people is that, under stress, the higher brain areas involved in "executive functioning"—planning for the future, anticipating the consequences of one's actions, and inhibiting inappropriate responses—become less active (van der Kolk, in press). Just like small children loose the veneer of socialization and throw temper tantrums when they are frustrated, traumatized adults are prone to revert to primitive self-protective responses when they perceive certain stimuli as a threat. Once sensory triggers of past trauma activate the emotional brain to engage in its habitual protective devices, the resulting changes in sympathetic and parasympathetic activation interfere with effective executive function: The higher brain functions have less control over behavior, causing a behavioral "regression." Without well-functioning rational brains, individuals are prone to revert to rigid "fixed action patterns": the automatic behavioral flight, fight, or freeze responses that are our evolutionary heritage of dealing with threat, and our individual implicit memories of how our own bodies once attempted to cope with the threat of being overwhelmed. The legacy of trauma is that these somatic (i.e., endocrine and motoric) patterns can be triggered by the slightest provocations, reactivating the physical response of the organism to past terror, abandonment, and helplessness, sometimes in exquisite detail.

Psychology and psychiatry, as disciplines, have paid scant attention to the behavioral (i.e., muscular, organic) responses that are triggered by trauma reminders and, instead, have narrowly focused on either the neurochemistry or the emotional states associated with the reminders. They thereby may have lost sight of the forest for the trees: Both neurochemistry and emotions are activated *in order to* bring about certain bodily postures and physical movements that are meant to protect, engage, and defend. The dramatic advances in pharmacotherapy have helped enormously to control some of the neurochemical abnormalities caused by trauma, but they obviously are not capable of correcting the imbalance.

The fact that triggers reinstate some of the hormonal and motoric responses to the original trauma raises some important issues: The DSM-IV definition of posttraumatic stress disorder (PTSD) emphasizes physiological hyperarousal in response to traumatic reminders. However, trauma is not simply a physiological response. The essence of trauma is utter helplessness combined with abandonment by potentially protective caregivers. Probably the best animal model for this phenomenon is that of "inescapable shock," in which creatures are tortured without being unable to *do anything* to affect the outcome of events (van der Kolk, Greenberg, Boyd, & Krystal, 1985). This causes them to collapse and stop trying to fight or escape. For human beings the best predictor of something becoming traumatic seems to be a situation in which they no longer can imagine a way out; when fighting or fleeing no longer is an option and they feel overpowered and helpless. As Darwin already pointed out: the emotions of fear, disgust, anger, or depression are signals to communicate to others to back off or protect. When a person is traumatized, these emotions do not produce the results for which they were intended: The predator does not back off, desist, or protect, and whatever action the traumatized person takes fails to restore a sense of safety.

After one or more confrontations with the futility of their emotions and automatic action patterns to restore safety and control, many traumatized children and adults seem to lose the capacity to utilize their emotions as guides for effective action. Their emotions may get activated, but they don't recognize what they are feeling. This is called an inability to verbally identify the meaning of physical sensations and muscle activation, *alexithymia.* This inability to recognize what is going on inside—to correctly identify sensations, emotions, and physical states—causes individuals to be out of touch with their needs and incapable of taking care of them, and often extends to having difficulty appreciating the emotional states and needs of those around them. Unable to gauge and modulate their own internal states, they habitually collapse in the face of threat or lash out in response to minor irritations. The hallmark of daily life becomes futility.

When contemporary trauma studies rediscovered the profound disruptions in the subjective experience of physical sensations and the automatic activation of fixed action patterns in traumatized children and adults (the French psychiatrist Pierre Janet had done extensive research on this issue a century ago, but we did not recognize his contribution till later), the mainstream therapeutic community found itself at a loss as to how to address the deficits in those areas. One point was clear: The rational, executive brain—the mind, the part that needs to be functional in order to engage in the process of psychotherapy—has very limited capacity to squelch sensations, control emotional arousal, and change fixed action patterns. The problem that Damasio (1999) articulated had to be solved:

> We use our minds not to discover facts but to hide them. One of things the screen hides most effectively is the body, our own body, by which I mean, the ins and outs of it, its interiors. Like a veil thrown over the skin to secure its modesty, the screen partially removes from the mind the inner states of the body, those that constitute the flow of life as it wanders in the journey of each day. The elusiveness of emotions and feelings is probably . . . an indication of how we cover to the presentation of our bodies, how much mental imagery masks the reality of the body. (p. 28)

Given that understanding and insight are the main staples of both cognitive–behavioral therapy (CBT) and psychodynamic psychotherapy, the principal therapies currently taught in professional schools, the discoveries in neuroscience research have been difficult to integrate with contemporary therapeutic practice. Neither CBT nor psychodynamic therapeutic techniques pay much attention to the experience and interpretation of physical sensations and preprogrammed physical action patterns. Given that Joseph LeDoux had shown that, at least in rats, "emotional memories are forever" and that the dorsolateral prefrontal cortex, the center for insight, understanding, and planning for the future, has virtually no connecting pathways to affect the workings of the emotional brain, the best verbal therapies can offer is to help people inhibit the automatic physical actions that their emotions provoke. In short, verbal therapies can help people with "anger management" (i.e., quieting themselves down before blowing off the handle) such as in counting to ten and taking deep breaths.

The realization that insight and understanding are not enough to keep traumatized people from regularly feeling and acting as if they were traumatized all over again forced clinicians to explore techniques that offer the possibility of reprogramming these automatic physical responses. It was only natural that such techniques would have to involve methods that address people's awareness of their internal sensations and their physical action patterns. Of course, many different cultures have healing traditions that activate and utilize physical movement and breath, such as yoga, chi qong, tai chi, and other Asian and African traditions. However, in the West, approaches that involve working with sensation and movement have been fragmented and have remained outside the mainstream of medical and psychological teaching. Nevertheless, working with sensation and movement has been extensively explored in such techniques as focusing, sensory awareness, Feldenkrais, Rolfing, the F. M. Alexander Technique, body-mind centering, somatic experiencing, Pesso–Boyden psychotherapy, Rubenfeld synergy, authentic movement, the Hakomi method, Middendorf breath work, and many others. Although each of these techniques involves very sophisticated approaches, the nature and effects of these practices are not easily articulated, and, as Don Hanlon Johnson noted, their meanings are not easily captured in the dominant intellectual categories. The most noteworthy integration of body work and mainstream science occurred when Nikolaas Tinbergen discussed the Alexander technique in his 1973 Nobel Prize acceptance speech.

During the past few decades, several body-oriented practitioners specifically have addressed the somatosensory impact of trauma. To my mind, the three outstanding teachers in this area—those who have had the most profound influence on myself and many of the clinicians I work with—have been Pat Ogden, the author of this book, Peter Levine, and Al Pesso. After decades of training in Rolfing, Hakomi, and other body-oriented techniques, Pat Ogden integrated the psychological and neurobiological effects of trauma with body work and has founded a new school of therapy that incorporates work with sensorimotor processes firmly anchored in attachment theory, neuroscience, and traditional psychotherapeutic practice.

Sensorimotor psychotherapy is sensitive to the fact that most trauma occurs in the context of interpersonal relationships. This reality means that trauma involves boundary violations, loss of autonomous action, and loss of self-regulation. When people lack sources of support and sustenance, such as is common with abused children, women trapped in domestic violence, and incarcerated men, they are likely to learn to respond to abuse and threats with mechanistic compliance or resigned submission. Particularly if the brutalization has been repetitive and unrelenting, they are vulnerable to ongoing physiological dysregulation (i.e., states of extreme hypo- and hyperarousal) accompanied by physical immobilization. Often, these responses become habitual. As a result, many victims develop chronic problems initiating effective, independent action, even in situations where, rationally, they would be expected to be able to stand up for themselves and "take care of things."

Many traumatized individuals learn to dissociate and compartmentalize: They may be competent and focused most of the time, but they may suddenly collapse into primitive and inflexible states of helplessness and immobilization when they are confronted with situations or sensations that remind them of the past. Some may remain aware of what they are feeling, what is going on around them, about potential escape routes, and physical impulses to protect themselves, whereas others space out and lose contact with both their internal sensations and what is going on in their environment. Many clinicians, when assessing for dissociative problems, focus on emotions and behaviors. However, sensorimotor psychotherapy specifically deals with dissociative symptoms that involve body sensations, movement disorders, dysregulated physiological arousal, lack of body sensations, and reexperiencing the trauma in somatosensory fragments.

Describing traumatic experiences in conventional verbal therapy is likely to activate implicit memories in the form of trauma-related physical sensations, physiological dysregulation, involuntary movements, and the accompanying emotions of helplessness, fear, shame, and rage, without providing the resources to process these nonverbal remnants of the past. When this sequence occurs, trauma victims are likely to feel that it still is not safe to deal with the trauma; instead they will tend to seek a supportive relationship in the present. The therapist thereby becomes a refuge from a life marked by ineffectiveness and futility.

Sensorimotor psychotherapy directly addresses the fact that the traumatic past continues to influence how people perceive themselves and their surroundings, and how they position themselves in relationship to the world around them. Rather than focusing on how people make meaning of their experience—their narrative of the past—the focus is on clients' physical self-experience and self-awareness. Body-oriented therapies are predicated on the notion that past experience is embodied in present physiological states and action tendencies: The trauma is reenacted in breath, gestures, sensory perceptions, movement, emotion, and thought. The role of the therapist is to facilitate self-awareness and self-regulation, rather than to witness and interpret the trauma. Therapy involves working with sensations and action tendencies in order to discover new ways of orienting and moving through the world.

Working with traumatized individuals entails the overcoming of several major obstacles. One is that, although human contact and attunement are cardinal elements of physiological self-regulation, interpersonal trauma often results in a fear of intimacy. For many people the anticipation of closeness and attunement automatically evokes implicit memories of hurt, betrayal, and abandonment. As a result, feeling seen and understood—which helps most people feel calm and in control—may precipitate a reliving of the trauma in individuals who have been victimized in intimate relationships. Therefore, before trust can be established, it is important to help clients create a *physical* sense of control by working on the establishment of physical boundaries, exploring ways of regulating physiological arousal (using breath and body movement), and focusing on regaining a physical sense of being able to defend and protect themselves. It may be useful to explore previous experiences of safety and competence and to activate memories of what it feels like to experience pleasure, enjoyment, focus, power, and effectiveness. Working with trauma is as much about the person remembering how he or she survived as it is about addressing what was broken. As Pat Ogden emphasizes in this book, "Discover[ing] the abandoned empowering active defenses that were ineffective at the time of the trauma."

Another problem is that, neurobiologically speaking, the only part of the conscious brain that is capable of influencing emotional states (which are localized in the limbic system) is the medial prefrontal cortex, the part that is involved in introspection (i.e., attending to the internal state of the organism). Various neuroimaging studies reviewed in this book have shown decreased activation of the medial prefrontal cortex in individuals with PTSD (Lanius, 2002; Clark & McFarlane, 2000). This means that traumatized individuals, as a rule, have serious problems attending to their inner sensations and perceptions. When asked to focus on internal sensations, they tend to feel overwhelmed or deny having any. When they finally do pay attention to their inner world, they usually encounter a minefield of trauma-related perceptions, sensations, and emotions (van der Kolk & Ducey, 1989). They often feel disgusted with themselves and usually have a very negative body image; as far as they are concerned, the less attention they pay to their bodies, the better. Yet one cannot learn to take care of oneself without being in touch with the demands and requirements of one's physical self.

Hence, Pat Ogden proposes that therapy is about learning to become a careful observer of the ebb and flow of internal experience, mindfully noticing whatever thoughts, feelings, body sensations, and impulses emerge. Traumatized individuals, first and foremost, need to learn that it is safe to have feelings and sensations. In this process it is critical for clients to become aware that bodily experience never remains static. Unlike at the moment of a trauma, when everything seems to freeze in time, physical sensations and emotions are in a constant state of flux.

In order to deal with the past, traumatized people need to activate their medial prefrontal cortex, their capacity for introspection. Therapy needs to help them develop a deep curiosity about their internal experience. This curiosity is essential in learning to identify their physical sensations and to translate their emotions and sensations into communicable language—communicable, most of all, to themselves. Once people realize that their internal sensations continuously shift and change, that they have considerable control over their physiological states, and that remembering the past does not inevitably result in overwhelming emotions, they can start to explore ways to actively influence the organization of their internal landscape. As patients learn to tolerate being aware of their physical experience, they discover physical impulses and options that they had abandoned for the sake of survival during the trauma. These impulses and options manifest themselves in subtle body movements such as twisting, turning, or backing away. Amplifying these physical impulses and experimenting with ways to modify them ultimately bring the incomplete trauma-related action tendencies to completion.

Traumatized people often lose the effective use of fight or flight defenses and respond to perceived threat with immobilization. Sensorimotor psychotherapy helps them reorient to the present by learning to attend to nontraumatic stimuli. This focus opens them up to learning from new experiences, rather than reliving the past over and over again, without modification by subsequent information. Once they learn to reorient themselves to the present, individuals can experiment with responding to perceived threats by rediscovering their lost capacities to actively defend and protect themselves.

Sensorimotor psychotherapy is based on the premise that, in order to overcome the tendency to be trapped in the past, the traumatized person needs to (1) become aware of old automatic maladaptive action tendencies, (2) learn to inhibit the initial impulses, (3) experiment with various alternatives to bring to completion the incomplete, frozen actions that proved to be futile at the moment of the trauma, and (4) practice ways to execute alternative, effective actions. Pat Ogden's book is the first work to integrate our knowledge of body-oriented therapy, neuroscience, and attachment theory into a composite treatment method. Hopefully, after this wonderful integration, therapy for traumatized individuals will take a giant leap forward and never be the same.

Introduction

THE BODY, FOR A HOST OF REASONS, has been left out of the "talking cure." Psychotherapists who have been trained in models of psychodynamic, psychoanalytic, or cognitive therapeutic approaches are skilled at listening to the language and affect of the client. They track clients' associations, fantasies, and signs of psychic conflict, distress, and defenses. They register the various narrative threads clients bring, bearing in mind how and where the childhood story repeats itself in the present. They are skilled in creating the therapeutic alliance, working within a therapeutic frame, and recognizing transference and countertransference nuances and enactments. They monitor physical symptoms, using psychopharmacological interventions when indicated. And they invariably take note of the physical presentation of their clients, such as the mannerisms, subtle changes in weight or choice of clothing, the slumped posture of a depressed client, or agitated movements of an anxious client. Yet although most therapists are trained to notice the appearance and even the movements of the client's body, working directly with the client's embodied experience is largely viewed as peripheral to traditional therapeutic formulation, treatment plan, and interventions.

Sensorimotor psychotherapy builds on traditional psychotherapeutic understanding but approaches the body as central in the therapeutic field of awareness and includes observational skills, theories, and interventions not usually practiced in psychodynamic psychotherapy. Theoretical principles and treatment approaches from both the mental health and body psychotherapy traditions are integrated in this approach. Sensorimotor psychotherapy draws heavily from the Hakomi method, a form of body-oriented psychotherapy pioneered by Ron Kurtz (Kurtz, 1990), as a foundation for therapeutic skills and incorporates theory and technique from psychodynamic psychotherapy, cognitive–behavioral therapy, neuroscience, and theories of attachment and dissociation. The premise of this book is that traditionally trained therapists can increase the depth and efficacy of their clinical work by adding body-oriented interventions to their repertoire.

We use the term *sensorimotor psychotherapy* generically to indicate an approach that incorporates somatic interventions that are used by most body psychotherapists. However, sensorimotor psychotherapy is also a school that has developed body psychology theory to guide the use of somatic interventions, so the term is also used to refer to the synthesis unique to this school. The school teaches working with body sensation and movement, but generally excludes the use of touch. The judicious use of touch in psychotherapy may occasionally be helpful in specific situations, but is also potentially problematic, and is not a necessary component of this method (see Chapter 9 for further explanation).

We know that trauma has profound effects on the body and nervous system and that many symptoms of traumatized individuals are somatically driven (Nijenhuis & Van der Hart, 1999; Van der Hart, Nijenhuis, Steele, & Brown, 2004; van der Kolk, 1994; van der Kolk, McFarlane, & Weisaeth, 1996). Clients suffering from unresolved trauma nearly always report unregulated body experience; an uncontrollable cascade of strong emotions and physical sensations, triggered by reminders of the trauma, replays endlessly in the body. This chronic physiological arousal often is at the root of the recurring posttraumatic symptoms for which the client seeks therapy. The capacity to assimilate the traumatic experience within a life narrative is not yet available for these individuals, both because traumatic memories are not encoded in autobiographical memory and because the recurring trauma-related arousal continues to create a somatic sense of threat—a "speechless terror" (van der Kolk, Van der Hart, & Marmar, 1996; see also Siegel, 1999).

Traditional therapeutic models are based primarily on the idea that change occurs through a process of narrative expression and formulation in a "top-down" manner. For example, one principle of psychodynamic treatment models, stated simplistically, is that successfully facilitating affective connection to painful past experience and addressing the accompanying cognitive distortions within the context of a therapeutic relationship will bring about a positive change in sense of self and thereby a relief of suffering and improvement in well-being. The working premise is that a significant change in the client's *cognitions* and *emotions* will effect change in the physical or embodied experience of the client's sense of self. The prime target for therapeutic intervention is therefore the client's *language*; that is, the narrative is the entry point into the therapeutic process. The client's verbal representation, beliefs, and affects are engaged, explored, and reworked through the therapeutic relationship.

Improving ego functioning, clarifying meaning, formulating a narrative, and working with emotional experience are fundamentally helpful interventions that accomplish real gains for the client. To these already useful cognitive and dynamic practices and techniques, we propose the addition of "bottom-up" interventions that address the repetitive, unbidden *physical* sensations, movement inhibitions, and somatosensory intrusions characteristic of unresolved trauma. Traumatized clients are haunted by the return of trauma-related sensorimotor reactions in such forms as intrusive images, sounds, smells, body sensations, physical pain, constriction, numbing, and the inability to modulate arousal. By including body sensation and movement as a primary avenue in processing trauma, sensorimotor psychotherapy teaches the therapist to use body-centered interventions to reduce these symptoms and promote change in the cognitions, emotions, belief systems, and capacity for relatedness in the client.

The practice of sensorimotor psychotherapy blends theory and technique from cognitive and dynamic therapy with straightforward somatic awareness and movement interventions, such as helping clients become aware of their bodies, track bodily sensations, and implement physical actions that promote empowerment and competency. Clients are taught to observe the relationship between their physical organization and beliefs and emotions, noticing, for example, how a self-representation uttered in a here-and-now therapy moment, such as "I'm a bad person," affects physical sensation, posture, autonomic arousal, and movement. They also learn how their physical sensations, postures, and movements affect their emotional state and influence the words and content they describe in therapy. Such interventions actively incorporate the body into therapy, providing a more unified mind–body approach to the treatment of trauma. Within the context of a relationally attuned therapy, clinicians can help clients become curious and interested in how the body's responses to past trauma continue in the context of present-day life, and in how to change these responses to enable more adaptive functioning.

Most psychotherapeutic approaches do not provide a methodology that directly addresses trauma-related bodily responses and chronically activated somatic symptoms. Instead they focus primarily on cognitive, behavioral, psychodynamic, and psychopharmacological interventions that, despite having been validated through research, are only somewhat successful in treating the trauma-related disorders seen in clinical practice (Bradley, Greene, Russ, Dutra, & Westen, 2005; Foa et al., 1999; Marks, Lovell, Noshirvani, Livanou, & Thrasher, 1998; Tarrier, Sommerfield, Pilgrim, & Humphreys, 1999; Ursano et al., 2004). Therapists of all disciplines are often puzzled and frustrated by the limitations of existing treatment modalities to resolve the symptoms of trauma in their clients.

This book responds to the need for a somatic approach to trauma therapy that addresses the scarcity of literature on this subject and is accessible and appropriate for use by psychotherapists. The primary audience to whom this book is addressed includes psychologists, psychiatrists, social workers, psychotherapists, counselors, and family doctors who are treating traumatized individuals. In addition, we provide guidelines to help practitioners understand how the body contributes to both the maintenance and resolution of trauma-related disorders—information that may be valuable to psychiatric nurses, occupational therapists, rehabilitation workers, crisis workers, victim advocates, disaster workers, body therapists, as well as graduate students and interns entering the fields of mental health and trauma treatment. Furthermore, with the understanding that knowledge is empowering, this book is designed to be accessible to, and informative for, traumatized clients who are seeking to understand the causes and cures for their suffering.

Trauma and the Body: A Sensorimotor Approach to Psychotherapy is divided into two sections, theory and treatment. Part I explores the theoretical foundation and rationale for sensorimotor psychotherapy interventions, drawing on the century-old insights of Pierre Janet as well as the work of contemporary experts in the areas of trauma treatment, neuroscience, attachment, affect regulation, dissociation, and the body.

Chapter 1, "Hierarchical Information Processing: Cognitive, Emotional, and Sensorimotor Dimensions," provides a rationale for a somatic treatment approach, describing how traumatic experience disrupts the body's physiological and emotional regulation, causing profound effects on information processing. The hierarchical information-processing model is described and related to maladaptive patterns of "top-down" and "bottom-up" processing common to survivors of trauma. The requirements for effective treatment of traumatic experience, including attention to how mind and body process information and the role of bottom-up processing, are discussed.

Chapter 2, "Window of Tolerance: The Capacity for Modulating Arousal," describes the low tolerance for arousal and affect dysregulation as core symptoms of trauma-related disorders. Focusing on the central role of autonomic dysregulation in perpetuating the symptoms and complicating the treatment of trauma, this chapter examines the regulatory patterns of hypo- and hyperarousal related to the survival-oriented functions of the sympathetic and parasympathetic nervous systems. These posttraumatic regulatory patterns challenge information processing by interfering with optimal arousal states and integrative capacity: Under conditions of arousal that are either too high or too low, traumatic experiences cannot be integrated. These regulatory parameters provide a foundational premise for the "modulation model" of sensorimotor psychotherapy.

Chapter 3, "Attachment: The Role of the Body in Dyadic Regulation," describes regulatory role of attachment experience, its disruption by early traumatic experience, and its effect on the body. Literature from the field of attachment research, Allan Schore's (1994) work on affect regulation, and the distinction between interactive and autoregulation are utilized to describe the specific tendencies of self-regulation and autonomic dominance embodied in each of the four childhood attachment patterns. An example of how to address the dysregulatory effects of attachment failure in treatment at a bodily and autonomic level is described.

Chapter 4, "The Orienting Response: Narrowing the Field of Consciousness," explains the process of orienting whereby we select sensory stimuli from the myriad possible cues from the environment and from internal experience. Various kinds of orienting are described and the stages of the orienting response are delineated in a detailed case example. For the traumatized individual, the ability to orient to, interpret, and integrate sensory stimulation in an adaptive fashion is notably impaired and must be addressed as part of effective trauma treatment.

Chapter 5, "Defensive Subsystems: Mobilizing and Immobilizing Responses," describes various animal defensive subsystems, their origin and physical components, that ultimately may contribute to posttraumatic symptoms. The stages of the defensive response are explained in relation to the case example introduced in the previous chapter. In treatment, traumatized persons are helped to (1) reorganize survival-related defensive responses that exacerbate their symptoms, and (2) achieve more adaptability and flexibility in their defensive patterns.

Chapter 6, "Adaptation: The Role of Action Systems and Tendencies," describes the psychobiological systems that have evolved to support adaptive responses that optimize survival. These systems provide the impetus to explore the world, play, participate in social relationships, regulate energy, form pair bonds, and care for others. Traumatized individuals typically experience difficulty in effectively utilizing these systems because chronic deployment of defensive subsystems takes precedence over other systems. The purpose of this chapter is to describe these action systems and their associated physical tendencies, examine how they relate, and consider how therapists can work with them so that clients can satisfactorily fulfill their objectives. This chapter also describes why there is a propensity to implement actions at a particular level of organization, ranging from reflexive to adaptive. The impact of trauma and early life experiences on the action systems and on physical action tendencies is also addressed.

Chapter 7, "Psychological Trauma and the Brain: Toward a Neurobiological Treatment Model," authored by Ruth Lanius, Ulrich Lanius, Janina Fisher, and Pat Ogden, draws upon the neuroscience research to illuminate the effects of trauma on brain structures and functioning, as well as to explore the implications for treatment using body-based interventions. Neuroimaging technology has made possible the detailed study of how trauma impacts both cortical and subcortical processing of information; this research has profound implications for the treatment of trauma-based symptoms. An understanding of how treatment interventions may affect brain areas implicated in trauma can enhance both the specificity and the effectiveness of psychotherapy. This chapter also describes the differences observed in brain activity related to hyper- versus hypoarousal responses to trauma.

Part II of *Trauma and the Body: A Sensorimotor Approach to Psychotherapy* describes the treatment philosophy and techniques of sensorimotor psychotherapy. Because clients with complex trauma can be triggered by interventions that access the body too quickly, attention is given to approaches and techniques that promote pacing, boundaries, and safe, gradual reconnection with the body. Clinical examples and explanations throughout the second section illustrate and clarify sensorimotor psychotherapy theory and practice.

Chapter 8, "Principles of Treatment: Putting Theory into Practice," translates the theoretical material described in previous chapters into practice, providing an orientation to the principles underlying sensorimotor psychotherapy and applying hierarchical information-processing theory to clinical intervention. Working in the present moment is emphasized, and transference and countertransference concepts are related specifically to the somatic experience of the client in treatment. Janet's (1898) pioneering work on phase-oriented treatment for traumatized individuals is integrated with contemporary theoretical perspectives to provide an umbrella under which to position sensorimotor psychotherapy interventions and treatment planning.

Chapter 9, "The Organization of Experience: Skills for Working with the Body in Present Time," describes specific techniques, drawn primarily from the Hakomi method (Kurtz 1990), that allow client and therapist to safely observe, articulate, and explore present experience. With an emphasis on working with the organization of experience rather than insight, mindfulness techniques that facilitate the regulation of arousal and allow exploration of the client's organization of present experience are described. How these skills are integrated and utilized in sensorimotor psychotherapy is explored along with a section for clinicians on the pitfalls and benefits of the therapeutic use of touch.

Chapter 10, "Phase 1 Treatment: Developing Somatic Resources for Stabilization," describes the use of somatic resources to facilitate the management of traumatic triggers, the modulation of arousal, self-soothing, tolerance of therapeutic attachment and collaboration, and improvement in daily functioning. The challenge for the therapist during this phase is that of bringing autonomic dysregulation under greater conscious control so that hyper- and hypoarousal do not exacerbate the symptoms. The concept of the physical core/periphery is introduced as it relates to auto- and interactive self-regulation. This chapter explains how the development of somatic resources contributes to gradual expansion of self-regulatory skills and paves the way for the processing of traumatic memories at the next phase of treatment.

Chapter 11, "Phase 2 Treatment: Processing Traumatic Memory and Restoring Acts of Triumph," describes how the client, having attained sufficient integrative capacity in the first phase of treatment, is now ready to develop a sense of mastery or triumph over the intense feelings, body sensations, and impulses associated with traumatic memories. This chapter explores the nature of traumatic memory and delineates how the client is enabled to process these memories somatically in order to experience a sense of success and triumph. How memory is safely reevoked, how resources are retrieved, and how empowering actions are discovered and executed are discussed.

Chapter 12, "Phase 3 Treatment: Integration and Success in Normal Life," describes how the focus of treatment now shifts to establishing a life beyond trauma. Somatic interventions are used to help the client resolve relational issues, reengage in society, and tolerate increased intimacy, risk taking, and change. At this stage the therapeutic relationship can be used as a laboratory or template for trying out new actions/options, which can be practiced until they become automatic tendencies. The dynamic relationship between the client's physical core and periphery is a template and metaphor for enabling somatic integration and the capacity for flexible adaptation to life in the present. The transformation of cognitive distortions that impede full engagement with life and increasing positive affect tolerance and capacity for pleasure are explored in this chapter.

Traditionally trained therapists who are new to the idea of working with the body may hesitate to incorporate a sensorimotor approach. It may seem that utilizing the body states and movements that manifest during a psychotherapeutic session necessitate learning a whole new language and method of observation. These concerns are natural and many psychotherapists find this new terrain to be intimidating. However, what we have found in teaching this method to clinicians since 1981 is that attuning to body cues is something that is already built into virtually every therapist's method of working with clients and their internal states. The majority of human communication is not through verbal language but rather through body language: facial expression, eye contact, movement, behavior, posture, autonomic arousal, gestures, muscular tension, and so forth. In other words, the meaning and interpretation of each conversation that we have with another human being is built on observing, inferring, compiling, and making meaning of the other person's body movement, posture, and expression, and much of how we communicate in response is through our body reactions to the other.

Indeed, at this juncture, the reader may actually be asking the opposite question: If this book is discussing a method that is based on a seemingly innate and highly sophisticated skill of interpreting body language and interactively regulating our co-conversant through this language, why are we not already adept at the method described in this book? The art and science of the sensorimotor psychotherapist lies in making this unconscious processes conscious, thus giving language to the non-verbal communication that is so integral to our interactions with others, including our clinical practice, that we have almost completely overlooked it as a primary object of study. In sensorimotor psychotherapy, understanding and translating the language of the body's communication is central. Thus the process of learning sensorimotor psychotherapy includes the mindful study of how another's physical states and communications resonate in and affect our own body experience, and how they can be interpreted as a useful basis for consciously formulating both our verbal and non-verbal responses to our client. This book expresses the thoughtful study of this interactive process over the last two-and-a-half decades.

Weaving sensorimotor psychotherapy theory and practice into psychodynamic or cognitive–behavioral models of therapy, including EMDR and exposure treatments, helps to unify body and mind in the treatment of trauma. Moreover, this work can be effectively used as an adjunct to already existing psychotherapeutic modalities. It should be noted that the methods introduced in this book are not only applicable to trauma; a sensorimotor approach is equally applicable to the normal, non-traumatic range of childhood and family dynamics that shape the development and formation of the client's personality and interactive capacity. The ultimate aim of combining somatic and cognitive interventions is not only to alleviate symptoms and resolve the traumatic past, but also to help clients experience a new, reorganized sense of self. The sense of self develops not only in the context of beliefs, metaphors, and emotional responses but evolves organically as the physical organization of the client's body changes. Some traumatized clients have a habitually collapsed, frozen, or immobilized body and an accompanying sense of self as ineffectual. Others experience chronic hyperaroused, affect-dysregulated bodies and a sense of a self that seems "out of control." Sensorimotor psychotherapy helps these clients regulate their physical experiences and learn more adaptive actions so that their corresponding sense of self *feels* grounded, competent, and oriented toward present experience. As the arousal level, sensation, posture, and movement of the body adaptively change, a different, more positive, sense of self emerges, supported by these physical changes. Thus, by synthesizing bottom-up and top-down interventions, we hope to combine the best of both worlds to help chronically traumatized clients find resolution and meaning in their lives as well as develop a new, somatically integrated sense of self.

Trauma and
the Body

Part I

Theory

Chapter 1

Hierarchical Information Processing: Cognitive, Emotional, and Sensorimotor Dimensions

FOR TRAUMATIZED INDIVIDUALS, THE DEBILITATING, repetitive cycle of inter-action between mind and body keeps past trauma "alive," disrupting the sense of self and maintaining trauma-related disorders. Many people are left with a fragmented memory of their traumatic experiences, a host of easily reactivated neurobiological responses, and baffling, intense, nonverbal mem-ories—sensorimotor reactions and symptoms that "tell the story" without words, as though the body knows what they do not know cognitively. They are often unaware that these reactions—intrusive body sensations, images, smells, physical pain and constriction, numbing, and the inability to modu-late arousal—are, in fact, remnants of past trauma. Frequently uncertain of what happened and how they endured it, traumatized individuals tend to interpret these reactivated sensorimotor responses as data about their iden-tity or selfhood: "I am never safe," "I am a marked woman," "I am worthless and unlovable." These beliefs are reflected in the body and affect posture, breathing, freedom of movement, even heart rate and respiration (Aposhyan, 2004; Caldwell, 1997; Heckler, 1993; Keleman, 1985; Kepner, 1987, 1995; Krueger, 2002; Kurtz, 1990; Kurtz & Prestera, 1976; Lowen, 1975; Reich, 1945/1972; Rosenberg, Rand, & Asay, 1985). And each somatic adaptation to trauma, in turn, influences how traumatized people respond to the envi-ronment and make meaning of all subsequent experience.

3

Rather than helping to resolve these symptoms, attempts to process traumatic events by describing them in words or venting the associated feelings can precipitate "somatic remembering" in the form of physical sensations, numbing, dysregulated arousal, and involuntary movements. These intense bodily responses, in turn, can fuel trauma-related emotions of terror, dread, helplessness, hopelessness, shame, and rage. Attempting to describe traumatic events thus brings the past suddenly into the present, and orientation to current reality may be partially or temporarily lost (Tarrier et al., 1999; Burnstein, Ellis, Teitge, Gross, & Shier, 1986; McDonough-Coyle et al., 2000; Pitman et al., 1991; Scott & Stradling 1997; Devilly & Foa 2001; Tarrier, 2001). "Remembering" the trauma is experienced as "It's happening *again*—I'm still not safe." At those moments of feeling under threat, the "thinking" mind—the frontal cortex—is compromised. Accordingly, subsequent decisions and actions based on the bodily experience of threat tend to be impulsive, dangerous, or otherwise inappropriate to current reality. Yet again trauma-related beliefs—that is, beliefs that exacerbate somatic symptoms—feel confirmed: "It must be true that nothing good can happen to me"; "It must be true that I don't deserve to be safe."

The complexity and variety of symptoms affecting both mind and body are perplexing to therapists and clients alike. Highlighting the role of dissociation in trauma symptoms, Pierre Janet (1889) emphasized that unresolved trauma results in profound deficits in the ability to integrate experiences. Processes that are normally unified, such as emotions, thoughts, identity, memory, and somatosensory elements, are separated (Spiegel & Cardena, 1991). This integrative failure leads to an undue "compartmentalization of experience: Elements of a trauma are not integrated into a unitary whole or an integrated sense of self" (van der Kolk, Van der Hart, & Marmar, 1996, p. 306). One form of compartmentalization is apparent in the propensity of traumatized individuals to alternate between (1) emotional and bodily numbing and avoidance of cues reminiscent of the trauma and (2) intrusive reliving of the trauma via flashbacks, dreams, thoughts, and somatic symptoms (Chu, 1998; Meyers, 1940; Spiegel, 1990, 1997; van der Hart et al., 2004; van der Kolk & Van der Hart, 1989). In the words of James Chu, "This biphasic pattern is the result of dissociation: traumatic events are distanced and dissociated from usual conscious awareness in the numbing phase, only to return in the intrusive phase" (1998, p. 33).

Markedly different symptoms occur in each dissociative phase. In the intrusive phase, the person is plagued by unintegrated fragments of traumatic memories that return unbidden. In the numbing phase, these fragments are kept at bay, but the individual feels numb and detached, living "on the surface of consciousness" (Appelfeld, 1994, p. 18). The dissociative symptoms in each phase are further complicated by being both psychological, or psychoform, *and* sensorimotor, or somatoform (Nijenhuis & Van der Hart, 1999; Van der Hart, Van Dijke, Van Son, & Steele, 2000). Psychoform symptoms involve dissociation of mental functions and manifest as overwhelming affects, concentration difficulties, amnesia and other memory problems, and altered systems of belief. Somatoform dissociative symptoms involve body sensation, movement, and the senses, and include sensory distortions, dysregulated physiological arousal, lack of body sensation, pain, movement disorders, and reexperiencing the trauma in somatosensory fragments. Van der Hart and colleagues aptly noted that the psychoform and somatoform symptoms should be viewed as two sides of the same coin, because "they are both expressions of underlying dissociative processes that transpire within the inseparable union of psyche and soma" (2000, p. 35). The complicated mix of somatoform and psychoform symptoms begs for a treatment approach that directly addresses the effects of trauma on both the body and the mind.

THE TRIUNE BRAIN

The capacity of human beings for self-awareness, interpretation, abstract thought, and feeling exists within a developmental and hierarchical relationship to the instinctual and nonconscious responses of the body. These hierarchically organized evolutionary responses range from instinctual arousal and physical defenses to feelings and emotional experience to thoughts, self reflection, beliefs, and meaning making.

Wilber's (1996) notion of hierarchical information processing described the evolutionary and functional hierarchy among three levels of organizing experience: cognitive, emotional, and sensorimotor levels. In neuropsychology a parallel understanding of this hierarchy was articulated by MacLean, who portrayed the concept of the triune brain as a "brain with a brain within a brain" (1985, p. 8). The reptilian brain, first to develop from an evolutionary perspective, governs arousal, homeostasis of the organism, and reproductive drives, and loosely relates to the sensorimotor level of information processing, including sensation and programmed movement impulses. Correlating with emotional processing, the "paleomammalian brain" or "limbic brain," found in all mammals, surrounds the reptilian brain and mediates emotion, memory, some social behavior, and learning (Cozolino, 2002). Last to develop phylogenetically is the neocortex, which enables cognitive information processing, such as self-awareness and conscious thought, and includes large portions of the corpus callosum, which bridges the right and left hemispheres of the brain (MacLean, 1985) and helps consolidate information (Siegel, 1999). Thus the three levels of information processing—cognitive, emotional, and sensorimotor—can be thought of as roughly correlating with the three levels of brain architecture.

Different kinds of knowledge originate from each of these brains. The reptilian brain produces "Innate behavioral knowledge: Basic instinctual action tendencies and habits related to primitive survival issues" (Panksepp, 1998, p. 43). The limbic system provides "Affective knowledge: Subjective feelings and emotional responses to world events" (Panksepp, 1998, p. 43). The neocortex generates "Declarative knowledge . . . propositional information about world" (Panksepp, 1998, p. 43). Panksepp further clarified the behavioral and functional interface of these three "brains":

> The inner most reptilian core of the brain elaborates basic instinctual action plans for primitive emotive processes such as exploration, feeding, aggressive dominance displays, and sexuality. The old-mammalian brain, or the limbic system, adds behavioral and psychological resolution to all of the emotions and specifically mediates the social emotions such as separation distress/social bonding, playfulness, and maternal nurturance. The highly expanded neomammalian cortex generates higher cognitive functions, reasoning, and logical thought. (p. 43)

Each of the three levels of the brain thus has its own "understanding" of the environment and responds accordingly. A particular level may become dominant and override the others, depending on the internal and environmental conditions. At the same time, these three levels are mutually dependent and intertwined (Damasio, 1999; LeDoux, 1996; Schore, 1994), functioning as a cohesive whole, with the degree of integration of each level of processing affecting the efficacy of other levels. Fisher, Murray, and Bundy (1991) noted:

> The brain functions as an integrated whole but is comprised of systems that are hierarchically organized. The "higher level" integrative functions evolved from and are dependent on the integrity of "lower-level" structures and on sensorimotor experience. Higher (cortical) centers of the brain are viewed as those that are responsible for abstraction, perception, reasoning, language, and learning. Sensory integration and intersensory association, in contrast, occur mainly within lower (subcortical) centers. Lower parts of the brain are conceptualized as developing and maturing before higher-level structures; development and optimal functioning of higher-level structures are thought to be dependent, in part, on the development and optimal functioning of lower-level structures. (p. 16)

In many ways sensorimotor processing is foundational to other types of processing and includes the features of a simpler, more primitive form of information processing than do its more evolved counterparts. More directly associated with overall body processing, sensorimotor processing includes physical changes in response to sensory input; the fixed action patterns seen in defenses; changes in breathing and muscular tone; and autonomic nervous system activation. With its seat in the lower, older brain structures, sensorimotor processing relies on a relatively higher number of fixed sequences of steps in the way it works. Some of these fixed sequences are well known, such as the startle reflex and the fight/flight response. The simplest sequences are involuntary reflexes (e.g., the knee-jerk reaction), which are the most rigidly fixed and determined. More complex are the motor patterns that we learn at young ages, such as walking and running, which then become automatic. In the more highly evolved cognitive and emotional realms, we find fewer and fewer fixed sequences of steps and more complexity and variability of response. Panksepp (1998) likened this variance in complexity to the operating systems of a computer:

> Higher functions are typically more open, while lower ones are more reflexive, stereotyped, and closed. For instance, the basic vital functions of the brain—those that regulate organic bodily functions such as respiration—are organized at very low levels. Higher levels provide increasingly flexible control over these lower functions. . . . To use [a] computer analogy . . . the lower functions resemble read-only memory (ROM) "operating systems," which are essential for computers to do anything coherent, while the higher functions resemble random-access memory (RAM) space where increasing complex computations can be done. As more RAM space becomes available, the same operating systems can accomplish more and more. The relative abundance of RAM-like space in humans helps explain the complexity and sophistication of human abilities. (p. 77)

Flexibility and abstraction of response increase at the higher cognitive level of processing; greater fixity and concreteness of response increase at the sensorimotor level. Emotional processing falls in the middle, being neither as flexible as cognitive processing nor as fixed as sensorimotor processing.

The three levels of the brain may not always work well together (MacLean, 1985). In the aftermath of trauma, the integration of information processing on cognitive, emotional, and sensorimotor levels is often compromised. Dysregulated arousal may drive a traumatized person's emotional and cognitive processing, causing emotions to escalate, thoughts to spin, and misinterpretation of present environmental cues as those of a past trauma (van der Kolk, 1996a). For example, a client whose heart rate escalates at the sight of a tall, overweight, middle-aged man (who is similar in physical appearance to her abusive uncle) and who experiences a somatic sense of wanting to run, is likely to interpret these sensorimotor reactions as meaning that she is not safe. She might then find herself having the thought, "This man is dangerous." This thought, in turn, is likely to increase her heart rate and the tension in her legs and feet, provoking more thoughts, such as "I have to get out of here" and fueling trauma-related emotions of fear and dread. These emotions and sensorimotor reactions further sabotage her ability to appraise current reality accurately.

Although recent authors (Cozolino, 2002; LeDoux, 2002) have challenged the notion of a "limbic system" and emphasized that the neural networks responsible for social, emotional, attachment, and traumatic experiences are found throughout the brain, the concept of the triune brain nevertheless "serves a valuable function of providing a connective metaphor among the artifacts of evolution, the contemporary nervous system, and some of the inherent difficulties related to the organization and disorganization of human consciousness" (Cozolino, 2002, p. 9). We draw on this metaphor to help illustrate how experience is organized on the three levels of information processing and how the synergistic relationship among these levels is chronically impaired by unresolved trauma.

LEVELS OF INFORMATION PROCESSING AND THE BODY

Cognitive and emotional processing strongly affect the body, and sensorimotor processing strongly affects cognitions and emotions. In clinical practice, we find it useful to both examine each level of information processing separately and consider the interweaving of cognitions, emotions, and sensorimotor responses. It is especially important for the therapist to observe how the body affects and is influenced by the processing of information on each of these levels of experience. Specific somatic techniques can then be selected and integrated with cognitive and emotional interventions so that adaptive information processing is increased on all three levels.

Cognitive Processing

The term *cognitive processing* refers to the capacity for conceptualizing, reasoning, meaning making, problem solving, and decision making. It encompasses the ability to observe and abstract from experience, weigh a range of possibilities for action, plan for the accomplishment of goals, and evaluate the outcome of actions. Our actions as adults often reflect the hierarchical relationship of volitional cognitive processing over sensorimotor and emotional responses. We can decide (cognitive function) to ignore the sensation of hunger and not act on it, even while the physiological processes associated with hunger, such as the secretion of saliva and contraction of stomach muscles, continue. In cognitive theory this dominance of cognitive functioning is called "top-down processing" (LeDoux, 1996, p. 272), indicating that the upper level of processing (cognitive) can and often does override, steer, or interrupt the lower levels by elaborating upon or interfering with emotional and sensorimotor processing.

Much adult activity is based upon top-down processing. Schore (1994, p. 139) noted that, in adults, "higher cortical areas" act as a "control center," and that the orbital cortex dominates subcortical activity. We might think about what to accomplish for the day, outline plans, and then structure time to meet particular goals. While executing these plans, emotions and sensations (e.g., frustration, fatigue, physical discomfort) may be overridden. It is as though we hover just above our somatic and emotional experience, knowing it's there, but not allowing it to be the primary determinant of our actions. For the traumatized individual, however, the intensity of trauma-related emotions and sensorimotor reactions hinders the ability of top-down processing to dominate subcortical activity.

Additional difficulty with cognitive processing occurs because traumatized people typically form inflexible, maladaptive interpretations of the trauma or other life experience. Such interpretations take the form of inadvertent, generalized thoughts that are negatively biased and erroneous, such as "I am bad," "It was my fault," "All men are dangerous," and so on. Each thought is an action (Maturana & Varela, 1987)—that is, a mental action (Janet, 1926; Van der Hart, Nijenhuis, & Steele, 2006)—that generates not only more negative cognitions but also corresponding emotions and sensorimotor reactions. These thoughts play a part in the way traumatized people continue to organize their experience, which is shaped by pervasive patterns of cognitive distortions; these distortions result in persistent experiences of low self-esteem and defeat, as well as a chronic perception of a lack of safety.

Cognitive processing is inextricably linked with our bodies. Bodily feelings, or "somatic markers," influence cognitive decision making, logic, speed, and context of thought (Damasio, 1994, 1999, p. 41). The background body sensations that arise during cognitive processing form a biasing substratum that influences the functioning of the individual in all decision-making processes and self-experiences. The "very structure of reason itself comes from the details of our embodiment. The same neural and cognitive mechanisms that allow us to perceive and move around also create our conceptual systems and modes of reason" (Internet Encyclopedia of Philosophy, 2005). The circuits of the brain that are used for mental action are the same ones that are used for physical action (Ratey, 2002). The movement of the body as a child matures is essential for the optimal development of memory, language, and learning. Ratey (2002) speculated that motor neurons may even drive our sense of self-awareness. Thus, how we think and what we think are literally shaped by the body, and vice versa. According to Lakoff and Johnson (1999):

> The embodiment of reason via the sensorimotor system . . . is a crucial part of the explanation of why it is possible for our concepts to fit so well with the way we function in the world. They fit so well because they have evolved from our sensorimotor systems, which have in turn evolved to allow us to function well in our physical environment. . . . Our concepts cannot be a direct reflection of external, objective, mind-free reality because our sensorimotor system plays a crucial role in shaping them. (p. 4344)

All early relational dynamics with primary caregivers, traumatic or nontraumatic, serve as blueprints for the child's developing cognition and belief systems, and these belief systems influence the posture, structure, and movement of the body, and vice versa. If a child grows up in a family that values high achievement and encourages the child to "try harder" at everything she undertakes, her posture, gesture, and movement will be shaped by this influence. If this value is held at the expense of other values, such as "You are loved for yourself, not for what you do," the child's musculature will probably be toned and tense; her body will be mobilized to "try harder." In contrast, a child who grows up in an environment where trying hard is either discouraged or seen as maladaptive and where everything he achieves is undervalued, might have a sunken chest, limp arms, and shallow breath; his body will reflect a childhood experience of not feeling assertive and confident, of "giving up." It may be difficult for this child to mobilize consistent energy or sufficient self-confidence to complete a difficult task. Chronic postural and movement tendencies serve to sustain certain beliefs and cognitive distortions, and the physical patterns, in turn, contribute to these same beliefs.

If the body shapes reason and beliefs—and vice versa—then the capacity for insight and self-reflection—our ability to "know our own minds"—will be correspondingly limited by the body's influence (Lakoff & Johnson, 1999). How, then, can we begin to know our own minds? If the *patterns* of the body's movements and posture influence reason, cognitive self-reflection might not be the only or even the best way of bringing the workings of the mind to consciousness. Reflecting on, exploring, and changing the posture and movement of the body may be as valuable. For example, Terry came to therapy with a body "filled with fear": His shoulders were hiked up, his head was retracted, his chest was tight with held breath, his eyes darted around, and he had an exaggerated startle reflex. His chronic experience of his body did not support the "reasonable" belief that his past trauma was over and he was not currently in danger. Terry reported that he *knew* he was safe, but he *felt* as if he were unsafe. In therapy, the sensations and movements of his body were addressed in order to reveal their impact on his beliefs as well as to change both his body and beliefs. In the course of therapy, Terry became aware of this mind–body interface; he worked both cognitively and physically to change his embodied belief by relaxing his shoulders, deepening his breathing, and feeling his legs as firmly grounded and supporting his upper body. During this exploration, memories of his trauma emerged and were dealt with and resolved. After several sessions, Terry described a shift in his body and his beliefs: "Now my body feels like it supports me! I feel safer when my shoulders are more relaxed and my breathing is not so shallow and tense."

Emotional Processing

Emotions add motivational coloring to cognitive processing and act as signals that direct us to notice and attend to particular cues. Emotions help us take adaptive action by calling attention to significant environmental events and stimuli (Krystal, 1978; van der Kolk, McFarlane et al., 1996). The "emotional brain directs us toward experiences we seek and the cognitive brain tries to help us get there as intelligently as possible" (Servan-Schreiber, 2003, p. 26). According to Llinas, "As with muscle tone that serves as the basic platform for the execution of our movements, emotions represent the premotor platform as either drives or deterrents for most of our actions" (2001, p. 155).

Traumatized people characteristically lose the capacity to draw upon emotions as guides for action. They might suffer from alexithymia, a disturbance in the ability to recognize and find words for emotions (Sifneos, 1973, 1996; Taylor, Bagby, & Parker, 1997). They may be detached from their emotions, presenting with flat affect and complaining of a lack of interest and motivation in life and an inability to take action. Or their emotions may be experienced as urgent and immediate calls to action; the capacity to reflect on an emotion and allow it to be part of the data that guides action is lost and its expression becomes explosive and uncontrolled. Through nonverbal remembering triggered by reminders of the event, traumatized individuals relive the emotional tenor of previous traumatic experiences, finding themselves at the mercy of intense trauma-related emotions. These emotions can lead to impulsive, ineffective, conflicting, and irrational actions, such as lashing out physically or verbally, or feeling helpless, frozen, and numb. Emotional arousal in an individual with unresolved trauma thus often provokes action that is not an adaptive response to the present (nontraumatic) environment, but is more likely a version of an adaptive response to the original trauma.

The term *emotional processing* refers to the capacity to experience, describe, express, and integrate affective states (Brewin, Dalgleish, & Joseph, 1996). Emotions usually follow a phasic pattern with a beginning, middle, and an end (Frijda, 1986). However, for many traumatized individuals, the end never arrives. Emotional responses to very strong stimuli, such as trauma, do not appear to extinguish (Frijda, 1986)—a phenomenon that has been demonstrated in animal research by LeDoux, who noted that emotional memory may be forever (LeDoux, 1996). Traumatized individuals are often fixated on trauma-related emotions of grief, fear, terror, or anger. There might be a variety of reasons for this fixation: denial or lack of awareness of the connection between current emotions and past trauma; attempts to avoid more painful emotions; the inability to "think clearly" (Leitenberg, Greenwald, & Cado, 1992); or the inability to distinguish emotions from bodily sensations (Ogden & Minton, 2000). Moreover, the emotions may relate to a variety of past events rather than only one (Frijda, 1986). All these elements contribute to a circular, apparently never-ending reexperiencing of trauma-related emotions.

Like Damasio, Frijda emphasized that emotions are inseparable from the body: "Emotions are . . . matters of the body: of the heart, the stomach, and intestines, of bodily activity and impulse. They are of the flesh and sear the flesh. Also, they are of the brain and the veins" (1986, p. 5). Whether we are aware of these internal sensations or not, they both contribute to, and are the result of, emotions. Butterflies in the stomach tell us we are excited, a heavy feeling in the chest speaks of grief, tension in the jaw informs us we are angry, an all-over tingling feeling indicates fear.

Damasio stated that emotions have two features: first, the internal sensation, which is "inwardly directed and private," and second, visible feature, which is "outwardly directed and public" (1999, p. 40). Internal emotional states are thus experienced as subjective bodily sensations and are reflected in our outward presentation, giving signals to others around us about how we feel. Anger might be visible in the purse of the mouth, clenched fists, narrowed eyes, and general bodily tension. Fear may be communicated in hunched shoulders, held breath, and a pleading look in the eyes or in a bracing or moving away from the frightening stimulus. These bodily stances might be an immediate response to a current situation or a chronic, pervasive emotional state.

In therapy we can utilize the outwardly directed physical manifestations to clarify, work with, and resolve trauma-related emotions. One client who presented with visible tension across her shoulders was directed to notice this tension and explore it for meaning. She reported that it felt like the tension was holding back anger—an insight gleaned from awareness of her body rather than from cognition. This insight led to the realization of an erroneous belief that she had no right to be angry at her abusive father. Working with the anger through the tension itself (slowly executing the movement the tension "wanted" to make, processing the associated memories, beliefs, and emotions, and learning to relax the tension) assisted this client on her road to fuller self-expression and resolution of the emotions related to her past traumatic events.

In the previous example, working with the client's emotion simultaneously with its cognitive component was effective. However, despite the inextricable involvement of emotions with the body and cognitions, when trauma-related emotions such as terror are coupled with body sensation, such as trembling, the client is encouraged to distinguish body sensations and movements from emotions. In these instances, we help clients differentiate emotional processing from sensorimotor processing. In our vernacular, *emotional processing* pertains to experiencing, articulating, and integrating emotions, whereas *sensorimotor processing* refers to experiencing, articulating, and integrating physical/sensory perception, body sensation, physiological arousal, and motor functioning. This differentiation between these two levels of processing is important in trauma therapy because clients often fail to discriminate between body sensations of arousal or movement and emotional feeling, which can lead to the escalation of both. This lack of discrimination is partly due to the fact that sensation and emotion occur simultaneously and suddenly, and partly because affect dysregulation and degrees of functional alexithymia are characteristic of posttrauma symptoms. Clients often find themselves struggling with the effects of overwhelming emotions, with little awareness of how the body participates in creating and sustaining these emotions.

Conflating trauma-related emotions and the body sensations of physiological arousal can thus complicate the client's capacity to process and resolve the emotions related to traumatic events. If body sensations (e.g., trembling, rapid heart rate) are interpreted as an emotion (e.g., panic), each level of experience—sensorimotor and emotional—inflates and compounds the other. Both the rapid heart rate and the panic are exacerbated when experienced simultaneously. If cognition in the form of a belief is then added, such as "I am not safe," physical sensation and emotion will further intensify. In such a situation, arousal can escalate beyond the person's tolerance, and integrative capacity will be compromised. By working with the client to differentiate the sensation of physiological arousal from emotional arousal, the amount and kind of information are reduced and more ably processed by the client. Physiological arousal can be addressed, and often diminished, by uncoupling trauma-related emotion from body sensation through attending exclusively to the physical sensations of the arousal (without attributing meaning or emotion to them). Then, after the physiological

arousal returns to a tolerable level, the client can look at the emotional contents of the traumatic experience and integrate both.

For example, a Vietnam veteran, Martin, came to therapy to "get rid of"
his nightmares and feelings of being chronically emotionally overwhelmed.
In the course of sensorimotor psychotherapy, Martin learned to sense his
physiological arousal as he experienced it in his body. He learned to pay
active attention to his rapid heart rate and the shaking and trembling that he
first experienced following the original combat and later reexperienced all
too frequently in his daily life. Over several therapy sessions, he learned to
describe his inner body sensations, noting the tingling in his arms that
occurred prior to the shaking, the slight acceleration in heart rate, and the
increase of tension in his legs. As his capacity to observe and describe his
subjective bodily sensations developed, he gradually learned to accept these
sensations without trying to inhibit them. The therapist instructed him to
simply track these sensations as they progressed or "sequenced" through the
body. When a client becomes mindfully aware of such internal sensations,
the sensations themselves often spontaneously transform into ones that are
more tolerable (Levine, 1997). Martin learned to mindfully follow the
sequence of sensations as they progressed through his body, until the sensations themselves settled down. He noticed that his shaking gradually dis-
sipated, his heart rate eventually returned to baseline, and the tension in his
legs released on its own. After he learned to quiet his arousal in this way, the
therapy progressed to address the emotional responses related to the trauma.

Sensorimotor Processing

In contrast to the top-down processing used in the organization of normal
adult day-to-day life, the activities of very young children (and many individuals with trauma-related disorders) are dominated by sensorimotor
(Piaget, 1962) and emotional systems (Schore, 1994)—in other words, by
bottom-up processes. Tactile and kinesthetic sensations guide early attachment behavior as well as help regulate the infant's behavior and physiology
(Schore, 2003a). Infants and very young children explore the world through
these systems, building the neural networks that are the foundation for later
cognitive development (Hannaford, 1995; Piaget, 1962). Hard-wired to be
governed by somatic and emotional states, infants and toddlers respond
automatically to sensorimotor and affective cues and are unregulated by cognition or cortical control (Schore, 1994). The infant is a "subcortical creature
. . . [who] lacks the means for modulation of behavior which is made possible by the development of cortical control" (Diamond, Balvin, & Diamond,
1963, p. 305). Similarly, traumatized people frequently experience themselves as being at the mercy of their sensations, physical and sensory reac-

tions, as well as emotions, having lost the capacity to effectively regulate these functions. In the clinical practice of sensorimotor psychotherapy, we identify three general components of sensorimotor processing: inner-body sensation, five-sense perception, and movement.

INNER-BODY SENSATION

The term *inner-body sensation* refers to the myriad of physical feelings that are continually created by movement of all sorts within the body. When a change occurs in the body, such as a hormonal shift or a muscular spasm, this change may be felt as an inner-body sensation. The contraction of the intestines, circulation of fluids, biochemical changes, the movements of breathing, or the movements of muscles, ligaments, or bones all cause inner-body sensations. The capacity to have some awareness of sensation was referred to as the "sixth sense," first described by Charles Bell in the early 1800s and later by William James in 1889. Today, the sixth sense is understood as resulting from *interoceptors*, the sensory nerve receptors that receive and transmit sensations from stimuli originating from the interior of the body.

There are many different kinds of interoceptors. The kinesthetic sense of the movement of the body as a whole relies on *proprioceptors*, the sensory nerves that terminate in joints, muscles, and tendons. Proprioceptors provide a sense of the body's position in space without having to rely on the visual sense to know where and what position the body is in (Tortora & Anagnostakos, 1990). They relay the position of body parts, the degree of force used in movement, the velocity and timing of movement, and the speed and degree to which a muscle is being stretched (Fisher et al., 1991). The *vestibular system*, a subset of the proprioception that is located in the mechanisms of the inner ear, informs us about the relationship of the body to gravity and controls our sense of balance. This system maintains our equilibrium, primarily of the head, when we are standing still and in response to sudden movements or changes in speed of movements.

The visceral sense, called *enteroception*, tells us about the movements occurring within our internal organs, such as racing of the heart, butterflies in the stomach, nausea, hunger, or that "gut feeling." We have a variety of *nociceptors*, most numerous in the skin and less numerous in tendons, joints, and organs, which relay various kinds of physical pain. *Thermoceptors* respond to temperature. Whereas we are generally unaware of information coming from interoceptors, we can usually turn our attention toward this information at will and detect body sensation: for example, most people can become aware of their heartbeat or the sensation in the viscera after a few minutes of attention.

Through interoceptors, a variety of inner-body sensation is constantly being generated, contributing to internal states of well-being or distress.

However, sensation is usually experienced globally rather than specifically (Janet, 1907). Damasio wrote: "The background body sense is continuous, although one may hardly notice it, since it represents not a specific part of any thing in the body but rather an overall state of most everything in it" (1994, p. 152) As the ongoing background, body sensation is significant in our sense of self: "Consciousness of the 'self' most likely depends to a substantial extent on awareness (however vague, ill-defined, and folded into a larger consciousness) of the body per se, including its visceral organs and functions" (Cameron, 2001).

Although most sensations, unless quite pronounced, do not reach awareness, those that do are influenced by both emotions and cognition. Cioffi (1991, as cited in Bakal 1999) argued that our experience of specific body sensations is strongly determined by meaning and interpretation even when irrelevant to the actual physiological sensations themselves. Bakal (1999) and Cioffi (1991) gave the example of the sensation of cold hands, which could be interpreted as a problem with circulation, or as a normal response to cool air, or as a response to fear. Each interpretation evokes a particular emotional response, which, in turn, contributes to the development of the actual sensation. For example, an interpretation of lack of circulation could promote anxiety, with thoughts of potential medical problems. Anxious reactions may evoke additional body sensations and even colder hands. Thus the experience of sensation—how it develops and whether it increases or decreases—is organized in part by how it is interpreted and the accompanying emotional response.

People with trauma-related disorders suffer from both "feeling too much" and "feeling too little" (van der Kolk, 1994). They often experience inner-body sensations as overwhelming and distressing. The "rush" of adreneline or the sensations of a rapid heartbeat or of bodily tension are felt acutely and become more disconcerting when interpreted as indicating current danger (Thakkar & McCanne, 2000). These sensations may be even stronger for traumatized people, because interoceptive sensitivity is increased under stress Cameron (2001). Conversely, traumatized individuals commonly suffer from an inability to be aware of body sensation, or an inability to put words to sensation, known as *alexisomia* (Bakal, 1999; Ikemi & Ikemi, 1986). The absence of body sensation and the accompanying interpretation (e.g., "There is something wrong"; "I can't feel my body"; "I feel dead") can be just as distressing as experiencing too much sensation.

The intervention of facilitating awareness of bodily sensation has a long history in the treatment of trauma, and many practitioners believe that helping clients gradually, safely, and comfortably experience their sensations may contribute to resolving symptoms (Aposhyan, 2004; Bakal, 1999; Eckberg, 2000; Janet, 1925; Levine, 1997; Ogden & Minton, 2000; Rothschild,

2000; Sollier, 1897). The capacity to sense and describe sensation and to uncouple it from trauma-related emotions and cognitions enhances the possibility of clients' reintegrating the somatic experience of their trauma in order to establish new meanings and understandings of their past and themselves, as illustrated in the previous example of Martin.

FIVE-SENSE PERCEPTION

Sometimes called *exteroception*, the sensory nerves of our five senses receive and transmit information from stimuli in the external environment. The process of taking in information through the five senses can be thought of as having two components: the physical act of sensing and the individual's perception of the sensory input (Cohen, 1993). Sensory perceptions may dominate traumatized individuals' capacity to think rationally. Dealing with the peritraumatic sensory distortions and the posttraumatic intrusive sensory memory fragments is a necessary component of treatment.

Sensory input from all five senses enters the brain as electrical impulses that are not initially differentiated by the brain (Carter, 1998). What commands our attention from the massive amount of sensory stimulation received each moment is an extremely complex question. Ayres (1989) described the integration of sensory information as

> the neurological process that organizes sensation from one's own body [which occurs from sensory input] and from the environment and makes it possible to use the body effectively within the environment. The spatial and temporal aspects of inputs from different sensory modalities are interpreted, associated, and unified. Sensory integration is information processing. . . . The brain must select, enhance, inhibit, compare, and associate the sensory information in a flexible, constantly changing pattern. (p. 11)

Through this enormously intricate process, we select and filter information, determining what to pay attention to and what to disregard. All learning depends upon our ability to (1) receive sensory information from the environment and the interior of our bodies, (2) synthesize this information, and (3) to organize subsequent behavior. Because this process is influenced by our individual associations with what we sense, it overlaps with the other levels of processing. Llinas described perception as "the functional comparison of internally generated sensorimotor images with real-time sensory information from an organism's immediate environment" (2001, p. 3). Once this subcortical, unconscious comparison has taken place, movement is planned and executed.

Because it is based on the comparison of sensory input with internal frames of reference, our perception—and thus our behavior—is self-referential (Damasio, 1994). Our beliefs and emotional reactions to previous similar sensory stimuli condition our relationship with current stimuli. Without the expectations that influence perceptual priming, each sensory experience would be novel, and we would be quickly overwhelmed. Instead, we fit sensory input into learned categories. Ratey pointed out that "we are constantly priming our perceptions, matching the world to what we expect to sense and thus making it what we perceive it to be" (2002, p. 55). This priming function becomes maladaptive for traumatized individuals, who repeatedly notice and take in sensory cues that are reminiscent of past trauma, often failing to notice concomitant sensory cues indicating that current reality is not dangerous. These real-time trauma-related cues from both the environment and the body are compared to internal sensorimotor images, beliefs, and emotions, ultimately fueling behavior that would be appropriate for threatening situations but not for current nonthreatening situations (Brewin et al., 1996).

MOVEMENT

Movement is included in the sensorimotor level of information processing because of its obvious somatic component, although the frontal lobes of the cortex, rather than the subcortical areas of the brain, are home to the motor cortex and premotor cortex and are responsible for many forms of movement. The same areas of the brain that generate reason and help us solve problems are also involved in movement. Thus movement has shaped, and continues to shape, our minds (Janet, 1925), and vice versa, as articulated by Llinas: "The mind . . . is the product of evolutionary processes that have occurred in the brain *as actively moving creatures* developed from the primitive to the highly evolved" (2001, p. ix, italics added). Movement is essential for the development of all brain functions: Only organisms that move from one location to another require a brain; organisms that are stationary do not (Ratey, 2002).

Movement ranges from voluntary to involuntary, conscious to unconscious, and occurs in many different forms. It includes the rise and fall of respiration, internal movements of organs, pulsation of blood, and pumping of hormones, as well as the small, sometimes imperceptible, vibratory movements such as trembling or twitching. Motor skills range from gross motor movement involving large muscle groups, such as crawling, walking, and running, to fine motor movements of smaller, more refined actions, such as picking up objects with our hands or wiggling our toes. Movement also includes nonverbal interpersonal communications, such as facial expressions, changes in posture or the tilt of the head, or gestures of the hands and arms.

Most overt movement results from sensory perception and in turn helps to shape sensory perception. Movement or motor memory is "achieved from a sophisticated feedback system that detects errors made as the movement is learned. The feedback system uses these errors as a basis from which to generate a new, more accurate sequence of commands, eventually leading to a successful performance. We modify and learn through movement every second of our waking day whether we are active or inactive" (Ratey, 2002, p. 205). Movement memory is apparent in tasks such as tying shoelaces or learning to play a musical instrument. The subtler movement adjustments to environmental and interpersonal cues are less obvious but crucial in determining action tendencies. For instance, if a child is repeatedly met with parental disapproval when he enthusiastically gesticulates and puffs up his chest while describing his success at a game, his expanded chest will deflate and his movements become more restricted. If the criticism is repeated, this constrained movement may become an automatic tendency in interpersonal interactions, in turn affecting perception.

Todd (1959) taught that function precedes structure: The same movement made over and over again ultimately molds the body. For example, when the muscular contractions that prime defensive movements are repeated many times, these contractions turn into physical patterns that affect the body's structure, which in turn, further affects function. Over a long period of time, this chronic tension interferes with the body's natural alignment and movement, creates physical problems (most notably, back, neck, and shoulder pain), and even sustains corresponding emotions and cognitions. Kurtz and Prestera noted: "Such physical patterns become fixed by time, affecting growth and body structure, and characterizing not just the moment, but the person. Rather than simply a present disappointment, the crushed posture of hopelessness could be pointing to a lifetime of endless frustration, and bitter failure" (1976, p. 1).

Repetitive movements and postures thus contribute to the maintenance of cognitive and emotional tendencies by creating a position from which only select emotions and physical actions are possible (Barlow, 1973). We often notice the posture of the startle response in traumatized clients: shoulders up, breath held, head pulled down and forward into the shoulder girdle, similar to a "deer in the headlights." The action of the startle response disturbs the aligned balance between head and shoulders and is usually temporary, but if this normal response to a sudden novel stimulus becomes chronic, the physical organization itself may predispose the individual to experience emotions of fear and distrust and thoughts of impending danger on a chronic basis.

Physical action precedes cognitive and even emotional reactions in acute traumatic situations. Hobson (1994) stated that movement

> takes precedence in times of emergency, when it is advantageous to short-circuit the cortex and activate a motor-pattern generated directly from the brain stem. If we suddenly see a car careening toward us, we instantly turn our car away; we react automatically, and only later (even if it is only a split second later) do we realize there is danger and feel afraid. (p. 139)

When danger is imminent, a person responds with sequences of motor actions that are involuntary and largely predictable (Cannon, 1953). Llinas described these fixed action patterns as "sets of well defined motor patterns, ready made 'motor tapes' . . . that, when switched on, produce well defined and coordinated movements; the escape response, walking, swallowing, the prewired aspects of birdsongs, and the like" (2001, p. 133). Fixed action patterns comprise a variety of simultaneous and sequential movements. When a car appears unexpectedly in our headlights, our adaptive fixed action pattern consists of a variety of movements that enable the fastest defensive action possible: a sudden intake of breath, widening of the eyes, gripping of the steering wheel, slamming on the brakes, and turning the car to avoid a collision.

The evolutionary advantage of these fixed action patterns lies in their automatic engagement, which allows for the development of more complex actions on all levels of information processing. Because we can do them without thinking, fixed action patterns allow us to perform complex tasks automatically, such as walking, and with lightening speed, such as avoiding a deer in the road. Action tendencies are economical and adaptive, leaving the mind free for other tasks (Frijda, 1986; Hobson, 1994; Llinas, 2001; Ratey, 2002; Van der Hart et al., 2006). When we are driving along the highway, we may be thinking about all sorts of things unrelated to driving, while our physical movement mechanically negotiates the complex actions of steering, regulating speed, braking, perceiving other cars/drivers, and so on. If there is danger, our bodies respond without thought to the threat. The speed and automatic nature of fixed action patterns are crucial to survival. It is the recurrence of components of the fixed action patterns as sensorimotor fragments (e.g., intrusive sensations, movement impulses) that reappear after the danger is over that contributes to traumatic reexperiencing.

When the cascade of defensive actions to threat is evoked, some of the actions that constitute an adaptive response may be ineffective, interrupted, or incomplete. An automobile accident victim might have felt the impulse to turn the steering wheel but was unable to execute the action before she hit the oncoming car. The sexual abuse survivor might have wanted to fight her perpetrator but was overpowered. These incomplete actions of defense subsequently may manifest as chronic symptoms. As Herman noted, "Each component of the ordinary response to danger, having lost its utility, tends to persist in an altered and exaggerated state long after the actual danger is over" (1992, p. 34).

If a person is attacked and experiences the urge to fight back but is overpowered by the attacker, the sequence of possible defensive actions may persist in distorted forms, such as muscles held in a chronically tightened pattern, an exaggerated tendency to be triggered suddenly into aggression, or a chronic lack of tone or sensation in a particular muscle group. Janet gave the example of clients who exhibited symptoms of "contraction of the abductor muscles (the guardians of virginity) brought about by the memory of rape or by that of unwanted sexual relationships" (1925, p. 502). When the components of the defensive response to trauma persist in these altered forms, individuals react inappropriately to perceived threat or reminders of past threat in the present. They may become too aggressive (e.g., the client who turns violent when challenged by his wife) or too passive (e.g., the client, abused as a child, who cannot defend herself from unwanted sexual advances as an adult). Either way, the adaptive execution of a sequence of defensive actions remains truncated, incomplete, and dissatisfying to the individual. Without treatment, these tendencies may indefinitely prevent adaptive action in the present.

Whereas top-down processing is dependent on lower levels, sensorimotor processing can function independently of top-down regulation. During flashbacks or the reliving of past trauma, integrated cognitive processing is inhibited, and the person temporarily loses the capacity to recognize that present reality is safe. Instead, he or she identifies the sensations of hyperarousal and the impulse for physical action as indicators of danger. This bottom-up "hijacking" (Goleman, 1995) is a frequent source of daily life problems and self-blame for trauma survivors: They are unable to reflect on events from a critical distance, which engenders a sense of instability, loss of control, psychological incompetence, and a lack of confidence in coping with daily life. "I should be over this" or "I must be crazy" are two common complaints of traumatized clients, stemming from the conviction that they are psychologically inadequate rather than functioning with sensorimotor systems that are primed for threat and reacting to danger long since over (Allen, 2001).

COGNITIVE, EMOTIONAL, AND SENSORIMOTOR ACTION TENDENCIES

An action tendency is a propensity to implement or carry out a particular action. Action tendencies are formed on cognitive, emotional, and sensorimotor levels. Tendencies stem from procedural memory of processes and functions, reflected in habitual responses and conditioned behavior (Schacter, 1996). Procedural learning involves repeated iterations of movements, perceptions, cognitive and emotional processes, or combinations of these (Grigsby & Stevens, 2000). The original events from which these automatic personal processes and routines are learned have usually been forgotten. Actions that are procedurally learned "do not require conscious or unconscious mental representations, images, motivations or ideas to operate" (Grigsby & Stevens, 2000, p. 316). Operating nonconsciously, procedural learning on all three levels of information processing turns into automatic action tendencies that become crucial organizers of behavior.

Long after environmental conditions have changed, we remain in a state of readiness to perform the mental (cognitive and emotional) and sensorimotor actions that were adaptive in the past. For example, the child who learns that it is safer to back away from adults when either she or they are distressed, instead of seeking proximity, might develop action tendencies of avoidance-oriented postural adjustments (turned away, looking at the ground to avoid eye contact), movement impulses that lead to backing away, emotional responses such as fear, and cognitive belief systems such as "It's not safe to seek comfort." These action tendencies "have the character of urges or impulses. They lie in waiting for signs that they can or may be executed; they, and their execution, tend to persist in the face of interruptions; they tend to interrupt other ongoing programs and actions; and they tend to preempt the information processing facilities" (Frijda, 1986, p. 78). In broad terms, an action tendency is a readiness for specific behavior. This "readiness" means that the action tendency exists within the person in latent form and becomes activated in response to specific internal or external stimuli.

Maladaptive actions tendencies conditioned from the past are triggered by internal and environmental reminders of the past and take precedence when other actions might prove more adaptive. Once procedures become automatic tendencies, we no longer use top-down processes to regulate them. Ratey (2002) clarified how this works in terms of the levels of the brain:

> Processes that are fundamental and mastered are stored in and executed from the brainstem, basal ganglia, and cerebellum in the lower brain. Actions and cognition that are increasingly more complex, or very new, are managed further up in the brain, increasingly toward the frontal cortex, so that more brain regions are employed along the way that can offer input or provide delay for consideration. (p. 158)

When working effectively, we can "shift back and forth between deliberate and automatic movements and deliberate and automatic cognition" (Ratey, 2002, p. 160). This capacity is suboptimal for traumatized people, who have

difficulty suspending their strong action tendencies to engage in more deliberate, reflective actions (Fonagy et al., 1995).

THE INTERFACE BETWEEN TOP-DOWN
AND BOTTOM-UP PROCESSING

Top-down and bottom-up processing represent two directions of information flow, and their interplay holds significant implications for the occurrence and treatment of trauma. In clinical practice the therapist (1) notices
the client's information-processing tendencies on each of the three related
yet distinct levels of experience, (2) identifies which level of processing will
most successfully support the integration of traumatic experience at any particular moment of therapy, and (3) applies specific techniques that facilitate
the processing of traumatic experience at that particular level. For example, consider a survivor of childhood loss and sexual abuse who complains
of "feeling unsafe" and simultaneously experiences strong emotions of grief
accompanied by trembling and a rapid heart rate. The therapist could
choose to use the client's cognitions as an entry point, helping her to use
logic to recognize that she is now safe. Or the therapist might decide to deal
with the emotions of grief, using interventions that facilitate the client's
experience of the unresolved traumatic grief of loss and absence of safety in
her childhood. A third option would be to focus on the somatic reactions:
The therapist might temporarily disregard the cognitions and emotions and
focus exclusively on the physical trembling, accelerated heart rate, and associated movement impulses until they are resolved.

Thus action tendencies on all levels of information processing are viable
targets for therapeutic intervention. Any of these entry points would potentially have a positive therapeutic effect. However, it is important to note that
the most effective intervention will affect the client not only on the particular level at which the intervention is directed, but also on the other two
levels. Changing a cognitive tendency, or belief, can soothe the emotions and
the physical experiences; focusing on the emotion of grief can help calm the
body and change beliefs; addressing sensorimotor tendencies by tracking
physiological arousal until the body settles, or helping the patient explore a
previously inhibited physical action, can lower emotional arousal and help
shift beliefs.

Psychotherapy has traditionally harnessed top-down techniques to manage disruptive bottom-up processes through the voluntary and conscious
sublimation of sensorimotor and emotional tendencies. Such top-down
management of arousal is as old as the field of psychology itself and can be
an effective therapeutic intervention. When sensorimotor experience is disturbing or overwhelming, conscious top-down regulation can allow a person

to pace him or herself, modulating the degree of arousal or disorganization in the system. For example, a traumatized person who is triggered into high arousal by an innocuous environmental stimulus can manage this arousal by identifying the stimulus as innocuous and reassuring himself until the activation settles. Or he can manage the arousal by engaging in behavior that will distract him, such as watching television, or engaging in behavior that will discharge the arousal, such as going for a jog. Both of these indicate top-down management—deciding cognitively to undertake an activity that takes the edge off the distress associated with an overwhelming experience. The arousal is voluntarily and consciously sublimated through physical activity, behavioral discharge, cognitive override, or mental distraction.

Although top-down distraction or discharge techniques offer effective *management* of hyperarousal and provide significant relief, they may not fully address the entire problem (Allen, 2001), especially the somatic elements. Similarly, changing one's interpretations can engage cognition but ignore sensorimotor processes. Top-down processing alone may manage sensorimotor reactions but may not enable their full assimilation. For instance, a client can learn to mitigate arousal temporarily by convincing herself that the world is now safe, but the underlying tendency for arousal to escalate to overwhelming degrees has not been fully resolved. The traumatic experience and arousal from the sensorimotor and emotional levels may be redirected through top-down management, but the processing and assimilation of sensorimotor reactions to the trauma may not have occurred.

In sensorimotor psychotherapy, top-down direction is harnessed to support sensorimotor processing rather than just manage it. The client might be asked to mindfully track (a top-down, cognitive process) the sequence of physical sensations and impulses (sensorimotor process) as they progress through the body, and to temporarily disregard emotions and thoughts that arise, until the bodily sensations and impulses resolve to a point of rest and stabilization. In much the same way that a client who comes to therapy with unresolved grief can identify and experience the grief (emotional processing), a client who exhibits unresolved sensorimotor reactions can identify and experience these reactions *physically* (bottom-up sensorimotor processing). The client learns to observe and follow the sensorimotor reactions that were activated at the time of the trauma, as well as to mindfully execute physical actions that interrupt maladaptive tendencies.

CONCLUSION

Optimal functioning of the higher levels of the brain and of information processing is dependent, to some degree, upon the adequate functioning of the lower levels. There are extensive interconnections among all parts of the brain and among all levels of information processing. Ratey noted that "when we smile we feel happier and when we feel happier we smile. . . . The feedback between layers or levels of the brain is bidirectional; if you activate a lower level, you will be priming an upper level, and if you activate a higher level, you will be priming a lower level" (Ratey, 2002, p. 164). The client's awareness and processing of sensorimotor reactions exert a positive influence on emotional and cognitive processing, and vice versa. Movement and body sensation, as well as thoughts and emotions, are viable targets for intervention that can support resolution of the traumatic experience. Top-down approaches that attempt to regulate overwhelming sensorimotor and affective processes are a necessary part of trauma therapy, but if such interventions overmanage, ignore, suppress, or fail to support adaptive body processes, these traumatic responses may not be resolved. Similarly, bottom-up interventions that result in bottom-up hijacking, or fail to include cognitive and emotional processing, can sabotage integration and may lead to endless repetitive flashbacks, secondary retraumatization, or chronic trauma kindling (Post, Weiss, Smith, Li, & McCann, 1997). In order to treat the effects of trauma on all three levels of processing, somatically informed top-down management of symptoms, insight and understanding, and bottom-up processing of the sensations, arousal, movement, and emotions must be thoughtfully balanced.

Chapter 2

※•※•※

Window of Tolerance: The Capacity for Modulating Arousal

UNRESOLVED SURVIVAL-RELATED ACTION TENDENCIES include not only chronic postural and movement patterns related to defense, but also the rapid mobilization of the autonomic nervous system in response to trauma-related stimuli. People with trauma-related disorders are characteristically vulnerable to hyperarousal (i.e., experiencing "too much" activation) and/or hypoarousal (i.e., experiencing "too little" activation) and often oscillate between these two extremes (Post et al., 1997; Van der Hart, Nijenhuis, & Steele, 2006; Van der Kolk et al., 1996). Triggered by traumatic reminders, both autonomic tendencies leave clients at the mercy of dysregulated arousal. When hyperaroused, clients experience too much arousal to process information effectively and are tormented by intrusive images, affects, and body sensations. But when hypoaroused, clients suffer another kind of torment stemming from a dearth of emotion and sensation—a numbing, a sense of deadness or emptiness, passivity, possibly paralysis (Bremner & Brett, 1997; Spiegel, 1997; Van der Hart et al., 2004), and/or may be too distanced from the experience to be able to process information effectively. In both cases, top-down regulation is compromised and meaning making becomes biased by the perceived danger signals. Whereas these extremes of arousal may be adaptive in certain traumatic situations, they become maladaptive when they persist in nonthreatening contexts.

In order to put the past in the past, clients must process traumatic experiences in an "optimal arousal zone" (Wilbarger & Wilbarger, 1997). Falling between the two extremes of hyper- and hypoarousal, this zone is described as the "window of tolerance" (Siegel, 1999). Within this window, "various intensities of emotional and physiological arousal can be processed without disrupting the functioning of the system" (Siegel, 1999, p. 253). When clients are working within a window of tolerance, information received from both internal and external environments can be integrated. They can continually process the ongoing barrage of sensory information because they can receive and integrate current sensory input even while assimilating prior input (Williamson & Anzalone, 2001). They can think and talk about their experience in therapy and simultaneously feel a congruent emotional tone and sense of self. In an optimal arousal zone, cortical functioning is maintained—a prerequisite for integrating information on cognitive, emotional, and sensorimotor levels.

Window of Tolerance

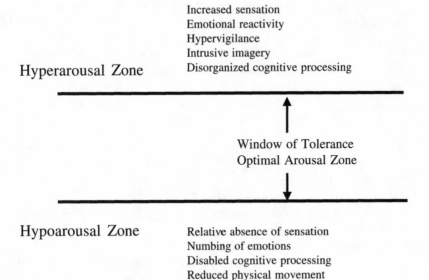

Figure 2.1. The three zones of arousal: A simple model for understanding the regulation of autonomic arousal.

VARIATIONS IN THE WINDOW OF TOLERANCE

As the modulation model diagram in the figure illustrates, three general "zones" of arousal can be delineated as optimal arousal, hyperarousal, and hypoarousal. Within the optimal zone, arousal naturally fluctuates in response to environmental cues and context and according to the individual's immediate internal condition (such as energy level, degree of fatigue or hunger). However, sympathetic and parasympathetic activity remain in relative balance, with each system achieving only a slight dominance over the other at any given moment (Wenger & Cullen, 1958). These minor adjustments help us to modulate arousal appropriately in order to make the best possible adaptation to the immediate task: If we are trying to fall asleep, low arousal helps us achieve a relaxed, drowsy state; if we are preparing for an important challenge, higher arousal helps us remain alert and mentally energetic.

Each person has a habitual "width" of the window of tolerance that influences his or her overall ability to process information. People with a wide window can cope with greater extremes of arousal and can process complex and stimulating information more effectively. People with a narrow window experience fluctuations as unmanageable and dysregulating. Most traumatized clients have a narrow window and are more susceptible to becoming dysregulated by normal fluctuations in arousal (Taylor, Koch, & McNally, 1992).

The width of a window of tolerance is directly related to how much stimulation is required to elicit the "threshold of response." When the threshold is low, a person's nervous system is aroused with very little input; when the threshold is high, more input is required. For optimal functioning, the threshold should be "high enough that we can tolerate the complexity and stimulation inherent in the environment, yet low enough that we can perceive subtle changes and novelty in the environment" (Williamson & Anzalone, 2001, p. 28). Thresholds vary from person to person and are influenced by several factors: (1) the kind of sensory stimuli (e.g., some people are more sensitive to visual input, whereas others are more sensitive to auditory input), (2) how long the effect of the stimulus lasts (i.e., the rate of recovery), (3) the person's initial arousal level, (4) previous experience (Williamson & Anzalone, 2001), and (5) temperament (Siegel, 1999). Thresholds also vary with the type of stimulation. Some people have a high threshold for cognitive stimulation, such as intellectual debate, but a low threshold for emotional stimulation, as in the context of a marital disagreement.

Traumatized individuals typically experience unusually low or unusually high thresholds, or both. Clients' thresholds are important indicators of their particular sensitivities, traumatic distortions, and capacity for effective information processing. The therapist helps them become aware of their thresholds and identify the somatic signs of arousal that exceeds the optimal zone, eventually expanding the width of their window of tolerance through somatic interventions. For example, Jim, who grew up with critical, abusive parents who frequently raised their voices in anger, became aware that his threshold for "negative feedback" was unduly low, especially when the other person's voice was raised, which was a problem at work. His boss used a "loud" voice when critiquing Jim's performance. At the slightest indication that his boss had negative feedback for him, Jim became hyperaroused and defensively reactive. He learned to identify his low threshold, recognize the somatic signs (tension in his shoulders, shortness of breath, and increase in heart rate) of his escalating arousal, and utilize physical action (taking measured, deep breaths, maintaining eye contact with his boss, and sitting back in his chair) to return his arousal to within a window of tolerance.

THE POLYVAGAL HIERARCHY

Porges (1995, 2001a, 2001b, 2004, 2005) discussed the complex interplay between the parasympathetic and sympathetic nervous systems in his "polyvagal theory," which takes a more sophisticated and integrative view of the autonomic nervous system than previous arousal theories that attributed all occasions of arousal to the engagement of the sympathetic nervous system (Cannon, 1928; Grinker & Spiegel, 1945). Porges's theory suggests that the nervous system can be better described in terms of a hierarchy of response rather than in terms of balance. The polyvagal theory describes three hierarchically organized subsystems of the autonomic nervous system that govern our neurobiological responses to environmental stimulation: the ventral parasympathetic branch of the vagus nerve (social engagement), the sympathetic system (mobilization), and the dorsal parasympathetic branch of the vagal nerve (immobilization). Each of these subsystems corresponds to one of the three arousal zones of the modulation model: The social engagement (ventral vagal) system correlates with the optimal arousal zone, the sympathetic system with the hyperaroused zone, and the dorsal vagal system with the hypoaroused zone.

The most evolutionarily recent and sophisticated of the subsystems is the ventral vagal complex, involving the ventral branch of the vagus nerve—the myelinated vagus—which originates in the nucleus ambiguous in the brainstem, one of several tiny patches of specialized neurons that make up the reticular activating system. This system determines an individual's level of consciousness or wakefulness. The ventral vagal complex is usually activated when arousal is in the optimal zone of the modulation model. Porges

(2003b) calls this system the "social engagement system" because it provides humans with a great degree of flexibility in communication and regulates areas of the body that are utilized in social and environmental interaction:

> The social engagement system has a control component in the cortex (i.e., upper motor neurons) that regulates brainstem nuclei (i.e., lower motor neurons) to control eyelid opening (e.g., looking), facial muscles (e.g., emotional expression), middle ear muscles (e.g., extracting human voice from background noise), muscle of mastication (e.g., ingestion), laryngeal and pharyngeal muscles (e.g., prosody), and head tilting and turning muscles (e.g., social gesture and orientation). (Porges, 2003b, p. 35)

Collectively, these components of the social engagement system enable rapid engagement and disengagement with the environment and in social relationships by regulating heart rate without mobilizing the sympathetic nervous system. For instance, in conversation, we can talk rapidly and animatedly in one moment and be quite still while listening in the next, fine-tuning our facial, vocal, and middle ear muscles accordingly. The sophisticated "braking" mechanism of the social engagement system can rapidly decrease or increase heart rate, allowing us to slow down and then remobilize, while inhibiting primitive defensive reactions (Porges, 2005). This system thus fosters more tranquil, flexibly adaptive overall states (Porges, 2004, 2005) and thereby helps arousal to remain within the window of tolerance.

In nonthreatening contexts the social engagement system regulates the sympathetic nervous system, facilitates engagement with the environment, and helps us form positive attachment and social bonds. Even under threat, a well-adapted person may utilize the social engagement system, for example, by trying to reason with a potential attacker. If this approach were ineffective, however, the social engagement system would automatically give way to the mobilizing fight/flight responses of the sympathetic nervous system. The dominance of the social engagement system, which helps to maintain arousal in a window of tolerance, is overridden under traumatic conditions when sympathetic responses would be more adaptive.

The activation of the sympathetic nervous system, evolutionarily more primitive and less flexible than the social engagement system, increases overall arousal and mobilizes survival mechanisms (flight and flight behaviors) in response to threat. When sympathetic nervous system tone is high, arousal increases toward the upper edges of the window of tolerance. As danger is perceived and interpreted by the brain, a mind–body chain reaction is set in motion: the amygdala "sounds the alarm," and the sympathetic nervous system is "turned on" by the hypothalamus, causing the release of a cascade of neurochemicals that increase arousal (McEwan, 1995; van der Kolk, McFarlane, & Van der Hart, 1996; Yehuda, 1997, 1998).

These "emergency reactions" (Cannon, 1929) mobilize energy in anticipation of the vigorous activity needed to meet the threat and include both energy-mobilizing and energy-consuming processes: accelerated, deeper respiration in response to the need for more oxygen; increased blood flow to the muscles (Frijda, 1986); decreased blood flow to the cortex; increased vigilance toward the environment; and the suppression of all physical systems not essential for defense. By enabling us to carry out vigorous fight/flight responses, hyperarousal maximizes our chances of survival (Levine, 1997; Rothschild, 2000). When vigorous physical responses, such as running or fighting, are successful, not only is the level of threat reduced but the cascade of danger-related neurochemicals is metabolized through these energy-consuming actions. Both of these factors help arousal to return to the window of tolerance. In the absence of vigorous action, hyperarousal may gradually return to an optimal zone when the threatening stimulus has receded or disappeared.

If both social engagement (mediated by one branch of the parasympathetic system, the ventral vagal complex) and fight/flight responses (mediated by the sympathetic nervous system) are unsuccessful in assuring safety, the other branch of the parasympathetic nervous system, the dorsal vagal complex, becomes the next line of defense. The dorsal branch of the vagus nerve, the unmyelinated vagus, also originating in the brainstem (at the dorsal motor nucleus of the vagus), is the most primitive of these systems. It is triggered into action by hypoxia (a lack of oxygen in the tissues of the body) and serves to decrease arousal toward the hypoarousal zone. The dorsal vagal branch enables survival-related immobilization, such as feigning death, behavioral shutdown, and syncope.

In contrast to the energy-consuming processes mediated by the sympathetic nervous system, increased dorsal vagal tone is associated with energy conservation: Many functions of the body begin to slow down, leading to "a relative decrease in heart rate and respiration and accompanied by a sense of 'numbness,' 'shutting down within the mind,' and separation from the sense of self" (Siegel, 1999, p. 254). Extreme dorsal vagal arousal can result in fainting, vomiting, or loss of control of the rectal sphincter, all of which seem to occur when action is not feasible (Frijda, 1986). Although this immobilization can assure survival, it can lead to bradycardia, apnea, and cardiac arrhythmias, and can actually be lethal for mammals if it is maintained over a prolonged period (see Figure 2.2; Seligman, 1975).

Arousal Zones

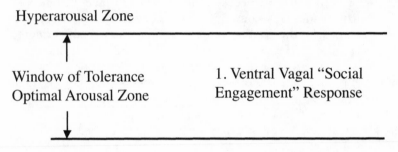

2. Sympathetic "Fight or
Flight" Response

Hyperarousal Zone

Window of Tolerance
Optimal Arousal Zone

1. Ventral Vagal "Social
Engagement" Response

Hypoarousal Zone

3. Dorsal Vagal "Immobilization"
Response

Figure 2.2.   The correlation of the three arousal zones and the polyvagal
hierarchy.

The dominance among these three autonomic subsystems normally fluctuates, but human beings generally respond hierarchically in the face of environmental challenges. The more sophisticated, sensitive, and least primitive
social engagement system (increased ventral vagal tone) might be the first
line of defense for individuals who have a wide and flexible window of tolerance. This type of response capacity is illustrated by a client who managed
to engage a potential rapist in a discussion about his sister, distracting him
from harming her. Our "backup" system for threatening situations in which
social engagement fails is the increased sympathetic arousal that mobilizes
fight or flight responses—for example, a woman trapped in a car by a potential rapist tried to talk him out of it. When this failed, she struck the man and
jumped out of the car, effectively escaping. The evolutionary "last resort"
backup system is the most primitive response (increased tone in the dorsal
vagal complex), employed when the sympathetically mediated fight or flight
strategies are ill-advised or unsuccessful. Many clients abused as children
at first attempted to fight back, which often increased the danger. In time,
they succumbed to the abuse, becoming passive and numb.
    During traumatic events, the neural hierarchy provides survival-related
advantages: It is "hard-wired," instinctive, and has alternatives built into

it. Additionally, because the social engagement system governs, and can inhibit, both the sympathetic responses and the dorsal vagal complex, this sophisticated "braking" mechanism facilitates the regulation of overall arousal in nontraumatic daily life as well. But when chronic failure of the social engagement system to negotiate safety and protection is experienced, as is often the case in chronic childhood trauma, the system habitually shuts down. Unchecked by the "brakes" of the social engagement system, the sympathetic or the dorsal vagal nervous systems remain highly activated, causing arousal to exceed the window of tolerance.

THE IMPACT OF TRAUMA ON AROUSAL
AND THE WINDOW OF TOLERANCE

When the social engagement system has repeatedly failed to avert danger in situations of chronic trauma, the long-term availability of this system may tend to decrease, thus diminishing the individual's future capacity for relationships. As Sahar, Shalev, and Porges (2001) explained:

> The defective vagal regulation of heart rate observed in PTSD may index a compromised integrated social engagement system. Thus, several of the behavioral features observed in PTSD (i.e., poor social behavior, lack of positive emotional expressivity) may be dependent on difficulties in the neural regulation of the muscles of the face and head, whereas several of the features related to autonomic state regulation may be due to difficulties in the vagal regulation of the heart and bronchi. (p. 642)

When safety is perceived, we readily engage with the environment, but this engagement will not take place when we misinterpret environmental cues as dangerous—a misinterpretation that triggers physiological states that support defensive strategies (Porges, 2004). Clients suffering from trauma-related disorders may have a functional loss of the fine-tuning that enables positive environmental and social interaction to regulate heart rate and viscera without sympathetic or dorsal vagal arousal, that is, without hyper- or hypoarousal.

Having survived the trauma, the inability to utilize the social engagement system to inhibit defensive strategies and maintain arousal within a window of tolerance prevents future adaptive responses. When traumatic experiences are chronic, the most adaptive survival responses for a specific set of circumstances are repeatedly activated, either as a result of actual threat or in preparation for anticipated threat triggered by traumatic reminders. Traumatized people are usually so sensitized by past traumatic events that they have a very low thresholds for relatively minor stressors, responding with the extreme arousal adaptive in the past, either becoming hyperaroused or becoming hypoaroused. In either case, because the window of tolerance has become functionally narrowed by repeated traumatic responses, the individual is now increasingly more vulnerable to perceived traumatic triggers. Many traumatized individuals are unable to prevent wide swings of dysregulated arousal, fluctuating between the extreme zones of hyperarousal and hypoarousal. This recurring "bottom-up hijacking" is experienced as sudden ruptures in the window of tolerance, after which the individual is unable to easily or quickly return to the optimal arousal zone (Siegel, 1999).

Chronic hyperarousal "creates a vicious cycle: State-dependent memory retrieval [triggered by trauma-related stimuli] causes increased access to traumatic memories and involuntary intrusions of the trauma, which lead in turn to even more arousal" (Van der Kolk, Van der Hart, & Marmar, 1996, p. 305). Hyperarousal is often accompanied by the fragmentation of perceptual experience into emotional and/or sensory elements. These dissociated perceptual memory fragments recur as symptoms in the form of flashbacks and nightmares and contribute to the rapid heart rate, elevated blood pressure, and altered skin conductance that are associated with hyperarousal. Somatoform symptoms of increased body sensation, tension, and involuntary or uncontrolled movements may accompany hyperarousal. Lanius et al. (2004) have demonstrated in functional magnetic resonance imaging (fMRI) studies that traumatic reevocations occur in conjunction with subjective descriptions of fear and panic. The individual becomes estranged from present reality, believing and acting as though the past event were happening again (Van der Kolk, Van der Hart, & Marmar, 1996).

The effects of chronic hyperarousal can be far-reaching, impairing overall ability to make adaptive choices. Hyperaroused individuals have difficulty using emotions as signals from which to make meaning, because hyperarousal leads them to construe innocuous stimuli as dangerous. The intensity and accelerated pace of emotions, sensations, and sensory stimuli disrupt reasoning and the ability to engage in reflective "reality checks." Hyperarousal causes traumatized people to "be unable to trust their bodily sensations to . . . alert them to take appropriate action" (Van der Kolk, Van der Hart, & McFarlane, 1996, p. 421). Thus the hyperaroused person's ability to respond adaptively to subsequent threat is suboptimal, and his or her behavior is often reactive and impulsive rather than reflective and adaptive.

Although hyperarousal symptoms are commonly considered the hallmark of trauma, not all traumatized clients report hyperarousal. Lanius et al. (2002) noted in her study, in which script-driven imagery of clients' traumatic event was used to elicit trauma activation, that hypoarousal rather than hyperarousal was experienced by nearly one-third of subjects. Instead of hyperarousal-related reactions, these clients respond to traumatic reminders with hypoarousal and behavioral shutdown.

Unlike the hyperarousal-related intrusive symptoms, hypoarousal reexperiencing causes similar losses in memory, motor or affective functions, and somatosensory awareness as those that occurred during the trauma (Van der Hart et al., 2004). Chronic hypoarousal frequently involves somatoform dissociative symptoms such as motor weakness, paralysis, ataxia, and numbing of inner-body sensation, as well as psychoform dissociative symptoms, such as cognitive abnormalities, amnesia, fugue states, confusional states, and deficits in attention (Nijenhuis & Van der Hart, 1999; Van der Hart et al., 2004a and 2004b). Clients may report a subjective sense of separation from the body, an absence of sensation in parts of the body or even in the entire body, and delayed or weakened physical responses. Hypoarousal can reduce the capacity to sense emotions and experience emotional reactions to significant events, thus diminishing effective emotional processing. Cognitive processing is also disabled, because hypoarousal interferes with the ability to think clearly and hinders appropriate evaluation of dangerous situations. The likely increase in dorsal vagal tone may correspond to passivity and "[an] absence of muscular activity, abandoning readiness for such activity, relinquishing focused attention" (Frijda, 1986, p. 159). The sensorimotor action tendencies associated with hypoarousal resemble passive inaction or slow movements that do not provoke much attention from others. The deficits of hypoarousal are often confusing to therapist and client alike and are frequently misinterpreted as depression, resistance, or passive–aggressive behavior. Instead, these deficits need to be considered as a hypoarousal response to trauma.

Hyper- and hypoarousal usually coexist with extreme thresholds for sensory stimulation. As noted, most people with trauma-related disorders have a narrow window of tolerance and are unable to withstand much stimulation (a low threshold). Others are counterphobic and seek extreme stimulation but have difficulty assimilating the accompanying arousal. Some have a high threshold because of the "buffering" effects of hypoarousal, which interferes with their responsiveness to the environment. Whereas one person might have little response to unusually loud noises in the immediate vicinity, another might be terrified and overwhelmed by the sound of a car in the distance. McFarlane, Weber, and Clark (1993) found that many traumatized individuals do not register stimuli noticed and responded to by nontraumatized participants. In this study, as the stimuli presented increased in intensity, normal participants responded proportionately, whereas participants with PTSD did not respond until a certain threshold was reached, but then they responded with inordinately high arousal to seemingly innocuous stimuli.

When arousal remains in the hyper- or hypoarousal zones, behavior tends to become less structured, and reflexive defensive tendencies appear to be random and disorganized. "In states of mind beyond the window of tolerance, the prefrontally mediated capacity for response flexibility is temporarily shut down. The 'higher mode' of integrative [cognitive] processing has been replaced by a 'lower mode' of reflexive responding" (Siegel, 1999, pp. 254–255). When a person remains in the hyper- or hypoarousal zones, traumatic experience is not integrated into a unitary whole or into an integrated sense of self. Over time, prolonged experiences of disorientation result in increasing fragmentation of perception, action, and self-state: In hyperaroused states, the individual may be reactive and defensive, whereas in hypoaroused states, the same individual may be meek and compliant. This fragmentation of a unified sense of self, in turn, results in further disorientation, dissociation, and greater difficulty in modulating arousal.

DISSOCIATION AND AROUSAL ZONES

In a state of hyper- or hypoarousal, individuals are unable to integrate their thoughts, emotions, memories, and/or sensorimotor responses to traumatic events. As survival and safety are achieved in the aftermath of trauma, arousal may gradually return to a window of tolerance, and dissociated elements may gradually be reintegrated and assimilated. However, clients who are easily reactivated by trauma-related stimuli into hyper- or hypoaroused zones may remain chronically unable to integrate past traumatic events. Fragments of these events are reactivated by triggers but not processed and integrated. Whereas some authors (Perry, Pollard, Blakely, Baker, & Vigilante, 1995) describe dissociative responses as aspects of the detachment and lowering of consciousness associated with hypoarousal, and do not associate dissociation with hyperarousal, Janet's (1889, 1907) description of dissociation as a failure of integrative capacity applies to both hypoaroused and hyperaroused states (Allen, 2001; Krystal, Bremner, Southwick, & Charney, 1998; Van der Hart et al., 2004).

When arousal falls within the window of tolerance and the individual is not traumatized, dissociative responses do not ordinarily occur. Arousal may fluctuate within the optimal zone, but the person is able to integrate elements of experience on cognitive, emotional, and sensorimotor levels of information processing. However, when hyper- or hypoarousal states become extreme and/or enduring, as is often the case during and after trauma, responses and processes that are normally unified and integrated may become chronically dissociated, hindering the individual's ability to process trauma-related information even when arousal is within the window of tolerance.

For example, during a childhood filled with traumatic neglect and abuse at the hands of many different caregivers Annie developed dissociative tendencies. She alternately experienced fear and terror with concomitant hyper-arousal, and foggy, "spaced out" states of hypoarousal, both of which interfered with daily life activities associated with marriage, work, play, and rearing children. When Annie was not experiencing either of these extreme arousal states, her arousal returned to the window of tolerance. She did her best to avoid reminders of the trauma in order to keep arousal within the optimal zone and meet the demands of her daily life. However, even when her arousal level was within the window of tolerance, her unintegrated traumatic experience remained compartmentalized, or dissociated, from her awareness. For decades after her childhood trauma, Annie cycled between periods of time when she was reliving the trauma (experiencing fear and terror, impulses to flee, states of shame and self-disgust, spaciness and motor weakness) and periods of time when she felt detached from and avoidant of the trauma, attempting to "get on with life." Annie reported little connection or integration between reliving and avoiding the trauma, saying that in each of these experiences, she "felt like a different person."

As Janet pointed out a century ago, individuals with complex trauma-related disorders develop "a tendency to the dissociation and emancipation of the systems of ideas and functions that constitute personality" (1907, p. 332). With such undue compartmentalization, even when a person experiences arousal within a window of tolerance, he or she remains dissociated from elements of the traumatic memory—from its context and its related action tendencies—all of which come to the fore when arousal occurs in the overactivated (hyper) and underactivated (hypo) zones.

Van der Hart and colleagues (2006) describe dissociation as a division of the personality into at least two dissociative aspects: one aspect that "goes on going on" after the trauma is primarily engaged in daily life functioning, remaining avoidant of the traumatic memories and their reminders; and the other aspect that encompasses the traumatic memories, experiences sensitivity to traumatic reminders and extremes in arousal, and engages in defensive actions against threat.

At times, Annie avoided the traumatic memories in order to participate in daily life activities: marriage, creating a home, raising two children, and going to graduate school. The associated symptoms that accompany this state could be described as dysthymia and emotionally flattened affect, but her arousal remained within a window of tolerance during these times. At other times, Annie was triggered by reminders of the trauma, and her arousal alternated between hyper- and hypoaroused zones. During these times she had great difficulty functioning in her daily life.

Thus, even though traumatized people can maintain arousal within a window of tolerance when avoiding the memories and reminders of the trauma, they are still dissociated from the other part of the self that relives the trauma. Like Annie, they remain dissociatively compartmentalized and distanced from the part of the personality that experiences the trauma-related arousal, affects, and defensive responses.

Annie's internal experience included not only the "going on going on" part and the overwhelmed part; she also observed other parts of herself that had very different "consciousness, memory, identity, or perception of the environment" (American Psychiatric Association, 2000) and with these, markedly different somatoform and psychoform dissociative symptoms. For example, the aspect of Annie that was submissive and compliant perceived the environment to be dangerous unless others were pleased. The aspect of her that engaged the defensive response of flight became hyperaroused and searched the environment for ways of escape. However, when she was avoidant of the trauma, her arousal remained in the optimal zone and she was able to function relatively adaptively, although she felt depressed and reported that she was "just going through the motions." During these periods, Annie anticipated having little control over the states of hyper- and hypoarousal that threatened at any moment to usurp her ability to carry on daily life activities, and she did her best to keep her arousal in the window of tolerance by avoiding trauma-related cues.

For Annie, and many people with trauma-related disorders, the integration of the markedly different consciousness, memory, identity, and action tendencies of different parts of the self into a unitary whole is profoundly hampered: When triggered by trauma-related stimuli, hyperarousal responses evoke some aspects of self; hypoarousal responses are associated with other aspects of self; and optimal arousal states are achievable at the cost of continuing dissociative disconnection. Thus, when trauma is severe, integrative capacity can fail in all three arousal zones.

TREATMENT ISSUES

A primary goal of treatment is to raise the integrative capacity of the client so that dissociated elements of past traumatic experiences can be assimilated. A major focus must be on increasing the functioning of the social engagement system and "decreasing the disorganizing effects of [any] particular episode of emotional [and physiological] arousal" (Siegel, 1999, p. 260). The individual's capacity to reason and reflect upon current reality and assess traumatic reminders must be reengaged, lowering the intensity of arousal in the case of hyperarousal and raising it in the case of hypoarousal. For example, Tracy had recently been in a severe car accident and came to therapy complaining that she was "jittery and jumpy" and could not "calm herself down." Hearing traffic noise evoked exaggerated startle reactions, and her arousal level remained in the hyperaroused zone much of her daily life. The hyperarousal that accompanied her assessment of danger when there was none disrupted her ability to engage in ordinary life activities. The initial sensorimotor psychotherapy treatment interventions focused on helping Tracy become aware of the sensations of hyperarousal (heart racing, tingling, slight trembling) and the related physical action tendencies (muscular tension in her back, arms, and legs) that she experienced in this zone. From there, Tracy learned meditative and mindful movement exercises (grounding and centering exercise; see Chapter 8), which helped to bring her arousal within the window of tolerance and enabled her to assess environmental cues more accurately. Gradually, as she learned to practice these exercises on her own whenever she felt "jumpy," her arousal remained within the optimal zone for longer and longer periods of time.

On the other hand, Victoria, who suffered from early sexual abuse, complained of a lifelong pattern of being withdrawn, "spaced out" and unable to sense her body or emotions. She reported that her previous therapist had diagnosed her with depression and prescribed antidepressants. Victoria had developed action tendencies that kept her in a hypoaroused zone: She described herself as "passive," with difficulty initiating action, and reported that she spent long periods of time sitting on her couch "spacing out." The primary sensorimotor psychotherapy interventions that assisted Victoria included standing during therapy rather than sitting, and engaging active, sometimes even vigorous, physical movements (e.g., pushing with the arms, stomping her legs, walking rapidly around the therapy office), which increased her energy and arousal. At first Victoria expressed fear and even terror of moving, remembering that if she moved during the abuse, things always got worse. As these memories were processed, Victoria was able to tolerate the increased arousal that emerged from physical movement, and with encouragement, clinical support, and modeling, was able to practice moving more in daily life. Gradually, Victoria's increased tolerance for movement and taking action enabled her to maintain arousal within the optimal zone for increased time intervals.

Sensorimotor psychotherapy is conducted within the context of an attuned therapeutic relationship that promotes collaboration and engagement between therapist and client. When the therapist's manner and interventions are mindfully responsive, and attuned to the client's long-term and moment-by-moment therapeutic needs, the client's social engagement system is elicited and then repeatedly strengthened. If movement exercises, such as those described above, are conducted simply as rote physical exercises, therapeutic benefit would be minimal. Within the context of a socially engaged, collaborative relationship, however, we observe an increase in the client's social engagement, information-processing capacity, and a growing ability to maintain optimal arousal even in the face of trauma-related stimuli.

CONCLUSION

The modulation of arousal requires sophisticated mental and physical abilities that traumatized clients often lack to varying degrees, especially when faced with trauma reminders that evoke unconscious procedural learning, action tendencies, and extremes of arousal. Many such clients find it challenging to accurately differentiate the various elements of their own internal cognitive, emotional, or sensorimotor action tendencies. Instead, propelled by undifferentiated, overwhelming emotions and physiological arousal, they may react impulsively, causing further dysregulation. Conversely, others remain at the mercy of chronic hypoarousal, appearing passive, emotionally "flat" and withdrawn, whereas others may experience dramatic biphasic alternation between the two extremes. Unable to separate the past from the present, many clients cannot accurately assess if internal reactions and physical action tendencies (bodily tension, movement, or arousal) are based on present reality, on extremes of trauma-related arousal, or on outdated defensive responses. Without adaptive regulatory strategies that help them regulate arousal within the window of tolerance and maintain cortical functioning, traumatized individuals cannot accurately interpret their own behavioral and emotional responses, or those of others, and subsequently react in inappropriate and disproportionate ways.

Regulating arousal within a window of tolerance necessitates the capacity to tolerate affective and autonomic activation without loss of the cortically mediated self-witnessing function. In such a state of optimal arousal, access to cognitive, emotional, and sensorimotor levels of information is maintained, ensuring integrated top-down and bottom-up processing. As integrative capacity increases, so does the width of the window of tolerance—and as the width of the window of tolerance increases, so does integrative capacity. A central task of the therapist in the treatment of traumatized clients is therefore to facilitate the development of increased integrative capacity, which initially is in the service of expanding tolerance for normal life and present reality and then, as a sufficiently broad window of tolerance is achieved, for the even more challenging task of integrating the traumatic past. If, as Janet (1907) suggests, traumatization is a failure of the integrative capacity, then the first priority in the treatment of trauma must be to restore clients' capacity to tolerate and integrate their own thoughts, feelings, and bodily sensations, to bear witness to their own experience, to be able to process significant life events—past and present, painful and pleasurable, ordinary and traumatic—within a window of tolerance.

Chapter 3

❊❖❊❖❊

Attachment:
The Role of the Body
in Dyadic Regulation

ALL HUMAN BEINGS, FROM INFANTS TO ADULTS, require an effective social engagement system in order to build attachment and affiliative relationships (Porges, 2004, 2005). In turn, early attachment experiences influence the development of the social engagement system and teach us how to regulate internal and external stimulation (Beebe & Lachmann, 1994; Bowlby, 1973, 1980; Fonagy, Gergely, Jurist, & Target, 2002; Hofer, 1984; Schore, 1994; Siegel, 1999). Born with limited capacities for self-regulation, human infants are dependent on the externally mediated interactive regulation of their primary attachment figures to maintain their arousal within the window of tolerance. Whether that attachment relationship is consistent or inconsistent, secure or insecure, it provides the context within which the infant develops lifelong tendencies for regulating arousal and affect. Early disruptions in attachment have enduring detrimental effects, diminishing the capacity to modulate arousal, develop healthy relationships, and cope with stress (Sable, 2000; Schore, 1994; Siegel, 1999).

Available to the full-term infant, the social engagement system is evident as the baby vocalizes, cries, and grimaces to signal distress, or smiles, gazes, or coos to interact with the caregiver (Porges, 2004, 2005). This "neural regulation of [facial] muscles that provide important elements of social cueing are available to facilitate the social interaction with the caregiver and function collectively as an integrated social engagement system" (Porges, 2005, p. 36). These kinds of behaviors serve to increase proximity between infant and caregiver. Through the repeated experiences of attuned dyadic interaction with the mother or primary caregiver, the child becomes increasingly effective at signaling, engaging, and responding to the other (Brazelton, 1989; Schore, 1994; Siegel, 1999; Stern, 1985); these responses, in turn, shape the social engagement system. The activation of this system leads to experiences of safety and helps maintain or return arousal to a window of tolerance by dampening both sympathetic and dorsal vagal activation. A competent social engagement system that effectively regulates these neural circuits fosters a wider window of tolerance and ultimately provides the child, and later the adult, with the capacity to tolerate, process, and even transform difficult experiences into opportunities for growth.

The social engagement system is initially built upon a series of face-to-face, body-to-body interactions with an attachment figure who regulates the child's autonomic and emotional arousal; it is further developed through attuned interactions with a primary caregiver who responds with motor and sensory contact to the infant's signals long before communication with words is possible. This interactive, dyadic regulation facilitates the development of the part of the brain responsible for the self-regulation of arousal: the orbital prefrontal cortex (Schore, 1994).

The capacity to self-regulate is the foundation upon which a functional sense of self develops (Beebe & Lachmann, 1994; Schore, 1994; Stern, 1985). The sense of self is first and foremost a bodily sense, experienced not through language but through the sensations and movements of the body (Damasio, 1994, 1999; Janet, 1929; Krueger, 2002; Laplanche & Pontalis, 1998; Mahler & Furer, 1968; Stern, 1985). The primary sensations at the very beginning of life are physiological and tactile, and the primary form of communication immediately after birth between parent and newborn is through touch, with visual and auditory stimuli having a stronger role as time goes on (Krueger, 2002). The physical experience of the caregiver's gentle, attuned ministrations to the infant's signals pertaining to sensation, touch, movement, and physiological arousal, as well as to his or her sensitivities/vulnerabilities regarding sensory input and other physical needs (e.g., food, warmth, fluids) establishes the infant's initial sense of self and sense of his or her body (Gergely & Watson, 1996, 1999). Thus, "the close and careful attunement to all the sensory and motor contacts with the child forms an accurate and attuned body self in the child" (Krueger, 2002, p. 7). When this occurs, social engagement, secure attachment, and regulatory abilities are adaptively supported.

Early interpersonal trauma is not only a threat to physical and psychological integrity, but also a failure of the social engagement system. Moreover, if the perpetrator is a primary caregiver, it includes a failure of the attachment relationship, undermining the child's ability to recover and reorganize, to feel soothed or even safe again. The child's opportunity to effectively utilize social engagement for care and protection has been over ridden, and he or she experiences overwhelming arousal without the availability of attachment-mediated comfort or repair. Without adequate attunement and development of the social engagement system within a secure attachment relationship, "[c]hildren . . . are not able to create a sense of unity and continuity of the self across the past, present, and future, or in the relationship of the self with others. This impairment shows itself in the emotional instability, social dysfunction, poor response to stress, and cognitive disorganization and disorientation" (Siegel, 1999, pp. 119–120).

Understanding how self-regulatory capacities are formed through early attachment relationships is helpful to therapists, who also provide a similar relational context in which dysregulated clients can develop adaptive regulatory capacities (Beebe & Lachmann, 1994; Schore, 1994). In therapy, fostering clients' social engagement and regulatory abilities is a top priority. Nonverbal cues are typically the first indicators of the client's experience of safety or danger in response to the therapeutic relationship, the environment, and internal cues (Lanyado, 2001). The therapist's attuned response to these nonverbal expressions is imperative in developing the client's social engagement system. For example, if a client's face expresses fear and his body tenses and pulls away, the attuned therapist may gently inquire about these nonverbal cues and take action to restore safety. If the client feels unsafe in the relationship, these actions might include increasing or decreasing physical proximity or other actions that give clients a sense of safety. Through these interventions, social engagement is reestablished and arousal is returned to a window of tolerance.

ATTACHMENT, SELF-REGULATION, AND RECIPROCAL INTERACTION

The primary caregiver, usually the mother, modulates her child's arousal by both calming the infant when arousal is too high and stimulating the infant when arousal is too low, thus helping the baby remain in an optimal state (Schore, 1994). The caregiver is attuned to the infant's need for stimulation as well as for disengagement via gaze aversion, which allows the infant to go to the edges of his or her window of tolerance without becoming hyperaroused. Or when, despite his or her best efforts, the infant experiences regulatory ruptures, the relationally attuned caregiver provides the interactive repair that enables the infant to return to a zone of optimal arousal (Beebe & Lachmann, 1994; Schore, 1994; Siegel, 1999; Stern, 1998; Tronick, 1998).

Because attachment needs are initially experienced and expressed primarily as body-based needs, the quality of the attachment relationship is originally founded on the caregiver's consistent and accurate attunement and response to the infant's body through their reciprocal sensorimotor interactions. The caregiver's ministrations, sensory joining, and quality of physical handling of the infant links body and mind experiences in the child and forms the basis for self-regulation (Krueger, 2002). This reciprocal interaction between the attuned caregiver and the infant is reenacted again and again (Schore, 1994; Siegel, 1999; Stern, 1985), expanding the child's internalized template of safe relatedness and consequently solidifying his or her ability to regulate, manage, and predict the environment.

Bion (1962) used the term *containment* to describe the primary caregiver's provision of a psychological environment that fosters the infant's self-regulating capacities. Winnicott's "holding environment" describes a similar concept that includes details about the type of physical care and environment that promote "the mental health of the infant" (1990, p. 49). By *containing* the child and providing a *holding environment*, the mother is able to hold the child both literally and in her mind in such a way that demonstrates her recognition of the child's physiological and affective states and also her ability to deal with them effectively. She can tolerate and "stay with" the child through his or her dysregulated states (Schore, 2003a).

Containment is communicated by the mother's holding and physical soothing of her infant's body with her touch and voice, which thereby modify the baby's physical sensations and motor activity (Brazelton, 1989). As the child develops, he or she acquires the capacity to experience security and comfort by means other than direct physical ministrations. Eye contact and words eventually "bridge the gap" between mother and child, and the child learns to calm down as the mother walks into his or her line of vision or is conjured in fantasy by the child as a comforting, calming presence.

The "good enough" mother/caregiver (Winnicott, 1945) is able to "mentalize" (Fonagy et al., 2002) her child. The caregiver who recognizes the child as a separate person with his or her own motivations, desires, and needs demonstrates a capacity to mentalize. This capacity in the caregiver enables the child to develop a secure sense of self and understand his or her own and others' motivations, desires, and needs as separate but negotiable.

One of the skills that enables mentalizing is the ability of the mother to perceive the child's world, identify with it, and align with it, while simultaneously realizing that the child is a separate person. Alignment—the empathic matching of one's own state to that of another Siegel (1999)—is a sensorimotor event that promotes social engagement communicated through prosody, voice tone and volume, touch, expression, pace, gestures, and so on. As the mother "gets closer to the child's state and then brings the child 'down' to a calmer state" (Siegel, 1999, pp. 280–281), through sensorimotor and emotional alignment, both mother and child experience a sense of calm and relaxation (Jaffe, Beebe, Feldstein, Crown, & Jasnow, 2001; Schore, 1994; Siegel, 1999; Stern, 1985). In psychotherapy, attuned therapists need to provide *alignment* for clients, conveyed through voice tone, body language, and emotional "resonance" (Siegel, 1999), and *containment*, by helping them maintain arousal within the window of tolerance. As one client said, "I need to know that you won't let me go there [to the memories of the abuse]."

An Ever-Changing Body-to-Body Dialogue

At the beginning of life, the newborn is dependent on its sensorimotor capacities (e.g., vocalizing, movement) to interact with the environment. However, social and emotional capacities quickly develop so that, by the end of the second month, the infant is able to engage in face-to-face interactions with the mother via intense and prolonged eye contact (Schore, 2003a). At this time, interactive play also begins, a highly arousing emotional and sensorimotor exchange in which the infant's rhythms and vocalizations are mirrored and elaborated by the mother (Schore, 2003a, p. 75; Trevarthen, 1979). This body-to-body, brain-to-brain dialogue, described as "affect synchrony," is a give-and-take somatic exchange during which the mother facilitates the infant's information processing by "adjusting the mode, amount, variability, and timing of the onset and offset of stimulation to the infant's actual integrative capacities" (Schore, 2003a, p. 76). As the infant's affective body "language" is responded to in a pleasure-enhancing manner by an attuned caregiver, the positive experience of nonverbal communication fosters the development of the infant's sense of self and conditions his or her future relationship to somatic expression as a means of communication.

For this development to occur, caregivers must adapt to the infant's ongoing development: The "maturation of the nervous system, accompanied by increasing differentiation of skills, drives infants to reorganize their control systems. At each step, parents must also readjust, finding a new more appropriate way of reaching out" (Brazelton, 1989, p. 105). The caregiver's empathic discernment of the child's changing physical and emotional needs ensures a balance between an environment that is safe and secure and one that is sufficiently enriching to simulate the child within his or her developmental capacity and to provide experiences of both enjoyment and mastery (Bradley, 2000; Emde, 1989).

Regulation of Positive Affect

The infant's developing experience of regulating a wide range of arousal states is facilitated by the mother's sensitivity to both positive and negative affective states. The good enough mother (Winnicott, 1945) actively engages in playful experiences with her infant, repeatedly pairing high arousal states with interpersonal relatedness and pleasure, thereby helping the child learn to tolerate rapid shifts in arousal: "During the imprinting of play episodes mother and infant show sympathetic cardiac acceleration and then parasympathetic deceleration in response to the smile of the other, and thus the language of mother and infant consists of signals produced by the autonomic, involuntary nervous system in both parties" (Schore, 2003a, p. 277). These interactions teach the infant to tolerate joy and excitement and encourage a "positively charged curiosity that fuels the burgeoning self's exploration of novel socio-emotional and physical environments" (Schore, 2003a, p. 78). Thus, "affect regulation is not just the reduction of affective intensity, the dampening of negative emotion. It also involves an amplification, an intensification of positive emotion, a condition necessary for more complex self-organization" (Schore, 2003a, p. 78). When the window of tolerance is restricted and the child cannot regulate affect effectively, he or she will have little tolerance for both pleasant and unpleasant sensations.

Good enough caregivers are inevitably somewhat inconsistent in their attunement with their children, but they promote recovery from breaches of attunement by providing interactive repair (Tronick, 1989). For example, when parents must interrupt the child's play for bedtime, they provide support to manage the frustration. When the child falls and bruises a knee, good interactive repair provides both comfort and reorienting of attention to play. Upon reunion with the caregiver following separation, a "source of joy" (Bowlby, 1980, p. 40) to both parties, the caregiver responds with, and encourages, the child's pleasure. This transitioning between negative and positive affect helps the infant develop resiliency and, later, flexible adaptive capabilities. As Schore stated: "The process of re-experiencing positive affect following negative experience may teach a child that negativity can be endured and conquered" (2003a, p. 143).

ATTACHMENT PATTERNS AND THE BODY

Ainsworth, Belhar, Waters, and Wall (1978) identified prototypes of three attachment patterns in children: secure attachment, insecure-avoidant attachment, and insecure-ambivalent attachment. In 1990 Main and Solomon (1990) identified a fourth pattern: disorganized-disoriented. Subsequently, various additional researchers and authors in the attachment field have elaborated on how these four patterns reflect the habitual regulatory tendencies observed in children in an interpersonal context (Lyons-Ruth & Jacobvitz, 1999; Sroufe, 1997; Van Ijzendoorn, Schuengel, & Bakermans-Kranenburg, 1999). Attachment patterns, formed in infancy, usually remain relatively stable throughout childhood and adulthood (Brennan & Shaver, 1995; Cozolino, 2002; Hazan & Shaver, 1990). A child's primary attachment pattern is usually formed in relationship to the mother, and this pattern is usually generalized to subsequent relationships. However, if the child forms different attachment patterns with each attachment figure, those patterns that are not primary may be also be triggered by similar situations or relationships in the future. Procedural triggering of these latent, non-dominant attachment patterns can lead to specific action tendencies relevant to a particular person but not generalized to all relationships.

Although attachment is described as "patterns of mental processing of information based on cognition and affect to create models of reality" (Crittenden, 1995, p. 401), attachment patterns are also held in place by chronic physical tendencies reflective of early attachment. Encoded as procedural memory, these patterns manifest as proximity-seeking, social engagement behavior (smiling, movement toward, reaching out, eye contact) and defensive expressions (physical withdrawal, tension patterns, and hyper- or hypoarousal). It is important to remember that these patterns are stereotypes, describing clusters of behavior, and that there are wide variations within each pattern (Bowlby, 1980; Fonagy, 1999b; Main, 1995; Sable, 2000; Slade, 1999).

Of particular interest in a sensorimotor approach are the physical tendencies of each pattern observed in infancy, versions of which are evident in our adult client population. Although each attachment pattern translates uniquely in each client on a somatic level and any attempt to stereotype these tendencies is only generalization, understanding the attachment patterns and their corresponding possible physical tendencies can help therapists devise somatic interventions to challenge them and repair attachment disturbances.

Secure Attachment

Bowlby (1982/1969) emphasized that the basic task of the first year is forming attachment, and Schore wrote that this is a "bond of emotional communication between the infant and the primary caregiver" (submitted). As we reviewed previously, the good enough mother accomplishes the task of creating secure attachment through reciprocal, attuned somatic and verbal communication with her infant. The child engages in exploratory behavior in the presence of the parent, shows signs of missing the parent upon separation, approaches the parent without ambivalence upon reunion, and often initiates physical contact. Quickly soothed upon distress, infants with secure attachment patterns return easily to exploratory activities. A secure attachment is both a psychological and physically mediated achievement that provides the "the primary defense against trauma-induced psychopathology" (Schore, in press; see also Ainsworth et al., 1978). These children have a relatively wide window of tolerance, are able to mentalize, form effective social engagement systems, and achieve overall adaptive functioning of parasympathetic and sympathetic systems. These attributes enable them to sustain arousal in the optimal zone or quickly return to that zone when arousal is momentarily excessive. As adults, these individuals can generally seek proximity to others with little or no avoidance or angry resistance and can tolerate relational frustrations and disappointments (Cassidy & Shaver, 1999). Their physical tendencies reflect integrated, tempered movements of approach that are context-appropriate, such as actions of moving toward, reaching out, or otherwise seeking contact. When their arousal exceeds the window of tolerance, they are able to seek and receive soothing and calming, without ambivalence, and are also able to self-regulate.

Congruence between movement and internal states is observed in the behavior of the child who has experienced secure attachment. The match between the child's interior psychological need and physical goals are congruent, and demonstrated through harmonious movements of the body. For example, when the attachment system is aroused, the child's movements are geared to unambiguously secure sufficient proximity with the parent to bring arousal back within the window of tolerance. In congruent behavior, the cognitive, emotional, and sensorimotor levels of information processing are aligned. When these children are observed, their intention for proximity to the mother, exploration away from the mother, desire for play, and so forth are easily detected and seen in the harmonious, cohesive movements of the child's body. These congruent behaviors are noticed in adults as well. Children with secure attachment patterns usually become adults who are comfortable being autonomous as well as comfortable seeking help and support from others. Clients who have experienced a secure attachment can use their therapist as a secure base once rapport is established, and their external physical movements match and reflect their internal state. They can unambiguously and congruently display their intentions, mood, desires, and even motives on cognitive, emotional, and sensorimotor behavioral levels.

Insecure Attachment

The two insecure patterns, insecure-avoidant and insecure-ambivalent, contain clear deficits. However, they, like secure attachment, are considered to be relatively adaptive and organized and predict future capacity for more or less adaptive behaviors (Ainsworth et al., 1978; Bowlby, 1920; Main, 1995; Siegel, 1999).

INSECURE-AVOIDANT ATTACHMENT

Mothers of insecure-avoidant infants actively thwart or block proximity-seeking behavior of the infant, responding instead by withdrawing or even pushing the child away (Ainsworth et al., 1978; Schore, 2003a). These mothers appear to have a general distaste for physical contact except on their terms and may respond to the infant's overtures with wincing, arching away, or avoiding mutual gaze (Cassidy & Shaver, 1999; Schore, 2003a; Siegel, 1999). The child adapts to this affectively laden somatic communication of unavailability by expressing little need for proximity, and apparently little interest in adult overtures for contact. And, when contact is made, the avoidant child does not sustain it, focusing instead on toys and objects rather than on the mother. He generally avoids eye contact with her and shows few visible signs of distress upon separation, although some researchers (Fox & Card, 1999; Main, 1995) have found evidence of autonomic arousal in these toddlers even when they appear behaviorally indifferent to the mother. Upon reunion, they actively ignore or even avoid the mother by moving or leaning away when picked up (Main & Morgan, 1996). They generally do not seek proximity with caregivers and are reserved emotionally.

Children with insecure-avoidant attachment patterns are described as having a dismissive stance towards the importance of attachment in adulthood. They often distance themselves from others, undervalue interpersonal relationships, become self-reliant, and tend to view emotions with cynicism. Clients with insecure-avoidant attachment histories tend to withdraw under stress and avoid seeking emotional support from others. With a compromised social engagement system and limited access to internal states, these clients typically minimize their attachment needs. Preferring autoregulation to interactive, they may find dependence frightening or unpleasant and avoid situations that stimulate attachment needs. The body tendencies vary; through muscular tonicity or rigidity these clients might show that they are more comfortable with defensive movements than with reaching out or moving toward. For example, one adult client found it unfamiliar and uncomfortable to reach out with her arms and did so awkwardly and stiffly, saying that it was easier to push away than to reach out for contact when no one had ever responded. As they are approached, these clients may pull back or become more armored. Others withdraw through a demeanor of passivity, often reflected in low muscular tonicity, and lack of response to relational overtures. Many clients demonstrate mixed tone: high tone in certain areas of the body, and low tone in other areas, as in the client who was strong and muscular through her legs but weak and flaccid through her arms. A lack of emotional expression and eye contact and a lower level of overall arousal are also correlated with this attachment group (Cozolino, 2002, p. 209). In a sensorimotor approach, somatic interventions that strengthen interactive regulation and social engagement (reaching out, seeking proximity, eye contact) provide effective avenues of exploration.

Children with insecure-avoidant attachment histories have a more complicated balance to attain between their need for caregiver proximity and their tolerance of anxiety; this adaptation may be subsequently reflected in a disjunction or disconnection between their interior needs and their external behavior. These incongruent patterns are apparent in our adult clients, too. For instance, the client who sits on the couch, visibly uncomfortable, may respond to the question "How are you doing?" or "How are you feeling in your body" with a smile and "Fine." This client's disconnection between her physical or emotional discomfort and her reported psychological state demonstrates an incongruence or mismatch between her inner psychological and somatic states, of which she is frequently genuinely unaware. Treatment for these clients includes becoming aware of internal states and practicing physical movements that accurately correspond to these states.

INSECURE-AMBIVALENT ATTACHMENT

The mother of the infant who develops insecure-ambivalent attachment patterns is inconsistent and unpredictable in her response to the infant. She may either over-arouse the infant or fail to help the infant engage. Because her interactions are often a response to her own emotional needs and moods rather than the infant's, this caregiver might stimulate the infant into high arousal even when the infant is attempting to down-regulate by gaze aversion. Thus, when the mother's own emotional need for engagement overrides the infant's need, her behavior intrudes on the infant causing dysregulation of the infant's arousal. Because the cargiver is inconsistent in her availability, sometimes allowing and encouraging proximity and sometimes not, the child is unsure of the reliability of the caregiver's response to his or her somatic and affective communications (Belsky, Rosenberg, & Crnic, 1995; Carlson, Armstrong, Lowenstein, & Roth, 1998; Main, 1995). This uncertainty results in infants who appear cautious, distraught, angry, distressed, and preoccupied throughout both separation from, and reunion with, the mother. Upon reunion, they typically fail to be comforted by the caregiver's presence or soothing (Main & Morgan, 1996), often continuing to cry. These infants characteristically appear irritable, have difficulty recovering from stress, show poor impulse control, fear abandonment, and engage in acting-out behavior (Allen, 2001). One example of the ambivalence such infants show with the unpredictable parent is to alternate between angry, rejecting behaviors and contact-seeking behaviors upon reunion with the mother after separation. Children with insecure-ambivalent patterns have a "difficult temperament" with "tendencies to intense expressiveness and negative mood responses, slow adaptability to change, and irregularity of biological functions" (Schore, 2003a, p. 29).

Children with insecure-ambivalent attachment histories are described as having a preoccupied stance toward attachment in adulthood. They are preoccupied with attachment needs, overly dependent on others, and might have a tendency toward enmeshment and intensity in interpersonal relationships, with a preference for proximity. They focus excessively on internal distress, often pursuing relief frantically (Cassidy & Shaver, 1999). With a compromised social engagement system, these clients are often unable to recognize safety within the relationship. Preoccupied with the availability of attachment figures (including the therapist), they frequently experience increased affect and bodily agitation and increase or loss of muscular tone at the prospect of separation. A sensorimotor approach would facilitate autoregulatory capabilities through a development of grounding, boundaries, and core internal support as well as promote adaptive interactive regulatrory abilities (see Chapter 10).

Children with insecure-ambivalent attachment patterns may demonstrate more congruency between internal states and external physical movement than insecure-avoidant children, but their behavior is often dysregulated. Their physical movement may be uncontained, geared more toward discharge of high arousal than toward the purposeful achievement of a specific goal. For example, a child may frantically cry and flail when the attachment system is aroused, rather than execute directional, purposeful movement toward the caregiver. The movement may take the form of agitation that does not translate into a tempered, purposeful movement that accomplishes a particular goal. In a sensorimotor approach with adult clients with insecure ambivalent attachment histories, learning to tolerate high emotional and physiological arousal and execute thoughtful, purposeful action rather than dysregulated, non-directional movement is essential.

Disorganized/Disoriented Attachment

Main and her colleagues (Main, 1995; Main & Hesse, 1990; Main & Solomon, 1990) observed a group of children who had puzzling and contradictory sets of responses to their mothers upon reunion after separation. The researchers also observed the mothers, whose behavior they evaluated as "frightening" (e.g., looming behaviors, sudden movements, sudden invasion, attack postures) or "frightened" (e.g., backing away, exaggerated startle response, retraction in reaction to the infant, a fearful voice or facial expression) (Main & Hesse, 1990). In addition, these mothers may exhibit role confusion (e.g., eliciting reassurance from the child), disorientation (e.g., trance-like expression, aimless wandering in response to the infant's cries), intrusive behavior (e.g., pulling the child by the wrist, mocking and teasing, withholding a toy) or withdrawal (e.g., not greeting the infant, not interacting verbally, gaze avoidance) (Lyons-Ruth, 2001). These caregivers often provoked sudden state switches without providing interactive repair. Sometimes the caregivers (usually the mother) of these children may be abusive or neglectful or both. Such a caregiver

induces traumatic states of enduring negative affect. Because her attachment is weak, she provides little protection against other potential abusers of the infant. . . . This caregiver is inaccessible and reacts to her infant's expressions of emotion and stress inappropriately and/or rejectingly, and shows minimal or unpredictable participation in the various types of arousal-regulating processes. Instead of modulating, she induces extreme levels of stimulation and arousal, either too high in abuse or too low in neglect, and because she provides no interactive repair, the infant's intense negative emotional states last for long periods of time. (Schore, submitted)

Because this misattuned caregiver shows little or no attempt to recognize or repair breaches in relatedness, the infant is left in hyper- or hypoaroused zones for extended periods of time.

Main and Solomon (1986, 1990) named the attachment pattern that developed from such caregiving the *disorganized/disoriented* style and identified seven categories of behavior indicative of this style:

1. Sequential contradictory behavior; for example, proximity seeking followed by freezing, withdrawal, or dazed behavior.
2. Simultaneous contradictory behavior, such as avoidance combined with proximity seeking.
3. Incomplete, interrupted, or undirected behavior and expressions, such as distress accompanied by moving away from the attachment figure.
4. Mistimed, stereotypical, or asymmetrical movements, and strange, anamolous behavior, such as stumbling when the mother is present and there is no clear reason to stumble.
5. Movements and expressions indicative of freezing, stilling, and "underwater" actions.
6. Postures that indicate apprehension of the caregiver, such as fearful expressions or hunched shoulders.
7. Behavior that indicates disorganization or disorientation, such as aimless wandering around, labile affect, or dazed, confused expressions.

Main and Solomon observed that these infants' "approach movements were continually being inhibited and held back through simultaneous activation of avoidant tendencies. In most cases, however, proximity-seeking sufficiently 'over-rode' avoidance to permit the increase in physical proximity. Thus, contradictory patterns were activated but were not mutually inhibited" (1986, p. 117).

Versions of these incongruent behaviors are observed in traumatized adults, especially in the context of discussing past relational trauma or past or current attachment relationships, including the relationship with the therapist. In clinical contexts, therapists often are confused by what seem like paradoxical responses to contact and apparent relational discontinuity. For example, Lisa frequently complained that "no one is there for me" and begged her therapist for more contact: to sit closer, to hold her hand if she cried, to call to see how she felt during the week. Yet, in sessions, Lisa consistently seated herself in such a way that she was facing away from the therapist and orienting toward the floor and sofa, and her body stiffened when the therapist moved her chair closer (at Lisa's request). Proximity seeking emerged in her verbal communication, whereas avoidance was communicated physically: her body held back the approach, avoiding even eye contact.

The often confusing incongruent and contradictory behavior observed in these infants, and in clients such as Lisa, can be understood as the result of simultaneous or alternating stimulation of two opposing psychobiological systems: attachment and defense (Liotti, 1999a; Lyons-Ruth & Jacobvitz, 1999; Main & Morgan, 1996; Ogawa, Sroufe, Weinfield, Carlson, & Egeland, 1997; Van der Hart et al., 2004). An infant predictably seeks proximity to the caregiver when distressed, but if the caregiver further distresses the infant instead of providing comfort and safety, an irresolvable paradox ensues (Main & Solomon, 1986). The infant cannot satisfactorily approach, flee, or reorient his or her attention. When the attachment system is aroused, proximity-seeking behaviors are mobilized. But when the defensive system is aroused, flight, fight, freeze, or hypoarousal/feigned death responses are mobilized. The disorganized/disoriented infant experiences the alternating or simultaneous stimulation of these two opposing psychobiological systems.

Steele, Van der Hart, and Nijenhuis (2001) have challenged the notion that this attachment paradigm is, in fact, "disorganized" (see also Jaffe et al., 2001). They have proposed that, in the context of frightened and/or frightening caregiving, disorganized/disoriented attachment is actually an organized, logical response caused by the concurrent activation of both the defensive and attachment systems: the social engagement system and the sympathetic and dorsal vagal systems are thought to be simultaneously or alternately stimulated. In childhood trauma and neglect, disorganized/disorientated attachment as a strategy is a logical outcome. The ongoing threat of frightened and frightening caregiving evokes the action tendencies of both proximity seeking and defense. This attachment behavior has been demonstrated in 80% of maltreated infants (Carlson et al., 1998) and is a statistically significant predictor of both dissociative disorders (Carlson et al., 1998; Liotti, 1992) and aggressive behavior (Lyons-Ruth & Jacobvitz, 1999).

The therapist notes the physical manifestations of relational tendencies that reflect this attachment pattern in adults and works with them directly. For example, Kathy presented in therapy with a profound distrust of the therapist, expecting betrayal and even attack. Her body was stiff, her eyes never wavered from the therapist's face, and she exhibited little movement. Whenever the therapist moved, Kathy's arousal increased. Yet she had sought therapeutic help, wanted to tell her story, and even called her therapist between sessions. She reported a childhood of extreme abuse from a primary attachment figure, which naturally evoked the alternation or simultaneous stimulation of attachment and protective or defensive impulses characteristic of disorganized/disoriented attachment. Her conflict between social engagement—seeking therapy, telling the therapist her story, calling the therapist for contact between sessions—and defense—fear, "frozen" body, and hyperarousal—reflects the early attachment disturbances from childhood trauma. The therapist, understanding this dynamic, worked first to increase Kathy's ability for social engagement by helping her have more control of her interactions in therapy. Because Kathy often felt threatened when the therapist moved, the therapist encouraged Kathy to notice when she felt her arousal begin to increase, and request that she (the therapist) sit still at those times. The therapist also told Kathy when she was about to move, so that her unexpected movements would not surprise Kathy. As Kathy's sense of control and safety increased, her arousal remained more often within the window of tolerance. The therapist then worked directly with both of Kathy's tendencies (defense and proximity seeking) by first discussing them with her, then asking her how her body would demonstrate both tendencies simultaneously. Kathy reached out toward the therapist with one hand while putting her other hand up in a defensive position. With this gesture, she took a deep breath, saying, "This is exactly how it is. I need both in all my relationships—I need contact, and I need to be on guard." Throughout Kathy's treatment, she and her therapist tracked when proximity-seeking, social engagement tendencies were prominent (through approach movements) and when proximity-avoiding tendencies were prominent (through defensive movements) and explored options for integrated action appropriate to current context.

ATTACHMENT PATTERNS AND SELF-REGULATION

The hierarchical relationship between social engagement, sympathetic, and dorsal vagal parasympathetic systems is established early in life and forms enduring overall arousal tendencies, reactions under stress, and even vulnerability to psychiatric disorders (Cozolino, 2002; Lyons-Ruth & Jacobvitz, 1999; Schore, 2001, p. 209; Sroufe, 1997; Van Ijzendoorn et al., 1999). As the infant's affect regulatory structures develop through attuned interactive regulation, they progress from dependence on external regulation to the capacity for internal regulation (Schore, 2001). For the infant in a secure attachment relationship, interactions with the caregiver "[facilitate] right brain development, promote efficient affect regulation, and [foster] adaptive infant mental health" (Schore, 2001, p. 204). The child's immature brain is continually stimulated in ways that "prune" the neurons of the orbitoprefrontal cortex, a structure that is especially important because of its profound effect on self-regulation. We depend upon the right orbitoprefrontal cortex for its ability to regulate emotional and autonomic arousal (Schore, 1994; Siegel, 1999), and this area of the brain depends reciprocally upon interactive regulation in infancy for its development. The early socioemotional context directly influences the prefrontal areas of the right brain that are "dominant for the unconscious processing of socioemotional information, the regulation of bodily states, the capacity to cope with emotional stress, and the corporeal and emotional self" (Schore, 2003, pp. 271–272).

Self-regulation comprises two strategies—auto and interactive—described by Schore as, respectively, "autoregulation in autonomous contexts via a one-person psychology" and "interactive regulation [via social engagement system] in interconnected contexts via a two-person psychology" (2001, p. 204). With both auto- and interactive regulatory abilities, a person can observe, articulate, and integrate emotional and sensorimotor reactions in solitude and can equally utilize relationships to achieve a similar end. These capacities are founded upon early attachment dynamics: "Early interactive experiences determine whether, in later times of crisis, the individual can allow himself to go to others for interpersonal support, that is, to avail himself of interactive regulation within an intimate or psychotherapeutic relationship when his own autoregulatory mechanisms have temporarily failed" (Schore, 2001, p. 245).

Secure Attachment and Regulation

Each of the four attachment patterns reflects specific tendencies of self-regulation and autonomic dominance. In the context of secure attachment, the child develops increasingly sophisticated autoregulatory abilities appropriate to his or her developmental age. Concurrently, the child is able to seek others for regulation, as needed, and has little or no resistance to utilizing interactive regulation to bring arousal into the window of tolerance. In a secure attachment relationship the child learns a balance of autoregulatory and interactive regulatory strategies that are internalized via the development of regulatory areas of the orbital prefrontal cortex. These regulatory areas of the orbital prefrontal cortex support social engagement and condition a balanced relationship between sympathetic and parasympathetic arousal (Schore, 1994). The child has an optimal ability to evaluate safety, danger, and life-threatening situations and can shift adaptively between the three arousal zones.

Insecure-Avoidant Attachment and Regulation

The child with an insecure-avoidant history may depend upon autoregulation and parasympathetic (dorsal vagal) dominance (Cozolino, 2002; Schore, 2003a) to self-regulate, most likely experiencing increased dorsal vagal tone characterized, in the extreme, by feelings of helplessness and lower levels of activity (i.e., a state of conservation and withdrawal) (Schore, 2003a). With a tendency to curtail the expression of emotion (Cassidy & Shaver, 1999), this "overregulation" indicates a reduced capacity to experience either positive or negative affect and may contribute to a low threshold of arousal in socioemotional contexts and to modulation imbalances (i.e., difficulty shifting out of low arousal states and moderating high arousal) (Schore, 2003a). This child, in the relative absence of an available caregiver, is robbed of the opportunity for satisfying social engagement and typically develops a preference for autoregulatory tendencies that do not depend on another's presence. He or she may learn to modulate arousal in solitude, turning inward through reading, daydreaming, and worlds of fantasy. Although generally compliant, the child may express frustration in peer relationships where avoidant attachment behaviors are sometimes associated with hostility, aggressiveness, and conduct problems (Allen, 2001; Crittenden, 1995; Sroufe, 1997; Weinfield, Stroufe, Egeland, & Carlson, 1999). Interactive regulatory and social engagement abilities necessary for resolving interpersonal conflicts are often underdeveloped in such individuals.

Insecure-Ambivalent Attachment and Regulation

On the other hand, children with insecure-ambivalent attachment patterns tend to have a sympathetically dominant nervous system (Cozolino, 2002; Schore, 2003a) with a low threshold of arousal and concurrent difficulty maintaining arousal within a window of tolerance. The inconsistent responsiveness of the primary caregiver has taught the child to increase signaling for attention, escalating distress in order to solicit caregiving (Allen, 2001). These children are biased toward undercontrolled high-arousal states, with increased emotional reactivity combined with an inability to modulate distress, leaving them vulnerable to underregulatory disturbances (Schore, 2003a). Less able to autoregulate, as adults these individuals find isolation stressful: Because they have trouble tolerating solitude, they cling to relational contact, becoming overly dependent on interactive regulation but simultaneously experiencing a lack of ability to be easily calmed and soothed in a relationship. Although social engagement is sought, the person remains biased toward hyperarousal, in part due to hypervigilence developed from previous experience of intrusive behavior by the primary attachment figure.

Disorganized-Disoriented Attachment and Regulation

Hyper- and hypoarousal are both involved in the infant's psychobiological response to frightened or frightening caregivers, with whom the social engagement system is functionally off-line for much of the time. Disorganized/disoriented attachment patterns in children has been associated with elevated heart rates, intense alarm reactions, higher cortisol levels, and behavior that may indicate increased dorsal vagal tone, such as stilling, going into a brief trance, unresponsiveness, and shutting down (Schore, 2001). In the initial stage of threat, infants demonstrate sympathetic activation accompanied by startle reactions, elevated heart rate, respiration, and blood pressure, and usually crying or screaming (Schore, submitted). However, when sympathetic arousal cannot be regulated, a quick shift to hypoarousal may occur. The body undergoes "the sudden and rapid transition from an unsuccessful strategy of struggling requiring massive sympathetic activation to the metabolically conservative immobilized state mimicking death associated with the dorsal vagal complex" (Porges, 2001a, p. 136).

Thus sympathetically mediated responses quickly change "from interactive regulatory modes into long-enduring less complex autoregulatory modes" (Schore, submitted). During these hypoaroused conditions, observed in newborns (Bergman, Linley, & Fawcus, 2004; Spitz, 1946), the infant is unresponsive to interactive regulation (Schore, submitted). Early relational trauma generates prolonged negative affective and physiological states in the infant, which, in turn, "generate immature and inefficient orbitofrontal systems, thereby precluding higher complex forms of affect regulation" (Schore, submitted). These negative states also leave the child with a compromised social engagement system.

Tramatogenic environments that produce disorganized-disoriented attachment behaviors in children typically include both neglect and abuse: Children living in conditions of neglect are often at the mercy of abusive and/or unprotective adults, and abusive environments usually include neglect. Whereas physical, emotional, or sexual abuse typically produces either chronically heightened autonomic arousal or biphasic alternations between hyper- and hypoarousal states, neglect typically leads to a flattening of affect (Gaensbauer & Hiatt, 1984), which has a more negative effect than abuse alone (Cicchetti & Toth, 1995) due to the decreased arousal and behavior associated with chronic increase in dorsal vagal tone. Whereas overstimulation and inadequate repair are inevitable outcomes of trauma, inadequate stimulation, insufficient mirroring, and a lack of responsiveness by the caregiver accompany neglect. Such inadequate stimulation can be life-threatening to an infant, forcing the child to autoregulate by becoming disengaged and hypoaroused (Carlson et al., 1998; Perry et al., 1995; Schore, 2001). In chronic and extreme hypoarousal, the child may even enter persistent conditions of conservation and withdrawal, with profoundly reduced affect, loss of postural and muscular tonicity, and disengagement from the environment. Individuals who have experienced chronic childhood trauma characteristically suffer from a compromised social engagement system, underdeveloped or ineffective interactive regulatory abilities, as well as impaired autoregulatory capacities; they remain in, or alternate between, hyper- or hypoarousal zones for extended periods of time.

SENSORIMOTOR TREATMENT

Attachment to the therapist "serves as a base from which to explore both the inner world and the outer environment, offering a haven of refuge at times of fear and anxiety, and a source of information for understanding the underlying meanings of troubling symptoms" (Sable, 2000, p. 334). Each attachment pattern poses particular challenges for both client and therapist.

Treatment of Insecure-Avoidant Attachment

As we stated above, individuals with insecure-avoidant attachment histories have a dismissive stance toward attachment in adulthood, and may have a tendency toward a parasympathetically (dorsal vagal) dominant autonomic nervous system as well as a tendency to autoregulate. Therapeutic goals for these individuals include fostering interactive regulation and the ability to engage in social interaction when their arousal is higher than they are used to. The clients often turn away from social interaction when they are anxious, and practice managing this higher arousal state during interpersonal interaction fosters a wider window of tolerance. These goals are approached in a titrated manner because pushing too quickly for change may trigger both psychological and somatic defenses and cause the client to feel more withdrawn and possibly less open to treatment and change. Therefore, a slow collaborative approach is taken, using a combination of psychoeducation about the client's attachment history and the creation of a collaborative atmosphere of exploration about the way the elements of the attachment group are experienced in movement and sensation.

Sally demonstrated dismissive attachment patterns and behaviors that indicated unresolved trauma. She came to her first session complaining about "intimacy problems" with her partner. She said that she had always felt emotionally remote in relationship to her partner, though she loved and appreciated her. The therapist immediately noted the affective "flatness" with which Sally discussed these concerns. Her body was slumped and showed little spontaneous movement. The therapist asked Sally to choose a pillow that could represent her partner, and to notice what happened in her body as she imagined her partner in the room with her (a typical starting point with a client with an insecure-avoidant attachment history). Sally said that she felt nothing in her body whatsoever, which is common for such individuals. The therapist asked Sally to notice what happened in her internal experience as he moved the pillow closer to her. Sally found that she felt "claustrophobic." The therapist asked her to notice how "claustrophobia" related to her body. Sally said she felt as if her whole body tightened, and she reported feeling smaller and more distant as the therapist moved the pillow closer. Over the course of several sessions, Sally became more aware that her body would spontaneously tighten and that often her emotions would become unavailable to her when her partner approached her. She and her therapist explored this in the therapeutic relationship as well, and Sally discovered the same response when the therapist increased proximity. Sally described this as a "numbing of her emotions" and inability to feel her body in response to physical closeness. To work on this, the therapist encouraged her to openly discuss these physical and emotional feelings as they arose, thus utilizing the social engagement system and creating links between cognitive, emotional, and sensorimotor levels of processing.

Sally also learned to pay attention to times she felt uncomfortable in the therapy hour, and to ask her therapist to stop when he came close physically (by leaning forward) or verbally/emotionally (by asking questions), and to request more time to explore and report her internal experience. Over the course of many sessions, Sally began to trust that she could control the physical and psychological proximity to the therapist and began to feel like she was "less numbed out" for longer portions of the session. She said she felt like she was able to sense her body and her emotions and be in a relationship for the first time. Eventually, Sally became more comfortable "being in her body" while relating emotionally and exploring closer psychological proximity to her therapist, and eventually her partner.

Treatment of Insecure-Ambivalent Attachment (preocupied)

The wounding of the child with a history of insecure-ambivalent attachment also disrupts intimate capacity and interactive regulation, but through different somatic mechanisms and for different reasons. The person with this attachment history is "ambivalent" because of the inconsistent attunement and unpredictable intrusiveness of the caregiver and the undeveloped capacity for autoregulation. As noted, these children develop a preoccupied stance toward attachment in adulthood. The emotional lability and irritability of this attachment pattern (which was distinctly absent in the insecure-avoidant attachment pattern) often manifest as dysregulated behaviors that may be an attempt to "discharge" strong affect and arousal.

Tom demonstrated a preoccupied stance toward attachment needs, and also behaviors that indicated unresolved trauma. He was unable to regulate his emotions and expressed an inability to trust his wife. As he spoke, the therapist noticed that he moved around in the chair and nervously jiggled his legs. He spoke quickly, in an impulsive rather than thoughtful manner, and was emotionally labile and intense. Over the course of several sessions, the therapist intervened by 1) helping Tom feel more grounded physically, and therefore emotionally (see Chapter 10); 2) working directly with the physical sensations of emotional and physiological activation and stress by bringing his mindful awareness to them and encouraging him to refrain from behaviors that served to discharge this arousal; and 3) tracking these sensations as they slowly progressed through his body, allowing the sensations of arousal to manifest, build, autonomically discharge (through trembling, shaking, temperature changes, etc.), and eventually come to rest—rather than utilizing behavior, such as aggressive outbursts and excessive exercise, to dissipate it. As Tom became more proficient at recognizing his own physical and emotional discomfort during the therapy session, he learned to contain his feelings of anxiety by remaining aware of his body sensation, grounding himself, and practicing other physical actions that helped him develop his capacity to contain his emotional experience and calm down. Over time he found that he could talk about very intimate aspects of himself and his relationship while feeling more grounded and comfortable with physiological and emotional arousal. This allowed him to interact with his therapist (and his partner) without displaying uncomfortable emotional outbursts.

Treatment of Unresolved Disorganized-Disoriented Attachment

In the context of trauma treatment, the unresolved disorganized-disoriented attachment pattern poses the most extreme challenge for both client and therapist: Attachment to the therapist in the context of the therapeutic alliance inevitably mobilizes the client's defensive system, whereas distancing by either client or therapist inevitably mobilizes the client's attachment system. Unresolved trauma results in a "blockage in the flow of energy and information between two minds" (Siegel, 2001, p. 88). With a compromised social engagement system, clients suffering from childhood relational trauma understandably have great difficulty utilizing relationships, including the therapeutic relationship, for interactive regulation. Herman (1992) pointed out that although traumatized individuals desperately need to form a trusting relationship, they are beleaguered by fears and suspicions learned from, and relevant to, their traumatic past. These fears and suspicions often prevent clients from engaging in adaptive relational behavior. As much as the therapist might wish to provide good interactive regulation for the client, an interpersonal trauma history disrupts the client's ability to experience the therapist as safe and reliable. In the words of Hedges, "Contact itself is the feared element because it brings a promise of love, safety, and comfort that cannot ultimately be fulfilled and that reminds [the client] of the abrupt breaches of infancy" (1997, p. 114). One of the first tasks of therapy is to strengthen the social engagement system by helping clients overcome "the phobia of attachment to the therapist" (Steele et al., 2005b, p. 26).

With this challenge in mind, the therapist, like an attuned caregiver, attempts to keep the client within the window of tolerance by taking a number of precautions to assure that the information evoked in the therapy hour is within the client's ability to integrate. Like the good enough mother who observes and contains the child through psychophysiological dyadic regulation, the sensorimotor psychotherapist observes or "tracks" the subtle movements and somatic "expressions" that accompany the client's words and emotions, linking body and mind experiences and helping the client to down-regulate hyperarousal and counteract the numbing effects of hypoarousal. Understanding the crucial importance of nonverbal, bodily cues in regulating the client, the therapist experiments with changes in pace, tone, and volume of voice, body posture, movement, and physical distance from/closeness to the client, tracking closely for dysynchrony and reestablishing synchrony. Therapists must consistently employ techniques facilitating interactive repair to keep clients' arousal within a window of tolerance.

It bears repeating that as clients attempt to manage states of overwhelming negative affect, their recognition and experience of positive affective states is inevitably impaired. Most traumatized clients lack the capacity to experience pleasure and joy in their lives. Overwhelmed by negative affects and triggered by reminders of trauma, these clients invariably find that even their capacity to become *aware* of pleasurable experience is compromised. In addition, positive affective states often have become associated with danger in tramatogenic childhood environments: Pride in accomplishment may have been shamed; laughter may have been punished; relaxation may have meant a loss of hypervigilence leading to exploitation. This phobia of positive affect can be gently challenged by the therapist by facilitating experiences of curiosity, exploration, humor, empowerment, and play (see Chapter 12).

With the help of the therapist's thoughtful interactive regulation of both positive and negative affect, the client's social engagement system is stimulated and developed. As the availability of the social engagement and attachment systems facilitates successful experience of regulatory repair, clients learn the autoregulatory capacities of observing and tracking their own emotional, cognitive, and sensorimotor reactions. Paradoxically, the therapist's ability to interactively regulate the client's dysregulated arousal creates an environment in which the client can begin to access his or her own ability to regulate arousal independent of relational interaction. As Schore (2003b) explained: "Over the course of the treatment, the therapist's role as a psychobiological regulator and coparticipant in the 'dyadic regulation of emotion' (Sroufe, 1997), especially during clinical heightened affective moments and episodes of projective identification, can facilitate the emergence of a reflective capacity and an 'earned secure' attachment" (p. 102). Additionally, the therapist is cognizant of the fact that both the client's attachment and defensive systems will be evoked within the therapeutic relationship and tracks for the behavioral indicators of both of these systems.

Louise and Frank came to sensorimotor psychotherapy because of marital problems, which both reported as stemming from Louise's recurrent history of sexual abuse between ages 5 and 8. Louise and Frank had not had sexual relations in over a year, and Frank complained that Louise's behavior was "unpredictable." He described how painful it was for him when Louise invited him to be close, then suddenly and unexpectedly pulled away physically—behaviors that may indicate sequential arousal of attachment and defensive systems. Though Louise generally seemed well adjusted and able to modulate her arousal level, the topic of sex immediately evoked autonomic arousal and emotions that would swing from high to low, with little ability on her part to self-regulate. Demonstrating conflicting action tendencies typical of disorganized-disoriented attachment, she engaged in attachment-related, proximity-seeking behavior at the thought of intimacy with her husband (evident in a soft, open, inviting facial expression, eye contact with Frank, slight smile, open body posture and movement toward him), but then quickly experienced two different defensive responses: accelerated heart rate and tension in her body, especially her legs, which Louise described as indicating that she wanted to "run away;" as well as "spacing out," vacant eye contact, and losing interest in the exchange.

Evoking Louise's social engagement system, the therapist, a male, helped her notice her physical tendencies of attachment and defense and the extremes of autonomic arousal she experienced, and he asked her to pause when arousal became high until it was back within the window of tolerance. Louise became curious about these physical tendencies and learned to notice when her defensive reactions usurped her desire to be close to her husband. The therapist helped her assemble several strategies to use both during therapy and with Frank at home. In the initial session interventions were focused on helping Louise experience control and choice: She was encouraged to stop the discussion when any topic (including the topic of sexuality) triggered her defensive reactions. Once Louise realized she had this control, she no longer felt the need to "withdraw" or "run away," and she observed that her autonomic arousal began to stabilize, enabling her to socially engage. She reported that her body sensations became less overwhelming and turbulent, and also less numb. She could feel her feet literally touching the ground.

Louise's therapist encouraged her to become aware of other stimuli that were triggering to her and to notice her physical reactions to them. Louise reported that being in the presence of two men (her male therapist and her husband) was frightening for her, and she correlated the fear with stiffness in her neck, trembling throughout her body, and tension in her legs. Louise, Frank, and the therapist decided that Louise could try moving her chair closer to the door and open the door slightly. Her therapist suggested that she would have the option to leave the room if she became more triggered and afraid. As she sat near the door, Louise slowly stopped trembling and her stiff neck began to relax.

In this initial session, Louise continued to feel somewhat distressed and unable to fully calm herself. A third intervention was suggested by her therapist and proved useful. When Louise experimented with holding a large square pillow that covered her entire torso and genitals, she felt more relaxed. Her therapist encouraged her to use the pillow when she experienced autonomic arousal or defensive strategies, thus facilitating Louise's closer observation of her bodily experiences—which in turn enabled her to self-regulate during the session with greater competence. With the addition of the pillow, Louise experienced a returning sense of physical calmness and greater capacity for social engagement.

Through understanding her defensive tendencies and learning these somatic strategies that calmed her physiological arousal, Louise began to experience greater trust in the therapist and the therapeutic process. Through her social engagement with, and the interactive regulation of, her therapist, combined with her use of these strategies, Louise's capacity to self-regulate during the sessions was enhanced. She mentioned that she felt able to find the words to tell the therapist about her internal experiences and that she actually liked working with him. Thus the first session enabled the formation of a therapeutic alliance. Additionally, Louise and her therapist designed homework to help her notice her defensive tendencies and to engage in conscious, adaptive behaviors, such as verbalizing her needs or placing a pillow in front of her body when physically close to her husband. These strategies enabled her to increase her contact with Frank without becoming physically aroused or defensive.

During a later session, the idea of physical and sexual contact between Louise and Frank was explored. The therapist suggested that they imagine physical (nonsexual) touch between them. Prior to the onset of treatment, Louise had been having startle responses any time she even imagined Frank touching her without her explicit permission. No contact during sleep and little contact around the house was tolerable. Work with this issue began slowly. The therapist asked them both to think of a place that might foster their exploration of physical, sensual, but non-sexual contact. When Frank suggested the bedroom, Louise physically braced and pulled back, triggering her into what she called a "freeze" and then "shutting down" mode. Despite Frank's frustration at her reaction, they began to brainstorm other possibilities. Frank suggested the couch. Again Louise found her body bracing instinctively. Finally, Louise suggested somewhere public, such as a park. When she visualized this scenario, it still seemed "like a lot," but it led to another idea: "How about when we're in a park watching something else, like a game or something, and we start holding hands and touching each other (non-sexually)." She closed her eyes and noted that her body relaxed when she imagined this interaction. Frank was disappointed but agreed to give it a try.

The following week, Louise was pleased. She was beginning to work with these "sensual" exercises in a way that did not provoke her defensive tendencies, and she reported that she could keep her arousal within a window of tolerance. She and Frank had gone to a park to watch children play and were physically affectionate there, hugging, holding hands, and occasionally kissing. The therapist asked Louise if she actually felt pleasure. The first week her answer was "No," leading the therapist to suggest that Louise initiate and direct more of the contact. As the weeks progressed, Louise felt increasingly greater control over their physical contact and gradually began to feel pleasure. As time passed and her ability to interactively (by talking with Frank) and autoregulate increased, Louise was able to maintain her autonomic arousal within a window of tolerance as her trust and enjoyment of Frank's closeness became greater and more pleasurable. Strategies, boundaries, and structure were essential ingredients to Louise's developing sense of attachment and ability to modulate her arousal.

CONCLUSION

Because the ability to modulate arousal and develop healthy, adaptive relationships requires sophisticated mental and physical abilities that are dependent on early attachment and social engagement experiences, clients with histories of neglect, abuse, and attachment failure are often challenged relationally, especially when faced with unexpected reminders of their trauma. Autonomic dysregulation evoked by trauma-related relational stimuli drive intense hyper- and hypoarousal responses and fixed action tendencies, such as hypervigilance, fight, flight, freeze, or submit responses, associated with early experience. Misinterpretation of their own responses and those of others results when procedural survival-related learning from the past usurps awareness of the present. Social engagement suffers as sympathetic and dorsal vagal responses predominate over ventral vagal responses. In treatment, sensorimotor therapeutic interventions address habitual action tendencies and practice to establish more adaptive capacities. As the therapist facilitates an attuned, collaborative "dyadic dance" with the client, the experience of interactive psychobiological regulation allows the individual to modulate his or her arousal and achieve states of pleasure and calm, rather than extremes of arousal. Practice of new actions in the context of attuned social engagement with the therapist leads to the development of more adaptive relational capacities and the strengthening of both interactive regulatory skills and autoregulatory abilities. Through the successful accomplishment of previously feared or unfamiliar actions, as illustrated in the case of Louise, feelings of mastery emerge. Finally, as the attachment and social engagement systems become more accessible to the client, other transformations begin to occur in the orienting and defensive systems.

Chapter 4

✕✕✕

The Orienting Response: Narrowing the Field of Consciousness

LONG AFTER THE ORIGINAL TRAUMATIC EVENTS ARE OVER, many individuals find themselves compelled to anticipate, orient to, and react to stimuli that directly or indirectly resemble the original traumatic experience or its context. These individuals unconsciously and reflexively narrow the field of consciousness to reminders of the trauma, thereby failing to perceive cues indicative of safety and inadvertently maintaining an internal sense of threat. Alternatively, they may experience hypoarousal-related interference with the innate ability to orient to cues signaling either pleasure or danger; they may report feeling "shut down," unable to perceive their own emotions or body sensations, and fail to notice threatening stimuli (which can result in increased vulnerability to revictimization). Because the act of orienting is "fundamental to human learning and cognitive functioning," changing trauma-related maladaptive orienting tendencies is essential to successful treatment (Kimmel, Van Olst, & Orlebeke, 1979, p. xi).

Physical and psychological responses to both internal and external stimuli are predicated on, and extrapolated from, orienting responses. What we turn our attention to, or orient to, determines not only our physical actions but our mental actions as well. We sustain a preparation to orient at all times, during sleep as well as during wakefulness (Sokolov, Spinks, Naatanen, & Heikki, 2002), and this preparation is both physical and psychological. The

65

components of orienting include turning the head and focusing the sensory organs on the object of orientation. In addition, "perceptual enhancement, motor preparation, and appropriate sensorimotor tuning" occur and "the nature of these changes [are] mapped onto a prognosis of future events, action, or information processing" (Sokolov et al., 2002, p. 239). Thus, the constant preparation for, and the act of, orienting are fundamental to information processing. Orienting determines the quality, kind, and amount of data received by sensorimotor, emotional, and cognitive processing systems that then serve to guide our actions (Kimmel et al., 1979; Sokolov et al., 2002).

Orienting entails turning attention toward whatever is most compelling or interesting at any given moment. When an external stimulus is found engaging (e.g., a beautiful painting or a thrilling novel) or demands attention (e.g., threatening stimulus), we orient to, or direct our sensory "radar" toward, this stimulus. We also orient toward internal events that clamor for attention, such as emotions or physical sensations.

Orienting is the first step in gathering information pertaining to significant stimuli. Sokolov et al. wrote that orienting has its functional value in "enhancing aspects of information processing, so that environmental [and internal] stimuli can be more efficiently analyzed. . . . This facilitation occurs particularly at moments in time that are likely to convey information to the organism . . . where an unusual or a novel stimulus . . . has occurred, or where a significant . . . stimulus . . . has occurred" (2002, p. 218). Thus orienting primes the person to become aware of potential survival-related environmental and internal cues, and to further assess those cues as neutral, beneficial, or dangerous.

OVERT AND COVERT ORIENTING

Orienting occurs on both overt and covert levels. Overt orienting involves visible physical actions of turning the sensory organs, particularly the eyes, and often the head and body, in the direction of an environmental stimulus. This form of orienting is often highly automatic, largely independent of conscious awareness, and commonly generated reflexively via an unexpected or novel stimulus (Fisher et al., 1991; Levine, 2004; Sereno, 2005). However, as the cortex matures over the course of development, overt orienting also comprises top-down components whereby we voluntarily select certain objects in an active, strategy-driven process. In contrast, covert orienting does not require muscular change. Instead, an "inner" or "mental" shift in attention from one environmental stimulus to another indicates an internal orienting that is often invisible to an observer (Posner, Walker, Friedrich, & Rafal, 1984).

These two forms of orienting are closely related: A sudden change in the environment will normally induce both overt (observable) and covert (nonobservable) orienting simultaneously. An initial response of overt orienting is often immediately followed by covert orienting, when internal attention is also focused on the object of orientation, and the visible behavioral changes of overt orienting then may cease (Sereno, 2005). Overt and covert orienting can also operate independently of one another; for example, we can overtly orient by looking at one object in the environment while simultaneously focusing our internal attention on something else altogether.

People with trauma-related disorders often have difficulty in synchronizing overt and covert orienting. They may overtly orient toward everyday stimuli while covertly orienting toward trauma-related internal stimuli: their rapid heartbeat, an intrusive image, or thoughts of inadequacy and failure. For example, after a motor vehicle accident, Mary appeared to orient toward objects in her environment; however, internally she was overwhelmingly oriented toward both intrusive memories of the accident and internal sensations of trembling.

Different orienting behavior manifests in different body responses. The therapist can track overt orienting through observable changes in the client's musculature, especially in movements of the eyes, face, and neck (Levine, 1997). Changes in overt orienting are detected as clients turn their heads and/or eyes to look at the therapist or at an object in the office. Covert orienting is usually indicated in much subtler bodily changes, such as a slight change in facial expression or angle of the head. These moment-by-moment alterations are important in sensorimotor psychotherapy because orienting changes often indicate different sensorimotor sequelae and subsequent modifications in the organization of the client's experience. Internal changes in a traumatized client's ability to process immediate information may often be so sudden and dramatic that observing the precursors—overt and covert orienting—is essential to implementing effective interventions.

For instance, while discussing an interpersonal conflict in therapy, Tahlia found it difficult to follow the conversation and did not immediately respond to questions that the therapist asked, although her gaze remained focused on him. Even though her overt orienting had not changed, Tahlia was covertly orienting to internal associations to her traumatic past. When the therapist asked Tahlia what she was orienting toward internally, she reported three foci: an image of her abusive father, the immobility and stiffness in her neck, and a feeling of impending danger accompanied by increased heart rate. The therapist asked Tahlia to look around the room, orient to various objects in the office, and then reorient to his face. This shift in movement, albeit simple, disrupted the rigid immobility of her neck, facilitating flexibility in Tahlia's overt orienting, which had been fixed. Subsequently, Tahlia reported that she could now "see" her therapist along with the image of her father, resulting in her heart rate slowing and her fear diminishing.

THE FIELD OF CONSCIOUSNESS

Being able to orient in a flexible and adaptive way to current reality is crucial for information processing and integration of new data from the environment. At times it is most adaptive to orient narrowly toward a very limited range of stimuli, retracting the field of consciousness, whereas at other
times it is most adaptive to orient to a broader range of stimuli, thereby
widening the field of consciousness. This *field* of consciousness refers to the
quantity of perceptual stimuli, both internal and external, that is included or
excluded from awareness (Steele, Dorahy, Van der Hart, & Nijenhuis, in
press; Van der Hart et al., 2004). The extent of this field of consciousness
varies in relation to our state of mind, and we are limited in what we can orient toward at any one time (Janet, 1907). We naturally retract (narrow)
our field of consciousness by orienting toward selected stimuli.

We are continually bombarded with enormous amounts of information
from our surroundings and from our internal milieu, far too much to
process at any given moment. The deluge of information that enters our
senses each moment could easily overwhelm our integrative capacity if we
were unable to filter out irrelevant or insignificant information. Narrowing
our field of consciousness by selecting relevant cues is fundamental to organizing goal-directed behavior. If we cannot select what we give our attention
to effectively, we may fail to notice relevant stimuli, or we may flit from
one stimulus to another, with no ability to concentrate our attention. On the
other hand, if we filter out too much information or become compulsively
focused on a certain stimulus, we may filter out pertinent stimuli and fail to
respond to important information.

Traumatized people typically have trouble sorting out relevant, significant cues from inconsequential ones (McFarlane et al., 1993; Van der Kolk
et al., 1996, p. 14). Their selection process may be biased by hypoarousal
states and a corresponding dulling of the senses that interferes with the ability to select and orient to relevant cues. Alternatively, a felt sense of danger
and the accompanying hyperarousal may make trauma-related stimuli the
dominant objects of their orientation, thereby relegating new information
about the environment to the background. Traumatized individuals sometimes underorient to cues that could provide information about potential
new threats in the current environment. Holly, a young woman who was
incestuously abused as a child, rarely slept during the hours from midnight
to 5:00 A.M.; she lay awake orienting to every sound as potentially threatening. On nights that she became fed up with lying awake, she would sometimes decide to go out jogging without any consideration of the potential
risks and with little overt orienting to her surroundings.

The tendencies of traumatized individuals to narrow the field of consciousness in predictable and maladaptive ways significantly hamper adap-

tive information processing and the consequent behavior (Levine, 1997). As a result, the ordinary joys of everyday life may be filtered out and only stimuli that match traumatic schema are noticed (Van der Kolk et al., 1996).

Helping clients identify and change their overt and covert orienting tendencies to include previously excluded stimuli, while filtering irrelevant or retraumatizing stimuli, alters their experience of the present and influences their subsequent actions toward more adaptive outcomes. We suggest that these potential changes in orienting are more easily developed in the client by helping them *practice* changing their orienting process on a sensorimotor level rather than through discussion. For example, Tahlia learned to practice looking around and orienting to different objects in her environment when she was triggered by reminders of the trauma—a simple physical exercise that helped her orient to the here-and-now and bring her arousal back within the window of tolerance.

THE ORIENTING REFLEX

A novel or unanticipated stimulus evokes an overt orienting response that helps to assure survival: An environmental change might indicate threat or the promise of food. Pavlov first described the involuntary response to novel or unexpected stimuli as the "orienting reflex" in 1910 and defined it as "the immediate response in man and animal to the slightest changes in the world around them" (Pavlov, 1927, as cited in Van Olst, 1971, p. 5). When a sudden change in the environment occurs, a series of internal events takes place to help us "orientate [the] appropriate receptor organ in accordance with the perceptible quality in the agent [stimulus] bringing about the change, making full investigation of it" (Pavlov, 1927, as cited in Van Olst, 1971, p. 5). For example, the receptor organ could be the eyes, caught by the sight of an unexpected falling object; or the receptor organ could be the ears of a combat soldier tuned to the sound of distant thunder or gunfire; or several receptor organs may respond simultaneously, especially when the stimulus is threatening: "The moment that the first shells whistle over and the air is rent with the explosions there is suddenly in our veins, in our hands, in our eyes a tense waiting, a heightening alertness, a strange sharpening of the senses" (Remarque, 1929/1982, p. 54). The new stimulus that commands attention replaces previous objects of orientation until enough information is obtained to determine one's relationship to the novel stimulus. In the above example, the sounds of shells and gunfire replace the combat soldier's previous orientation to conversation with his comrades.

Pavlov and colleagues emphasized the observable physical movements of the orienting reflex: the rotating of the eyes, the pricking of ears (in animals), and the turning of the head and body in the direction of the stimulus

(Sokolov et al., 2002). Changes in heart rate, breathing, blood flow, pupil size, and skin resistance also occur (Gottlieb, 2005).

Because the orienting reflex is an automatic and involuntary bottom-up process, it occurs much faster than it would if cognition were required (Hobson, 1994; LeDoux, 1994). The orienting reflex has an inhibitory, immobilizing effect because it momentarily arrests ongoing behavior in order to facilitate information gathering, yet, at the same time, it also has an activating effect as it stimulates the receptor organs and movements that support information gathering (Sokolov et al., 2002).

Although orienting reflexes are usually elicited by novel stimuli, they can also be evoked by any stimuli that might carry important information, for example, "changes in stimulation, stimuli too complex to be perceived fully on a single presentation, and stimuli that 'signal' significant or informative events to follow" (Graham, 1979, p. 138). An orienting reflex can also be evoked by the unexpected *omission* of familiar or ongoing sensory stimuli, such as the sudden, unexpected termination of the sound of a television that has been accommodated to as "background" noise. Similarly, stimuli that evoke the orienting reflex in some situations may not in others. If you encounter the dog you left at home while walking downtown, the orienting reflex will occur, whereas the sight of your dog at home may not elicit the reflex.

For the traumatized individual, maladaptive orienting tendencies include (1) a hypersensitivity to minor environmental or internal changes; (2) a tendency to overorient to archaic trauma-related stimuli; and (3) an inability to discriminate and evaluate the context of stimuli, especially regarding cues that may indicate danger in certain contexts but not in others (McFarlane et al., 1993; Shalev & Rogel-Fuchs, 1993).

The orienting reflex assists us in remaining appropriately open and responsive to information-carrying events in the environment (Sokolov et al., 2002). However, the orienting reflex is not continually reevoked by stimuli that have become familiar and ordinary. When we no longer orient to a stimulus, it means that we have become desensitized or habituated to it (Deese, 1958). Sokolov (1960, 1963) studied the effects on the orienting reflex of repeated exposure to inconsequential stimuli, finding that the reflex grew weaker with each exposure until it was no longer evoked; the threshold of response evocation had increased and habituation had occurred.

The counter capacity to overcome habituation—to become resensitized to newly salient stimuli—ensures survival benefit by enabling sensory discrimination of familiar yet potentially important stimuli in a different context. For example, being awakened by the sound of a door opening when no one else is home motivates us to take immediate action to determine whether or not we are in danger. Thus the orienting reflex is frequently evoked when there is a discrepancy between the stimulus and the individual's contextual expectation. However, many trauma survivors, especially those with maladaptive thresholds for stimuli due to their hypoarousal patterns, fail to orient or "dishabituate" to stimuli that are potentially important, and these stimuli are ignored.

Both habituation and sensitization are necessary if we are to cope with the multitude of available stimuli in each moment and still appropriately focus our attention and keep arousal within a window of tolerance. Traumatized individuals have typically established dysfunctional orienting tendencies that are overhabituated or oversensitized. In either case, these responses are embedded in posture and movement tendencies. Bettina developed orienting tendencies in the context of a violent early family history. These tendencies of ignoring her surroundings helped her to regulate her arousal: She predictably oriented inward, rather than outward, away from what she perceived as a threatening environment. Postural habits of looking down and away further diminished her ability to orient toward and evaluate environmental stimuli, leaving her preoccupied with distressing internal sensations, thoughts, and emotions.

[handwritten margin note: Example w/ personal application]

TOP-DOWN ORIENTING

As noted, because the orienting reflex is an automatic and involuntary bottom-up process, it occurs much faster than it would if cognition were required (Hobson, 1994; LeDoux, 1994). However, the full spectrum of orienting behavior also includes more general, continuous processes of orienting to internal and external environments as well as conscious, cognitive decision-making processes about objects of orientation. Top-down orienting takes place as objects of orientation are determined and selected based on planning or goal setting or other rational, conscious processes together with perceived emotional salience. For example, a person may intentionally decide to engage in a particular activity, such as a compelling debate, and temporarily ignore hunger cues. In this case, orienting to hunger cues is consciously overridden by a top-down "executive" decision that purposely narrows the field of consciousness. Another example: At the beginning of the day, we may prioritize objects toward which to orient by choosing certain activities over others: for example, making sure we get to work on time, establishing a list of chores to be done that day, and so on. In this way, we consciously decide to retract our field of consciousness in order to focus on stimuli of predetermined interest. In other words, we orient toward stimuli that support achieving certain preselected goals.

Orienting can be disturbed or interrupted by either external stimuli or internal cues, thereby initiating a reorientation (Sokolov et al., 2002). Physical requirements such as fatigue, hunger, pain, or illness may compete with these conscious-orienting choices by claiming priority in commanding our attention. Obviously, at the time of traumatic events, survival needs dictate orienting: For prisoners of war, for example, narrowing the field of consciousness to orient toward their guards is an adaptive strategy that may have top-down as well as bottom-up components.

Hobson pointed out that the more "rational" elements of orienting are closely related to the orienting reflex (1994, p. 88). Whereas general orienting "occurs more slowly, has at least some voluntary aspects and is cognitive," the orienting reflex is "completely automatic, involuntary, and precognitive." A complex and interactive relationship exists between involuntary, reflexive orienting and voluntary, cognitive orienting, and between overt orienting and covert orienting. As both sequential and parallel processes, they are intimately related. Conscious orienting and reflexive orienting continually interact and partially transform into the other. When the orienting reflex is evoked, it soon changes to encompass cognitive decisions about orienting, which transforms again into reflexive orienting. Examination of peritraumatic reactions, posttraumatic action tendencies, and interventions used in the therapeutic processing of trauma entails working with both reflexive/innate/bottom-up orienting and more cognitive/rational/top-down orienting.

EXPLORATORY ORIENTING

Pavlov (1927) and Sokolov (1969) both described the relationship between orienting and exploration as a survival mechanism that has "evolved into a specific system for collecting information," information necessary for continued existence (Sokolov et al., 2002, p. 2). Orienting facilitates active exploration as the organism searches the environment for new information. In contrast to the orienting reflex, exploratory orienting is more volitional and more susceptible to inhibition (Hunt & Kingstone, 2003). Exploratory orienting is influenced by the individual's predominant needs: If hunger predominates, the individual will orient toward stimuli that might provide a source of food. If no pressing need is experienced, exploratory orienting will be less specific. For example, orienting is open-ended when nothing in particular is going on in our environment as we take a summer evening walk. Safe, with nothing in particular commanding our attention, we stroll along, checking out the trees, looking at our neighbor's gardens, smelling the warm air. We orient as our sensory attention is caught for a moment and reorient to the next object of our fleeting interest.

Many of the objects of orientation are so ordinary or insignificant that they do not demand additional attention. The decision about what is important enough to require further attention and analysis is influenced by learning and past experiences; we may give additional attention to our neighbor's gardens if we also tend a garden. Obviously, if a sudden unexpected stimulus, such as a growling dog, appears, exploratory orienting is curtailed and the orienting reflex is evoked, dramatically and suddenly narrowing the field of consciousness and focusing our attention.

ORIENTING AND ATTENTION

Attention is a related, but different, phenomena from orienting, and is often problematic for people with trauma-related disorders, who may be plagued by distractions and attention deficits (Krystal, 1988; Stien & Kendall, 2004; van der Kolk, McFarlane et al., 1996). In the process of directing attention, the person first disengages from whatever he or she is attending to, then reorients toward the new object, and then focuses attention on the new object (Posner, 1980). The first two steps involve either the bottom-up orienting reflex, if the new stimulus is novel, sudden, or surprising, or voluntary top-down orienting, if the person "decides" to orient to a particular stimulus. The third step that occurs after orienting involves focusing attention, which requires immediate or prolonged concentration.

The degree of concentration or alertness brought to the awareness of a stimulus is referred to as the quality of attention or *level* of consciousness (Van der Hart et al., 2004); that is, whether attention is intense and highly focused or more diffuse and less focused (Kurtz, 1990; Steele et al., submitted). Attention can be prolonged and highly focused on stimuli that have personal relevance and are intellectually or emotionally engaging. Highly focused attention may also occur with top-down control, wherein we decide to concentrate on something, even if it is not particularly engaging (Jensen, 1998), such as doing our taxes. In order for attention to be *adaptive*, the ability to maintain both alert concentration and top-down (executive) control is required (Posner, DiGirolamo, & Fernandez-Duque, 1997; Posner & Petersen, 1990; Posner & Raichle, 1994)—and both are problematic for traumatized people (Putnam, 1994, 1995). Sustained attention is needed to make plans and set goals, identify the series of tasks required to enact the plans or achieve goals, and monitor progress and adjust accordingly along the way. Traumatized individuals frequently have trouble sustaining attention, which impedes their ability to carry tasks through to completion (Janet, 1907).

Hobson wrote that "attention . . . must remain centered in dynamic tension between distraction and obsession if our behavior is to stay on a moderate course" (1994, p. 167). Adaptive attention enables an active balance between being too distracted, unfocused, erratic, or flighty and being overly focused, compulsive, obsessive, or fixated. Achieving this dynamic equilibrium is particularly difficult for traumatized people, whose arousal is often not within the window of tolerance necessary for adaptive attention. To sustain attention, arousal should be fairly high, toward the upper limits of the window of tolerance, but not so high that it interferes with concentration. Many traumatized individuals are both reflexively fixated *and* reflexively inattentive; they alternate between the extremes of fixation and distractibility. They may scan the environment hypervigilantly, orienting briefly to a variety of stimuli without discrimination, or they may become involuntarily and compulsively fixated on a particular stimulus and unable to redirect attention. Shifting orientation and attention from external to internal stimuli, or from internal to external, presents further difficulty, because the traumatized person is often strongly distracted by both internal and environmental stimuli.

Psychotherapeutic interventions must help clients reorient and redirect attention in an effort to become "unstuck" from particular stimuli and more concentrated on others of immediate relevance. Directing clients to physically orient their body toward new stimuli and asking them questions that help to focus attention, such as "What do you see there?", "What color is it?", "Can you see the little patterns in the fabric?", "What do the patterns look like?" may move them out of the impasse. To help clients focus attention on the body, the therapist can ask them questions that can only be answered by giving acute attention to sensations in the body: "How big is the sensation? About the size of a grapefruit? Baseball? Pinprick? Which way is the tension pulling: in or out, left or right?"

As a result of a recent rape, Molly was distracted from stimuli related to the present, disconnected from both her body and her environment, and preoccupied by memories of the incident. In order to disrupt these orienting and attentional tendencies and help her reorient to present-moment stimuli, the therapist first redirected her orientation and requested that she give sustained attention to her body. She asked Molly to stand, notice which foot had more weight on it, and notice if the weight was more on the ball of that foot or the heel. Then Molly was instructed to rapidly orient to various objects in the room and name each object and its color: for example, blue pillow, red lamp, white tile. These interventions increased Molly's ability to focus her attention during the therapy sessions. Moreover, she had learned exercises that she could implement on her own to disrupt the tendencies that kept her feeling lost in the memories of rape while helping her focus more attentively on current circumstances.

THE IMPACT OF BELIEFS ON ORIENTING AND ATTENTION

Adaptive behavior requires anticipation of significant information-carrying events and preparation of responses in advance. We have an evolutionary advantage if we can predict meaningful events and prepare beforehand by deciding how to process, and respond to, the upcoming information (Sokolov et al., 2002). Orienting is thus "characterized by an active search for new information based on comparison and re-evaluation of working hypotheses present in the brain" (Sokolov et al., 2002, p. xiii). Guided by preformulated, primarily implicit hypotheses or beliefs, we orient toward particular stimuli related to a particular belief and then assess if these stimuli are congruent with our belief. The more strongly the person holds a particular belief, the more likely it is to be aroused, the less information will be needed for its confirmation, and the more information will be needed for its negation (Brewin et al., 1996; Bruner, 1951).

Much of what we see is colored and organized by what we expect to see. The cues toward which clients are compelled to orient, and which sustain their attention, are likely to be those that verify implicit beliefs held about the self and the world. Susan had tendencies of orienting and attention that stemmed from the beliefs formed through early relationship dynamics. She grew up with parents who were preoccupied with their careers and each other, and she reported feeling unsupported and uncared for throughout her childhood. She said that she felt "on her own" for most of her life and described a childhood of fixing her own meals, telling her parents when she needed new clothes, and becoming self-sufficient at a very young age. The hypothesis, or belief, she formed was, "No one will ever be there for me, so I have to do it all myself." Her body posture and language reflected this belief: Susan's body was highly toned and fast moving; her arms hung with her palms facing backward (which she described in therapy as indicating a reluctance to reach out to others), and she had difficulty looking people in the eye. Her belief, supported by her physical posture and movement, caused Susan to habitually orient away from cues that indicated the availability of reliable support. She did not notice the offers of help from other people. Susan complained that her husband failed her in ways similar to those of her parents; however, her frustrated husband stated that he repeatedly extended support to Susan but that she consistently refused, or simply did not respond, so he had finally given up trying. Susan clearly was not orienting or attending to cues that would disprove her belief; instead she focused on cues reminiscent of her past that verified her belief that no one would support her.

Clients typically orient and attend to stimuli reminiscent of traumatic events, without conscious recollection that the stimuli are, in fact, reminders of the past (Bargh & Chartrand, 1999; Kirsch & Lynn, 1999). Jennifer was not consciously aware that her therapist's sweater was similar to that worn by her rapist. But all her attention was fixated on his sweater, and as she did so, she experienced her therapist as a potential threat. She became temporarily unaware of all the other stimuli that would indicate that he and her rapist were different people. Orienting to, and sustaining attention on, the traumatic reminder caused a somatic reliving of the past, and she could not realize that she was currently safe with her therapist. Without being consciously aware of it, Jennifer had developed an implicit hypothesis ("Perpetrators wear a particular kind of sweater; people wearing that kind of sweater will harm me") that directed her attention and orienting behavior. Such conditioned procedural learning is unconscious, extremely robust, easily evoked, and challenged only with difficulty (Charney, Deutch, Krystal, Southwick, & Davis, 1993; Cowan, 1988; Grigsby & Stevens, 2000; Pitman, Orr, & Shalev, 1993; Shalev, Orr, Peri, Schreiber, & Pitman, 1992).

The tendency to orient toward conditioned stimuli intensifies trauma-related procedural learning. In Jennifer's treatment it became important to explore orienting behavior that allowed her to gather new information about her environment and the males who wore that particular kind of sweater, to explore orienting toward and away from the conditioned stimulus, and to work toward modulating her arousal when she chose to orient toward the sweater.

STAGES OF THE ORIENTING RESPONSE

Orienting (whether overt or covert, exploratory, top-down, or reflexive) is not composed of just one behavioral, mental or somatic response. A number of authors have differentiated several stages of orienting and attention, each with its own characteristic mental and physical actions (Arnold, 1968; Levine, 1997; Pavlov, 1927; Siegel, 1999; Van Olst, 1971), and Levine (1997, 2004) particularly notes the importance of working with orienting processes in treatment. The following stages of the orienting response have been compiled from these authors as well as from clinical experience. Although the stages are presented in a linear fashion for clarity of explanation, they occur simultaneously or follow each other in a split-second sequence.

1. Arousal
2. Activity arrest
3. Sensory alertness
4. Muscular adjustments
5. Scanning
6. Location in space
7. Identification and appraisal
8. Action
9. Reorganization

The following case study illustrates how each stage contains mental and physical actions that can become targets of interest, exploration, understanding, and intervention in therapy. Dorothy, a 19-year-old college student survived an assault in the apartment she shared with two other students. She initially came to therapy to resolve a recurring sleep disturbance after this event. Addressing her tendency to orient, even while sleeping, to unintegrated fragments related to this incident proved to be a key element in integrating the trauma.

1. *Arousal.* The first stage of the orienting response involves an increase in arousal, which can range from slight to extreme. Siegel wrote that this "initial orienting response" is a sign of heightened activity in the brain (1999, p. 124). Arousal is experienced as body sensation (often described as a slight feeling of excitement), small changes in respiration and heart rate, and other reactions of the autonomic nervous system (Levine, 1997; Rossi, 1993; Sapolsky, 1994; Van Olst, 1971). The degree of arousal is paired with the level of curiosity, excitement, and interest evoked by the stimulus (Levine, 1997). If the stimulus is not immediately perceived as threatening, arousal will remain within the window of tolerance. Dorothy reported that on the evening of the event, she was absorbed in her studies when she heard a noise downstairs. Not knowing what the sound was but expecting her roommates to return later in the evening, Dorothy became interested and curious, but not anxious, upon hearing this noise. The stimulus (in this case, the noise) was not particularly intense or unfamiliar. Dorothy was in a relaxed state of mind and had no traumatic or negative associations with the sound downstairs. Thus her arousal elevated only slightly, remaining within the window of tolerance.

2. *Activity arrest.* The second stage of orienting involves a modification of activity, described as "activity arrest," in which ongoing actions are temporarily and abruptly diminished or halted completely (Levine, 1997; Sokolov et al., 2002). If the stimulus is startling or compelling, activity may cease altogether in order to eliminate or minimize any distractions to orienting to the novelty and gathering information about it (Sokolov et al., 2002). If the stimulus is not particularly surprising or interesting, activity may slow down but not cease altogether. The activity arrest response is most obvious in animals when they hear an unfamiliar noise and pause, motionless. This pause continues until the stimulus is assessed, at which point action is taken. Arrest is differentiated from the freeze response (explained in the next chapter), which is an immobilizing defense that occurs *after* the stimulus is assessed as dangerous. Dorothy stopped studying to focus her attention on the source of this new sound. She was curious, her field of consciousness retracted, and she became still and motionless to listen more attentively.

3. _Sensory alertness_. This third stage takes place concurrently with activity arrest. The sense organs are refocused and become increasingly alert. Siegel explained that the "brain and other systems of the body enter a state of heightened alertness with an internal message of 'something important is happening here and now'" (1999, p. 124). All five senses are tuned to the novelty, ready to learn about it through smell, sight, sound, and sometimes taste and touch (Rossi, 1993; Van Olst, 1971). The nostrils might flare, the pupils might change, and the ears may "prick up." In humans, hearing and seeing become particularly acute, whereas in other animals the sense of smell may be more central. Of note is that all the other senses become heightened with the stimulation of one sense organ: If there is a loud sound, vision becomes more acute, not just hearing (Sokolov et al., 2002; Van Olst, 1971). Acutely attuned senses, initially a reflex, prepare us for further assessment and action (Hobson, 1994). The field of consciousness narrows so that we can fully attend to the novel cues, and nonrelevant internal and external sensory cues are excluded as objects of orientation or attention. In Dorothy's case, the textbook she had been reading and the sensation of thirst she had noticed before the interruption were automatically ignored. Her auditory awareness was particularly heightened, as she "strained her ears" to listen from upstairs to the noise downstairs.

4. _Muscular adjustments_. The visible movement and postural adjustments of covert orienting and shifts in attention are accompanied by subtle muscular changes that may not be noticeable. These muscular changes occur within the salient response modality: For example, if the visual modality is involved, changes include neck movements and adjustments in gaze (Kuiken, Busink, Dukewich, & Gendlin, 1996). General muscular adjustments of flexion and extension that occur primarily in the spine characteristically accompany activity arrest and increased alertness (Levine, 1997, 2004; Van Olst, 1971; Veronin, Luria, Sokolov, & Vinogradova, 1965). When a person is startled by an event, muscular flexion occurs initially, often accompanied by a pulling up of the viscera in response to a tightening of the diaphragm, abdominal wall, and pelvic floor. Breathing may become shallow or cease momentarily. A lengthening of the spine and neck may follow to give the person or animal a better view of the environment in preparation for the next step (Levine, 1997). When Dorothy heard the noise downstairs, her body tightened, her spine lengthened almost imperceptibly, and her breathing became slightly shallow.

5. _Scanning_. This fifth stage pertains to overt orienting: physical movements of turning the head, neck, and spine, searching the environment for the novel stimulus (Babkin, 1949; Sokolov et al., 2002; Van Olst, 1971; Veronin et al., 1965). Eye movement is often a primary component of this stage (Hobson, 1994), and the muscles of the feet, legs, back, and neck may

work together so that the whole body turns in search of the stimulus (Levine, 2004). Other versions of scanning may also take place, depending on the form of the sensory input—for example, turning the head to better hear a piece of music, lifting the chin to smell baking bread, even shifting the spine to attend internally to a feeling of grief. Turning her spine and widening her eyes, Dorothy oriented toward the door of her bedroom and focused her attention on the doorway.

6. _Location in space_. The sixth stage entails locating the novel stimulus in a particular place in the environment (Levine, 2004). The stimulus is situated in physical space in relation to the objects in the surroundings. Dorothy recognized that the sound was coming closer, moving toward her room. She remained in an arrested state, alert and still, aware of the approaching proximity of the footsteps, and continued to orient and sustain attention toward the door. A young man appeared in the doorway.

7. _Identification and appraisal_. The identification and evaluation of stimuli as safe, dangerous, or life-threatening initially occurs without conscious awareness. Up to this stage of orienting, qualitative judgment has been less central. At this point, a meaning of significant or insignificant, safe, dangerous, or life-threatening is ascribed to the stimulus.

Siegel (1999) referred to the initial evaluative stage as _elaborative appraisal and arousal_. The preliminary appraisal and arousal mechanisms comprise sensorimotor and emotional responses that are neither conscious nor cognitively directed (Arnold, 1968; Frijda, 1986; LeDoux, 1996; Siegel, 1999). In other words, core brain structures make the initial determination of the goodness or badness of the stimulus, and whether to move toward or away from it, based on instinct and/or previous experience of similar stimuli. After the initial appraisal, a more elaborate evaluation occurs: Automatic responses, such as the sensation of fear, begin to become conscious and cognitive assessment may take place, refining the unconscious appraisal.

The appraisal is influenced by expectancy and context (Frijda, 1986); it incorporates relevant past experiences of the stimulus, including emotional and representational elements of memory, as well as the person's current internal emotional and bodily state, the external environment, the intensity and familiarity of the stimulus, and expectations of the future (Siegel, 1999). These expectations "form a cognitive background that holds relevant coding categories in readiness and upon which the events impinge" (Frijda, 1986, p. 326). Appraisal thus depends upon the integrative capacity of an individual to separate past from present, and his or her ability to remain optimally aroused in order to think, feel, and attribute appropriate meaning to a present experience.

We may be biologically predisposed to evaluate a novel stimuli too hastily as dangerous—as LeDoux (1994) effectively noted, it is better to mistake a stick for a snake than a snake for a stick. All the senses process at "a 'lower' level—before complex processing and long before conscious awareness," often setting off the alarm signaling "danger" when there is none (Siegel, 1999, p. 213). Furthermore, value attribution is intimately connected to emotional valence and body sensation, which are available prior to the full processing of the stimulus (LeDoux, 1996)—a reality that is painfully apparent for traumatized people, who react to their first impression of danger without further appraisal (LeDoux, 1994).

A full appraisal thus involves both subcortical and cortical mechanisms, and is both immediate and extended. When there is no time to consider cognitive elements or when the appraisal is not the result of an integrative process, then it remains rudimentary (Frijda, 1986). If attention can be sustained, then more information can be gathered and the initial appraisal revised—provided that the individual is receptive to revision. If the stimulus is appraised as benign, then the individual will move to the next stage of the orienting response. However, if a stimulus is judged to be dangerous, the focus changes to an "appraisal of the possibilities of escape as opposed to attack or of some other attempted solutions to the threat" (Lazarus, 1968, p. 249). Trauma-related expectations of impending danger often disrupt extended appraisal and revision processes in traumatized individuals, and they are therefore prone to respond to perceived threat cues and traumatic reminders with defensive action.

When the man appeared at her door, Dorothy identified him as a stranger and was wary and slightly fearful. However, because he was young and dressed in a down jacket, like most of her friends, she quickly assumed he was a fellow college student—a context-appropriate assessment. This appraisal was validated by his politeness as he inquired about the whereabouts of one of her roommates. Any apprehension she felt decreased, her arousal lowered, her body relaxed slightly, her breathing normalized, and her physical arrest changed to increased movement.

8. *Action*. Following appraisal, explicit action is initiated, which in its most basic form involves either *approach*, including sustained and top-down control of attention, or *avoidance*. The initial physical action occurs instinctively when the first precognitive appraisal is made; then comes action mediated by cognition and the refinement of the initial appraisal and emotional response. The precognitive appraisal "narrows the response options available to a few choices that evolution has had the wisdom to connect up with the particular appraisal mechanism" (LeDoux, 1996, pp. 69–70). In contrast, cognitively mediated action is characterized by greater flexibility of responses.

At this stage Dorothy relaxed a little and told the intruder that her roommate had not yet returned from vacation but was expected later in the evening. Her social engagement system was activated, and she continued to orient and sustain attention toward the intruder with an attitude of interest and curiosity rather than fear. If she had evaluated him as dangerous, her action would have been characterized by avoidance and defense rather than approach and engagement.

9. *Reorganization.* In the final stage reorganization occurs; the system returns to homeostasis, reorienting to other objects. There may be muscular relaxation or slight tremors, depending on how much arousal, sensory alertness, and muscular mobilization have occurred. In Dorothy's case, her arousal, which had risen toward the top edge of the window of tolerance, dropped, her alert senses returned to their previous level, and her body relaxed. Dorothy had oriented to the novel stimulus, progressed through all the stages of orienting, and taken appropriate verbal action. She had concluded that the novelty of an unknown man in her building was of no particular danger or interest. She began to disengage her attention from him and to orient toward her books, refocusing her attention back toward her studies.

Had the young man left, Dorothy would have continued to direct her attention to her studies. Instead, the man moved closer to her and drew a knife from his pocket. In response to his increasing proximity and the weapon, Dorothy's orienting immediately heightened: her arousal escalated, her senses suddenly became acute, her body tightened, she held her breath and oriented exclusively to the knife, retracting her field of consciousness to the threat cue. She reappraised the man as dangerous and engaged in further appraisal to determine the most appropriate action to assure her safety. The defensive systems, in general, and Dorothy's particular defensive actions in this instance are described in the next chapter.

ORIENTING TENDENCIES, ATTENTION, AND UNRESOLVED TRAUMA

As we have discussed throughout this chapter, traumatized clients often react to novel or conditioned stimuli with responses characterized by defensive instead of adaptive orienting. Traumatic events spur a conditioned learning that pairs previously benign stimuli with feelings of fear (LeDoux, 1996). Hyper- or hypoarousal becomes easily triggered, and these clients begin orienting toward either internal and external cues that are associated with past trauma, or they fail to orient to significant cues. For months after this incident, Dorothy was highly sensitized to down jackets similar to the one the intruder had worn and found herself hyperorienting to anyone who wore such a jacket. Her expectation was that anyone wearing down jackets was dangerous, and she responded with alarm and avoidance behavior.

Clients may also feel "spaced out" and fail to orient, especially in hypo-aroused states. It is as though they cannot move through the stages of the orienting response to resolution and reorganization and instead become "stuck" in defensive responses and the accompanying extremes of arousal.

As noted, traumatization has been described as a failure of integrative capacity (Janet, 1907). We propose that an inability to progress adaptively through the stages of orienting both hinders integrative capacity and is the effect of its failure. The activity-arrest stage of orienting may turn into a freezing reaction wherein the client feels paralyzed and unable to take appropriate action. Or the senses may remain alert long after the stimulus has passed, and the posture may remain hyperflexed or hyperextended. At least partly due to the dysregulated arousal tendencies, a traumatized individual may demonstrate either hyperorienting tendencies, continually scanning the environment for threat cues, or hypoorienting tendencies, with the eyes fixed and neck immobile, failing to scan the environment. At the stage of taking action, tendencies of hyperactivity or hypoactivity may be apparent: Some clients take impulsive action and cannot stop, whereas others have trouble taking any action at all. Tendencies to avoid orienting to certain trauma-related stimuli are as debilitiating to the traumatized individual as are tendencies to repeatedly orient to reminders of the trauma (Frijda, 1986, p. 315).

In treatment, therapists can observe clients' orienting and attentional tendencies as different internal or external stimuli are perceived and teach traumatized clients to become aware of the physical, emotional, and cognitive components of these tendencies as well as to evaluate their efficacy. Once client and therapist have noted how and at what stage orienting responses are stuck, the therapist can redirect the client's orienting in ways that promote more adaptive responses.

For example, prior to the attempted assault, Dorothy had a lifelong desire to marry and have children. She was generally oriented toward cues that were connected to this desire: young men, children, families, dating opportunities. Following the incident, she developed an aversion to young men who resembled the man who attacked her. Having thought the intruder intended rape, she shunned sexual relationships, had difficulty broaching the subject of sexuality, and was clearly conflicted when discussing dating.

Her therapist noticed that when their discussion approached sexual content, Dorothy's arousal increased, her shoulders and neck tightened, and she avoided looking at her therapist. Instead, she appeared fearful, and her eyes were glued to the door. Dorothy had clearly jumped to an appraisal of the situation or topic as dangerous without fully participating in all the stages of the orienting response. The therapist directed Dorothy to orient to her immediate surroundings by looking around the room; this intervention interrupted Dorothy's fixed gaze and reinstated the turning movements of the neck and spine that are indicative of the "scanning" stage. The therapist then directed Dorothy to orient toward him and to focus her attention on the therapist's face, noticing what happened in her own body. Dorothy noted her impulse to look away, a slight feeling of fear, and thoughts of the therapist as dangerous. The therapist encouraged Dorothy to experiment with looking away and then reorienting to his face and continue with extended appraisal. This intervention enabled Dorothy to gather more information and cognitively assess the situation's dangerousness or safety instead of merely reacting to her initial sensation and emotion. Through mindful experimentation with new orienting behavior and by learning to sustain her attention rather than respond instinctively, Dorothy began to engage her cognitive capacity to appropriately assess current situations.

The new experience of (1) making voluntary choices about how and where to orient and (2) taking in new information from the environment facilitates the process of engaging new orienting responses. Dorothy had felt very safe with her boss and was successful at her part-time job at the college co-op prior to the incident. Nevertheless, following the assault, she found herself inexplicably panicky in his presence. She was not able to make eye contact or to notice his warm smile. She fled to the restroom, where she sat with her heart and head pounding, trying to catch her breath. In treatment focused on understanding the trauma-related beliefs, expectations, and habitual orienting responses evoked by the sight of her boss, Dorothy began to become aware of how her orienting tendencies interfered with her ability to distinguish friend from foe. First she learned to notice and tolerate her retraction of consciousness, and then she learned to change it by voluntarily allowing her gaze to linger on a new stimulus. At subsequent meetings with her boss, Dorothy was able to work with her orienting and defensive tendencies, first orienting to objects in the room (i.e., reinstating flexible scanning), then orienting to her boss from a distance, studying his facial expression and body language and noticing her own tendency to overlay her past experience on the present moment. As Dorothy's self-awareness and field of consciousness enlarged, her arousal remained within her window of tolerance, and she could realistically appraise the environment.

In summary, the process of orienting allows us to take in critical information from the environment and organize subsequent perception, action, and behavior. The orienting that occurs during trauma typically precedes a cascade of defensive responses that are necessary and adaptive in the context of survival. However, trauma-related orienting tendencies become maladaptive if the client is subsequently prevented from orienting to additional information that confirms the absence of current threat. These orienting tendencies also have profound effects on cognitive tendencies: Traumatized clients develop habits of attention in which they orient and attend to trauma-related beliefs, such as beliefs in their worthlessness or beliefs that they will never be safe or happy, orienting only to stimuli that confirm these beliefs, unable to take in other information. This maladaptive sequence leads to further somatic changes and bottom-up processes that directly alter cognitive and emotional processing. With compromised orienting responses that are not adaptive for their current lives, traumatized individuals typically fail to assess danger adequately and repeatedly find themselves either in threatening situations or are in isolated situations, too fearful of danger to engage with the world.

In treatment, as illustrated in the case study of Dorothy, the therapist observes the way in which orienting responses are affecting the client's ability to (1) evaluate threat, (2) integrate a wide array of stimuli, both new and old, and (3) rework old trauma-related cognitive schemas. In this context the therapist can begin to assist the client in reorienting toward those stimuli that hold potential for resolving chronic patterns of traumatic orienting, and, in so doing, lay the foundation for more adaptive behaviors.

The sensorimotor psychotherapy practitioner helps clients slow down and become mindful observers of the components of their orienting and attentional processes, increasing their awareness of how and toward what they focus their attention. This observational position allows them to become less fixated on the traumatic stimuli that reflexively command their orienting and attention and more attentive to the orienting and attentional tendencies themselves. By observing the stages of orienting as they emerge in the therapy hour, clients begin to understand these tendencies and become more effective in changing them so that they can orient in ways that facilitate their successful resolution of the past trauma. This process appears to be most effective when, through "dual processing," the client is able to engage in orienting and attentional behavior while simultaneously observing the effects on mind, emotion, and body. When dual processing occurs, the traumatic stimuli do not dominate and co-opt orienting, and clients become more focused on tracking their progress through the stages of the orienting response. Mindfulness of the orienting process places a therapeutic gap between stimulus and response (Kurtz, 1990): Rather than orienting unconsciously to traumatic stimuli, the client learns to observe the process of orienting and to witness the stages of the orienting response. Rather than be driven by habitual responses, the client becomes curious and increasingly observant—the first step toward changing the trauma-related orienting tendencies and habitual defensive responses that are bound to follow.

Chapter 5

✖•✖•✖

Defensive Subsystems: Mobilizing and Immobilizing Responses

DEFENSIVE RESPONSES HAVE EVOLVED TO ENSURE SURVIVAL in a world that historically has contained several different types of threat: the danger of predatory animals, the menace of natural disasters, the violence from other human beings, and in the past century, the peril of potential vehicular and machinery accidents, human-made disasters, and mechanized warfare. The instinctive defensive and protective reactions to these perils turn maladaptive for traumatized individuals, whose defensive responses persist decades after the original threatening events are over. These individuals are "caught in a vicious cycle of inadequate efforts to cope with a stressor, lose their ability to disengage from so doing, fail to use all available resources and become increasingly distressed" (Shalev, 2005). The repetition of defensive action tendencies inappropriate to current reality is debilitating to individuals who, as time goes on, lose more and more confidence in their capacity to navigate the challenges of ordinary life. Over time, they become unable even to imagine positive endings to current situations that evoke old defensive tendencies.

REACTIVATED DEFENSIVE RESPONSES

Orienting responses allow us a means of evaluating stimuli in terms of their potential danger to us. When a stimulus is evaluated as threatening, both

85

physical and psychological defenses work together to reduce the danger and maximize the chances of survival. Like orienting responses, these defensive responses consist of a series of relatively fixed sequential sensorimotor reactions whose expression depends on the nature of the stimulus, the capacities and experience of the individual, and the external environment. In human beings the components of the defensive system also include conscious cognitive and emotional elements. This combination provides the advantage of speed in the unconscious defensive response, along with the capacity for consciously fine-tuning the response to specific elements of the danger. For example, if a hiker turns a bend in a wilderness trail and comes upon a bear, the defensive, precognitive instinct—the evoked fixed action tendency—is a startle response and fleeing. This action tendency is further organized by the context of the experience: A split-second later, there may be a more organized conscious response, as a cognitive decision is made about how to flee, which direction to run in, how quickly to run, whether to yell at the same time, and so forth (LeDoux, 1996; Llinas, 2001). This conscious response may incorporate past learning experiences such as the possibility that "It might be safer to stand still rather than run when you see a bear." These adaptive options are nevertheless all modifications of, and improvements on, the instinctive action tendency to flee in the face of danger. The ability to amend a fixed action tendency—to make voluntary, top-down, conscious decisions while under the command of an action tendency—is an attribute most unique to the human species, a characteristic of well-adapted individuals (Llinas, 2001).

If defensive actions are effective and danger is successfully averted, we customarily experience a sense of relief and victory over the threat. These feelings of mastery are notably absent for traumatized individuals. Janet stated, "The patients who are affected by . . . traumatic memories have not been able to perform any of the actions characteristic of the stage of triumph" (1925, p. 669). More colloquially, we would say that traumatized individuals get stuck in the particular repetitive action tendencies of defense that were evoked at the time of the original trauma and are evoked again and again by environmental cues reminiscent of that trauma (Krystal, 1988). These individuals are driven by bottom-up hijacking to reenact those same defensive responses long after their survival value has disappeared. Clinically, we have observed that clients tend to repeat a defense that was evoked at the time of the original trauma even though it may have been unsuccessful or only partially successful in conferring safety. As Janet noticed long ago, "[Traumatized] patients . . . are continuing the action, or rather the attempt at action, which began when the thing happened, and they exhaust themselves in these everlasting recommencements" (1925, p. 663).

This tendency to reenact defensive responses manifests in many forms. The adult survivor of childhood incest may freeze instead of refusing an unwanted sexual advance; the victim of childhood beatings may react with uncontrolled aggression toward her own children when she feels threatened; the war veteran may feel the urge to run or withdraw whenever he feels even slightly anxious. While recognizing that they are "overreacting," traumatized individuals are nevertheless frequently unable to moderate their responses. Each time these repetitive defensive tendencies are evoked, the individual becomes unable to make use of options and solutions available in his or her present, nontraumatic situation. A defensive action, such as freezing or fighting, becomes a generalized response to perceived threat, causing traumatized clients to feel that they cannot cope with everyday challenges.

The term *defensive reaction* was originally coined by Pavlov (Van der Kolk, 1987). The function of the defensive reaction, as Pavlov observed, is to initiate immediate, self-protective, and survival-oriented behavior. When the traumatized individual is faced with reminders of the trauma and experiences a defensive response, the function of that defensive response has shifted from reacting to an immediate threat to reacting to anticipated threat (Misslin, 2003). What began as a necessary defense in the face of a real threat becomes a pervasive, unrelenting reaction to the *anticipation* of a threat, with all the concomitant changes in physiology (Czeisler et al., 1976; Sumova & Jakoubek, 1989). Individuals caught in a pattern of anticipating danger and reenacting old defensive responses possess only a limited ability to modify their action tendencies according to context and cannot access top-down thinking to inhibit defensive actions. Vera, for instance, had a history of childhood sexual abuse during which she learned that any attempt to fight or flee would be overpowered by the perpetrator. Subsequently, as an adult, she would repeatedly freeze in the presence of male authority figures. Vera knew that the freezing defense was not adaptive in her adult work relationships, but she was unable to modify it, no matter how often she told herself (top-down) that the situation was now different. Despite her insight, her intellectual competence in solving complex problems, her recognition of her current safety, and her capacity to contribute usefully to the organization that employed her, she would shrink from speaking up to her boss. When asked her opinion in meetings, she often became incapable of articulating her point of view. She reported feeling "paralyzed" and "unable to breathe," as though her mind said one thing while her body did something else. She was trapped by the bottom-up defensive action tendencies related to her traumatic past.

In treatment it is essential to work with defensive responses in order to reinstate their adaptive and flexible functioning. By definition, traumatized individuals have experienced a failure of their defensive responses to assure safety. As Herman noted, "Traumatic reactions occur when no action is of avail" (1992, p. 34). The individual is forced to abandon active, mobilizing defenses (fight or flight) in favor of defenses that are immobilizing: freeze or "feigned death." Levine noted that "the bodies of traumatized people portray 'snapshots' of their unsuccessful attempts to defend themselves in the face of threat and injury" (2005, p. 2). These failed defenses can be rediscovered and revitalized by giving attention to the body and thereby reestablishing a sense of mastery and competence.

In therapy clients learn to mindfully observe their defensive tendencies. Through awareness of the body, they are able to put a gap between the trigger and the defensive tendency to notice increasingly more detailed somatic components of their defensive responses (Kurtz, 1990). They often discover the abandoned empowering defenses that were ineffective at the time of the trauma. For example, as Vera became aware of the somatic components of her tendency to freeze, she noticed tension throughout her body, especially in her legs. When her therapist asked her if there were words that accompanied the tension, Vera first said, "I can't move," which was a necessary, adaptive freezing response to childhood sexual abuse: If she had struggled at that time, the abuse would have worsened. As Vera was instructed to focus her attention on the tension in her legs, she commented, "My legs want to run away." She had discovered the empowering defensive action that she could not execute during the abuse. With this realization, Vera became more aware of the impulse to run and experienced "power" in her legs. Encouraged by the therapist to stand and walk around the therapy office in order to feel the capacity of her legs to move, Vera said she wanted to run in place. She began to breathe deeply, color came to her face, and her eyes brightened. After "running," Vera verbalized a different feeling in her body—it felt powerful, energized, and alive—saying, "My body has caught up with my mind!" This felt experience of the restoration of an active defensive response emerged spontaneously from Vera's awareness of her somatic tendency to freeze. As clients become aware of the body, they often discover previously abandoned bottom-up defensive possibilities that can mitigate current maladaptive bottom-up tendencies. Actions that were incomplete, previously discarded as ineffective or useless, can be executed in the context of an attuned therapeutic relationship and thus completed, restoring a physical capacity that was previously abandoned.

COMPONENTS OF THE DEFENSIVE RESPONSE

All mammals are equipped with a cascade of defensive reactions in a hierarchical system that enables them to respond accordingly to both mild and severe levels of threat (Cannon, 1953; Fanselow & Lester, 1988). Mimicking phylogeny, we divide these defensive reactions into three general defensive subsystems: (1) a subsystem that involves directly calling upon others for help (attachment system and the social engagement system), (2) the mobilizing defenses (fight or flight) that activate the body, and (3) the immobilizing defenses (freezing, collapse, or feigned death) that result in motionlessness and submissive behaviors.

Animals may follow a sequential pattern in the use of a particular defense, which varies according to availability of protection, physical distance between predator and prey, and the frequency of prior threat in specific locations (Fanselow & Lester, 1988). Threat falls along a continuum of predator immanence from total safety to deadly attack (Fanselow & Lester, 1988; Nijenhuis & Van der Hart, 1999b; Nijenhuis, Vanderlinden, & Spinhoven, 1998), and "behavior changes will occur as a function of changes in the prey's perception of its location on the continuum" (Fanselow & Lester, 1988, p. 187). Animals typically curtail their ordinary activities of exploring, foraging, mating, and playing when predators are likely to be in the area. "The human counterpart might be the child who restricts her activities (e.g., stays in her room or stays out of the house) when her abusive father is home" (Allen, 2001, p. 170). Sudden and specific changes in behavioral and physiological defenses occur in response to different stages of imminence in attempts to reduce or thwart further increases in immanence (Fanselow & Lester, 1988). Animals may attempt flight after spotting a predator. A baby animal or a weaker pack animal may first cry for protection when endangered under certain circumstances. However, freezing is often the preferred defensive response, even when an escape route is available (Nijenhuis et al., 1998), particularly if the predator has not yet spotted the prey. Because movement cues activate predator behavior in animals, immobility may prevent detection, and the predator may orient instead to other moving objects. If the predator comes near the prey, frantic, explosive fight behavior is typically evoked. If this defense is unsuccessful, "feigned death," in which the animal's body becomes limp and immobile, is used as a "last resort" survival response. Feigned death may prevent further attack because animals are programmed not to devour unmoving prey; animals that are not moving or cannot move may be diseased (Perry et al., 1995; Seligman, 1975). It should be noted that the same versions of these animal defensive responses are found in humans as well.

These defenses are not always engaged in a sequential manner; any defense may be evoked depending on the immanence and characteristics of the threat as well as on other important variables, such as the resources of the individual and which defenses have "worked" for the person in the past. Each defensive response is typically definitive, primitive, and inflexible (Nijenhuis et al., 1998; Nijenhuis et al., 1999), but no one defensive response is "better" than another: All are potentially adaptive and effective at diminishing threat, depending on the particular circumstances. It is not the use of a particular subsystem, per se, but the *inflexibility* among these defensive subsystems and their overactivity that contributes to the traumatized person's distress after the traumatic event is over.

Relational Defensive Strategies:
Social Engagement and Attachment

The social engagement system may provide the first line of defense prior to the mobilizing, sympathetically mediated defenses of fight or flight. It also appears to be used simultaneously with other defensive subsystems at times. As described in Chapter 2, this system enables subtle, fine-tuned recognition of relational threats. Communication in social situations relies on the sending and receiving of subtle signals (via facial expression, tone of voice, body language and movements) and has many functions, including the evaluation of safety. Interpersonal communication that is perceived as threatening can be modified by the use of the social engagement system that manages, modulates, and eventually disarms or neutralizes the threat from the other person. A client who felt she prevented a potential rape by "talking him down" illustrates the use of social engagement to reduce threat; simultaneously she experienced increased sympathetic nervous system arousal and impulses to flee.

The attachment system is instinctively activated in children when they are endangered, and this system is often aroused as the initial defense in certain dangerous situations for adults as well. Children cry and call for their parent; it is said that one of the most common words uttered by frightened combat soldiers is a version of *mother*. Adults turn to their cell phones in order to find their primary attachment relationships when they feel under threat. However, in traumatic situations, attachment figures may not be available to respond, and social engagement may provide insufficient protection or even increase the threat under some circumstances. Under such conditions, other defensive subsystems are engaged. The sympathetically mediated defenses of flight and fight mobilize the body by bringing increased blood flow to the gross large muscles groups used in overt acts of protection or escape. The immobilizing defenses provide another defensive response that relies on a *lack* of motor action, such as being completely still, hiding, freezing, or becoming submissive.

Mobilizing Defenses

When the mobilizing fight or flight responses are aroused, the orienting response is simultaneously heightened. The field of consciousness is narrowed to include only those elements in the environment pertinent to survival— the threat and possibilities of escape routes—and to exclude cues that are not essential to survival. The senses become hyperalert in order to better smell, hear, see, and taste the danger (Levine, 1997; Van Olst, 1971) in preparation for further assessment and response. Emotional states that support the particular defense might also emerge to the forefront of consciousness (Frijda, 1986; Hobson, 1994; Rivers, 1920). For example, fear is predominant in the flight response, and anger may accompany a fight response.

The mobilizing defenses of fight and flight are characterized by increased activation of the sympathetic nervous system and the corresponding neurochemically mediated physical reactions, such as heightened respiratory rate and increased blood supply to skeletal large muscles in preparation for action. Defensive systems are designed to be economical and to facilitate our utilization of the safest, most effective response available to us; for example, flight is often the most common response to threat when successful escape is probable and the threat warrants it (Fanselow & Lester, 1988; Nijenhuis et al., 1998; Nijenhuis et al., 1999).

Immobilizing defenses will not usually emerge in definitively escapable situations because animals, including humans, will fast discover escape routes through trial and error (Scaer, 2001, p. 16). As the large muscles are primed and readied for flight, the cascade of neurochemicals diminishes awareness of any pain so that the mind and body are focused only on flight. According to Fanselow and Lester, this reduced nociception has its survival advantage when mobilizing defensive responses are still possible because it "attenuates pain-elicited disruption of defensive behavior" (1988, p. 203).

Flight sometimes involves not only a running away from danger but also a running toward a person or place that can provide safety (a basic premise of attachment behavior; Bowlby, 1988). Flight impulses can be observed in clients' leg movements and also in a variety of subtler movements, such as twisting, turning, or backing away.

If the chance of escape is unlikely and the threat closes in, the victim's attempts at flight may become increasingly frantic. In the animal kingdom, if flight becomes impossible as the predator is about to strike the prey, dramatic changes in behavior usually occur as the prey shifts to "circa-strike defensive behaviors" that occur immediately before, during, and just after attack (Fanselow & Lester, 1988, p. 202). The animal might engage in a last-second explosive leap away, but if this desperate effort to get away also fails, mobilizing defenses of fight are stimulated. Aggressive actions are engaged as the prey/victim tries to fight off the predator/perpetrator by scratching, biting, hitting, kicking, or otherwise struggling (Fanselow & Lester, 1988; Nijenhuis et al., 1998; Nijenhuis et al., 1999). The fight response is characteristically provoked when the prey feels trapped, under attack, or when aggression is perceived as capable of securing safety. These statements hold true for humans as well. Impulses for fight behavior are often experienced somatically by clients as tension in the hands, arms, shoulders; hands beginning to tighten or curl into a fist; lifting of the hands or arms; narrowing of the eyes; clenching of the jaw; impulses to kick or struggle.

Mobilizing defenses also include innumerable patterns of skilled defensive responses—action tendencies that are both learned and spontaneous and enacted automatically in the course of safely performing physical activities, such as operating machinery, driving automobiles, and engaging in sports. These are mobilizing defensive subsystems that are not *purely* fight or flight responses. For example, the ability to drive requires complex movements. Through repetition, these become learned action tendencies that can be executed without thought, such as suddenly slamming on the brakes and turning the steering wheel to prevent an accident.

> [Humankind] in the vast majority of cases, neither flees nor adopts an attitude of aggression, but responds by the special kind of activity, often of a highly complex kind, whereby the danger may be avoided or overcome. From most of the dangers to which [humankind] is exposed in the complex conditions of our own society, the means of escape lie in complex activities of a manipulative kind. . . . The hunter has to discharge his weapon, perhaps combined with movements, which put him into a favourable situation for such an action. The driver of a car and the pilot of an aeroplane in danger of collision have to perform complex movements by which the danger is avoided. (Rivers, 1920)

Other examples of defensive actions that anticipate and correct for possible difficulties without invoking the full flight/fight systems include engaging the righting reflexes during a near fall, raising an arm for protection from a falling object, avoiding a rock in a downhill ski run, and so on. Many sports call on these kinds of defenses: Skiing and skateboarding, for example, necessitate the smooth incorporation of defensive reflexes as well as learned actions, not only to assure safety but also as a part of the acquisition of competence. In martial arts, defensive responses are honed in precise ways that involve immobilization of the opponent and counterattack using the opponent's flow of energy to knock her off balance, and so forth. Even individuals in actually dangerous situations might protect themselves by incorporating learned actions: for example, a fighter pilot attends not only to the "predator" shooting at him, but equally to the myriad of dials and instruments that keep his plane aloft and his artillery engaged.

Immobilizing Defenses

When the mobilizing defenses have failed entirely or produced only partial success in preventing trauma, the person may become traumatized. "The traumatized individual has been overpowered and made helpless—unable to avert trauma by defensive aggression and unable to escape" (Allen, 2001, p. 169). The mobilizing defenses give way to immobilizing defenses when the former are ineffective or not the best strategy to ensure survival (Allen, 2001; Misslin, 2003; Nijenhuis et al., 1998; Nijenhuis et al., 1999; Rivers, 1920; Schore, submitted). As Nijenhuis and Van der Hart noted: "[Attempting to fight or flee] would be inevitably frustrating and nonproductive for a child being physically or sexually abused or witnessing violence. In some situations, active motor defense may actually increase danger and therefore be less adaptive than passive, mental ways of coping" (1999b, p. 50). In these situations a fight response might provoke more violent or sadistic actions from the perpetrator. Additionally, flight responses such as outrunning the assailant or fleeing from home may not be possible for a child. Instead, clients suffering from chronic childhood trauma have been forced to resort to immobilizing defenses, and they continue to use them in present time particularly in the context of posttrauma reminders.

These immobilizing defenses are described in a variety of terms: freezing, feigned death, deep freeze, animal hypnosis, tonic immobility, cataleptic immobilization, playing possum, mesmerism, surrender, submission, collapse, and floppy immobility. They are less clearly explained or differentiated in the literature than the mobilizing defenses, and some confusion about their delineation remains. The following section describes them as we have observed them in clinical contexts, identifying two main immobilizing defenses: freezing (two types) and limp passivity or feigning death.

TYPES 1 AND 2 FREEZE RESPONSES

Misslin (2003, p. 58) described freezing as "alert immobility" wherein there is complete cessation of movement, except for respiration and eye movements. Although the respiratory rate is increased, it is shallow (Hofer, 1970) and almost imperceptible, which helps reduce the likelihood of detection. In animals, once the predator has been detected, freezing is the prevailing defensive response (Fanselow & Lester, 1988). In humans, freezing appears to involve a highly engaged sympathetic system in which the muscles become stiff and tense, heart rate is elevated, sensory acuity is increased, and the person becomes hyperalert. The high sympathetic tone of freezing seems similar to the arrest stage of the orienting response, during which temporary cessation of movement occurs until the stimulus is located, identified, and evaluated. However, freezing is markedly different from the arrest stage of orienting because the stimulus has already been assessed as dangerous and autonomic responses have already been significantly mobilized. Although the arrest stage of the orienting response also involves physical stilling, the stimulus has not yet been appraised as dangerous; if it is appraised as threatening, freezing may be evoked. Fanselow and Lester emphasized that freezing is not simply movement inhibition: "Rather it is an integrated, functional behavioral pattern. Inactivity is to freezing as locomotion is to flight" (1988, p. 192). Freezing occurs in an organized fashion, as seen in rats who freeze next to walls, in corners, and in the darkest area of the room, to maximize the survival advantage of preventing detection.

Clients describe two types of freezing, similar to the two types of freezing described in animals. In type 1 freezing, clients report that they were very aware of the environment, especially of threat cues, potential escape routes, or protective impulses, feeling energized and tense, ready and able to move or run if needed. They describe being motionless, panic-stricken with pounding heart, but ready and able to act. Occurring after the appraisal of danger, the distinguishing element in this version of freezing is that the individual still feels able to move. Fanselow and Lester describe type 1 freezing in animals: "It is as if the freezing animal [or person] is tensed up and ready to explode into action if the freezing response fails [and it is detected]" (Fanselow & Lester, 1988, p. 202). Frequently, type 1 freezing occurs when the predator or perpetrator is still at a distance and when motionless behavior may prevent detection. The individual is waiting for more data about the source of danger before taking action. In these cases, freezing occurs prior to the mobilizing defenses, if detected or if danger suddenly increases, the individual is ready and able to erupt into "explosive behavior" (Fanselow & Lester, 1988)—into versions of fighting or fleeing. In traumatogenic environments type 1 freezing may also occur in combination with submissive behavior, exemplified in the "frozen watchfulness" of a child who "waits warily for parental demands, responds quickly and compliantly, and then returns to her previous vigilant state" (Schore, submitted).

Clients also describe a second type of freezing as feeling "paralyzed"— terrifyingly incapable of moving and unable to breathe. This type 2 freezing is associated with a sense of utter entrapment with no possibility of action successfully averting the threat. A similar paralysis is provoked in animals by confinement, harnessing, entrapment, and restraint, and may follow struggle (Gallup, 1974). A version of type 2 freezing is eloquently described by E. M. Remarque (1929/1982):

> My forehead is wet, the sockets of my eyes are damp, my hands tremble, and I am panting softly. It is nothing but an awful spasm of fear, a simple animal fear of poking out my head and crawling on farther. All my efforts subside like froth into the one desire to be able just to stay lying there. My limbs are glued to the earth. I make a vain attempt; they refuse to come away. I press myself down on the earth, I cannot go forward. (p. 211)

Siegel (1999) postulated that with this kind of freezing, both the sympathetic and the parasympathetic systems are aroused simultaneously, which produces muscular constriction paired with a feeling of paralysis.

FEIGNED DEATH: "TOTAL SUBMISSION"

The immobilizing defense of feigning death, limp passivity, behavioral shutdown and/or fainting ensues when all other defenses have failed (Lewis, Kelly, & Allen, 2004; Nijenhuis et al., 1998, 1999; Porges, 2004, 2005; Scaer, 2001; Schore, submitted). Also called "total submission" (Van der Hart, Nijenhuis, & Steele, 2006), this condition of surrender occurs in dire conditions of extreme hopelessness. Scaer (2001) describe this condition:

> The racing heart slows to a crawl, blood pressure drops precipitously, tense muscles collapse and become still as a result of the assumption of an apparent enforced vegetative state. The focused and alert mind becomes numb and dissociated, at least in part due to high levels of endorphins. Memory access and storage are impaired, and amnesia may be expected. (p. 17)

In short, this response is characterized by profound inhibition of motor activity (Misslin, 2003) coupled with little or no sympathetic arousal. The individual experiences a dramatic increase in dorsal vagal tone, extreme hypoarousal, and a profound state of helplessness (Porges, 2001a; Scaer, 2001). In this variant of the immobilizing defensive responses, the muscles become flaccid rather than tense and stiff as they do in freezing (Levine, 1997; Nijenhuis et al., 1998, 1999; Scaer, 2001). Also called "floppy immobility" (Lewis et al., 2004), in this collapsed state the "muscles go limp, eyes look glazed, and heart rate slows down—just the opposite of what happens with the adrenaline burst of the freeze response" (Lewis et al., 2004, p. 53). Breathing may be shallow, and clients often describe this condition as "trancelike." This response appears to be associated with increased levels of endogenous opioids that render the person insensitive to pain (Lewis et al., 2004, p. 53). At this final stage of surrender, analgesia prevents nociception of injury—which may account for the fact that many clients report that they felt no pain during the abuse (Van der Kolk et al., 1996). Krystal (1988, p. 116) describes the feigned death response as "a complex pattern of surrender, necessary and prevalent in the entire animal kingdom and carrying its own means of merciful, painless death."

This totally passive condition is markedly different from freezing, because both types of freezing are highly engaged states accompanied by hypervigilance, whereas feigned death/submission is a completely detached state

(Lewis et al., 2004). The ordinarily flexible orienting response, which includes effective use of the senses, scanning mechanisms, and evaluative capacities, becomes dulled or severely impaired during feigned death/submission, whereas it becomes heightened during freezing. The impaired orienting is accompanied by a reduced capacity to attend to either the external environment or to internal phenomena. Anesthesia, analgesia, and the slowing of muscular/skeletal responses (Levine, 1997; Nijenhuis et al., 1998, 1999; Nijenhuis & Van der Hart, 1999a) may occur. Darwin (1872) called this type of immobility in animals a "sham death" to describe the death simulation behavior that permitted survival (Misslin, 2003) when predators were close at hand.

SUBMISSIVE BEHAVIORS

Submissive behaviors are distinct from full feigned death/submission. Although they involve action, they are placed in the category of immobilizing defenses because of their characteristic subservient and compliant qualities that optimize survival in certain situations. Submissive behaviors serve a protective function because they "aim at preventing or interrupting aggressive reactions" (Misslin, 2003, p. 59). The musculature involved in the gross motor actions in subservient behavior is not tight in readiness for assertive or aggressive action, and the action that occurs is not actively defensive. The physical movements are characterized by nonaggressive action, automatic obedience, and helpless compliance. These behaviors are common among traumatized individuals and include crouching, ducking the head, avoiding eye contact, bowing the back before the perpetrator, and generally appearing physically smaller and consequently less noticeable and threatening. A version of this condition, described as "robotization" (Krystal, 1978) and noted in Nazi death camp survivors, is characterized by mechanical behavior and automatic obedience, without question or thought, to the demands of the perpetrators. An even more pronounced version is observed in the extreme and complete passivity of some death camp survivors who "no longer attempted to find food or to warm themselves, and they made no effort to avoid being beaten" (Herman, 1992, p. 85).

As a result of chronic abuse, it is not uncommon for traumatized people to respond to threat cues with mechanistic compliance or resigned submission. It is important to recognize this submissive tendency as defensive behavior rather than as conscious agreement. For example, a woman who mechanically allows a male relative to enter her apartment, despite knowing he will undoubtedly rape her, as he has done before, is most likely enacting a submissive defense learned after many such repetitions of threat and danger. Predatory or abusive individuals often seek to evoke these behaviors in others, thereby taking advantage of this instinctive defensive response to elicit automatic compliance with the abuse (Herman, 1992).

IMMOBILIZING SUBSYSTEMS IN TRAUMATIZATION

Porges's polyvagal hierarchy theory reminds us that the dorsal vagal complex comes into action when all other defenses fail to ensure safety. Individuals who suffered chronic abuse as children, especially during a developmentally vulnerable period, and who may not have been able to capitalize on social engagement, attachment, or mobilizing defenses for survival, generally have come to rely on immobilizing defenses. It is inevitable, given their dependent status and developmental vulnerability, that children will submit to abuse at least until the adolescent years; victims of childhood sexual abuse seldom report actively resisting their perpetrators (Nijenhuis et al., 1998).

Although the freeze responses are not available until the second half of the first year (Schore, submitted), the increase in dorsal vagal tone has been observed even in newborns who become hypoxic (Bergman et al., 2004; in Schore, submitted). The hypoarousal of the submissive response leads to a subjective detachment from emotions as well as an evacuation, so to speak, of emotional experience; remarks such as "I just wasn't there" seem to suggest a reduction in, or respite from, the individual's emotional pain and suffering. Clients frequently describe depersonalization experiences: being outside their body, watching themselves from a distance as though they were someone else. One client reported the following: "I would leave my body and watch her [herself, the client] from the crack in the ceiling. I felt sorry for her during the abuse. I wouldn't go back into the body until it was all over." In other cases, a person continues to act but is also separated from the body, as in the following example of a combat soldier:

My mind left my body, I went ahead and stood on a hill. From there I watched, quite objectively and with some amusement, the struggles of this body of mine staggering over the duckboards and wading through the mud where the duckboards were smashed. I watched it duck when a salvo of German shells came over. I saw it fall flat on its face when a concealed battery of our own whizzbangs opened up within a few yards of it. I saw it converse with the gunners, who, stripped to the waist, loaded, pulled the lanyards of their guns and jumped away from the leaping recoil. (Cloete, 1972, p. 242)

When physical escape proves impossible, these immobilizing defenses are the physiological and psychological measures that are thought to protect the person against further suffering. Earlier we wrote about distinguishing hyperarousal-related dissociative conditions characterized by intrusive reexperiencing of the trauma from dissociative conditions that involve a subjective numbness (hypoarousal) and submission. Although hyperarousal-related flashbacks (in which the present is disconnected from a vivid reliving experience) are also dissociative in nature, they are markedly different from the dissociative phenomena that inform the submissive defenses. Hyper-arousal-related flashbacks involve a heightening of subjective emotional states and somatosensory awareness, in sharp contrast to the deadening of subjective emotional states and somatosensory awareness that often accompanies the submissive, hypoarousal-related defenses (Van der Hart et al., 2006).

STAGES OF THE DEFENSIVE RESPONSE

In describing the order of stages in which defensive subsystems might be employed, a complex, instinctive, lightning-fast system must be oversimplified. These stages and the order in which they are engaged may differ, and some stages even omitted, depending on the specific variables of the event and the individual's resources and circumstances.

These stages of the defensive system are illustrated by Dorothy, the 19-year-old college student presented in the previous chapter; we resume her story at the point of the orienting response when Dorothy evaluated the intruder as dangerous. The following sequence has been compiled from a number of sources (Allen, 2001; Fanselow & Lester, 1988; Levine, 1997; Misslin, 2003; Nijenhuis et al., 1998, 1999; Pavlov, 1927; Porges, 2003; Schore, 1994, submitted; Siegel, 1999) and from clinical experience:

1. Marked change in arousal
2. Heightened orienting response
3. Attachment and social engagement systems
4. Mobilizing defensive strategies
5. Immobilizing defensive strategies
6. Recuperation
7. Integration

1. *Marked change in arousal.* When a stimulus is evaluated as threatening, an instant and automatic change in the level of arousal occurs, usually emerging as an *increase* in arousal. For example, Dorothy knew she was in danger when she perceived the visual stimuli, which conveyed the stranger's menacing motives: when he came too close to her and pulled out a knife. As she initially oriented to the sound of the intruder's footsteps, she went from experiencing a slight arousal and mild excitation related to curiosity, to feeling afraid and experiencing a sudden elevation of arousal. The sensations associated with the rush of adrenaline—her increased heart rate, her hair

"standing on end," and so on—were all evidence of sympathetic nervous system defense preparation for the motor actions involved in fight or flight.

Dorothy did not have an abusive childhood; other individuals who do have a history of abuse might have become immediately hypoaroused, engaging the immobilizing submissive defense in the same situation, especially if submission was the habitual and predominant defensive response to their past threat. Through previous experience of abuse these individuals will have learned that the mobilizing defenses are useless in promoting safety.

2. *Heightened orienting response.* In the face of threat, the orienting response becomes inseparable from defensive responses, and the various components of orienting are intensified. Irrelevant objects in the environment and awareness of internal experience fade to the background as the individual focuses narrowly and intensely on threat-related stimuli. Hobson (1994, p. 161) described this in the following way: "As we become alert we can process data faster and evaluate it more critically because our brain-minds are more highly activated. At the same time, we become more precisely oriented." Heightened physiological arousal is accompanied by emotions such as fear, producing an adaptive interaction between orienting tendencies, emotions, and attention to maximize chances of survival. Mujica-Parodi, Greenberg, and Kilpatrick (2004) summarized this interaction:

> Emotional arousal primes the organism for imminent danger by increasing the orienting response, which permits the organism to find and focus on the source of danger. Once oriented to the source of danger, emotional arousal strengthens attention to the source of danger and diminishes attention to stimuli unrelated to its source, narrowing the amount of peripheral information simultaneously accessible with the target. (p. 1)

As Dorothy entered a fearful state of amplified sensory vigilance, all her senses and attention were focused on the object of potential threat. Her field of consciousness was thus narrowed and her level of consciousness was high. Dorothy was oblivious to everything else as she oriented exclusively to the impending possibility of danger and to her prospects for defense and survival. In a state of alert type 1 freezing, she remained immobile, muscles contracted to prepare for action, eyes glued to the man and the knife as she assessed options for action. She was able to think clearly, and she rapidly evaluated whether running for the door or reaching for the phone was feasible. Another individual with pronounced feigned death/submission defensive tendencies might have had the opposite experience: decreased orienting, hypoarousal-related perceptual dulling, lowered levels of consciousness.

3. *Attachment and social engagement systems.* Once the orienting system has done its job of gathering information and has evaluated the degree of danger, overt defensive and protective actions are employed. Earlier we discussed that one line of defense in handling threat might be utilizing the attachment system, by crying out for help, or the social engagement systems, by attempting to negotiate with the perpetrator. Although the role of the social engagement system is to act as a brake on the sympathetic system by first engaging in communication behavior to elicit protection, in some cases the body has already activated mobilizing defenses before the individual begins to negotiate or attempts to negotiate with a potential assailant. (This is an example of how the defensive response stages may not follow a linear pattern in the context of complex real-life situations; rather, different defensive strategies come online, as needed.) Dorothy initially attempted to reason with her assailant, telling him that her friends would be home any minute and that he should leave immediately before he was caught.

4. *Mobilizing defensive strategies.* As noted in Porges's polyvagal hierarchy theory, when social engagement fails, the next line of defense is the sympathetically mediated fight or flight responses (although, as noted, the sympathetically mediated type 1 freeze often occurs prior to the mobilizing responses when the threat is at a distance). In spite of Dorothy's attempts to engage the intruder, he moved closer to her, brandishing the knife. With the stranger between her and the door, Dorothy realized escape was impossible. She thought about how she might be able to take the knife from him, and she thought of crying out for help—thoughts that occurred in a fraction of a second. As the stranger approached her, aiming the knife at her chest, Dorothy was mobilized to fight her assailant. She lifted her arm in self-protection, knocking his arm to the side, and the knife grazed her shoulder. After a brief struggle, the roles reversed. Dorothy managed to wrestle the knife away and stab him in the neck, which caused him to run away.

5. *Immobilizing defensive strategies.* As noted, mobilizing defenses such as the ones Dorothy employed are exchanged for immobilizing strategies when the former are likely to be ineffective or promote more danger. Although the immobilizing defenses have in common a full or partial cessation of physical action, there are also important differences between types 1 and 2 as described earlier. Dorothy, who reported no prior trauma, did not resort to immobilizing defenses during the incident, other than type 1 freezing while assessing the options for action. Another client, Petra, had experienced sexual assaults by her older brother over a prolonged period during childhood. At the time of that early abuse, her only defense was submission accompanied by hypoarousal. She reported feeling "nothing" in her body; no emotional response during the abuse and amnesia for much of what had happened. In later years, Petra instinctively depended on the same

submissive defense in the context of subsequent challenging situations. Sensitized by years of inescapable trauma, Petra's immobility response was triggered by ordinary life challenges (e.g., asking for a raise at work), which to Dorothy were minor and easily managed by her social engagement system.

6. *Recuperation*. Recuperation takes place when the threat is over and the perpetrator is not in proximity; thus recuperation is not inherently defensive, but it is a deviation from normal, everyday activities (Fanselow & Lester, 1988). It is at this point that the individual enters a stage of physiological and psychological recovery. Physiological recuperation starts with the deescalation of arousal back into a more optimal baseline state and a deactivation of those body systems that have been activated by the defensive responses. When submission or dorsal vagal responses have been the predominant defense, recovery occurs as arousal elevates from hypoarousal to a more optimal level within the window of tolerance. When hyperarousal accompanied by immobilization has been the response to the trauma, we often see arousal return to baseline through discharge and dissipation made possible by physical activity. For instance, to use a nontraumatic comparison, after an arousing activity such as watching a horror movie, an individual might find it useful to go for a jog, dance, or work out at the gym to help reinstate his or her baseline arousal level. When sympathetically mediated defenses have been employed during the frightening experience, this "discharge" might happen partly through uncontrollable trembling, thought to be caused by release of the energy not expended in fighting or fleeing (Levine, 1997). Physical shaking or trembling is a common reaction for survivors in the aftermath of a traumatic event. Levine (1997) pointed out that vibrating and trembling are also prevalent in all animals once they are out of danger. In humans, emotional catharsis often accompanies the physical trembling; there is often a need to cry. The social engagement or attachment systems may also be stimulated in the aftermath of trauma. Many people have the urge to tell someone, particularly attachment figures, about the experience.

Clinically, we have observed that clients who utilized mobilizing defenses or the sympathetically mediated freezing responses at the time of the trauma often report intense shaking and trembling afterward or begin to shake and tremble as they address the events in psychotherapy. In Dorothy's case, even though she had fought back successfully, she still trembled and cried intermittently while she was on the phone reporting the assault to the police and then later in the company of her sister as she described more fully what had happened. Petra, on the other hand, could not talk about what had happened to her because she remembered little about the incest and trying to do so evoked the hypoarousal-related defensive response again. In her early treatment sessions, when she called up what little she did remember, she merely reported vaguely that she felt numb, just as she had felt resigned and spaced out following each assault.

After the traumatic event, a period of psychological and physiological recuperation is required to recalibrate and restore optimal levels of arousal. In recuperation, the object of attention changes from the threat to the injury; rest behaviors and actions that support the recovery and healing of the injury are generally initiated (Fanselow & Sigmundi, 1982). The individual reacts to the injury once the threat is over because the analgesic system becomes quiescent, and pain is then experienced. Thus the return of nociceptive stimulation leads to recuperative behavior (Fanselow & Lester, 1988). Recuperation in the animal world typically takes place in isolation, but humans often initiate contact with a trusted other or seek medical help. Of note is that the individual does not fully resume normal activities and capacities until recuperation is complete. At this stage, risk may be increased (Fanselow & Lester, 1988). In situations of chronic traumatization, perpetrators may further abuse or otherwise exploit victims at this stage, taking advantage of victims' increased vulnerability.

Dorothy immediately called her sister and asked her to come over and then, together, they called the police. Petra's stage of recuperation from incidents of childhood sexual abuse was markedly different: She felt ashamed, believed the abuse was her fault, told no one, and received no help for the physical injuries she incurred. She resumed her normal activities, pretended that nothing had happened in the basement with her brother, and told herself that the physical pain in her genitals was nonexistent. Indeed, she told herself that she was stupid to even think of her body. The inability to complete the recuperation stage often results in chronic states of "licking the wounds" (feelings of exhaustion and prolonged periods in bed that are not restorative) or in deficits in the ability to care for the body and/or the self.

7. *Integration.* People subjected to chronic or severe trauma are often not only unable to complete the recuperation stage but fail to integrate what has happened to them over time. Instead, they wall off the parts of themselves that are hurt or scared and continue their everyday activities as if nothing happened. As previously described, this dissociative compartmentalization is characteristic of severe trauma-related disorders and indicates a profound failure in the person's integrative capacity (Janet, 1907).

The stage of integration occurs over a longer period of time than recuperation and varies depending on the severity of the threat, the kind of defense used, the success of the defense, the degree of completion at the recuperation phase, as well as the individual's history, abilities, and support system. Integration is a long-term process of reorganization that includes both the physical and the psychological assimilation of the traumatic experience. Integration includes "postprocessing" of the effects of the trauma—in other words, learning about, elaborating, integrating, and eventually turning off the powerful survival-related "stress" machinery (Shalev, 2001), the defensive subsystems. All important events, and particularly traumatic events, need to be "put it in [their] place in that life-history which each one of us is perpetually building up and which for each of us is an essential element of his personality" (Janet, 1925, p. 662).

The experience of trauma changes people in profound ways (Herman, 1992; Janoff-Bulman, 1992; Rieker & Carmen, 1986; Van der Kolk, 1996a). Even if mobilizing defensive systems have been effective and they have navigated the traumatic event successfully, they often no longer feel the same as they did before the event. Subjective feelings of either competence or incompetence may increase, depending somewhat on the success or failure of defensive endeavors at self-protection and escape. Van der Kolk pointed out that "the behavioral and biochemical sequelae of escapable shock are just the opposite of those of inescapable shock" (1987, p. 67). Whereas inescapable trauma hampers resiliency, in a situation of escapable trauma mobilizing defenses have been effective. The successful navigation of a threatening event may help human beings become more resilient and increase their integrative capacities.

A range of positive emotions—exuberance, gratitude, relief, joy, exhilaration, or optimism—may emerge in response to triumph over threat. Janet's (1919, 1925) "stage of triumph," noted earlier, includes a sense of pleasure in what he calls the completed action—in this case, the "pleasure" of using mobilizing defenses successfully. Research on animals further corroborates the theory that greater stress resistance develops when animals are subjected to escapable trauma and, like humans, demonstrate greater resilience. Janet (1919, 1925) also wrote about the necessity of "resignation": the acceptance of the traumatic events themselves, their irreversible effects, and perhaps the losses these may have incurred—all of which are a part of the integration process. Resignation is an important element of integration whereby the individual "makes peace" with the past.

The process of integration comprises several phases. Although Dorothy successfully defended herself, she still experienced nightmares and flashbacks of aspects of the event afterward. She also found that previously neutral environmental triggers, such as movies that contained scenes of similar assaults, news broadcasts of assaults on women, and jackets similar to the one her assailant wore, rapidly raised her anxiety. Although these symptoms were not severe enough to interrupt her capacity to function, Dorothy reported that, even years after the event, she was still occasionally upset by films or news that included an assault similar to the one she had experienced.

Dorothy's integration of the trauma she experienced was facilitated by an eventual sense of pride in her ability to "keep my wits about me" and fight back during the assault. She decided to take a challenging martial arts class to strengthen her confidence and capacity to defend herself physically. The process of executing physical defensive movements through martial arts or physical exercise contributes to an internal sense of rebuilding and repairing that facilitates healing. Through self-defense training, "survivors put themselves in a position to reconstruct the normal physiological response to danger, to rebuild the 'action system' that was shattered and fragmented by the trauma" (Herman, 1992, p. 198). As Dorothy's reorganization and integration of the traumatic event progressed over time, she talked about the incident with greater self-confidence and assurance, focusing more on her capacity to turn the tables on her assailant and force him to run away, rather than on the terror she had experienced.

In contrast, the aftereffects of Petra's incest experiences were much more debilitating because her submission defense turned into a longstanding habituated response pattern. She continued to feel a frequent sense of "collapse," a tendency to "give up" under relatively minor stress, a loss of enthusiasm, an absence of joy in living, and a lack of direction about her future. Her tendency toward hypoarousal continued into adulthood and prevented her from achieving her potential psychologically, occupationally, and socially. Her responses were in sharp contrast to those of Dorothy: Instead of greater confidence and a sense of mastery, she experienced shame and numbness; instead of being able to take active measures to integrate the experience, her immobilizing defense of submission and accompanying hypoarousal prevented her from marshaling recuperative and integrative capacities.

INCOMPLETE OR INEFFECTIVE DEFENSIVE RESPONSES

One's subjective experience of safety and security "depend[s] on a set of beliefs in one's own powers" (Krystal, 1988, p. 157). In conditions of trauma, these powers have failed to protect the person (Cole & Putnam, 1992; Herman, 1992; Janet, 1925; Levine, 1997, 2004; Pearlman & Saakvitne, 1995; van der Kolk, MacFarlane, et al. 1996). When a traumatic event is so severe that the individual has no recourse but to freeze or submit, the defensive system becomes disorganized afterward: "When neither resistance nor escape is possible, the human system of self-defense becomes overwhelmed and disorganized. Each component of the ordinary response to danger, having lost its utility, tends to persist in an altered and exaggerated state long after the actual danger is over" (Herman, 1992, p. 34). The common perpetuating factor in trauma-related disorders appears to be the persistence, even decades later, of altered defensive responses as well as maladaptive orienting responses. It is a basic contention of sensorimotor psychotherapy that over time, these habitual interrupted or ineffective physical defensive movement sequences function as powerful contributors to the maintenance of trauma symptoms, thereby deterring their resolution. Their dissociation from other aspects of the self keeps them separate and unintegrated from the individual's present life and experience.

The persistence of defensive subsystem components occurs in a variety of ways. Many somatoform symptoms, such as anesthesia and analgesia, are related to animal defenses (Nijenhuis et al., 1999). Van der Hart et al. (2000) speculate that "the high rate of somatoform dissociative symptoms in WWI combat soldiers was, at least in part, due to forced immobility in the face of threat to bodily integrity, thereby evoking chronic animal defensive states, in particular, freezing, with concomitant somatoform manifestations" Traumatized persons who tend toward freezing typically seem to feel easily "trapped" and unable to take action under possible threat. "In contrast to submission to unavoidable danger, [freezing] . . . is related to a chronic state of hypervigilance, a tendency to startle, and occasionally panic" (Krystal, 1988, p. 161). Since freezing involves sympathetically mediated hyperarousal, traumatized persons who tend toward these responses may become easily hyperaroused, exhibiting symptoms characteristic of the hyperaroused zone described in Chapter 2.

People who have responded with the parasympathetically mediated submissive defense tend to become easily hypoaroused. Petra frequently responded to feelings of anxiety by lapsing into a "zoned out" condition accompanied by a loss muscle tone. She described herself as "giving in" to men sexually during her adolescence and young adulthood. During emotionally and physically painful abusive encounters with her boyfriend, she was unable to fight or flee, utilizing instead the submissive response that had "worked" in childhood. Her response was similar to that found in animals repeatedly subjected to unavoidable pain: These animals tend to become helplessly submissive, lying down and whimpering instead of actively resisting, when exposed to pain (Seligman, 1975). Petra felt dissociated from herself and waited, mute, until the abuse was over.

A loss of an internal locus of control is common for clients who have relied upon any of the immobilizing defenses: freezing, submission, or submissive behaviors. Traumatized people often "cannot return to the previous personality type but assume submissive, slave like personalities, and their ability for assertive behavior becomes impaired to one degree or another" (Krystal, 1988, p. 157). Failing to understand that this loss is a common result of a bottom-up immobilizing defensive response, they then may feel ashamed and inadequate and berate themselves afterward for their lack of assertiveness. Not aware that their responses reflect instinctively driven immobilizing defenses, clients such as Petra blame themselves, as if their choices were voluntary and purposeful. In turn, the self-attribution and self-blame solidify the patterns of immobilization. Without a sense that they can trust themselves or their bodies, clients become identified with the habitual reactions; the immobilizing responses are experienced as "just who I am."

Whereas for many traumatized individuals, immobilizing defenses predominate and usurp adaptive functioning, for others, mobilizing defenses may continue to persist in the form of hyperactive defensive responses. Janet clearly described an extreme variation of a failed resolution of fight responses: "Certain patients plainly manifest anger; they strike, scratch, bite, and their cries are menacing. . . . The movements of defense of the arms stretched forward, the drawing back of the body, are quite characteristic" (1907, pp. 102–103). Although most of our clients might not demonstrate such extreme behavior, we do see subtler versions of what Janet describes. Many clients are quick to become emotionally reactive, angry, or even violent, and they experience significant bouts of rage with minimal provocation. This propensity toward anger may be attributed to both an unintegrated fight response and the suppression of anger in a traumatic situation, whereby the anger "only goes underground and returns as a permanent challenge to the [person's] future adjustment" (Krystal, 1988, p. 165). Fleeing behaviors, such as running away and avoidance, may continue to be employed long after the traumatic event. "Shell-shocked" veterans have been known to duck imaginary flying objects for years afterward; some clients who were near the World Trade Center when the planes hit the buildings also find themselves running for cover as a plane passes overhead, or they suffer from repeated nightmares in which they are attempting to escape danger. Thus mobilizing defenses also may persist long after the original traumatic event.

CONCLUSION

Defensive responses, much like the orienting responses, are governed by psychobiological action systems that are cued into effect thereby conferring the advantage of speed, by environmental danger. In humans there is also a cognitive component that enables previous learning and judgment to fine-tune the defensive response to the specific context. Modifications of these defenses enable us to develop physical skills that guarantee our safety while driving a car, skateboarding, skiing, or even just walking across the street. Constant motoric adjustment is necessary through orienting and appraisal of the present challenge in order to ensure safety, balance, and direction. Tragically, our traumatized clients are more likely to overuse the defenses habitually employed at the time of their trauma in response to current minor stressors or environmental reminders. Through sensorimotor psychotherapy interventions, these clients can be helped to first observe their maladaptive defensive responses simply as physiological, habitual phenomena—or better yet, as "survival resources," ingenious ways their evolutionary heritage preserved survival in a dangerous world. As clients begin to explore these defensive tendencies in a mindful way, a spontaneous phenomenon often occurs: the mobilizing defensive responses begin to present themselves in the body: a tightening of the jaw, arms, and fist or sensations in the throat accompanied by a feeling of wanting to speak or scream (see Chapter 11). Through the slow and painstaking work of observing what the body wants to do as the trauma is recalled, the possibility of a new response emerges, incipient during the original trauma, ready to be further developed into defensive responses that are more flexibly adapted to the present.

Chapter 6

※※※

Adaptation:
The Role of Action
Systems and Tendencies

ALL OF OUR EXPERIENCES, from still, contemplative moments to those of peak performance, involve physical as well as mental action. Even the simple and apparently passive experience of watching a sunset (a sensory, cognitive, and affective event) activates neurons in the motor system. Our cognitive, emotional, and sensorimotor responses are organized and shaped into action tendencies by evolutionarily prepared, psychobiological action systems that are (1) epigenetically hard-wired, (2) susceptible to classical conditioning, (3) self-organizing, (4) self-stabilizing, and (5) adaptive in nature (Cassidy & Shaver, 1999; Nijenhuis, Van der Hart, & Steele, 2002; Panksepp, 1998; Van der Hart et al., 2006).

Given the diversity of life challenges we encounter from infancy to old age, a wide range of potential, available action systems is needed for optimal adaptation to the environment. Whereas the action system of defense organizes our response to threat, other action systems govern facets of experience unrelated to danger and threat. These systems stimulate us to form close attachment relationships, explore, play, participate in social relationships, regulate energy (through eating, sleeping, etc.), reproduce, and care for others (Cassidy & Shaver, 1999; Marvin & Britner, 1999; Panksepp, 1998; Van der Hart et al., 2006).

Different terms have been used to describe concepts similar to action systems. Bowlby (1969/1982), Cassidy and Shaver (1999), and other attachment theorists have used the term *behavioral systems*, whereas Gould (1982) and Lichtenberg (1990; Lichtenberg & Kindler, 1994; Lichtenberg, Lachmann, & Fosshage, 1992) have used the term *motivational systems*. Fanselow and Lester (1988) used the term *functional systems*, and Panksepp (1998) described *emotional operating systems*, emphasizing the emotional motivators of systems and their evolutionary mission of ensuring survival. Following the lead of Van der Hart et al. (2006), we have chosen to use the term *action systems* because the engagement of each system stimulates particular physical actions—body sensations and movements—as well as corresponding mental actions—thoughts and emotions—relevant to each system.

The intent of the theory of action systems is to propose a paradigm that connects the internal realm of cognitive, emotional, and sensate experience to physical action. What we are calling *action systems* are not precisely what are referred to by the previous authors. What follows is an amalgamation of several theories and our own clinical experience. Our thoughts are more in the realm of informed speculation than they are reflective of well-researched models of psychophysical action. Our contention is that these hard-wired action systems may determine physical actions, sensations, emotions, and cognitions from the bottom-up. Although action systems do not inflexibly dictate or determine particular actions, they do affect and influence tendencies toward certain actions in particular situations (Steele, Van der Hart, & Nijenhuis, 2006). Sensorimotor psychotherapy emphasizes meticulous observation of the postures, actions, and inhibitions exhibited by the client's body and associated with the various action systems.

Action systems are interdependent and interrelated, yet each one is programmed into the brain and represented by neural circuits that, when activated, dictate somewhat predictable responses geared to achieve the particular goals of that system (Nijenhuis et al., 2002). An action system is activated by discrete internal and external stimuli that, in turn, inspire further orienting to system-related cues and also organize behavior to fulfill that system's goals. When a stimulus is perceived, a thought or feeling is evoked, along with a preparatory motor response, which then drives the direction of the next perception and/or evokes another thought or feeling. The relationships among these experiential components (thought, emotion, body sensation, five-sense perception, and movement) are interactive and organized around fulfilling the goals of the particular action system being engaged. These goals "extend over long periods of time, with the behavior needed to achieve [them] being adjusted flexibly, in a non-random fashion, to a wide range of environments and to the development of the individual" (Cassidy & Shaver, 1999, p. 651; see also George & Solomon, 1999). For example, the goals of the attachment system—such as proximity to, and security with, a trusted other—remain relatively constant throughout the lifespan, but the behavior required to accomplish these goals is modified and developed as individuals mature and as environments change. Over time, people build up their own manner and group of responding to the arousal of each system and fulfilling its goals—that is, they develop their own action tendencies in relation to each system—with varying degrees of breadth, richness, success, adaptability, and personal satisfaction.

Specific emotions are associated with each system and are coordinated with the behavior appropriate to accomplish the system's goals. For instance, curiosity is characteristic of exploration, joy is frequently aroused by play, anger and fear accompany defensive responses, and so on (Panksepp, 1998). Each emotion, in turn, is connected to discrete facial expressions, movements, sensations, and behavior. Sensory perceptions become biased by the stimulation of a particular action system and its emotional quality: For example, if exploration and its corresponding emotional tone of curiosity are aroused, our senses become heightened to novel, interesting stimuli, and our movements and postural adjustments are organized to increase our ability to perceive these stimuli. Our thoughts, as well, change in content to pertain to the process and objects of exploration. Thus all levels of information processing—cognitive, emotional, and sensorimotor—work in concert, systemically, in pursuit of the goals of a particular action system.

Although action systems are each unique, they are also mutually dependent, interconnected, and often complementary. Several action systems are normally evoked simultaneously and work together to achieve a variety of interrelated goals. For example, interaction with a spouse might simultaneously elicit systems of attachment, play, exploration, and sexuality. Experiencing *combinations* of action systems requires a higher-order integrative capacity that is often deficient in traumatized individuals. For example, balance in work, play, rest, friendships, spousal relationships, and parenting is difficult to achieve and requires flexibility, cooperation, and coordination among action systems (Steele et al., 2005). As we mature, cultivating integrative capacity involves "building" this interrelatedness by tending to the tasks and goals of various action systems simultaneously and executing the necessary, complex actions to achieve success. For example, in a marriage, activities such as attending a work-related party could simultaneously meet the goals of various action systems—e.g., the attachment system (proximity), exploration system (professional endeavors), play system (recreation), and sociability system (forming relationships outside of the marriage). In order to successfully respond to the potentially competing goals of all of these action systems at the party entails complex, sophisticated, and mutually empathic communication between partners, requiring sufficient integrative capacity from them both.

Eight Action Systems

Based on the work of Barkes, Cosmides, and Tooby (1992), Bowlby (1969/ 1982), Cassidy and Shaver (1999), Fanselow and Lester (1988), Gould (1982), Lichtenberg (1990; Lichtenberg & Kindler, 1994), Panksepp (1998), Steele et al. (2005b), and Van der Hart et al. (2006), eight fundamental and interrelated action systems governing human behavior have been delineated.

1. Defense (described in the previous chapter)
2. Attachment
3. Exploration
4. Energy regulation
5. Caregiving
6. Sociability
7. Play
8. Sexuality

These action systems fall into two main categories: one, those that promote defense in threatening contexts, which includes the defensive subsystems described in the previous chapter; and two, those that promote functioning in (nonthreatening) daily life (Steele et al., 2005b). These two categories tend to mutually inhibit each other: If the defense system is aroused, activities pertaining to the action systems of daily life cease, resuming once the danger has passed.

Because of its crucial role in ensuring survival and providing the necessary biopsychosocial regulation for optimal brain development, the attachment system provides the foundation for all other systems. Through attachment relationships, the child learns how to respond to the arousal of every other action system. The unique expression each system ultimately takes and the degree of adaptability of an individual's action tendencies in response to the arousal of any action system is largely founded upon the development of the attachment system early in life, as it is shaped by the child's major attachment figures.

Defense Action System

Attachment is intimately connected to the defense system because it is aroused whenever the child experiences insecurity, discomfort, or danger. As noted in the previous chapter, the defense action system serves the goal of survival and is activated whenever a stimulus is perceived to be potentially dangerous. The tendency of traumatized individuals to experience certain innocuous stimuli as threatening repeatedly sets off defensive subsystems even in situations where there is no threat. Eventually, these defensive action tendencies become default behaviors that take precedence over actions that could fulfill the goals of action systems pertaining to daily life unrelated to threat. For example, Annie, a 50-year-old woman who had suffered physical abuse and neglect by her alcoholic mother, remained vulnerable to traumatic activation when, later in life, relationships became close and more family-like. Her defense system mobilized, with its accompanying action tendencies, each time an individual's attempts at closeness activated her attachment system. Over time, this pattern of response not only resulted in chronic relational problems but also interfered with the elaboration and maturation of her attachment action system, in general.

The dominance of the defense action system in people with trauma-related disorders is a central theme in the treatment of these individuals. The clinician must be aware of the intrusion of defensive action tendencies into the behavior and movement of the client, which then overrides the functioning of other action systems. In sensorimotor psychotherapy, clients learn to recognize the physical signs indicating arousal of their defensive system, such as hyper- or hypoarousal and muscular tension or flaccidity. They learn to evaluate whether these responses are appropriate to their current situation, and they learn to inhibit or calm this arousal so that they can respond effectively to action systems governing the nonthreatening aspects of daily life.

Attachment Action System

As noted, the attachment system is linked to the defense system because of its crucial role in ensuring survival. Three important evolutionary needs operate to evoke the attachment system in children: the need for proximity, a safe haven, and a secure base (Simpson, 1999). The need for proximity is evoked when separation from the attachment figure exceeds the child's comfort zone, either in terms of time or distance. From an evolutionary perspective, the attachment function of proximity maintenance operates to decrease the risk of danger/injury to the vulnerable infant or child by ensuring closeness to a more powerful and competent caregiver. The attachment figure also offers the emotional "safe haven" of comfort and support when needed. Within the context of this "secure base," children experience the necessary security to learn regulatory capacities, which facilitates the development of all the other action systems. In the service of meeting the goals of these systems, attachment figures provide comfort, physical touch, communication, help when needed, physiological and interactive regulation, and a sense of belonging (Ainsworth et al., 1978; Bowlby, 1969/1982; Carlson, Cicchetti, Barnett, & Braunwald, 1998; Cassidy & Shaver, 1999).

For example, a mother may encourage the action system of exploration by holding the child securely while drawing his or her attention to interesting perceptual aspects of the environment. Or she may elicit the action system of play by initiating a game of peek-a-boo. Over time, even in adulthood, attachment relationships become a vehicle of support for the successful execution of other action systems. Although the attachment system becomes less critical to physical survival over the course of development, it continues to play a prominent role in daily existence over the lifespan through its connections to other action systems. As Bowlby stated, "Human beings of all ages are found to be at their happiest and to be able to deploy their talents to best advantage when they are confident that, standing behind them, there are one or more trusted persons who will come to their aid should difficulties arise" (1973, p. 359).

Numerous physical actions are characteristic of attachment behavior: proximity-seeking and -inducing behaviors, facial expressions such as smiling, responding to the mother's expressions and eye contact, crying and reaching for the caregiver, shaping (Stern, 1985), or automatically conforming, to the mother's body, and so forth (Ainsworth, 1963; Bowlby, 1988; Lyons-Ruth & Jacobvitz, 1999; Schore, 1994, 2003a). Schore (1994) noted that auditory signals, such as a certain verbal prosody, pitch, and sounds, induce many attachment-related behavioral sequalae.

As described in Chapter 2, these attachment behaviors coexist with defensive action tendencies for people with trauma-related disorders. Attachment-related, proximity-seeking action tendencies are often stimulated simultaneously or sequentially with defensive tendencies, as evidenced in the movement of children with disorganized-disoriented attachment patterns. The client's attachment movement sequences are observed and explored, often in the context of the client's developing attachment to the therapist, so that attachment behaviors are not confused with, overwhelmed by, or lost to defensive tendencies. The sensorimotor therapist may ask clients to mindfully observe, repeat, alter, or enhance movements that relate to attachment, such as reaching out. For example, Kat came to therapy complaining about ambivalence in her marriage. When she was asked by her therapist to imagine her husband in the room with her, Kat felt the impulse to reach toward him and take his hand; however, she simultaneously experienced defensive tendencies of tension in her chest and the impulse to pull away from him. This conflict between attachment and defensive physical actions is characteristic of clients such as Kat, who have experienced childhood relational trauma. Over the course of therapy, Kat learned to understand and inhibit the defensive tendencies related to her past trauma, so that she could engage in attachment-related movements of seeking proximity without experiencing conflicting impulses. This shift reinforced the comfort and security of a less conflicted attachment system, which further reduced her opposing impulse to defend.

Exploration Action System

The exploration system is not activated unless safety is assured; thus it too depends heavily on the attachment system in infancy and childhood. Ainsworth (1963) proposed that the attachment relationship provides the secure base from which a child can safely explore, stressing the importance of the "attachment–exploration balance" (Ainsworth, Bell, & Stayton, 1971; Cassidy & Shaver, 1999). These two systems are both complementary and inhibitory: When the attachment system is not activated—in other words, when the child feels secure—exploration increases; but when potential threat is perceived and the attachment system is activated, exploration ceases until the threat has passed or has been evaluated as a false alarm (Ainsworth & Wittig, 1969). In the context of secure attachment relationships, then, a child's exploratory habits reflect the experience of *secure exploration* (Grossman, Grossmann, & Zimmermann, 1999). The child experiences the safety of an attachment figure who will come to his or her assistance, which in turn enables him or her to explore.

Panksepp has eloquently described the exploration action system as the "foraging/exploration/investigation/curiosity/interest/expectant/seeking system" that "fills the mind with interest and motivates organisms to move their bodies effortlessly in search of the things they need, crave, and desire" (1998, pp. 145, 53). From an evolutionary perspective, exploration is the system that historically allowed men and women to investigate the environment, find the optimal hunting grounds, discover food sources. In modern times, exploration drives curiosity and learning and provides the basis for both educational and vocational activities. Panksepp maintained that the exploration system "drives and energizes many mental complexities that humans experience as persistent feelings of interest, curiosity, sensation seeking, and, in the presence of a sufficiently complex cortex, the search for higher meaning" (1998, p. 145).

Exploration is closely linked to other action systems because of its unique ability to participate in the fulfillment of the aims of any action system. For instance, if the energy regulation system is aroused, a person's behavior will become organized around gratification of that system's needs: if tired, he or she will seek a warm place to sleep; if hungry, he or she will look for food.

Physical actions that are typical of the exploration system include behavioral and facial expressions of curiosity and openness; tracking, seeking, and orienting movements that are geared toward discovering and investigating novel, interesting stimuli; and hand–eye coordination utilized to explore objects in the environment. The behaviors, expressions, and animated hand gestures that indicate interest and curiosity are also often evident in the exploration of abstract ideas and concepts. In clinical practice the exploration system is activated as clients are helped to become curious about, rather than identified with, how their action tendencies manifest in present time. In particular, the therapist stimulates clients' curiosity and willingness to observe their defensive tendencies as they are aroused by innocuous stimuli that are reminders of the trauma. This exploratory behavior may be induced by the therapist's voice prosody, modeling, mindfulness, and the arousal of the therapist's own exploration system and its accompanying curiosity. The interaction between the client and therapist fosters the development of the exploration action system within a reparative attachment relationship.

Energy Regulation Action System

As we discussed in Chapter 3, the attachment system plays a vital role in regulating the child's autonomic arousal by providing the interactive repair necessary so that the arousal of disruption is followed by a return to the window of tolerance. In addition to ensuring an optimal balance between states of activity and rest, the energy regulation system also modulates eating, drinking, sleeping, body temperature, elimination, the taking in of oxygen, physical activity, and responses to physical injury or pain. The attachment figure's timely response to the arousal of the child's energy regulation system is essential to the child's physiological and emotional well-being. Throughout the lifespan, the arousal of these fundamental survival-oriented functions that maintain homeostasis results in goal-directed actions aimed at either providing immediate satisfaction or time-limited postponement.

Energy regulation is maintained by a variety of mechanisms. Reflexive mechanisms include immediate modification of regulatory processes, such as changing breathing rate according to oxygen need, or shivering to maintain body temperature. Innate behavioral tendencies similar to these provoke animals to search for resources of warmth, food, water, and protective sleeping places needed for long-term survival (Panksepp, 1998). Thus actions of energy regulation interface with the exploration system. Additionally, interactive and autoregulatory behaviors that modulate emotional and physiological arousal, such as the exchange of a loving look between parents that soothes them both during a challenging encounter with their teenager, are actions of energy regulation that interface with caregiving, attachment, and sociability. Behaviors such as vigorous exercise or energetic play can also serve as energy regulatory actions that bring arousal back into a window of tolerance. Calming, restful actions, such as rhythmic rocking, tai chi, or yoga, may accomplish a similar purpose. Imbalances in internal homeostasis are accompanied by sensations of hunger, thirst, hyper- or hypoarousal, or fatigue—all signals to the organism to alleviate these sensations by taking action. Traumatized individuals are often insensitive to their energy regulatory needs, or form addictive tendencies in response to them, and treatment includes helping clients gradually become aware of the body sensations that signal these needs and then cultivating actions that appropriately satisfy them in a timely manner.

Caregiving Action System

Attachment is also intimately intertwined with the caregiving system. Bowlby (1969/1982, 1988) suggested that the responses of the attachment figure to the infant are organized by the caregiving system, the primary goal of which is the protection of offspring. The caregiving action system becomes activated in attachment figures when *they* perceive that the child is stressed, threatened, or in danger (George & Solomon, 1999), or when *the child* perceives an external stimulus or internal condition as threatening, uncomfortable, or stressful; the parent's caregiving action system is then deactivated when the child feels safe, content, and comfortable. Schore (2003b) described this reciprocal relationship between the attachment and caregiving systems, noting that the caregiver becomes dysregulated by the infant's cries and responds with caregiving. Modulating the child's distress reciprocally allows the caregiver to regulate him- or herself. This is the mechanism underlying the pleasurable emotions parents feel when they can protect and care for their children, and the fear, anger, and anxiety when they cannot.

When the caregiving system is aroused, the caregiver must determine whether and how to respond (George & Solomon, 1999, p. 652). His or her behavior depends upon assessment of the other person's signal and evaluation of threat. Close observation of mother–infant interactions have described an enormous range of caregiving movement patterns, including monitoring behaviors whereby the mother tracks the child's energy level, mood, and interactive capacity, as well as emotional soothing and nourishing behaviors (Tronick 1998). The nurturing emotions that accompany the caregiving systems are described as "subtle, warm and soft" (Panksepp, 1998, p. 247) and are evident as the mother attunes her behavior, voice, and perceptual apparatus to the infant's body and emotions.

Caregiving behavior naturally changes depending upon the developmental stage of the individual: infants, children, adolescents, adults, and the elderly all require different caregiving behaviors. The nature of the dyadic relationship also influences the form of caregiving: caregiving behavior between parent and child differs from that between friends, which differs from that between adult children and their aging parents. Clients often require therapeutic assistance to develop appropriate caregiving action tendencies toward their children, themselves, partners, elders, and friends.

In clinical practice therapists regulate, vary, individualize, and enact the caregiving behaviors that are appropriate and based on each client's needs and therapeutic goals. Similar to a child's caregiver, the therapist must be sensitively attuned to the client as well as be able to weather the storms of difficulty and provide interactive repair when the inevitable empathic failures occur (Steele, 2003; Tronick, 1998).

Sociability Action System

As the first social relationship, the attachment relationship lays the foundation for the sociability action system, also known as the "affiliation" (Murray, 1999) or "affectional" system. The sociability system is a much larger, or broader, system than attachment and does not pertain solely to behavior that is directed toward only one or two significant attachment figures but includes behavior directed toward the "tribe" or community (Bowlby, 1969/1982). A variety of relationships that are part of human experience, such as friendship, companionship, colleagueship, and group association, fall under the sociability system (Cassidy & Shaver, 1999). The sociability action system is fundamental to survival (Cassidy & Shaver, 1999; Panksepp, 1998). Without this relational interdependency, we would not have been able to function in the "packs" or groups that optimized the survival of the species.

Sociability contributes to psychological health: An individual may suffer significant negative consequences if social bonds are not adequately established in the childhood years. Moreover, if such bonds are established and subsequently lost, negative consequences may ensue (e.g., depression, fear of abandonment, anxiety) (Panksepp, 1998). The sociability system is interdependent with the other action systems. In addition to increasing defensive options, social groups (1) offer a "village" for caregiving of both children and adults, (2) support energy regulation needs for food and shelter, (3) foster exploration and play, and (4) provide the opportunity to develop attachment ties through pair bonding, sexuality, and reproduction.

As described in Chapter 2, the social engagement system governs facial muscles, the larynx, and the middle ear muscles and regulates both the sympathetic and dorsal vagal systems to enable effective social communication. Preprogrammed movement sequences that begin with attachment grow into the enormous range of social behaviors evident in humans. These include emotional expressions (e.g., smiling, crying, laughing), both verbal and nonverbal vocalizations, and the gestures, postures, facial and body expressions that punctuate interpersonal communication. The sociability behavior is developed and defined by the particular social environment that forms the cultural context of the individual. Individuals exhibit a wide spectrum of differential skills and abilities in forming a social connection with others (Goleman, 1995). With typically compromised social engagement systems, traumatized individuals bring an enormous range of problematic behaviors to the arousal of the sociability system, including agoraphobic tendencies, social phobias, inability to be alone, profound lack of social skills, and a general difficulty in forming social bonds. In sensorimotor psychotherapy, these tendencies are explored through awareness of the physical actions that interfere with the sociability system. For example, one client exhibited little affect facial expression or movement in social interaction, causing others to feel "disconnected" from her. Another had the habit of crossing his arms in front of his chest and leaning back when talking with others, a physical tendency that his partner interpreted as a superior attitude. Yet another froze and had difficulty talking in social interactions. These behaviors indicate the simultaneous activation of defense and sociability. Therapists observe physical tendencies that emerge when the sociability system is aroused, and help clients challenge the tendencies that interfere with meeting the goals of this system.

Play Action System

Competing feelings of discomfort or fear often impede an individual's ability to play, which depends on the subjective experience of safety to engage. If safety is threatened, play is instantly terminated, and if threat is prolonged, the ability to play is typically lost. This is evidenced in both human and animal behaviors. Abused or caged chimpanzees demonstrate similar symptoms and lack of playfulness seen in traumatized humans (Goodall, 1995).

Exploration and play are usually discussed under the same rubric, because they often co-occur or occur in such quick succession that they appear to happen simultaneously. Activities of exploration often lead to play; conversely, play can lead to new movements and ideas and thus to increased exploration. However, Panksepp (1998) argued that play activates different circuitry in the brain than does exploration and therefore play is an action system in its own right. Play is not "compliant or acquiescent" (Winnicott, 2005, p. 68), rather "a spontaneous, non-stereotyped intrinsically pleasurable activity, free of anxiety or other overpowering emotion" (Brown, 1995, pp. 7–8). Playing begins in infancy, as the baby is effectively mirrored, offered objects, and treated in such a way that he or she develops a sense of temporal continuity (Cannon, in press). It can include the rough-and-tumble play in which young animals and children often engage, other versions of physical play, and object play. "Contest" activities—sports, video games, competitions—are often described as play and can qualify if the excitement and pleasure accompanying these activities do not become anxiety-driven, which detracts from the spontaneity and joy of play itself and indicates the arousal of defense. As the cortex develops, more complex varieties of play emerge that are less physical and more cognitive in nature, such as jokes, puns, and other kinds of mental humor, comedy, and entertainment. According to Panksepp (1998), the hallmark of the play action system is laughter, which strengthens attachment and social bonds. Play reciprocally pairs increased arousal with pleasure and is associated with endorphin production, general well-being, and an increase in physical and mental health (Schore, 2003a). Both play and exploration action systems interface with sociability by contributing to social bonding, cooperation, communication, the determination of social rank, structure, and the development of leadership skills (Panksepp, 1998).

Therapists track movements characteristic of play and help clients expand on their ability to engage these actions. A variety of characteristic cross-cultural (and cross-species) movement patterns signal play behavior to other members of the social environment, including a relaxed, open body posture and a tilting of the head with a whimsical expression on the face (Beckoff & Allen, 1998; Caldwell, 2003; Donaldson, 1993). Play behavior also includes rapid changes from one behavior to another, which are absent in serious, nonplayful interactions (Beckoff & Byers, 1998; Brown, 1995). Basic, primitive play movements shift quickly and are random, nonstereotyped, and expressed in children and animals in a variety of leaps, rolls, and rotational movements (Goodall, 1995). Agitated or nervous movements usually serve to end play behavior, unless they are experienced and interpreted as part of the play (Brown, 1995).

The inability to play has debilitating consequences: "The forestalling of playing means living a life of impoverishment and isolation, developing a literalism that prevents connection and normal development" (Cannon, in press). Winnicott (1971) has stated that a primary task of the therapist is to help clients learn to play. Stimulating the play action system and the corresponding affects of fun and pleasure are particularly important in therapy with traumatized clients who typically are unable to engage in playful behavior. They characteristically find it difficult to relax enough to have fun, and often perceive the spontaneous, playful banter or quickly changing physical movements of play as awkward or threatening. Play behavior is often usurped by defensive tendencies: fear, agitated movements, freezing, tension, or collapse. As well, clients may find the spontaneous playful behavior of others threatening or uncomfortable. Finding access to the part of the client that may be ready and able to engage in play is a significant demarcation in the development of the therapeutic relationship. The therapist meticulously tracks for incipient playful actions—the beginning of a smile, a joke, or a spontaneous action—and capitalizes on those moments, drawing them out and becoming appropriately playful. As with exploration, inducing the state of play in clients allows them to begin to enjoy the process of healing, disidentify with traumatic associations, and engage a new range of possibilities.

Sexuality Action System

"Evolution has built uncompromising feelings of sexual desire into the brain" (Panksepp, 1998, p. 226), and such feelings are partial motivators for pair bonding and human reproduction (Belsky, 1999). However, rearing children to reproductive age requires much more of parents than a sexual relationship (Bowlby, 1969/1982). Relational bonds between couples of opposite or same sex who cohabitate and raise children comprise a complex intertwining of various action systems. The caregiving system, along with sexuality and attachment, are all involved in adult pair bonds (Bowlby, 1969/1982). Intimate friendship (sociability) is also an element of many pair bonds (Cassidy & Shaver, 1999; Panksepp, 1998). Adult attachment relationships, like early attachment bonding, fulfill the three criteria of attachment: provision of proximity, safe haven, and a secure base (Hazan & Zeifman, 1999). The difference is that these criteria are mutually fulfilled in adult attachment relationships. The attachment of adult pair bonds "cements an enduring emotional bond between individuals that translates . . . into differential survival and reproductive success" (Hazan & Zeifman, 1999, p. 348). Thus the attachment action system appears to be the foundational system for that of sexuality.

However, the sexuality system involves a variety of specific behaviors that are not found in the attachment system, such as courtship, seduction, pair bonding, and mating action tendencies and fixed action patterns apparent in almost all mammals when the sexuality/reproduction system becomes aroused. We typically think of sexuality as also involving the sociability system that includes affectionate or loving interactions between partners. However, "members of our species regularly demonstrate that sex and social warmth or nurturance need not go together, and in primitive areas of the brain that elaborate such feelings, confusion also prevails" (Panksepp, 1998, p. 226). Humans are capable of sexual activity that does not include the complex courtship behaviors that indicate affectionate, loving relationship, as well as sexual relationships that are uncoupled from reproduction. Thus sexuality includes a variety of actions that are not directly related to the actual reproductive act. Sexual pleasure-seeking behaviors such as masturbation or viewing pornography and Internet sites devoted to a range of sexual interests also fall into the realm of the sexuality action system behaviors.

In addition to explicit sexual actions, sexuality movement sequences include recognized courtship and flirting behaviors that indicate attraction—smiling, eye contact, higher-pitched vocalizations at a higher volume, animated, exaggerated gestures and facial expressions (Cassidy & Shaver, 1999)—and often include playful behavior that indicates the simultaneous arousal of the play action system. This initial flirtatious behavior is fundamental to the activation of the sexuality system, but attachment behaviors become evident as a relationship develops (Cassidy & Shaver, 1999). Comforting forms of physical contact, such as putting arms around one another, handholding, and speaking in a soothing vocal tone frequently develop as sexual attraction turns into an active sexual relationship, augmenting or replacing the flirtatious contact that characterizes encounters that are more purely sexual (Cassidy & Shaver, 1999). And, as new lovers form an attachment relationship over time, behaviors further change to include more sophisticated caregiving, attachment, and sociability behaviors; partners thereby transition from having an "arousal enhancing to an arousal moderating" effect on each other (Hazan & Shaver, 1999, p. 350).

Treatment of traumatized clients, especially those who have been sexually abused, often involves inquiry into how to return to, or for some even to experience, enjoyable sexual feelings. Focusing attention on dysregulated sexual arousal/inhibition or indiscriminant sexual activity is also a treatment imperative. Frequently, clients have trouble linking sexual attraction and desire with attachment and play. Difficulties may arise when engaging in a new relationship and attempting to tolerate the sensations, sensuality, and related actions. In treatment, clients learn to inhibit their habitual maladaptive action tendencies related to sexuality and to study and practice new actions that facilitate the gradual development of the reproduction/sexuality system so that it no longer is experienced as either dangerous or driven. For example, Ann, at the age of 50, came to therapy to address an action tendency pertaining to sexuality: Sexual experiences were not physically pleasurable for her but allowed her to feel a sense of power and conquest that ultimately prevented her from establishing a lasting sexual partnership. Though she could relate this tendency to her older brother's abuse, which gave her a feeling of importance and specialness, neither the insight nor her increasing dissatisfaction with being unmarried helped her to shift her behavior. In therapy, she and her male therapist used his presence and gender to simply study how she organized the experience of being with a male person with whom she wanted connection. Ann strained to avoid going into her "sexual mode" (tilting her head to one side, fluttering her eye lashes, holding the therapist's eye contact in alternation with demurely looking down, crossing and uncrossing her legs, frequent smiles, leaning forward) and noticed that she felt anxious and uncertain. She reported having no idea of how to move, to breathe, to "be" without using her sexual power, and her (nonsexual) arousal increased. The therapist encouraged her to continue to inhibit flirtatious behavior, helped her to study what it was like to not know how to be in a relationship with a male without flirting, and to tolerate the uncertainty. Although very uncomfortable, Ann continued to notice and track the unfamiliar anxiety and uncertainty until her physical sensations began to settle.

Over time, the therapist helped her explore a different kind of power: Rather than having power over the other (the man), she explored feeling power over her own state. By self-regulating and inhibiting the physical, emotional, and cognitive tendencies, she felt "successful" and powerful without depending on sexuality for power. In one session, as the therapy hour completed, Ann and her therapist decided to explore shaking hands as a good-bye gesture. Ann struggled with not sexualizing this action, experimenting with what it feet like to engage in a nonsexual relationship with a man. Ann reported "relief" and left the session experiencing a new kind of mastery over her old tendency.

HIERARCHICAL INTERACTION AMONG ACTION SYSTEMS

If, when, and how an action system comes into play in any given moment depends on a variety of factors. According to Cassidy, "Behavioral [action] systems have rules that govern the selection, activation, and termination of the behaviors as a specifiable function of the individual's internal state and the environmental context" (1999, p. 4). These rules involve the person's developmental level and internal condition as well as immediate environmental stimuli. For instance, if an individual is hungry (energy regulation), he or she will explore the environment for food. On the other hand, if the same person is just out for a walk and happens upon a pastry shop, he or she may become hungry at the sight of an appealing tart. In this case it is the arousal of the exploration system that led to noticing food that was appetizing enough to stimulate hunger; the energy regulation system functions here as a secondary action system. Play occurs when safety and energy regulation needs are met; caregiving occurs in the context of attachment and in social relationships where another person requires care. The arousal of any action system, then, is intimately linked with all the other systems. Whichever system or systems are aroused at a given time, the individual will inherently seek out the environmental options related to satisfying the goals of those systems.

Mario, for example, is 6 years old when he is taken to the zoo and sees a hippopotamus for the first time. At first he is scared of the hippo's big mouth and teeth, and he wraps his arms around his father's leg, hiding behind it.

His father reassures him and encourages him to see that the animals are kept safely away from him. Mario peers at the hippo and becomes fascinated by the big teeth and huge mouth; he laughs and points to the baby hippo in the pool, playfully imitating its actions, and after a while turns and asks his father for an ice cream. In this anecdote we see how behavior is "the product of the interaction among behavioral [action] systems (George & Solomon, 1999, p. 653). First, as Mario sees the novel stimulus of a big animal with a big mouth and big teeth, he experiences alarm; the action systems of attachment and defense are simultaneously activated, and Mario hides behind his father's leg. The safe base provided by Mario's attachment relationship with his father mitigates his need for defense and provides sufficient reassurance for the action system of exploration to engage, and Mario becomes curious. As he explores, initially from the safety of the attachment relationship—his father's body shielding him from the hippo—and becomes increasingly intrigued with this novel stimuli, the action system of play is activated. As the play system is terminated after a period of time, Mario's exploration system is again aroused, and he looks around, sees an ice cream stand, experiences the stimulation of his energy regulation system, and requests an ice cream.

Many factors play a part in the behavioral decisions we make: information from the body and the five senses, objects of immediate orientation, thoughts, beliefs, and emotional responses, and the reaction and feedback from the environment to each discreet action. The range and type of behavior relating to each action system and how it varies with age, gender, past experience, and current context, contribute to a versatility of response. Biological feedback, via both hormones and the central nervous system, allows us to monitor the internal and environmental cues that lead to each system's activation or termination. As the goals of one action system are fulfilled by our behavior, new goals that might involve additional action systems emerge, as in the above example. Mario moved from the goal of safety to curiosity about the hippo to the desire for an ice cream. This "goal-corrected" feature—meaning that when one goal is fulfilled, another emerges—of action systems permits variety and flexibility in response and enhances adaptive behavior.

Some action systems are available at birth, whereas others develop over time or come into play with maturity. Thus behavior is also influenced by the order in which action systems become available (Cassidy & Shaver, 1999; Maslow, 1970; Panksepp, 1998). Panksepp (1998) noted:

> All mammals, indeed all organisms, come into the world with a variety of abilities that do not require previous learning, but which provide immediate opportunities for learning to occur. . . . Emotional abilities initially emerge from "instinctual" operating systems of the brain,

which allow animals to begin gathering food, information, and other resources needed to sustain life. . . . Others, such as sexual lust and maternal devotion, emerge later to promote reproductive success. Additional social processes, such as play and the seeking of dominance, start to control behavior with differential intensities during later phases of life and help promote the establishment of stable social structures and the propagation of the most fortunate and most able. (p. 26)

The systems that develop first influence the "wiring" of both bottom-up and top-down processes and, in turn, strongly influence action systems that develop subsequently. For example, the attachment relationship shapes regulatory capacities and brain development before top-down, cortical regulation becomes available, as indicated by observation of toddlers, who instinctively utilize the secure base of the caregiver for exploration—a bottom-up strategy. Later in childhood, a preadolescent may utilize the attachment system to access top-down management: for example, by asking for advice or information about a science project that is causing the child anxiety. Although infants have a rudimentary sexuality system, as evidenced in masturbatory activity among infants, this system is augmented at puberty and comes online fully in young adulthood. The sexuality/reproduction system emerges fully through bottom-up processes of hormonal and physiological changes, but then is directed by a variety of cognitive considerations because it matures at a time in development when top-down regulation—insight, interpretation, reflection—is possible.

The activation of action systems and their corresponding behaviors is also influenced by hierarchical evolutionary imperatives. Janet (1925) suggested that action systems emerging earlier in development are characterized by greater "energy" or "force" than those that emerge later, making the former harder to regulate. Thus the defensive and attachment action systems, so crucial for survival, are activated with greater intensity than action systems that are less imperative for survival or that emerge later developmentally: Play, exploration, or sociability are not usually accompanied by such intense force or energy as the action systems of defense or attachment. If a current stimulus triggers a system that is survival-related and antecedently organized, "the tendency to react will be promptly charged with a large measure of vital energy" (Janet, 1925, p. 683). In other words, defense and attachment systems are organized to express or discharge their associated force or energy through immediate action. We often see this immediacy in traumatized clients who cannot delay or inhibit the arousal and accompanying action impulses evoked by attachment or defense systems and who then take impulsive or even destructive action. When aroused to a high degree, the energy regulation system may also be associated with greater energy and goal-directed action than other systems. Although human beings are capable of delaying the gratification of energy regulation needs for food, warmth, elimination, and sleep for considerable periods of time, eventually these needs will take priority over exploration, play, sociability, sexuality, and at times even attachment and defense.

Additionally, later-organized action systems are more easily supplanted by the earlier-organized ones than the other way around, because a greater degree of integrative capacity is required to inhibit reactive behaviors that are stimulated when early-organized systems are aroused. For example, parents teach their children to eat in socially appropriate ways even when the children are very hungry. The parents try to influence the basic actions of energy regulation so that its goals are satisfied with actions (such as good manners) appropriate to the sociability system. This training usually takes years of social prompting that only decreases as children develop more integrative capacity that helps them inhibit socially unacceptable eating behavior. In the wake of trauma, the ability to inhibit a flight response triggered by an autonomic "false alarm," in favor of initiating the action systems of exploration or sociability, requires high integrative abilities, including reflection and the ability to restrain bottom-up orienting and defensive tendencies.

THE OVERACTIVATION OF THE DEFENSE ACTION SYSTEM

The "rules" by which action systems are selected, enacted, and terminated are shaped not only by culture but also by traumatic experiences. In traumatogenic environments, the child's action system of defense is frequently stimulated, either in response to, or in anticipation of, an overwhelming or traumatizing event. The attachment system is likely to be compromised as a result of "frightened" or "frightening" caregiving. Energy regulation may give way to defense: Instead of sleeping at night, the child stays awake, listening for sounds that predict threat. Sociability, exploration, or play may be perceived as dangerous. In adult life, long after the traumatic events are over, the traumatized individual typically continues to experience conflict between the action system of defense and one or more action systems associated with (nontraumatic) daily living. Because the defensive system is antecedently organized, inherently endowed with a great deal of force, and chronically stimulated in those suffering from unresolved trauma, many traumatized clients experience difficulty overriding or inhibiting the defense system so that the goals of other actions systems can be fulfilled. In contrast, when a nontraumatized person is exposed to a threatening stimulus, the defensive system tends to recede when the threat has passed or when inaccurate perceptions of threat are revised, and as safety is restored, the individual can respond to the other systems that govern daily life.

Thus, for traumatized individuals, the tendency toward overactivation of the defense action system has become an unconscious reflexive habit woven into the fabric of their lives. A variety of the symptoms and problems of traumatized clients indicate their inability to respond effectively to other action systems. Disruption of energy regulation is apparent in sleeping and eating difficulties, nonorganic problems with breathing, a disturbed capacity to sense or respond to physical pain and injury, as well as chronic autonomic dysregulation of arousal. Almost invariably, clients are unable to play, finding that their capacity to experience pleasure, exuberance, and joy in playful interactions or activities has either diminished, disappeared altogether in the wake of trauma, or is experienced as paradoxically dangerous and threatening (Luxenberg, Spinazzola, Hidalgo, Hunt, & Van der Kolk, 2001; Luxenberg, Spinazzola, & Van der Kolk, 2001).

Similarly, the sociability system is often impaired by an inability to tolerate social stimulation or to use social relationships to self-regulate. Some clients with trauma-related disorders isolate themselves, avoiding social contact altogether; some experience freezing responses when they consider leaving their homes to explore the environment (obstructing the exploration system); some uncontrollably lash out at their children (disrupting the caregiving system); some complain that they have no safe person upon whom to depend (inadequate attachment); some want to become parents but experience defense-related hyperarousal at the thought of a sexual relationship. Although reliance on the defense system was probably adaptive in childhood, its continuing predominance long after the trauma is over results in an adult life that has become grossly limited and constrained for many traumatized individuals.

ACTION SYSTEMS AND TENDENCIES

Action systems govern both tendencies of fixed action patterns (i.e., the stereotyped movements germane to a species, such as the mobilizing and immobilizing defensive responses) and less stereotyped but still automatic tendencies associated with conditioned learning (e.g., a child who learns that the best way to prevent abuse is to be quiet and speak only when spoken to). The engagement of an action system "change[s] sensory, perceptual, and cognitive processing, and initiate[s] a host of physiological changes that are naturally synchronized with the aroused behavioral tendencies characteristic of [that system]" (Panksepp, 1998, p. 49). These changes include discrete mental and physical actions of orienting, information processing, and behavior that eventually become automatic tendencies in response to the arousal of a system.

All the action systems "organize diverse behaviors by activating or inhibiting motor subroutines and concurrent autonomic-hormonal changes that have proved adaptive in the face of life-challenging circumstances during the evolutionary history of the species" (Panksepp, 1998, p. 49). Subsequently, however, when the same action system is aroused in another set of circumstances, the person is primed to respond with the action tendencies learned earlier, without conscious attention or intention. These action tendencies are both physical (observed in habitual interoceptive, postural, gestural and movement responses) and mental (apparent in repetitive cognitive and emotional responses).

Given the enormous array of options for action at any given moment, action tendencies confer the advantage of limiting or constraining this extensive (and possibly overwhelming) "menu" of possibilities (Janet, 1935a). As Llinas (2001) stated:

> [motor] patterns respond somewhat selectively to an urgent event in the external world requiring a well-defined, overt strategy [related to an action system] such as attack and defense, finding food, reproduction and the like, and in a timely and appropriate fashion. A set of clear constraints must be superimposed on a [motor] system that is so extraordinarily rich and predictive and they must be very powerful. . . . The motor system is [thus] constrained, carved down out of its overcompleteness into (among many) this particular fixed action pattern so that when needed it is activated at once and perfectly so. (p. 145)

Thus, when an action system is aroused, the infinite possibilities for action are restricted by previously formed automatic action tendencies designed to expedite the fulfillment of the goals of that action system. The efficiency of any procedural learning restricts choice because it reduces the availability of other movement options. Once formed, these actions tend to remain relatively stable tendencies even when the situation that evoked or required them is no longer present (Cassidy & Shaver, 1999). Long after environmental, and internal, conditions have changed, we remain in a state of readiness to perform the mental and physical actions adaptive in the past. Action tendencies can become maladaptive when they continue to usurp other actions that would prove to be more adaptive in the current context or immediate environment. For example, when a young woman with a history of childhood abuse suddenly turns her face away from the kiss of her beloved boyfriend, she may be responding to his sudden proximity with a defensive action tendency rather than welcoming his proximity as a safe attachment figure and desirable sexual partner.

PREDICTION OF OUTCOME

Prediction of outcome is a strong factor in the development of action tendencies. The ability to forecast, or imagine, the effect of our actions influences which actions we execute and how we execute them. For instance, the sexually abused child who remains quiet and only "speaks when spoken to" may "predict" that these actions will decrease the chances of abusive treatment. Thus action tendencies are not only a readiness for executing a particular action, but also an expectation of a particular outcome (Frijda, 1986; Van der Hart et al., 2006). For instance, if we expect that exploratory actions will be ineffectual, humiliating, or dangerous, we will tend to avoid them; if we expect that exploration will lead to satisfaction, we will develop the tendency to be curious about the environment and to engage in "approach" exploratory actions.

The term *internal working models* refers to the complex systems of beliefs we have developed about our attachment figures, beginning as infants and very young children, in response to repeated experience (Bowlby, 1988). These working models help us anticipate and forecast the future and therefore serve to shape our actions (Bowlby, 1999, p. 135), eventually contributing to the development of action tendencies.

We perceive the external world through the senses, initially in relationship with our caregivers, and this perception is subsequently (and continually) compared to both past experience and current present moment internal experience. As Llinas noted, the "solution to [any discrepancy in] this comparison of internal and external worlds is then externalized: an appropriate action is taken, a movement is made. By this process, a spectacular transference has occurred: an 'upgrading' of the internal image of what is to come to its actualization into the external world" (2001, p. 38) Our internal working models have the potential to help us continually forecast the probable result of our actions—but what happens when the forecasts are not upgraded? Traumatic experience and consequent neuropsychological deficits prevent traumatized individuals from "upgrading the forecast," resulting in a repetition of past actions even when they are no longer adaptive.

In order for the action tendencies that accompany our working models and their associated predictions to be most effective, they must be geared to the needs of the present rather than to the past. Ideally, working models should be flexible, able to change in response to environmental and internal cues (Marvin & Britner, 1999, p. 48). A person's behavioral repertoire should expand through development, maturation, and learning gained from interactions with others and the environment. Although constrained by action tendencies and forecasts, our responses to the arousal of action systems still need creative "upgrading" so that our actions become progressively more complex, adaptive, and sophisticated (Janet, 1925, 1937a).

For example, the caregiver action system in a parent adapts continuously to changes in the child's developmental level and attachment needs, such that the general actions of caregiving change dramatically in character and tone over the course of the child's development. But trauma-related arousal and overactivated defensive subsystems interfere with the development of more flexible and creative tendencies. Therefore, many clients are unable to update their action tendencies, and their minds and bodies respond to the present with activation, interpretation, and forecasts based on past traumatic experience. Behaviors that therapists (and insightful clients) view as maladaptive to present circumstances are often "shadows" of previous actions, adaptive in earlier contexts, that have not been upgraded.

ACTION SYSTEMS, ACTION TENDENCIES, AND THE BODY

Action systems are inherently physical in nature. The body sensations indicating arousal of the energy regulation system are most obvious. A full bladder indicates the need to urinate, a growling of the stomach signals hunger, dryness in the mouth tells us we are thirsty, goose bumps indicate cold, sweating signals too much heat, and so on (Panksepp, 1998). Physical sensations accompany the arousal of other action systems as well: Tension in the arms or legs signals the fight or flight responses of defense; impulses to move toward or reach out occur in the presence of an attachment figure; butterflies in the stomach accompany separation from an attachment figure; the tugging of the heart that parents feel as they see their child struggle with a new challenge; the quickened energy that accompanies the excitement of exploration, and so on. When any of these sensations reach a certain intensity, they become so compelling that alleviating them may take priority over responding to other action systems. Along with sensations associated with the arousal of action systems, the prospect of fulfilling action system-related goals and experiencing the resulting pleasure can motivate us to make these goals a priority. And experiencing the sensations related to a particular system often induces the *feeling*, or emotion, of being in that action system, because the feeling is produced by the action that is happening (Damasio, 1999). Thus, when traumatized individuals experience the sensation of increased arousal and tension in the body (e.g., from the exploration or sexual systems), they often feel endangered, relating these sensations to the defensive systems.

In order for an action system to achieve its particular goal, it co-opts the physical capacities of the body. Specific physical actions serve more than one system: Locomotion, for example, can serve the attachment system (enabling an individual to walk toward an attachment figure), the defense system (enabling escape from potential danger), and the exploratory system (enabling movement toward an object of curiosity) (Marvin & Britner, 1999). However, as we have noted, each action system is also organized by particular beliefs and emotions—mental action tendencies—so the same movement or type of locomotion can take on very different qualities depending on which action system and corresponding beliefs are mobilized. Locomotion in the context of exploration has a different quality than locomotion in the context of flight behavior. When the defensive system is aroused along with action systems of attachment, sexuality, sociability, exploration, play, caregiving, or energy regulation, locomotion may reflect simultaneous or consecutive contradictory patterns: for example, walking toward while tensing the body; walking toward, then abruptly changing directions; halting movements while walking towards, and so on.

Our physical actions, such as those described in the previous paragraph, are generally thought to be under our conscious control, but most movement occurs from procedural memory, without reflection, in response to sensory stimuli and internal processes outside of our awareness. Each motor act is comprised of a series of precise actions strung together in a revolving sequence, a "sensorimotor loop" (Cohen, 1993). Sensory information is first received from the external world and internal experience. Then this incoming information is compared with past experience. This comparison results in an interpretation of the stimuli and a forecast of possible outcomes of various actions, followed by the organization of a motor response. Only after these sequences are completed does an actual movement occur, starting the loop over again. Cognitive and emotional processing are affected by the feeling of what's happening in the body (Damasio, 1999). These bottom-up sensorimotor loops create the context for mental experiences and actions. In turn, mental actions and top-down processes affect physical actions and bottom-up processes.

Action tendencies include both activation and inhibition of discrete movements (physical and mental) and generally fall into one of two categories: (1) a readiness to accept, receive, and approach, or (2) a readiness to defend, escape, and avoid (Frijda, 1986). These two poles are reflected in bodily posture and movement: Smiling, a relaxed body posture, or moving toward something are all actions that reflect acceptance, receptivity, and approach; defensive behaviors such as frowning, withdrawal, moving away, or constriction reflect avoidance, defense, and escape from potential threat. In moving toward something with a relaxed and open body posture, we stimulate relaxed but energetic (and often pleasurable) inner body sensations, heightened sensory perception, and emotions and cognitions related to interest and pleasure. In moving away from something with tightened facial muscles and narrowed eyes, we stimulate muscular tension, increased autonomic arousal, and cognitions and emotions related to danger and defense. The defensive and avoidance behavior adaptive in childhood has become habitual for many of our traumatized clients, interfering with the full execution of approach behavior (e.g., exploration and trials of new experience).

Instead, their action tendencies involve either simultaneous or sequential movements of approach and defense/avoidance.

We can make educated hypotheses about an individual's expectations and forecasts by observing the organization of his or her physical action tendencies as they emerge spontaneously in response to an immediate stimulus. Both approach and avoidance actions may be observed. For instance, if people are asked to consider exploring a challenging novel activity, such as performing in front of a group or going out on a date, each person will react with a tendency toward particular automatic physical and mental actions—and these actions may manifest in an individual at different moments, in different circumstances. Some individuals will become excited and curious, and their bodies may demonstrate increased arousal and overall tonicity, communicating an openness and "approach" attitude. Others might experience fear, irritation, or aversion, manifesting an "avoidance" or defensive attitude of constriction and shrinking. Some will hold their breath, others may lean forward in anticipation, and still others may respond with simultaneous approach and avoidance movement, such as leaning forward and pulling backward simultaneously. Each response holds specific meaning and tells a different story about the person's often unconscious forecasts of what outcome will result from action—in this case, performing or going on a date.

For chronically traumatized individuals, actions are often conflicted and include the simultaneous or sequential approach and avoidance/defense movements, similar to the actions of disorganized-disoriented attachment patterns described in Chapter 3. These conflicting movements are noticeable when clients respond with defensive action tendencies to the arousal of other action systems that were not available or safe in childhood.

LEVELS OF ACTION TENDENCIES

Physical and mental actions range from the most primitive, reflexive, and elementary to the complex and sophisticated actions that require a large degree of integrative capacity (Janet, 1925, 1937a). One of the evolutionary advantages of action tendencies is that they help us conserve energy and thereby allow for the development of newer, more complex actions. Once a tendency is formed, it is immediately available in the face of specific internal or external stimuli. For example, when young children first learn to use a spoon, all their energy is focused on getting the spoon to their mouth. In time, this action becomes a procedurally learned tendency that is so automatic that they are freed to engage in ever more complex actions, such as social interaction during mealtime. Over the course of development, our actions become increasingly sophisticated and complex as we learn more urbane skills and develop higher-order mental abilities, such as the ability to reflect on experience, weigh the possible effect of our actions, challenge maladaptive actions, and contemplate how we might act differently.

Lacking the integrative capacity to engage in these complex actions and driven by autonomic activation and defensive subsystems, traumatized individuals instead tend to revert to the well-worn pathways of older, more reflexive action tendencies. In Janet's words, "it is especially new [more complex] actions that will become difficult [for traumatized individuals], and, for a long time, the patients go on with old actions without being able to stop" (1907, p. 315). In the face of somatosensory reminders of trauma, reflexive lower-level mental and physical tendencies are triggered, even in contexts where higher-level mental actions would be more adaptive and might lead to more effective physical action. Reflexive action tendencies are highly stereotyped and immediate, associated with basic survival, and accompanied by the concomitant loss of higher-level tendencies. They tend to be repetitive, fail to develop or bring satisfaction, and are frequently uncomfortable for another person to witness (Caldwell, 1996). For example, traumatized clients may feel that it is "safer" to yell, withdraw, hit, submit, freeze, fight, flee, or engage in addictive behavior than to engage in less familiar, more complex actions that feel less safe and that challenge reflexive action tendencies. In short, their capacity for social engagement is overridden by more primitive defense actions.

For example, one client impulsively consumed great quantities of sugary foods, reporting that those foods had always helped in the past to temporarily regulate her chronic hypoarousal. This lower-order tendency to assuage her hypoarousal with food took precedence, and she was unable to reflect on the "cost" of eating those foods in terms of later irritability, blood sugar dysregulation, weight gain, and feelings of shame. These lower-order tendencies are easier to fulfill and harder to change, whereas the more recently acquired ones, such as the ability to thoughtfully consider the effects of actions, are more difficult to execute (Janet, 1937b). Reflection, being a later developed, more complex action, becomes a primary goal in treatment: that is, increasing the client's integrative capacity until more flexible, sophisticated actions are readily available to replace maladaptive, reflexive actions.

The complex process of executing mental and physical actions occurs rapidly and continually in discrete stages: planning (constructing the action), initiation, execution, and completion (Janet, 1903; Van der Hart et al., 2006). At any one of these stages the individual has the option to change course: to stop, resume, iterate, or continue, and evaluate if the outcome has been met. The capacity for recognizing and utilizing options reflects sophisticated integrative skills, such as (1) consideration of the action's effect on the environment, (2) monitoring of sensations, emotions, and cognitions, (3) evaluating if goals have been accomplished, (4) creating new goals, and (5) planning new actions. To gain access to these options necessitates complex mental actions that often must be taught to traumatized clients. Adaptive action requires that clients be able to reflect upon the accuracy of their forecasts, compare forecast to outcome, and evaluate the effect of the completed action on current and subsequent actions. In turn, this process requires noticing when an old, reflexive, or maladaptive action tendency arises; inhibiting the reflexive tendency; considering other, more adaptive possibilities; making a decision; and finding a way to execute an alternative, more adaptive, complex, and creative action. Furthermore, adaptive action requires monitoring how the action is affecting other people and how it is affecting oneself.

Some traumatized individuals are able to plan a new action but are unable to achieve the next stage of actually initiating it. Others can initiate but are unable to carry through the implementation of the new action to completion. Instead, under the sway of maladaptive tendencies, they abandon the new action or initiate another action before the original one is completed. Others complete the action but with little interest or satisfaction; they feel disconnected from the new experience and unable to ascribe meaning or value to the action (Janet, 1903). Still others are unable to step back from their reflexive action tendencies sufficiently to reflect upon the efficacy of the new action (Van der Hart et al., 2006), and some seem oblivious to the effect of their actions upon the environment or themselves.

Each and every action taken affects a person's integrative capacity in one way or another. The achieved and completed act raises integrative capacity, whereas an unfinished, failed, or curtailed act lowers it (Ellenberger, 1970; Janet, 1925). In therapy, clients are helped to become aware of the separate components that comprise their action tendencies, observe them as they unfold, and mindfully determine whether or not they are adaptive. Over time, they develop the ability to inhibit maladaptive tendencies and, through practice, develop new, more currently adaptive tendencies that, when practiced and actualized, initiate new, more creative and sophisticated tendencies (Janet, 1925).

ACTION SYSTEMS AND DISSOCIATION

As discussed in Chapter 1, trauma-related disorders are characterized by a biphasic pattern (Chu, 1998; Van der Kolk et al., 1996) in which individuals alternate between experientially reliving the trauma, thereby reengaging defensive tendencies, and avoiding potentially disturbing and dysregulating reminders in order to participate in daily life. The numbing and avoidance symptoms result from instinctive attempts to circumvent extreme arousal states and defensive actions stimulated by traumatic reminders in order to respond to the action systems of daily life.

Several authors discussed the separation or alternation between states of fear with periods of relative calm in severely traumatized individuals (Barach, 1991; Liotti, 1999b; Schwartz, 1994). Allen noted how the application of attachment theory assists our understanding of the development and need for compartmentalized aspects of the personality: "Discontinuous behavioral state switches are part and parcel of contradictory models of relatedness. Over time, these working models accrue a history on the basis of a long series of interactions in certain contexts. Thus working models become components of identity or, when dissociated, become associated with an illusory sense of separate identity" (2001, p. 193).

As we have reviewed earlier in this chapter, the defensive action system supports survival and adaptation under threat, whereas the other action systems promote engagement in daily life. Action systems comprise two general types: the defensive system that responds to danger, and all the other systems that promote engagement in daily life activities (Steele et al., 2005). When these biphasic alternations between defensive and daily life action systems occur repetitively and persist over time, we observe increasing compartmentalization between reexperiencing of the trauma (which arouses the defense system) and avoidance of traumatic reminders (which allows engagement with the other actions systems). As Steele et al. (2005b) put it:

> Metaphorically speaking, fault lines occur between action systems of daily life and those of defense, because they naturally tend to mutually inhibit each other. For example, one does not stay focused on cleaning the house or reading when imminent danger is perceived; instead one becomes hypervigilant and prepares for defense. Then, when danger has passed, one should naturally return to normal activities rather than continuing to be in a defensive mode. Integration between these two types of action systems will more likely fail during or following traumatic stress than will integration among internal components of each of these two complex action systems. (p. 17)

When the action system of defense is not integrated with other action systems, a type of biphasic dissociative pattern ensues. This was first noted by Janet, who wrote about the successive alternation of two "psychological existences" in traumatized individuals: "In one [condition], he has sensations, remembrances, movements, which he has not in the other, and consequently he presents, in a manner more or less clear . . . two characters, and in some sort two personalities" (1901/1998, p. 491). Janet's pioneering work on dissociation has helped pave the way for the formulation of the theory of structural dissociation of the personality (Nijenhuis et al., 2002; Steele & Van der Hart, 2001), which proposes that, in the wake of trauma, one self-state, or part of the personality, remains fixated on defense against threat, whereas the other self-state, or part of the personality, is dedicated to carrying out the activities of the other action systems: those of attachment, energy regulation, exploration, play, sociability, sexuality, and caregiving (Nijenhuis et al., 2002). The structural dissociation theory also has roots in the work of Charles S. Myers, a British military psychiatrist and psychologist who studied traumatized World War I combat soldiers. Myers (1940; see also Van der Hart et al., 2000), like Janet, was struck by the compartmentalization or separation of experience and identity observed in the wake of trauma: "The . . . normal [part of the] personality is in abeyance. . . . The recent emotional experiences of the individual have the upper hand and determine his conduct: the normal has been replaced by what we may call the "emotional" [part of the] personality" (p. 67). According to Myers's observations, this part of the traumatized soldier's personality "differed widely in physical appearance and behavior, as well as mentally, from the completely normal personality" (1940, p. 69). Driven by unintegrated fragments of the traumatic memories, one part of the personality, or self-state, remains fixated on the trauma and on surviving it, repetitively evoking and rekindling the defensive action system. Traumatic reminders and the arousal of the action system of defense preoccupy the individual at these times that the "emotional" part of the personality, which is caught up in reexperiencing the traumatic past, is dominant.

Current life experiences involving energy regulation, relationships, childrearing, and professional endeavors necessarily activate the action systems of daily life. If, for example, we are involved in a traumatic car accident, that part of us connected to the action systems of daily life will try to reengage in our normal life activities as soon as possible, even while the action system of defense is activated by car-related sights or sounds and we begin to shake and tremble as we put the key in the ignition. The part of the self that attempts to resume normal activity was described by Myers as an "apparently normal" part: "Gradually or suddenly an 'apparently normal' [part of the] personality usually returns—normal save for the lack of all memory of events directly connected with the shock, normal save for the manifestation of other ('somatic') hysteric disorders indicative of mental dissociation" (1940, p. 67). Thus the aspect of self that attempts to resume normal activity responds to environmental stimuli signaling the needs of the action systems of daily life (such as having to go to work in a car or needing to pick up the children from soccer practice), and the "apparently normal" part of the personality emerges to respond as best as possible to fulfill these objectives. Compartmentalization between engaging in daily life and reliving the trauma is clearly described in the following excerpt from an incest survivor:

> Who was my other self? Though we had split one personality between us, I was the majority shareholder. I went to school, made friends, gained experience [engaged in action systems of daily life], developing my part of the personality, while she [engaged in defensive action systems and] remained morally and emotionally a child, functioning on instinct rather than on intelligence. She began as my creature, forced to do what I refused to do, yet because I blotted out her existence, she passed out of my control as completely as a figure in a dream. (Fraser, 1987, p. 24)

Thus one part of the personality tries to keep the memory of the trauma at bay in order to conduct daily life activities and continue normal development, but with varying degrees of success. When the individual is confronted with reactivating stimuli, the defensive action system encroaches upon and interrupts the completion of the tasks pertaining to daily life. Each action system, whether of defense or daily life, has a particular organization of action tendencies that is unique to that system. As a result,

> in a given situation each dissociative part of the personality has a *propensity* to exhibit a particular pattern of behaviors, thoughts, feelings, sensations, and perceptions that may differ significantly from other parts, based on the action systems by which each is influenced. Thus, various parts are constrained to some degree by the specific action systems by which they are mediated, leading to relatively inflexible mental and physical actions. (Steele et al., 2005, p. 17)

Annie, the childhood abuse survivor described in Chapter 2, can recall the compartmentalization as it operated adaptively during her childhood and is aware that, even today, one part of her still avoids the traumatic memories in order to participate in daily life activities: marriage, creating a home, raising two children, and going to graduate school. At these times Annie remains dissociatively compartmentalized, distanced from the parts of her personality that still experience the trauma-related arousal, affects, and defensive responses. However, when she tries to sleep at night or when she is triggered by reminders of the trauma during the day, hyperarousal symptoms, activation of defensive subsystems of fight, flight, or compliance/submission, and hypoarousal-related isolative avoidance attest to the intrusion of the "emotional parts" of her personality that are still reliving traumatic procedural learning and engaging action tendencies of defense. During these times, she has great trouble engaging the action systems of daily life.

The structural dissociation between parts of the personality represents a profound integrative failure. Action systems are not integrated in the whole of the personality. For example, each self-part may be constructed around a different defensive subsystem with its accompanying action tendencies (Nijenhuis et al., 2002; Van der Hart et al., 2006). Some parts of the personality reflect different physical and mental tendencies characteristic of action systems of daily life, whereas other parts exhibit tendencies related to different defensive subsystems: A "fight" part might exhibit heightened overall arousal, tension, and readiness in the arms, an abrasive social demeanor, and hypervigilent orientation to threat cues, accompanied by anger and thoughts of aggression. This part of the individual might have a stronger, louder voice and a set of memories centering on stories of challenge and demand. An aspect of the self organized by the "flight" response might exhibit physical postures of pulling back, movement impulses in the legs and feet, and heightened orienting responses accompanied by fear and thoughts of escape. A part organized by the "freeze" response is likely to exhibit muscular tension and a rigid immobility, such as contraction of leg and arm muscles, accompanied by high anxiety. A "submissive" part might exhibit flaccidity in the musculature, numbness, collapsed immobility, and a dulling of the orienting response, reduced emotional and cognitive capacity. Another part might exhibit exaggerated movements of reaching or clinging, along with feelings of desperation and longing. Similarly, aspects of the individual engaged in daily life activities will exhibit physical and mental tendencies characteristic of each of these action systems.

It should be emphasized that *structural dissociation of the personality* is a theoretical construct that conceptualizes traumatic dissociation along the lines of action systems theory as an adaptive, neurobiologically organized response to trauma. The language of this theory is not intended to imply an actual division of the personality into discrete, separate entities but rather to describe the campartmentalization of the relationships between encapsulated action tendencies—a compartmentalization that reflects the repetitive activation of biphasic alternations between action systems. Terms such as *part of the personality* are "metaphoric descriptive labels of mental [and somatic action] systems that have failed to integrate" (Steele, Van der Hart, & Nijenhuis, 2004, p. 39).

The failure to integrate defensive action systems with action systems of daily living is inevitable in varying degrees in clients with trauma-related disorders. The concepts of structural dissociation and compartmentalization point to a number of important features crucial to a sensorimotor understanding and treatment of trauma: (1) the inherent conflict between action systems of defense and those of normal daily life; (2) the way in which action tendencies become encapsulated into self-states or parts of the personality; and (3) the essential role of integrative capacity in bringing past and present into harmony.

CONCLUSION

Therapists and clients co-create new levels of understanding by examining clients' unique actions tendencies as they respond to the arousal of each action system. Developing more adaptive action tendencies related to normal (nonthreatening) life, as well as to threatening situations, requires that we study the simultaneous arousal of both categories of action systems as they are evoked in the natural course of therapy or in normal life. In the context of long-term therapy, clients utilize the social engagement system to develop an attachment relationship with the therapist, which develops the sociability and attachment systems, models appropriate caregiving behavior, and provides the secure base for exploring their action tendencies, both habitual and potential, in response to the arousal of all the action systems. It is important for the therapist to assess which actions remain incomplete or unexpressed and help clients learn to complete these action potentials and thereby bring forth new capabilities. As defensive tendencies are inadvertently triggered, they can be studied and thereby demystified so that they no longer interfere with the functioning of daily life systems. When we help clients to become interested in, and curious about, their action tendencies by observing their physical, mental, and emotional reactions, the exploration system is evoked. In the context of curious, nonjudgmental exploration, significant moments of playfulness between therapist and client often unfold spontaneously. The goal in treatment is to improve upon the adaptive functioning of all action systems and to mitigate the unfettered arousal of the defensive system so that it is activated only when needed, no longer disrupting the functioning of other systems.

Chapter 7

❊❊❊

Psychological Trauma and the Brain: Toward a Neurobiological Treatment Model

Ruth Lanius, Ulrich Lanius, Janina Fisher,[1] and Pat Ogden

THE PREVIOUS CHAPTERS HAVE REVIEWED NUMEROUS ways that traumatic experience impacts both the mind and body of a developing child by affecting hierarchical information processing, attachment and social engagement systems, autonomic arousal and self-regulatory ability, and action tendencies related to systems of defense and of daily living. An understanding of the neurobiology of trauma may further enhance our conceptualization of the long-term sequelae of trauma and help to guide our therapeutic efforts toward increasing the accuracy and specificity of clinical interventions. In this chapter we review relevant brain areas that have been identified in recent neuroimaging research as being involved in traumatic stress syndromes, focusing specifically on the heterogeneity of response to traumatic reminders and on how different brain regions may relate to the biphasic

Ruth Lanius, MD, Ph.D., FRCPC, is Associate Professor in the Department of Psychiatry at the University of Western Ontario, London, Ontario, and Director of Traumatic Stress Service at London Health Sciences Centre. Ulrich Lanius, Ph.D., is a clinician in the Department of Psychiatry at Royal Columbian Hospital, New Westminster, British Columbia. Janina Fisher, Ph.D., is instructor and senior supervisor at the Trauma Center in Boston.

response to trauma. Finally, we use examples from the neuroscience literature to discuss how experience is processed on cognitive, emotional, and sensorimotor levels, as well as to examine the impact of unresolved sensorimotor responses on all levels of information processing.

TRAUMA, LEVELS OF INFORMATION PROCESSING,
AND THE TRIUNE BRAIN

As discussed in Chapter 1, the concept of hierarchical information processing (Wilber, 1996) proposes that there are intertwined, functional relationships among different levels of information processing. To work with this hierarchy in clinical practice, we must attend to all three levels: cognitive processing (thoughts, beliefs, interpretations, and other cognitions), emotional processing (emotion and affect), and sensorimotor processing (physical and sensory responses, sensations, and movement). Similarly, MacLean (1985) has conceptualized a "brain within a brain within a brain." The reptilian brain, first to develop from an evolutionary perspective, governs arousal, homeostasis of the organism, and reproductive drives. The "paleomammalian brain" or "limbic brain," found in all mammals, surrounds the reptilian brain and is concerned with emotion, memory, some social behavior, and learning (Cozolino, 2002). Last to develop phylogenetically is the neocortex, which enables self-awareness and conscious thought and includes large portions of the corpus callosum, which bridges the right and left hemispheres of the brain (MacLean, 1985).

Each of the three levels of the brain has its own perception of the environment and responds accordingly, such that a particular level may override the others, depending on the environmental conditions. Even when one level supercedes the others, however, cognitive, emotional, and sensorimotor processing are functionally mutually dependent and intertwined (Damasio, 1999; LeDoux, 1996; Schore, 1994); the three levels of the brain and the corresponding information processing interact and affect each other simultaneously, functioning as a cohesive whole, with the degree of integration of each level of processing affecting the efficacy of other levels.

THALAMUS

The interactive process among the three levels of the brain is likely facilitated by the thalamus, a structure that plays a key role in relaying sensory information to the limbic system and neocortex, thus eventually leading to the integration of sensory information (Lanius et al., 2005). All sensory information, except for olfaction, is routed through the thalamus to the cerebral cortex, and thus the thalamus is often referred to as the sensory gateway to the cortex. It has also been suggested that the thalamus might be involved in mediating the interaction between attention and arousal (Portas et al., 1998), both of which are clearly relevant to the integration of information and the phenomenology of traumatic stress syndromes. The thalamus is located at the "intersection" of the reptilian and mammalian brains on top of the brainstem, connecting the latter with the limbic system and the neocortex. Disruptions in thalamic functioning are likely to interfere with the relay of sensory information to the limbic system and neocortex, as well as with the integration of such information. In that the thalamus serves as a gateway that directly or indirectly modulates the access of sensory information to the cortex, amygdala, and hippocampus, Krystal et al. (1998) proposed that the thalamus facilitates transmission of sensory information to these brain areas. We therefore hypothesize that the thalamus has a crucial function in the interaction of the three brain layers and may be important for the interaction of cognitions, emotions, and behaviors.

Our research group has recently reported thalamic dysfunction in subjects with PTSD, as have some other laboratories (Bremner, Narayan, et al., 1999a; Liberzon, Taylor, Fig, & Koeppe, 1996). Disruptions in thalamic functioning would be likely to interfere with the relay of sensory information to the limbic system and neocortex, as well as with the integration of such information. Such a process could potentially account for the ongoing experience of sensory fragments in PTSD. That is, sensory input from the lower brain structures would remain unintegrated into normal consciousness because the information cannot reach either the limbic system or neocortex in the context of thalamic dysfunction. Thoughts, emotions, and physical sensations initially pertaining to a single event would remain split into separate representations, which are not recalled as an integrated whole. Thalamic dysfunction may therefore underlie PTSD flashbacks—traumatic memories that are often experienced as timeless, vivid sensory fragments of the original experience. To further complicate the clinical picture, these dissociated memory fragments are often associated with marked emotional liability, unexplained somatic symptoms, or negative self-evaluations and self-defeating behaviors (Brewin et al., 1996; van der Kolk et al., 1996).

Thus thalamic dysfunction may be one factor accounting for the inability to integrate traumatic memories into the present context so often observed in trauma-related disorders, a phenomenon that may be related to disruptions in thalamus-mediated temporal binding. Temporal binding refers to the 40 Hz oscillations of the thalamus that results in synchronous activity of "reentrant thalamocortical loops." In other words, when mental activity is clearly present in the alert mental state, nerve cells in the thalamus oscillate at a frequency of 40 Hz. The connections of thalamic nerve cells with nerve cells in the cortex have been proposed to lead to similar frequencies of cortical nerve cell oscillations, thereby creating reentrant thalamocortical feedback loops. Temporal binding has been suggested to be "a temporally coherent event that binds, in the time domain, the fractured components of external and internal reality into a single construct . . . the 'self' " (Joliot, Ribary, & Llinas, 1994, p. 126; see also Llinas, 2001). Such a lack of temporal binding and the resulting lack of thalamocortical dialogue may be a process that accounts, among others, for flashback experiences in PTSD (Lanius, Bluhm, Lanius, & Pain, 2005). In the absence of temporal binding, then, individuals experience an inability to integrate the totality of what is happening into personal memory and identity, such that these fragments of memory remain isolated from ordinary consciousness. Such a conceptualization raises the question of whether dynamic state changes in the corticothalamic system may account for the fragmented nature of memory observed in people with PTSD and whether PTSD is a neuropsychiatric disorder that can be characterized by thalamocortical dysrhythmia (Llinas, Ribary, Contreras, & Pedroarena, 1998). If PTSD results in interference with the relay function of the thalamus, that interference could partly account for the predominantly sensory nature of the intrusive phenomena noted in trauma-related disorders: Thalamic dysfunction would disrupt the integration of sensory information by interfering with its relay to the limbic system and neocortex. That is, the upper brain structures would become temporarily disconnected from lower brain structures each time the traumatic memory is accessed, simultaneously interfering with effective bottom-up, as well as top-down, processing.

TRAUMA AND LATERALIZATION

In addition to what may appear to be a horizontal disconnection between lower and upper brain structures, neuroimaging studies in PTSD also offer evidence of differences in lateralization secondary to trauma, with increased brain activity during recall of traumatic memories in the right hemisphere and decreased brain activity in the left hemisphere. Such differential activation may be attributable to the different nature and quality of a traumatic memory (Lanius et al., 2004), and to the involvement of different neural networks implicated in the recall of memories. For example, differences in brain networks engaged in traumatic memory recall have been observed in subjects with PTSD who experienced flashbacks versus subjects without PTSD who recalled the traumatic events as ordinary autobiographical memories. These differences suggest differences in episodic memory retrieval between the two groups (Figure 7.1).

Reexperiencing traumatic events in the form of flashbacks is very different from the recall of events as ordinary autobiographical memories (Brewin et al., 1996; van der Kolk & Fisler, 1995). Flashbacks most often occur spontaneously, triggered by internal or external events, and their occurrence usually cannot be controlled. They involve a subjective distortion in time and are much more vivid than ordinary recall; the event is often experienced as though it were happening again in the present. Flashbacks are experienced as fragments of the sensory components of the event, such as visual images or olfactory, auditory, or kinesthetic sensations (van der Kolk, McFarlane, & Weisaeth, 1996) and as unchanging over time (Brewin et al., 1996)—which differs from ordinary memories, which are altered by repeated recall (Brewin et al., 1996). Overall, flashbacks are vivid sensory experiences, whereas ordinary autobiographical memories are personal narratives that describe sensory elements of the experience (Brewin et al., 1996; van der Kolk, McFarlane, & Weisaeth, 1996) and are recalled rather than reexperienced.

Our laboratory has shown that subjects who did not suffer from PTSD showed brain activation patterns consistent with verbal episodic memory retrieval (Lanius et al., 2004). Comparison of the brain networks of the PTSD subjects and the non-PTSD subjects showed that the non-PTSD subjects had greater levels of brain activation in *left* prefrontal areas, whereas the PTSD patients showed more activation in *right* posterior areas. Activation

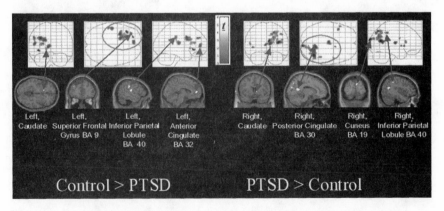

Figure 7.1. Brain regions with activation showing significantly greater connectivity/covariation with activation in the right anterior cingulate in traumatized subjects with PTSD than in traumatized subjects without PTSD during recall of a traumatic event.

of the left prefrontal areas of the brain has been proposed to play a role in more verbal forms of memory recall (Figures 7.2a and 7.2b), whereas the brain networks activated in PTSD patients showed patterns of neural activation associated with much more nonverbal patterns of memory retrieval (reviewed by Cabeza & Nyberg, 2000, 2003). These distinctly different neuronal network activations observed in PTSD versus non-PTSD subjects may help to explain the neuronal underpinnings of sensory-based, nonverbal flashback phenomena in PTSD. Based on these results, PTSD-related symptoms appear to be associated with differences in laterality, specifically right-hemispheric dominance.

The importance of lateralized responses in PTSD has been previously examined by using electroencephalography (EEG) and auditory probe-evoked potential attenuation. Schiffer, Teicher, and Papanicolaou (1995), for example, reported that subjects who had experienced early trauma displayed significant left-dominant asymmetry during neutral memory recall and relative right dominance during traumatic memory recall. In addition, psychological abuse has been shown to be associated with an increased

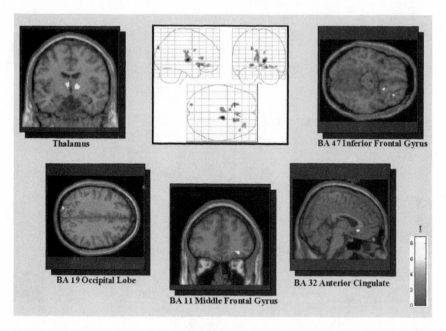

Figure 7.2a. Regions of activation during traumatic memory recall versus implicit baseline, where the comparison group (*n* = 10) shows greater activation than the flashback/reliving PTSD group (*n* = 11), k > 10.

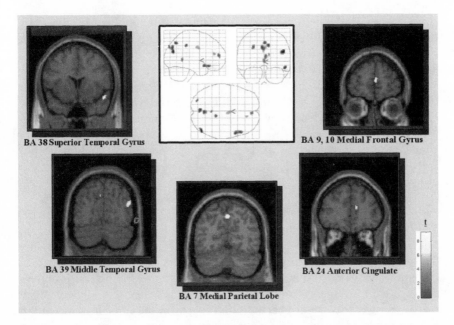

BA 38 Superior Temporal Gyrus

BA 9, 10 Medial Frontal Gyrus

BA 39 Middle Temporal Gyrus

BA 24 Anterior Cingulate

BA 7 Medial Parietal Lobe

Figure 7.2b. Regions of activation during traumatic memory recall versus implicit baseline, where the dissociated PTSD group (*n* = 10) shows greater activation than the comparison group (*n* = 10), k > 10.

prevalence of left-sided EEG abnormalities and an increased prevalence of right–left hemispheric asymmetries (Teicher, Ito, Glod, Anderson, & Ackerman, 1997). EEG coherence studies of abused versus nonabused children have also reported that abused children had greater average left-hemispheric coherence than did nonabused children but that the two groups had a comparable degree of right-hemispheric coherence. Teicher et al. (1997) suggested that these findings may be related to diminished left-hemispheric differentiation in the abused group and thus may provide evidence that childhood abuse has a significant effect on cortical development. Previous neuroimaging studies in PTSD, using the script-driven imagery symptom provocation paradigm, have also suggested lateralized responses. Using traumatic script-driven imagery, Rauch et al. (1996) found that in the traumatic condition, relative to the neutral condition, regional cerebral blood flow increases occurred in the right medial orbitofrontal cortex, insula, amygdala, and anterior temporal pole.

We have discussed what may appear to be a horizontal disconnection between lower and upper brain structures in PTSD as well as evidence supporting relative right dominance during traumatic memory recall. In treatment, the client and therapist may also be able to capitalize on the fact that the brain appears to have another alternate connection between the hemispheres, sometimes referred to as the "subcortical bridge," across which information can be exchanged (Austin, 1998). Despite the fact that the cortical structures are bifurcated into left and right hemispheres, the brain remains undivided at the level of the lower reptilian brain structures (Sperry, Zaidel, & Zaidel, 1979). Indeed, the existence of these subcortical connections may account for the fact that split-brain patients (whose corpus calossum has been severed) still behave in a unified manner during their everyday activities.

Generally, it appears that language-based information does not exchange readily across the subcortical bridge (Gazzaniga, Holtzman, & Smylie, 1987), whereas nonverbal information, including "unconscious or preconscious codes, nuances we can never attach a name to," cross most readily (Austin, 1998, p. 348). For example, the subcortical bridge can easily transmit emotionally linked subcortical messages that convey impressions of danger, sudden movements, and stimuli indicating potential violence. When these messages cross hemispheres from the right to the left side, they tend to engage a kind of "response readiness" for adaptive action, such as facilitating potential speech responses in the left hemisphere that reflect action tendencies necessary to invoke the social engagement system as a first response in ensuring survival.

Using somatic experience as an entry point in therapy and maintaining mindful awareness of the body may facilitate information processing by enhancing information transfer between the hemispheres. Traumatized clients frequently have difficulty regulating affect and arousal within the window of tolerance, and working at the body level enables fixed action tendencies to be evoked without unmanageable autonomic activation; thus "bottom-up hijacking" occurs less frequently and readily. It stands to reason that awareness of the body may also promote the exchange of somatosensory and nonverbal information between hemispheres; however, such a hypothesis is speculative at this point.

NEURAL CORRELATES OF PTSD

The study of the neural mechanisms underlying traumatic experiences was primarily a matter of conjecture until the advent of neuroimaging technology and the burgeoning interest in neuroscience research that took place in the late 1990s and early 2000s and served to transform the trauma treatment field. Neuroimaging has become an important technique in understanding the neurochemistry, as well as the functional changes, underlying various psychiatric disorders. Studies using positron emission tomography (PET) and functional magnetic resonance imaging (fMRI) in subjects with PTSD have attempted to elucidate which areas of the brain might be involved in the recall of traumatic events. The goal of these studies has been to examine regional cerebral blood flow (rCBF) changes during exposure to reminders of the traumatic event, using one of two paradigms: traumatic script-driven imagery symptom provocation, which involves remembering the traumatic memory after hearing a script of the experience, or exposure to photographs or sounds reminiscent of the traumatic experience. In addition, several studies have implemented pharmacological challenges, cognitive tasks, or emotional stimuli such as masked faces in order to examine the neuronal circuitry underlying trauma-related disorders. Using these paradigms, neuroimaging research has identified a number of brain areas that appear to be involved in traumatic stress syndromes: amygdala, medial prefrontal cortex, anterior cingulate gyrus, hippocampus, insula, and orbitofrontal cortex (Bremner, 2002; Hull, 2002; Lanius, Bluhm, Lanius, & Pain, 2006; Liberzon & Phan, 2003; Pitman, Shin, & Rauch, 2001; Tanev, 2003).

Amygdala

Located in the right and left temporal lobes, the amygdalae are considered to be part of the brain's emotional processing system (often referred to as the limbic system). The amygdala plays a profound role in fear conditioning (LeDoux, 2002) because of its function in "sounding the alarm" when a stimulus is perceived as threatening, and it may be involved in initiating sympathetic nervous system responses. Several neuroimaging studies have shown increased activation of the amygdala in PTSD (Bremner, 2002; Hull, 2002; Lanius, Bluhm, Lanius, & Pain, 2006; Liberzon & Phan, 2003; Pitman et al., 2001; Tanev, 2003). It has been suggested that an overactive amygdala in PTSD may result in generalization of the fear response, leading to an overall increase in fearful behavior.

However, the finding of increased amygdala activation in PTSD has not always been consistent. For instance, Lanius's findings, in script-driven symptom provocation studies with multiply traumatized individuals, suggest a lack of amygdala activation during traumatic recall (reviewed in Lanius, Bluhm, Lanius, & Pain, 2006). Similarly, Britton, Phan, Taylor, Fig, and Liberzon (2005) and Bremner (Bremner, Narayan, et al., 1999; Bremner, Staib, et al., 1999) have also observed a lack of amygdala activation during recall of traumatic events in PTSD subjects. Indeed, Perry et al. (1995) suggest that some traumatized individuals may develop "limbic irritability," with a tendency toward overactive amygdala responses to traumatic stimuli, whereas others may develop a propensity toward hypoactive amygdala responses. In support of this hypothesis, Chugani et al. (2001) reported an association between a history of neglect and a lack of amygdala activation.

The hypothesis that a lack of amygdala activation may indeed be adaptive under certain circumstances is born out by the animal literature, which suggests that a lack of amygdala activation may allow continued functioning in situations characterized by ongoing threat. For instance, it was observed that, when a rat intruded into another rat's territory and was defeated by that occupant, it remained quiet and frozen in a corner, not leaving, approaching, or challenging the victorious rat (Austin, 1998). Note the similarity with the immobilizing defenses described in Chapter 5 and the loss of ability to explore observed in human beings under threat conditions. Just like the child in a traumatogenic environment, who must adapt to a threat occurring in a context in which caregivers have dominance, the rat relies on the immobilizing defenses of avoidance, freeze, and submission to facilitate survival and adaptation in another rat's territory. In behavior that may resemble that of children with disorganized attachment, the rat maintains proximity to its cage-mate but uses autoregulatory, immobilizing strategies to avoid danger and increase safety. In contrast, rats whose corticomedial amygdala has been lesioned behave strikingly different after they have been defeated by another rat: They move freely about their cage and thrust out their muzzles, sniffing incautiously toward the victorious rat. These rats "seem oblivious of the proprieties, of their expected social boundaries. They have not learned their lesson" (Austin, 1998, p. 176). Monkeys have also been shown to become "strikingly fearless" after destruction of their amydalae; they have been described as "so naïve, that they will approach and handle a snake!" No normal monkey comes near a snake (Austin, 1998; Horel, Keating, & Misantone, 1975).

These animal behaviors bear striking resemblance to some of the behaviors often observable clinically in individuals with chronic trauma histories and may explain such phenomena as traumatic reenactments or the Stockholm syndrome. It is not uncommon for clients with chronic trauma histories to continue seeking abusive relationships without being aware of the dangers involved in such relationships. Future research therefore needs to address the clinical implications of altered amygdala activation.

Medial Prefrontal Cortex

The medial prefrontal cortex is considered part of the cognitive processing system and has been hypothesized to play a role in the extinction of conditioned fear responses (Morgan, Romanski, & LeDoux, 1993). By exerting inhibitory influences over the limbic system, including the amygdala, the medial prefrontal cortex thereby regulates the generalization of fear and overall increase in fearful behavior mediated by the amygdala. For example, PET studies have shown negative correlations between blood flow in the left prefrontal cortex and the amygdala (reviewed in Lanius, Bluhm, Lanius, & Pain, 2006; Pitman et al., 2001).

Medial prefrontal cortex dysfunction has been consistently described in the majority of PTSD neuroimaging studies and has been hypothesized to be associated with attentional and frontal deficits sometimes associated with a quasi dementia-like syndrome in PTSD (Markowitsch et al., 2000). The medial prefrontal cortex has also been shown to suppress the stress response mediated by the hypothalamic–pituitary–adrenal axis and thus plays a role in the regulation of cortisol, the stress hormone (reviewed in Lanius, Bluhm, Lanius, & Pain, 2006). Finally, a role of the medial prefrontal cortex in emotion regulation has been identified (Lane & McRae, 2004).

In addition, this region is thought to play an important role in the retrieval of episodic memory (Tulving, Kapur, Craik, Moscovitch, & Houle, 1994) and may also be involved in the temporal segregation of memories (Schnider, Ptak, von Daniken, & Remonda, 2000). The brain function of temporal segregation ensures that "currently relevant memories can be differentiated from memories that may have been relevant once but are no longer" (Moscovitch & Winocur, 2002, p. 187). Thus, altered levels of medial prefrontal cortex activation may be partly responsible for the "timeless" nature of the traumatic memories experienced by many PTSD patients.

Neuroimaging studies have also investigated the neural correlates of self-referential processing and have identified a network of brain regions, including the medial prefrontal cortex (Johns, Baxter, et al., 2002). This self-referential function is particularly relevant to the aspects of sensorimotor therapy that focus on awareness of present experience; for example, when the client is asked to mindfully track (a top-down, cognitive process) the physical sensations and impulses (sensorimotor process) as they progress through the body, and to temporarily disregard emotions and thoughts that arise, until the bodily sensations and impulses resolve to a point of rest and stabilization in the body. Generally, mindfulness (the ability to self-witness or to employ "observing ego") is thought to engage the medial prefrontal cortex.

Anterior Cingulate Gyrus

The anterior cingulate gyrus is a complex structure with multiple functions; it has been shown to play a key role in the representation of subjective experience, in the integration of bodily responses with behavioral demands (Vogt & Gabriel, 1993), and in emotional awareness. Lane, Fink, Chau, and Dolan (1997) have reported positive correlations between scores on the

Levels of Emotional Awareness Scale and cerebral blood flow in BA 24 of the anterior cingulate gyrus during film- and recall-induced emotion. These results indicate that the anterior cingulate cortex may also play a role in the experiential aspects of emotion as well as in the integration of emotion and cognition.

Animal research (Vogt, 2005) has suggested that the anterior cingulate gyrus has extensive connections with multiple brain structures, including the amygdala, hypothalamus, nucleus accumbens, ventral tegmental area, substantia nigra, raphe, locus coeruleus, periaqueductal grey, and brainstem autonomic nuclei. The anterior cingulate gyrus is thus part of a system that orchestrates the autonomic, neuroendocrine, and behavioral expression of emotion and may play a key role in the visceral aspects of emotion (reviewed in Lanius, Bluhm, Lanius, & Pain, 2006). On the basis of the key involvement of the anterior cingulate gyrus in the regulation of the autonomic as well as the experiential and/or expressive aspects of emotion, it is possible that disruption in its functioning, as observed in PTSD, may provide a neural basis of emotion dysregulation, including extremes of reexperiencing and avoidance of emotionally distressing memories, as well as generalized problems with physiological hyperarousal and emotional numbing. In addition to these functions, the anterior cingulate gyrus also plays significant roles in other responses crucial to preventing or surviving trauma, including pain, response selection, maternal behavior, vocalization, and skeletomotor control.

It is interesting to note that psychological trauma, including attachment trauma, in the first through third quarters of the first year of life has been observed to negatively impact the experience-dependent maturation of the anterior cingulate limbic circuits (Schore, 2001). Because the functions of the anterior cingulate gyrus are crucial to the optimal engagement of a number of action systems, its experience-dependent maturation may increase the likelihood that the action systems of daily life will be negatively impacted as a result of chronic childhood trauma and neglect. For example, the action system of exploration depends upon attentional focusing, response selection, autonomic regulation, and skeletomotor movement. The social engagement system also requires movement and response selection, along with vocalization. Thus both of these important systems, upon which other systems are dependent for their optimal development, may be compromised in the context of altered anterior cingulate development.

Helping clients to voluntarily orient and focus attention, as well as address cognitive, emotional, and sensorimotor elements, may help to optimize anterior cingulate functioning. Additionally, the use of movement may normalize anterior cingulate activation by evoking skeletomotor responses that would previously have been inhibited by trauma-related tendencies.

Lisa, who reported that she wanted to "get away" but froze during child-hood sexual abuse, repeated the tendency to freeze during subsequent unwanted sexual encounters. When working with the traumatic memory in therapy, she reported a freezing sensation but also the impulse to run. Her therapist asked her to stand and walk around the office, feeling the capac-ity of her legs to move—action that Lisa experienced as empowering. In this way, the motor responses (movement in her legs) were executed when she experienced a freezing sensation, whereas these responses were previ-ously inhibited by the trauma-dominated tendency. It should be noted, how-ever, that the hypothesis that such action may affect anterior cingulate func-tioning is highly speculative and warrants further research.

Hippocampus

The hippocampus, most commonly associated with memory function, is part of the temporal lobe and receives inputs from, and sends efferents to, both the amygdala and the cortex. The hippocampus plays an important role in declarative memory and may thus be involved in mediating learned responses to a constellation of cues. Furthermore, preclinical studies demon-strate death of hippocampal neurons and hippocampal shrinkage after expo-sure of animals to chronic stress. This reaction may be mediated, in part, by cortisol through action on hippocampal glucocorticoid receptors (Charney et al., 1993).

Given the multitude of trauma effects that include both vivid reexperi-encing of traumatic memories as well as amnesia, it is not surprising that the hippocampus has been implicated in traumatic stress syndromes. A num-ber of studies has demonstrated hippocampal involvement in PTSD (reviewed by Geuze in Bremner, Vermetten, Afzal, & Vythilingam, 2004; Geuze, Vermetten, & Bremner, 2005; Shin et al., 2004).

Magnetic resonance imaging (MRI) studies have also shown that both male combat veterans and women survivors of childhood sexual abuse with PTSD have shrunken hippocampal volumes (reviewed in Geuze et al., 2005). In some of these studies, decreased hippocampal volume correlated with trauma exposure or memory deficit. It is believed that this reaction is related to the effects of cortisol on hippocampal glucocorticoid receptors, leading to cell degeneration. At the same time, it should be noted that some researchers have also argued that small hippocampal volumes may not be a *result* of chronic stress exposure but rather represent a *preexisting risk fac-tor* for the development of PTSD (reviwed in Gueze et al., 2005).

Whether a preexisting condition or the result of traumatic exposure, or both, there are some beginning suggestions that, given the ability of the hip-pocampus to generate new cells, reduced hippocampal volume may be reversible through treatment. In one study hippocampal shrinkage was reversed through administration of the antidepressant paroxetine (reviewed in Geuze et al., 2005).

Insula

In previous chapters we have shown that traumatic experiences affect all three levels of information processing. Not only do autonomic responses drive habitual tendencies, but trauma-related cognitive distortions, perception, and emotion also play a role in perpetuating procedural learning once adaptive for traumatic situations. The insula, located within the cerebral cortex, "appears to be preferentially involved in the emotional response to potentially distressing cognitive stimuli, interoceptive sensory stimuli, and body sensations" (Reiman, Lane, Ahern, Schwartz, & Davidson, 2000, p. 399). Thus the insula plays a role in all three levels of information processing: It (1) mediates responses to cognitive stimuli; (2) plays a key role in body perception (interoception); and (3) it also affects perception of emotions. In fact, Craig (2003) hypothesized that the insula of the nondominant (right) hemisphere provides a neuronal basis for the subjective evaluation of one's condition, that is, for knowing "how one feels." The insula has also been shown to receive signals related to pain states, body temperature, and visceral sensations, as well as signals regarding the state of the smooth musculature in blood vessels and other viscera (described in Craig, 2003). Reiman et al. (2000) hypothesized that the insula may play a role in the evaluation of potentially distressing body sensations for emotional content and, in that role, may serve as an "internal alarm center" (Nijenhuis et al., 2002, p. 19) via its input–output relationship with the amygdala.

Damasio (1999) has also emphasized the role of the insula and the somatosensory cortices in processing signals regarding bodily state, suggesting that these signals form the basis for human emotions. In a PET study investigating brain activity during self-generated emotion, Damasio et al. (2000) found insula activation across a range of emotions. Bilateral activation of the insula was observed to be associated with recall of memories that caused feelings of sadness and anger, whereas right hemispheric activation was observed in the context of happiness and fear. Similar findings have been reported in conjunction with recall of traumatic memories: Rauch et al.'s 1996 study of subjects with PTSD demonstrated increased metabolism in the right insula when subjects were exposed to trauma memory scripts and became autonomically aroused. In a brain-imaging study comparing individuals with and without PTSD, Lanius, Bluhm et al. (2006) observed activation of different neuronal networks involving the insula in subjects with PTSD who experienced a dissociative response to the recall of traumatic memories, as compared to subjects who were not suffering from PTSD. Patients with PTSD in this study reported feeling removed from their own bodies as well as from the emotional content of the traumatic memory. This research has important implications for treatment: As traumatized clients learn to slowly increase awareness of body sensation, movement, and impulses and to tolerate sensation and emotional arousal, changes in activation of the insula and medial prefrontal cortex may take place, thus increasing their ability for self-referential processing of bodily states and emotions. Clinically, we have observed that this ability to mindfully observe present-moment internal experience, in most instances, allows for down-regulation of defensive action systems and increased engagement of action systems related to daily life, especially the attachment, exploration, and sociability systems.

Orbitofrontal Cortex

In the field of neuroscience, particularly in research related to trauma and/or attachment, the role of the orbitofrontal cortex has stimulated increasing interest. The orbitofrontal cortex is the part of the frontal lobe that lies just above the orbit of the eyes, in a position that facilitates direct inputs from a number of adjoining cortical and subcortical brain areas: the dorsomedial thalamus, temporal cortex, ventral tegmental area, olfactory system, and the amygdala. Its outputs also extend to both cortical and subcortical brain regions, including the cingulate cortex, hippocampal formation, temporal cortex, lateral hypothalamus, and amygdala. Its complex system of inputs provide the orbitofrontal cortex with a wealth of information about what is happening in the environment and what plans are being organized by other cortical areas. In turn, its communication outputs affect a variety of behaviors and physiological responses, including emotional and autonomic responses organized by the amygdala. The orbitofrontal cortex also plays a role in mediating autonomic and behavioral responses via its connections with the cingulate cortex. In sum, the orbitofrontal cortex is uniquely situated to mediate communication between subcortical and cortical systems.

The orbitofrontal system may also be involved in "the regulation of the body state and in the reflection of changes in that state" (Luria, 1980, p. 262; Schore, 2003a) and thus may play an important role in the regulation of arousal within the window of tolerance. In its function as part of the attachment action system, the orbitofrontal cortex is believed to enable cortically processed information concerning the environment (e.g., visual and auditory stimuli emanating from a facial expression) to be integrated with subcortically processed information in the internal visceral environment, thus facilitating the association of incoming information from the external environment with motivational and emotional states. In the mother–infant dyadic interaction, these experiences, in which the perception of facial expression is integrated with the sensations associated with optimal body states, become the basis for secure attachment and, in turn, facilitate the optimal development of the orbitofrontal cortex (Schore, 2003a).

It has been suggested that abuse and/or neglect over the first 2 years of life negatively impacts the maturation of the orbital prefrontolimbic system (Schore, 1994, 2003a, 2003b). Different theorists propose different mechanisms of action for this process. Martin, Spicer, Lewis, Gluck, and Cork (1991) suggested that in early postnatal life, maintaining critical levels of tactile input of specific quality and emotional content is important for normal brain maturation, whereas Greenough and Black (1992) proposed that multiple sensory inputs, derived from contact with the mother during feeding/ nursing, are crucial in shaping the development of the orbitofrontal cortex. Schore (2003a) argued that sensory inputs are just one aspect of a larger process of dyadic regulation of arousal and affect, within the context of secure attachment, that contributes to optimal synaptic pruning:

> The early social environment, mediated by the primary caregiver, *directly influences* the final wiring of the circuits in the infant brain that are responsible for the future social and emotional coping capacities of the individual. The ultimate product of this social–emotional development is a particular system in the [orbitofrontal cortex] of the right brain that is dominant for the unconscious processing of socioemotional information, the regulation of bodily states, the capacity to cope with emotional stress, and the corporeal and emotional self. (p. 219)

Thus the orbitofrontal cortex is thought to play a central role in capacities that contribute to the expansion of self-regulatory ability, sophistication of the social engagement system, development of the attachment system, and as a result, maturation of the exploration system. An interference in development or activation of this part of the brain may therefore contribute to the autonomic, emotional, and cognitive dysregulation observed in our traumatized clients.

EMOTION AND THE IMPORTANCE OF SUBCORTICAL PROCESSES

Panksepp (1998) and Damasio et al. (2000) have cogently argued that affect is largely a subcortical process. In a brain-imaging study of the phenomenology of emotion, subjects were asked to narrate personal reminiscences that evoked deep, existentially experienced feeling states of anger, fear, sadness, and happiness (Damasio et al., 2000). When subjects were judged by investigators to be experiencing those feelings, radioactive water was infused to obtain PET-scan images. The results demonstrated markedly increased arousal in subcortical brain regions, accompanied by substantial reductions of blood flow in many higher brain areas, suggesting a decrease in information processing in neocortical systems during intense emotional states along with an increase in subcortical activity. Specifically with regard to traumatic stress syndromes, Pissiota et al. (2002) suggested that traumatic symptom provocation in PTSD is associated with an emotionally determined motor preparatory response that may be subcortically initiated rather than cortically controlled.

Trauma treatment techniques that focus on increasing emotional arousal run the risk of escalating subcortically mediated autonomic activation, thus leading to hyper- or hypoarousal. In sensorimotor psychotherapy, integrative capacity is facilitated by separately attending to each level of information processing and tracking signs of dysregulation that could impede integration. By increasing mindfulness and focusing exclusively on body sensation, clients work first with the sensate precursors to emotion and are often able to expand their window of tolerance. As the window of tolerance increases, clients are often gradually able to reestablish integrative emotional and cognitive processing. That is, the initial focus on sensation, in the absence of accessing the full range of the traumatic experience, may paradoxically facilitate more integrated brain functioning and help to ensure that clients do not suffer the discomfort of activation with little integration or transformation of that distress.

THE HETEROGENEITY RESPONSE
TO TRAUMATIC REMINDERS

In trauma-related disorders fragments of traumatic memory take on a life of their own, able to intrude at any moment, thereby fueling hyper- and hypoarousal responses that are beyond cognitive control. In the context of trauma-related dysregulation, emotional experiences, which also activate the amygdala and insula, can become so overwhelming that the individual is further challenged to maintain arousal within the window of tolerance.

The preponderance of neuroimaging research has shown that subjects experiencing flashback/reliving responses when asked to recall a traumatic memory exhibit brain activity that is strikingly different from those who do not have PTSD and who can recall their traumatic memory as a memory of the past, a normal autobiographical memory (Lanius, Bluhm, et al., 2006). PTSD subjects typically demonstrate brain connection patterns that are consistent with a nonverbal pattern of memory recall (i.e., activation of the occipital lobes, right parietal lobe, and posterior cingulate gyrus), as compared to control subjects who activate neural networks more consistent with verbal patterns of memory retrieval (i.e., left prefrontal cortex and anterior cingulate) (Figure 7.3). These neuroimaging findings are consistent with what we often observe clinically: PTSD patients experience their traumatic memories as timeless, intrusive, sensory fragments that often cannot be expressed as a narrative, whereas people who have suffered a trauma but do not suffer from PTSD usually recall traumatic memories as an integrated whole that can easily be expressed as a narrative. This observation calls into question the benefit of purely verbal therapies as modalities for processing information that is experienced primarily at a sensory level and suggests the need to explore body-centered methods. Sensorimotor psychotherapy engages clients in the processing of such sensory fragments by encouraging careful tracking of sensations associated with the traumatic memories until such sensations are no longer fragmented and can be experienced as an integrated whole. Because the fragmentation of memory occurs on all three levels of information processing, the sensorimotor psychotherapist is alert to all the building blocks of present experience: cognitions, emotions, perceptual and sensory input, inner body sensations, and movement or movement impulses. For

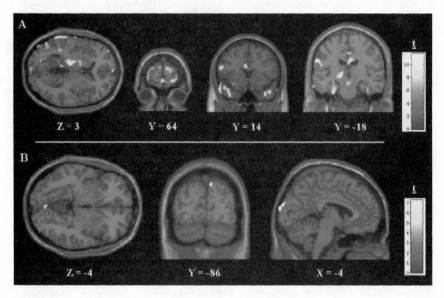

Figure 7.3. Regions of significantly increased brain activation during the traumatic memory recall. A = Male; B = Female.

example, fragmented sensory experiences can be associated with the urge to engage in certain movements, particularly movements in which the individual was not able to engage or which could not be completed as a result of the traumatic experience.

A woman abused in the context of domestic violence might have wanted to push away her abusive partner but instinctively relied on immobilizing defenses in a situation from which there was no immediate escape or hope of successful self-defense. As she and the therapist observe what happens in her body as she recalls being trapped with her enraged partner, she may find herself experiencing a particular sensory fragment associated with the urge to *push away*, such as a tightening in her jaw or upper arm or the curling of her hand into a fist. In a sensorimotor psychotherapy session, the client would be supported in studying the action tendency of the mobilizing defense until she could complete the movement of pushing away and reinstate a somatic sense of self reinforced by the ability to defend and protect the body. With the completion of the mobilizing defensive action, the sensory fragments related to both the immobilizing and mobilizing responses can be integrated; emotions such as elation or triumph can be tolerated; and cognitive meaning making can emerge, such as a new belief "I can protect myself now," to counter the physical experience of being overpowered. We would speculate that, in this type of body-oriented processing, the brain activation pattern associated with the recall of memory would become modified from a predominantly right, posterior activation pattern to a more left, prefrontal pattern.

Most symptom provocation studies have focused attention on patients who experience a hyperarousal/reliving response (reviewed in Lanius, Bluhm, et al., 2006). More recently, however, our laboratory has also begun to study a group of trauma patients with dissociative response patterns, to compare their brain activity in response to symptom provocation with that of the hyperarousal/reliving group. For example, Lanius et al. (2002) found that a small but significant percentage of patients responded to traumatic cues by showing classic symptoms of dissociation sometimes coupled with autonomic hypoarousal. In response to script-driven imagery provocation of traumatic memory, these patients reported feelings of numbness, of leaving their body, or of experiencing the traumatic memory "at a distance." Moreover, this subjective pattern of response to script-driven imagery was associated with patterns of brain activation distinctly different from those associated with the flashback/reliving response (see Figures 7.2a and 7.2b).

Sensorimotor-informed techniques can be equally effective with clients who demonstrate primarily dissociative responses to traumatic reminders. In the context of dissociative responses that can be coupled with hypoarousal, the goal of psychotherapy becomes to increase somatic awareness as a vehicle for bringing arousal into the window of tolerance; for example, teaching clients to slowly track the physical sensations connected to the numbing or depersonalization symptoms. Becoming mindfully aware of such sensations and feelings, heightening curiosity about how they are organized in the body, may lead to increased activation of higher brain areas, such as the prefrontal cortex, and thereby increase clients' ability to maintain optimal arousal and orient adaptively to both external and internal environments. Utilizing somatic resources that counteract numbing (such as movement, standing in a grounded, supported posture, or lengthening the spine) can also increase integrative capacity in the face of automatic tendencies toward dissociation or hypoarousal.

HETEROGENEITY OF RESPONSE: A CASE EXAMPLE

To appreciate the different challenges created by different action tendencies and activation patterns, we describe the case of a husband and wife who shared in the same traumatic event and evidenced two very different response strategies. In these two cases Lanius, Hopper, and Menon (2003) observed widely different subjective, heart rate, brain activation responses to traumatic script-driven imagery. The husband and wife were traveling together when they were involved in a serious motor vehicle accident—an accident that affected over 100 vehicles and caused multiple deaths and serious injuries. After crashing into the car in front of them, both subjects were trapped for several minutes, during which they witnessed a child in a nearby car burn to death and feared that they too would die. Neither sustained physical injuries.

Both subjects were assessed 4 weeks after the accident. The husband, a 48-year-old professional, reported having been completely healthy until the accident. During the accident, he recalled feeling extremely aroused and then becoming actively involved, both cognitively and behaviorally, in rescuing himself and his wife, ultimately breaking the windshield to allow their escape. The next day, however, he began experiencing flashbacks and nightmares, and these reexperiencing symptoms often included feeling as if the accident were recurring. He also became psychologically and physiologically hyperaroused when thinking or talking about the accident. Subsequently, he avoided driving on the highway where the accident had occurred, as well as avoiding thoughts and conversations about it. His sleep was very poor and his concentration severely impaired, rendering him unable to function at work. Other hyperarousal symptoms included irritability and startle reactions. He reported no complicating factors: no past or present substance abuse, past psychiatric history or current medical problems, no prescribed medications, and no family psychiatric history. He described his childhood as uneventful, stated that he had a good relationship with his parents, and reported no history of neglect or emotional, physical, or sexual abuse. He was sociable as a child and adolescent, completed an undergraduate accounting degree, and has since worked as an accountant.

His wife, a 55-year-old professional, was also healthy until the traumatic event. She described being "in shock" during the accident and, though trapped but not pinned in the car, reported, "I could hardly move because I was completely frozen." It was her husband's action of breaking the windshield and pulling her from the car that allowed their escape from the vehicle. Like her husband, she began experiencing flashbacks and nightmares the following day, often feeling "numb and frozen," as if the event were recurring. She avoided driving or reading newspaper stories about the accident. Her sleep was extremely poor, her concentration significantly impaired, and she was highly irritable and easily angered. Worst of all, her work functioning was completely impaired (she sold her business several months after the accident). She denied any past or present substance abuse but reported a postpartum depression after the birth of her first child and a past history of mild panic disorder. She had no medical problems and was not taking any medications. She reported no family psychiatric history but described her childhood as quite "traumatic." That is, though she denied any history of physical or sexual abuse, she reported that her father had died when she was 9 years old, leaving her to be raised by a mother described as a very "cold" and "distant" woman with whom she did not feel safe. Nonetheless, she was sociable while growing up, and her school performance was above average. She graduated from business school and had run a business for several years before the accident.

In response to script-driven imagery of the accident, the husband reported a vivid memory that included thoughts about how to escape, the physical urge to break the windshield, and feeling very anxious and "jumpy." His heart rate increased 13 beats per minute from baseline, and this experience corresponded with brain activation of areas that include the prefrontal cortex and the amygdala (see Figure 7.3). Planning how to get himself and his wife out of the car may have led to activation of the prefrontal cortex to mediate the functions of planning and problem solving. Activation of the amygdala in response to the script-driven imagery may have contributed to his hyperarousal symptoms (feeling "anxious and jumpy"), as well as his symptoms of PTSD, given the key role of the amygdala in both fear conditioning and PTSD.

In marked contrast, but consistent with her original peritraumatic response, the woman reported feeling extremely "numb" and "frozen" while recalling the traumatic memory, and her heart rate did not change from baseline. Increases in brain activation were found only in occipital regions, the brain areas involved with the processing of visual information, and may be a mechanism underlying the vivid visual images of the accident reported by the client during the brain-imaging procedure (see Figure 7.3).

In terms of subjective experiences, heart rate responses, and patterns of neural activation, these two survivors of the same traumatic event exhibited two distinct yet internally coherent peritraumatic and subsequent pathological responses to traumatic reminders. The husband's reports of cognitive and behavioral activation, along with physiological arousal, were consistent with the increases in activation observed in heart rate and in the prefrontal cortex and amygdala. In contrast, the wife's "numb" and "frozen" tendency, lack of heart rate increase, and very different pattern of neural activations, *despite having a severe case of acute and subsequent PTSD,* attest to the fact that hypoarousal responses are equally a reaction to trauma, and that the common denominator in trauma may be *autonomic dysregulation outside of the window of tolerance.*

CONCLUSION

Sensorimotor psychotherapy was developed entirely from clinical practice, and at this point in time the mechanisms underlying its interventions are unknown. These mechanisms will be an exciting area to explore in the future. However, anecdotal reports from both clients and therapists attest to the efficacy of utilizing somatic interventions. Professionals who have learned sensorimotor psychotherapy report that clients often experience a reduction in symptoms such as nightmares, panic attacks, aggressive outbursts, and general hyperarousal, and that the new ability to track body sensations helps clients experience present reality rather than reacting as if the trauma were still occurring. Sensorimotor psychotherapy provides clients with tools to deal with disturbing bodily reactions. They frequently report feeling increasingly able to remain present in the here-and-now as they begin to learn how to limit the amount of information they must process at any given moment by focusing their attention on movement and sensation. Clients also report that their feeling of safety is enhanced when they practice protective and defensive actions such as pushing away.

Sensorimotor psychotherapy techniques may facilitate the integration of traumatic material sequestered in subcortical or right brain areas by working bottom-up, deepening mindfulness (which may increase cortical activity), evoking and studying trauma-related fixed action tendencies, and then experimenting with the practice of new actions. Because of its emphasis on regulating arousal and expanding the window of tolerance, sensorimotor psychotherapy attempts to avoid excessive autonomic or emotional arousal that might interfere with the integration of information. The pronounced focus on the body often facilitates the experience of emotion within a window of tolerance. When the client is encouraged to track even minimal physiological sensations and movements, mindfulness of present-moment experience is enhanced. Orienting to the here-and-now, the body, and the self may increase prefrontal and medial prefrontal activity, which may mediate perceptions that the traumatic event is not occurring in present time. By allocating attention to both traumatic activation and somatic resources, tracking and modulating levels of arousal in response to internal and external stimuli, and teaching new, more adaptive actions, improved functioning and integrative capacity of both brain and body are facilitated. This improvement enables the traumatic events to be processed and a renewed experience of self to emerge.

However, accessing too much sensation too quickly, particularly before clients are able to observe their experience and put aside content and emotional states, may actually increase dissociation and exacerbate symptoms. Therefore, therapists must proceed in accordance with each client's pace and ability to integrate. Additionally, therapists using sensorimotor psychotherapy report that some clients are not interested in working with the body. Over time, such clients may slowly and painstakingly learn to be aware of their somatic experience and find value in that awareness. An occasional client may remain unable or unwilling to work with somatic interventions, finding body sensations and movements too overwhelming and distressing, or otherwise finding a somatic approach uninteresting, unappealing, or ineffective. In such cases, sensorimotor psychotherapy is contraindicated, and the therapist must employ other techniques.

Along with understanding the particular needs and capacities of our clients, awareness of the brain regions and systems involved in both top-down and bottom-up processing can contribute to our ability to select optimal approaches and techniques to help traumatized clients achieve mastery over symptoms and satisfaction in daily life pursuits. In this chapter we have given an overview of brain areas hypothesized or known to be implicated in trauma-related disorders with the aim of expanding understanding of the role of the brain in trauma-related disorders and providing food for thought in working toward a neurobiologically informed treatment model.

Part II

Treatment

Chapter 8

✕•✕✕

Principles of Treatment: Putting Theory into Practice

AS WE HAVE REVIEWED IN PREVIOUS CHAPTERS, important components of traumatic events are encoded and processed at a subcortical level. Past, present, and future are not differentiated, and aspects of previous traumatic experience are confused with current reality. The client's attempts to recall or acknowledge traumatic events may precipitate "remembering" in the form of physical sensations, autonomic responses, and involuntary movements. Terror, dread, helplessness, and hopelessness are fueled by these somatic reactions. Trauma-related cognitive distortions feel confirmed again and again: "The world is dangerous. I will never be safe." Effective information processing on cognitive, emotional, and sensorimotor levels is profoundly hampered.

In the face of posttraumatic flooding, despair, self-loathing, and autonomic dysregulation, all therapists try to assist clients in becoming more stable physiologically, emotionally, and functionally. Most therapists agree that sooner or later, once stability is achieved, most patients need to confront their traumatic experience directly in order to experience closure (Cloitre, Koenen, Cohen, & Han, 2002; Gold, 1998). Most therapeutic approaches help clients find words to describe the fearful experiences they have undergone, understand why these experiences remain so uncomfortably registered in their inner landscape, and develop new mental and physical actions that

165

are adaptive to current reality. By including the body as a primary avenue in processing trauma, therapists can work directly with sensation and movement to affect symptoms and promote change in the clients' cognitions, emotions, belief systems, and capacity for relatedness (Aposhyan, 2004; Bakal, 1999; Kepner, 1987, 1995; Kurtz, 1990, personal communication, August 14, 2005; Kurtz & Prestera, 1976; Levine, 1997; Ogden & Minton, 2000; Rothschild, 2000). This chapter describes basic therapeutic principles for the synthesis of somatic techniques with traditional top-down cognitive approaches that not only alleviate symptoms and resolve the traumatic past but also help clients experience a reorganized sense of self.

TOP-DOWN AND BOTTOM-UP INTERVENTIONS

As clients learn to observe, curiously and nonjudgmentally, their habitual action tendencies emerging in the therapy session, it becomes possible to experiment with developing new, more adaptive tendencies. The techniques involved in helping clients to effect this change require thoughtful differentiation and integration of top-down and bottom-up therapeutic approaches.

Top-down cortically mediated techniques typically use cognition to regulate affect and sensorimotor experience, focusing on meaning making and understanding. The entry point is the story, and the formulation of a coherent narrative is of prime importance. A linguistic sense of self is fostered in this process, and experience changes through understanding. In bottom-up approaches, the body's sensation and movement are the entry points, and changes in sensorimotor experience are used to support self-regulation, memory processing, and success in daily life. Meaning and understanding emerge from new experiences rather than the other way around. Through bottom-up interventions, a shift in the somatic sense of self in turn affects the linguistic sense of self. Sensorimotor psychotherapy blends these bottom-up interventions, which directly address movement, sensory experience, and body sensation, with top-down cognitive approaches and verbal dialogue.

Top-down interventions are employed to *observe and support* sensorimotor processing: Clients learn to mindfully track (a top-down cognitive process) the interplay of physical sensations, movements, and impulses (sensorimotor processes) and to notice their internal reactions to "experimental trials" of new physical actions. Integrating bottom-up and top-down interventions requires the client to prioritize sensory and motor experiences and observe their interplay with emotional and cognitive levels of information processing. Clients learn to notice how thought and emotion affect the body and also how different physical sensations and movements affect upper levels of information processing. By using the body (rather than only cognition or emotion) as a primary entry point and avenue of exploration of traumatic experience, the effects of trauma on the body and on procedural learning are addressed directly.

In a session, a topic or "story" discussed in ordinary conversation is the verbal introduction to the piece of work to be done. As the client narrates the experience or describes the issue, the therapist observes his or her present-moment organization of experience—body language, emotions, thoughts, movements—for "indicators" (Kurtz, 2004) of trauma-related tendencies. This careful observation of how the client is organizing internal experience when talking about past trauma or current issues directs the choice of which particular element of present experience should become the entry point to deeper exploration.

Even in this early stage of a session, the trauma-related tendencies are challenged by the mindful focus on each component, by the slowed pace and shifted concentration from "talking about" to observing what is occurring in the client's internal experience as he or she is talking. The therapist evokes the client's curiosity and mindfulness of the building blocks of present experience by querying him or her about emerging thoughts, emotions, exteroceptive information (five senses), interoceptive information (body sensation), and movement.

THE PRESENT MOMENT

Although most psychotherapeutic approaches "agree that therapeutic work in the 'here and how' has the greatest power in bringing about change" (Stern, 2004, p. 3), talk therapy has limited direct impact on maladaptive procedural action tendencies as they occur in the present moment. Although telling "the story" provides crucial information about the client's past and current life experience, treatment must address the *here-and-now experience* of the traumatic past, rather than its content or narrative, in order to challenge and transform procedural learning. Because the physical and mental tendencies of procedural learning manifest in present-moment time, in-the-moment trauma-related emotional reactions, thoughts, images, body sensations, and movements that emerge spontaneously in the therapy hour become the focal points of exploration and change.

Although traditionally trained psychotherapists are accustomed to working with a broad brush, attending to verbal accounts of past experiences or portions of experiences, working in the moment requires a narrower focus on "the felt experience of what happens during a short stretch of consciousness" (Stern, 2004, p. 32). The focus of therapeutic interventions shifts from ordinary conversation about the client's traumatic past or present difficulties to what is occurring in the client's behavior and internal experience, moment by moment (Chefetz, 2000). Kurtz (1990) notes:

> The client's present experience [body sensations, movement, sensory perceptions, emotions, cognitions] is a vivid example of how all experiences are organized and is an opportunity to study how and why experience gets organized in just that way. [Present] experiences are grist for the mill and studying them is very different from talking about them or getting caught up in them. (p. 11)

In therapy, when significant events occur or when the client is describing a significant past event, working in the present moment allows therapist and client to collaboratively discover the action tendencies and procedural responses that accompany these narratives. This present-moment organization of experience is unpredictable in its unfolding: "Each small world of a present moment is unique. It is determined by the local conditions of time, space, past experience, and the particularities of constantly shifting conditions in which it takes its form. Thus, it is not knowable in advance" (Stern, 2004, p. 38–39). The "self study" of the present moment (Kurtz, 1990) leads to increased knowledge and understanding of physical and mental action tendencies and to a wider repertoire of choices regarding changing them.

Engaging Exploration: Mindfulness of Present Moment Organization of Experience

As noted in Chapter 6, the exploration system "drives and energizes many mental complexities that humans experience as persistent feelings of interest [and] curiosity . . . (Panksepp, 1998, p. 145). Stimulating the client's exploration system in the service of becoming curious about action tendencies manifesting in the present moment is essential to effect change in procedural tendencies. For example, as a client discusses her traumatic motor vehicle accident in therapy, her therapist asks her to become interested in how she is organizing the experience—what is happening inside—in her thoughts, emotions, sensations, and movements, as she begins to talk, or even to think, about her accident:

> [Therapist and client] study what is going on, not as disease or something to be rid of, but in an effort to help the client become conscious of how experience is managed and how the capacity for experience can be expanded. The whole endeavor is more fun and play rather than work and it is motivated by curiosity, rather than fear. (Kurtz, 1990, p. 111)

✳️Through mindfulness of present-moment organization of experience, the client shifts from being caught up in the story and upset about her reactions to becoming curious about them (Siegel, 2007). She notices that as she talks about the accident, she has the thought, *I am going to die.* Next she observes her body tensing in response to the thought, and she describes feeling slightly panicky. Rather than reliving this experience, as she might have done if the therapist had not directed her attention to observation of the present-moment organization of it, she is learning to step back, observe, and report it. She is discovering the difference between "having" an experience and exploring the organization of that experience here and now, days or weeks or years after the event itself.

Mindful observation of here-and-now experience changes information processing. Rather than triggering bottom-up hijacking of cognitions or escalation of trauma-related beliefs and emotions about impending danger, ✳️the act of mindful exploration facilitates dual processing. Clients do not get caught up in their trauma-related beliefs or arousal but, rather, study the evocation of titrated components of internal experience, especially the body's responses. Arousal stays within the window of tolerance and associations with traumatic memories begin to shift from automatic and exaggerated reactions to mediated, observable responses.

The use of mindfulness has been shown to change brain function in positive ways, increasing activity in areas of the brain associated with positive affect (Davidson et al., 2003). Mindful exploration of present-moment experience is also thought to engage the executive and observing functions of the prefrontal cortex. The prefrontal cortices and cognitive functions often fail to inhibit the instinctive defensive actions kindled by unresolved past trauma (Van der Kolk, 1994), and the ability to self-observe is hindered. Activating the prefrontal cortex allows clients to maintain an observing presence.✳️The therapist's job is to "wake up" the prefrontal cortices through mindfulness, stimulating the curiosity typical of the exploration action system in service of discovering the organization of experience.✳️The capacity to maintain observation of internal experience is what can prevent clients from becoming overwhelmed by the stimulation of past traumatic reactions and develop "mental coherence" (Siegel, 2006).

SOCIAL ENGAGEMENT: BUILDING A COLLABORATIVE THERAPEUTIC RELATIONSHIP

Curiosity, the hallmark of exploration, is recognized as inherently conflict-engendering for a child in a confusing, dissembling, or unsafe environment (Berlyne, 1960; Bronson, 1972). On the one hand, curiosity gives rise to fascination and exploration; on the other, when exploration is perceived as potentially dangerous, curiosity may arouse fear and caution. Comparable to a "good enough" caregiver with a child, the therapist must demonstrate sensitivity to clients' needs for both safety and exploration of their inner organization of experience. By recognizing the challenges that emerge when clients explore, the therapist helps them stay within the window of tolerance, interactively regulating their anxiety so that the focus on the goal of exploration can be maintained (Cassidy & Shaver, 1999). In other words, when clients attempt exploration and become distressed, frustrated, or defensive, the therapist helps to alleviate the distress while simultaneously encouraging them to cautiously continue with the exploration: "Sensitive support during exploration is characterized by acknowledging the infant's [or client's] frustration and hinting toward a solution that is appropriate, given the infant's [client's] developmental level" (Grossman et al., 1999, p. 763).

Often in therapy, this sensitive support takes the form of continuing to observe trauma-related defensive tendencies and studying their effects on the client's thoughts, emotions, body sensations, and movement. The inevitable conflicts between curiosity and fear or frustration can gradually resolve as the skilled therapist helps maintain social engagement, using voice tone, pacing, mindfulness, and modulation of arousal, such that the client develops a wider window of tolerance. With each new experience of maintaining social engagement and regulating arousal in the face of increased challenge and activation, clients build confidence that their inner discoveries yield a positive outcome, which in turn compels them to continue to explore their internal landscape.

To illustrate: After several years of successful therapy, Jennifer walked into her therapist's office and experienced an unidentified stimulus triggering her "freeze" subsystem. Her body became tight, her eyes cast downward, her arms crossed in front of her, and she thought her therapist was going to hurt her. Attempting to maintain the social engagement system, her (male) therapist empathically acknowledged her feeling, reassured her and expressed both his concern and his curiosity that she would think he might hurt her. While her defensive system was still mobilized, he gently encouraged Jennifer to activate her exploration system: He asked if she would be willing to orient toward him and notice what happened in her body. She began slowly bringing her gaze toward the therapist and immediately reported feeling more frightened and paralyzed. Almost simultaneously she observed that she was unable to feel sensation in her body. In this exploration Jennifer's attention shifted from "having" her experience to observing it. Her therapist expressed his interest and surprise at her reaction, given their years of working together, but he did not try to talk her out of them, thereby modeled the exploratory behavior of curiosity and interest rather than fear or judgment. He asked Jennifer if she would be willing to tell him where in the room he might sit that would feel "right" to her, or at a safe distance from her. Again, the therapist slowed the pace, evoked mindfulness and curiosity, encouraged Jennifer to learn more about the organization of her defensive tendency, and stimulated the social engagement system by asking Jennifer to control the literal distance between them. Jennifer asked him to move to the other side of the room, and as he did so, she noticed that she calmed down.

Through the physical experience of orienting toward her therapist and by controlling the degree of physical distance she wanted between them, Jennifer increased her ability to appraise current reality: She no longer felt that her therapist was going to hurt her. It was only then that she was able to identify the trigger: her therapist's sweater. As discussed in Chapter 3, Jennifer's rapist had worn a particular kind of sweater, similar to the one her therapist had on that day, a conditioned trauma-related stimulus toward which she had oriented and on which she had focused all her attention, triggering her defensive tendency.

As she experienced control over the distance between herself and her therapist and identified why the sweater had frightened her, Jennifer reported that she could sense her body again and, for the first time, noticed how the physical tension associated with freezing was quite painful. With guidance from her therapist, she explored the tension, and as she did so, her arousal again increased. She reported that the tension and pain of the freeze response were related to feeling unable to move in order to protect herself, saying that just thinking about her past trauma brought up the freezing. Jennifer's therapist continued to help her explore these sensations of freezing, asking if the tension in her body could guide her into a physical action that felt "right." By staying aware of her body sensations and impulses, Jennifer noticed a physical impulse of wanting to make wide circular motions with her arms, defining what she described as "my space: [you] stay out." The therapist encouraged her to execute those motions and notice how this action changed her internal organization of experience. Jennifer observed a lessening of the tension and a feeling of satisfaction. From this in-the-moment exploration, Jennifer discovered actions she could make that were more adaptive to current reality. She understood the freeze response as her body's communication that she needed a personal boundary.

Engaging and practicing these circular motions helped Jennifer remain calm and relaxed. The more she worked consciously with setting appropriate personal boundaries, the more her arousal remained within the window of tolerance and the more reliably her social engagement system came online. This system helped to deactivate her habitual tendency to freeze in the face of perceived threat.

Jennifer, like many traumatized people, could not stay within her window of tolerance while orienting to a dissociated element belonging to the traumatic event that she had failed to integrate—in her case, the sweater. While she was concentrating on the sweater, her ability to orient toward nontrau-matic stimuli and perceptions, such as the support of her therapist, was notably impaired. She could neither widen her field of consciousness to include nontraumatic stimuli nor reduce her intense concentration upon the traumatic reminder. Other clients are phobically avoidant of traumatic reminders; in these cases coaxing them to explore "looking" directly at the current stimulus helps them realize the difference between past and present realities.

When Jennifer's defensive subsystem of freezing was inadvertently aroused in therapy, the therapist capitalized on the here-and-now opportunity to study her fixed action tendency and eventually find alternative actions. He worked with the simultaneous arousal of the social engagement system, the defensive system, and the exploration system, using curiosity and mindfulness to help Jennifer learn about the defensive tendency and what might mitigate its arousal. Carefully maintaining social engagement, he facilitated the turning of her awareness from the external stimulus to her internal organization of experience, explicitly stating that the locus of control was within Jennifer: He encouraged her to stop or change the focus, as she desired. This collaboration and the restoration of her internal locus of control created the safety Jennifer needed to allow herself to become aware of her present-moment experience and experiment with different actions.

This exploration could not have taken place without collaboration between client and therapist. The therapist engaged Jennifer as a collaborator, as an observer–reporter on her internal experiences, and a co-creator in deciding what to explore. Then client and therapist worked together, with equal attention and commitment, to notice, track, observe, consider, translate, and experiment with the action tendency of freezing. And finally, with equal care and collaboration, client and therapist worked together to discover more adaptive actions. Throughout this process, the therapist encouraged Jennifer to make conscious choices, rather than to comply passively, about how to respond to him and his suggestions.

Engaging the Play Action System

Exploration and play are closely related: Play can lead to new insights and increased exploration, and exploration can lead to playfulness. Playfulness and play activities are proposed to increase the capacity to cope with environmental stressors and to promote learning and creativity (Siviy, 1998). Integration of information is also thought to be enhanced through play behaviors (Beckoff & Byers, 1998). Activating the client's play action system usefully challenges trauma-driven tendencies, especially immobilizing defenses, cognitive schemas of danger and/or worthlessness, and phobic responses to pleasurable sensations and positive affect. Play is often accompanied by specific "play signals"—nonverbal gestures and postures such as increased eye contact, facial expression, spontaneous physical proximity, and enhanced social engagement (Beckoff & Byers, 1998). It is usually indicated by smiles, giggles, laughter, and other expressions of pleasure, fun, and social connectedness (Panksepp, 1998). Associated with comfort in one's sense of self, autonomy, and well-being, play arises spontaneously, and as we noted in Chapter 6, is inhibited immediately by the threat of danger and fear. Therefore, the emergence of the play system indicates a relative absence of fear and defensive subsystems.

The practice of psychotherapy must bring clients "from a state of not being able to play into a state of being able to play" (Winnicott, 2005, p. 50). However, therapists may feel that they must stay focused exclusively on resolving the symptoms and difficulties that clients bring. Thus they may fail to recognize the health and vitality that can surface in moments of playfulness, humor, and pleasure within the therapeutic relationship. Engaging the play system counters the often arduous work of trauma therapy and brings elements of humor, buoyancy, and resilience to otherwise distressing material, fostering a sense of overall well-being, if only for a moment.

Playfulness may be experienced as a challenge to the sense of safety. Winnicott (2005) emphasized that psychotherapists must provide opportunities for "formless experience, and for creative impulses, motor and sensory, which are the stuff of playing" (p. 86). However, for clients who experience a chronic feeling of impending danger, such a feeling diminishes their responsiveness to actions systems of daily life and increases their orientation to the action systems of defense. As with exploration, to be able to enter the "treacherous waters" of play, clients must experience a feeling of being in charge and in command of their participation; otherwise play will not be possible (Fisher et al., 1991; Levy, 1978). The therapist facilitates meticulous therapeutic collaboration so that clients experience an internal locus of control. Engaging in playful behavior, like exploration, requires the availability of the social engagement system and the therapeutic alliance as a secure base from which clients can comfortably experiment.

Encouraging play in therapy can lead to states of pleasure and positive affect that can support the client's healing (Caldwell, 2003). Even relatively early in the course of their work together there are small moments of triumph and playfulness between therapist and client. The therapist recognizes these moments and gently enables them to linger. Pausing with the client at these times and enjoying the moment together enables pleasure, connectedness, and further playfulness to surface as powerful allies in the task of relinquishing old trauma-related action tendencies. Through his or her ability to convey appropriate lightheartedness and see the humor in everyday life, the therapist also initiates playfulness in the context of therapy.

Cannon (in press) has written, "[t]he therapist must . . . be willing to engage in a kind of playing together which can lead to an alteration in the client's life world through present experience, which is different from that of the client's distant and more recent past." To illustrate, we will describe the conclusion to a session with Cate, whose sister was murdered when Cate was a teenager. In the beginning of the session the therapist's primary goal was to help Cate modulate her hyperarousal, provoked whenever she described the traumatic event. However, after the arousal was maintained within a window of tolerance, which enabled the memory to be effectively processed, playful moments emerged. As Cate sat facing the therapist, they both noticed that Cate's legs began to twitch. The therapist playfully mirrored these leg movements. Cate laughed at this, and exclaimed in a surprised and joyful tone of voice, "I feel good—I feel like dancing!" The therapist matched Cate's joyful tone, and capitalized upon the playfulness further by moving her arms and hands, as well as her legs, in a seated, "I feel good" dance that Cate happily mimicked. The therapist then mirrored and exaggerated Cate's movements, encouraging her to experiment with different "feel good" movements and phrases. Cate concluded the session expressing that she had gotten the tragic experience "out of my body," and reclaimed the joyful, alive, playful attributes she had lost after her sister's murder.

CHANGING ORIENTING TENDENCIES

In sensorimotor treatment, traumatized clients are taught to become aware of trauma-related tendencies of orientation and to redirect their attention away from the past and toward the present moment. Repeatedly "shifting the client's attention to the various things going on outside of the flow of conversation [evokes] experiences which are informative and emotionally meaningful" (Kurtz, 2004, p. 40). Redirecting orientation and attention from conversation to present-moment experience—that is, from external awareness to internal awareness, and from the past to the present—engages exploration and curiosity, and clients can discover things about themselves that they did not know previously (Kurtz, 2004).

When clients are hyperaroused or overwhelmed emotionally, voluntarily narrowing their field of consciousness allows them to assimilate a limited amount of incoming information, thereby optimizing the chance for successful integration. For example, as one client began to report her traumatic experience, her arousal escalated: Her heart started to race, she felt afraid and restless, and had trouble thinking. She was asked to stop talking and thinking about the trauma, to inhibit the images, thoughts, and emotions that were coming up, and orient instead to her physical sensation until her arousal returned to the window of tolerance. With the help of her therapist, she focused on her body and described how her legs felt, the physical feeling of anxiety in her chest, and the beating of her heart. These physical experiences gradually subsided, and only then was she encouraged to return to the narrative. The intervention of directing the client to narrow his or her field of consciousness to orient toward a manageable amount of information can be repeated whenever a client has difficulty processing the barrage of unassimilated stimuli and reactions from past trauma.

Conversely, when even a small amount of internal awareness is overwhelming, the field of consciousness can be expanded to include phenomena outside of the client's awareness that might prove to be stabilizing. For example, a client who was chronically anxious and preoccupied with his rapid heartbeat and confused thinking was asked to widen his field of consciousness by paying attention to the movement occurring in his legs. As a child, this client had been beaten by his father and attempts to get away had only made his father angrier. Subsequently, he had abandoned the defense of flight. In this session, he slowly became aware of the physical possibility of running and escaping as he oriented to the movement in his legs. As he paid attention to his urge to run, which had been "lost" in the chronic feelings of anxiety and immobility he associated with the rapid heartbeat, he noticed a settling of his heart rate into a calmer, more even rhythm, which helped him to feel more present in the here-and-now.

The redirection of orientation and attention can be as simple as asking clients to become aware of a "good" or "safe" feeling in the body instead of focusing on their physical pain or elevated heart rate. Or the therapist can ask clients to experiment with focusing attention away from the traumatic activation in their body and toward thoughts or images related to their positive experiences and competencies, such as success in their job. This shift is often difficult for clients who have habituated to feeling pulled back repetitively into the most negative somatic reminders of their traumatic experiences. However, if the therapist guides them to practice deeply immersing themselves in a positive somatic experience (i.e., noting the changes in posture, breath, and muscular tone that emerge as they remember their competence), clients will gain the ability to reorient toward their competencies. They experience their ability to choose to what they pay attention and discover that it really is possible to resist the somatic claims of the past. For instance, if a client experiences competence as a lift through her chest and a lengthening in her spine, orienting toward this sensorimotor experience may begin to counteract the negative associations she has had to her body, helping her gain a more distinct and cogent sense of competency.

This reorienting is not an attempt to avoid or discount clients' pain and ongoing suffering. Rather, it is a means to help them observe, firsthand, how their chronic orienting tendencies toward reminders of the past recreate the trauma-related experience of danger and powerlessness, whereas choosing to orient to a good feeling can result in an experience of safety and mastery. As clients become able to do so, the new objects of orientation often become more defined and vivid (Perls, Hefferline, & Goodman, 1951). Rather than attention being drawn repeatedly to physical pain or traumatic activation, the good feeling becomes more prominent in the client's awareness. This exercise of reorienting toward a positive stimulus can surprise and reassure clients that they are not imprisoned indefinitely in an inner world of chronic traumatic reexperiencing, and that they have more possibilities and control than they had imagined. These orienting exercises need to be practiced again and again for mastery.

Conversely having clients orient to the very stimulus on which they are fixated helps them consciously and directly attend to reminders of past trauma. This provides the opportunity for the reactions to the trauma-related stimulus to change from involuntary and reflexive to reflective awareness and assimilation. The client's sense of control and efficacy is often enhanced, whereas simply orienting to new, neutral, or pleasurable stimuli may not accomplish this (Ford, personal communication, August 12, 2005). For example, Jason, who had been traumatized in a car accident, avoided driving because he experienced fear each time he got behind the wheel of his car. He learned in therapy to orient directly toward the trauma-related stimulus: driving on the highway. His therapist asked him to simultaneously focus on his current body sensation. Eventually, as Jason practiced imagining driving while attending to body sensations, the fear decreased. He then practiced orienting to his body sensations when actually driving until he eventually experienced a sense of confidence and competence even at the wheel of his car.

Perls et al. observed that when attention is directed to an object—in this case, to body sensation—it "brightens as figure and the background darkens; the object simultaneously becomes more unified but also more detailed. While more and more details are noticed and analyzed one by one, at the same time they become more organized in their relations to each other" (1951, p. 63). As the orienting response is redirected, the stimulus—such as driving on the highway—no longer elicits the conditioned response of fear. A different response and new meaning to the stimulus emerge: in this case, a sense of competence and confidence in a previously traumatic situation.

A BRIEF INTRODUCTION TO SOMATIC TRANSFERENCE
AND COUNTERTRANSFERENCE

The work of sensorimotor psychotherapy, like all psychotherapies, is both enhanced and hampered by the transferential relationship established between the therapist and client (Pearlman & Saakvitne, 1995). Understanding the complexities of these powerful forces is as necessary when using somatic interventions as in any other therapeutic intervention. As the connection to the therapist is established, the therapeutic relationship offers an opportunity for the client to experience a secure present-time attachment, but it also brings up transferential tendencies associated with past attachment relationships (Sable, 2000). Informed by the experience of interpersonal trauma and betrayal, posttraumatic transferential relationships can be exceptionally potent and volatile. In response to the therapist, clients experience fear, anger, mistrust, and suspicion, as well as hope, vulnerability, and yearning, and they are acutely attuned to subtle signals of disinterest or interest, compassion or judgment, abandonment or consistency (Herman 1992; Pearlman & Saakvitne, 1995).

An example of difficult transference that became manageable occurred when a traumatized client in couples therapy began to experience her therapist as similar to her father. Her father had abused and neglected her, and often compared her to her sister, whom he preferred and treated well. The client felt a mixture of fear, anger, and frustration, and she claimed that the therapist was vilifying her and siding with her husband. At this point the therapist took her statements at face value and first explored all the ways that the client had felt wronged during the session. After a thorough exploration, the therapist understood the client's point and agreed that he had said some things that could be construed as biased. After this statement, which validated and somewhat assuaged the client's feelings, the therapist added, "In trauma treatment, when feelings arise or when you are triggered in a relationship, it can also be useful to explore the possibility that past relationships may be playing themselves out in the current relationship dynamics. Let's explore the precise body states that are evoked for you and be open to the possibility that these states have several layers. We may find the bodily feelings and responses summoned up by the current dynamics here in this room between you, your husband, and myself relate as well to the abuse you suffered at home that involved you and your parents." With that, the therapist had the client consider and re-evoke the somatic experience that accompanied the dynamic between the three of them that had just been explored cognitively. He asked her to pay attention to her body as she became aware of her husband at her right side (by whom she felt excluded and minimized), and the therapist (who had "made her feel" that he favored her husband). She felt her body states emerge as a mixture of tension, increased arousal, and a sense of "feeling lost" combined with fear and anxiety. The client recognized that she was feeling again an old sense of failure concerning her abusive and neglectful father who had idealized and favored her sister. With this insight, the therapist assisted her to further differentiate him from her abusive father by having a pillow represent the father. In the ensuing exploration, the client was encouraged to take a length of rope and place it in a circle around herself to indicate her boundary, and then make one paper sign that was directed toward her father, one directed toward her therapist, and another directed to her husband. She wrote on a paper, "Stay away," and "Enter my space only with my permission," placing this paper to face her father (the pillow). She wrote on another paper, "Listen to my side, too," and placed this paper facing her therapist. On the paper facing her husband, she wrote, "Please take my feelings seriously." Through this exploration the client became clear about what in her past had been stimulated and also what specific needs she had with regard to each individual involved both in her past and present.

Transference refers to the phenomenon of unconscious association and prediction: Salient characteristics of the therapist or of the therapeutic relationship evoke emotional, cognitive (Stark, 1999), and sensorimotor associational networks related to emotionally significant historical relationships. Treatment is impacted by negative transference reactions that may manifest as autonomic hyper- or hypo-arousal, undue physical tension, rebellion, suspicion, anger, fear, submission, and avoidance. Treatment is affected as well by positive manifestations of transference, such as feelings of idealization, seeking excessive proximity to the therapist, trust, and compliance. The client's unresolved childhood issues at different developmental stages impact the transference in different ways: Early issues related to neglect may result in a positive transferential reaction that includes viewing the therapist as nurturing; adolescent issues may evoke a "crush" on the therapist (Hunter & Struve, 1998) that manifests in the flirtatious courtship behaviors characteristic of the sexuality action system. Additionally, experience of interpersonal trauma leaves, as its transferential legacy, both the wish for rescue and the conviction of betrayal (Davies & Frawley, 1994; Herman, 1992). The client may experience the therapist as the perpetrator or rescuer, or react to the therapist's neutrality as if the therapist were an unprotective bystander. These responses must be treated as symptoms of experiences of neglect and/or trauma and taken seriously (Maldonado & Spiegel, 2002; Spiegel, 2003).

The client's body language typically conveys these powerful themes long before the client can articulate the unformulated or undifferentiated thoughts or feelings (Krueger, 2002). Movement, tension, or gesture tendencies are often the first indicators of transference phenomena. The wish for rescue, for instance, may manifest in a childlike somatic organization: head to one side, orienting downward in a helpless posture, or looking "up" at the therapist with idealization.

The therapist tracks the often subtle signs of defensive subsystems that indicate transference: submission (lowering of eyes, acquiescence and compliance, flaccidity in the musculature), freeze (overall tension, immobility), flight (pulling back) or fight (tensing of the arms and shoulders). As treatment progresses, the client's efforts to track, understand, identify, and express emotions often result in the expression of fearful, vulnerable, insecure, or angry affects to the therapist, reflecting the client's inner conviction that emotional experience is associated with threat. Both the somatic tendencies and the relational dynamics involved should be explored, helping the client to differentiate the therapeutic relationship from past relationships so that pathological traumatic reenactment and unworkable traumatic transference are prevented. For example, anger and mistrust toward the therapist may indicate the activation of lost or truncated active, mobilizing defensive responses that can then be worked with somaticallly, rather than interpreted as only transference to the therapist. At the same time that the therapist observes these phenomena, he or she should avoid minimizing the strength of the client's feelings toward him or her, which also requires attention.

Unresolved developmental issues are also naturally and unconsciously stimulated in the context of transference. Often, "early body self transferences are the somatic and sensory memories of either physical contact with the mother, or the sensory contact needs and attunement that were lacking. These nascent sensory and somatic early attachment experiences . . . become activated in the patient's transference experience, [as well as] the procedural memory for what did and did not originally happen" (Krueger, 2002, p. 181). These dynamics may manifest through childlike postures, dreams of being held or longings for closeness, such as "fantasies and sensations of access to the [therapist's] body and the mingling of bodies in a sensual not essentially sexual way, at times in a demand for physical responses by the [therapist]" (Krueger, 2002, pp. 181–182).

In alignment with most approaches, the sensorimotor psychotherapist attempts to make unconscious transference conscious. Treatment focuses both on working through transference in the context of the relationship, and on the exploration and clarification of the here-and-now cognitive, emotional, and somatic tendencies associated with the transference. Treatment allows transference phenomena to be explored without unduly activating autonomic arousal or disrupting the therapeutic relationship. The patient's capacity for maturity, autonomy, and an internal locus of control are fostered, while at the same time, allowing appropriate dependence upon the therapist (Steele et al., 2001).

Essential to elucidating transferential issues is the therapist's observation of the client's somatic and emotional reactions to any single therapeutic intervention or physical action on the part of the therapist; in response to such reactions, the therapist considers possible meanings and intervenes appropriately. For example, when the therapist leaned forward in her chair, the client, Jim, physically pulled back. This dynamic was verbalized and explored: What happens if the therapist adjusts her proximity by moving back slightly? (Jim relaxed and took a deep breath.) What happens if the therapist leaned forward again? (Jim again moved back, his body tightened, and his breathing became shallow.) Being curious about how Jim was unconsciously interpreting her action—the "message" communicated to Jim as she leaned forward—the therapist slowly repeated the action and asked Jim to notice the nonverbal communication of this action that caused him to move back. She said, "How do you translate this movement into words? If my leaning forward could speak in words, what would it say?" Jim immediately replied, "Your leaning forward tells me you want something from me." This exploration brought Jim's transference to light: His mother had molested him throughout childhood, and his belief was that the therapist, like his mother, might also want something from him. Jim and his therapist then continued to explore this issue, working with how his body held this response, and processing memories and emotions as they emerged. As Jim was able to separate past from present, he was also able to stay relaxed as the therapist leaned forward. Thus, in a somatic approach, tracking and finding the meaning of somatic communication occurring "body to body" are essential in uncovering and working with transferential dynamics.

Countertransference responses are often considered a valuable tool for the therapist in understanding the client. "It is neither possible nor even preferable to eradicate personal reactions to a patient. No one can be useful to a patient about whom he or she has no feelings at all, and repression of such feelings only creates blind spots" (Kudler, Blank, & Krupnick, 2001, p. 179). Listening to the pain, anger, and fear of a client may evoke not only empathy but similar feelings of suffering in the therapist, and may activate the therapist's own unresolved traumatic issues (Figley, 1995). Unexamined, these reactions can impinge upon and cloud the treatment, leading to distortions or disruptions of therapy. For example, if the therapist's leaning forward were an unconscious attempt to "mother" Jim, this physical action would reflect her countertransference and would require thoughtful recognition and consideration by the therapist. If unexamined, it would undoubtedly adversely affect the therapy. Therapists are best advised to stay aware of their own somatic reactions that might indicate countertransferential tendencies, which can manifest as "state changes of sleepiness, arousal, restlessness, boredom, or of desires to hold, shake, cradle, or direct various actions toward the patient" (Krueger, 2002, p. 186).

Somatic countertransference is particularly complicated when therapists join with, or "match," their clients, unconsciously imitating their physical posture and movements. If mirroring is done without mindful awareness, the therapist may "take on" the client's tension, arousal, movement, and posture without realizing it, which in turn affects the cognitive and emotional levels of processing. On the other hand, deliberate mirroring can provide the therapist with valuable information about the client's physical tendencies and help the client feel empathic rapport with the therapist.

The transference and countertransference between Peter and his therapist illustrates how to work somatically with these complicated dynamics. Peter, a young man who described himself as "genetically predisposed to failure" came to treatment after losing yet another girlfriend to whom he had become deeply attached. Despite his regret and self-loathing following the breakup, Peter continued to believe that he loved her. He wished passionately that she had not left him and persisted in trying to win her back. Peter was an only child who often was left to his own devices. His memories of his early home environment were of a depressed mother who was taken to the psychiatric hospital on several occasions for what sounded like psychotic features of a chronic depressive illness. His father was an energetic man who worked all the time.

Traditional psychotherapy had proven unsuccessful, and Peter began sensorimotor psychotherapy with skepticism. However, when he met his young female therapist, he became more hopeful, suddenly having the feeling that things might go better than he imagined. Soon after the onset of treatment, significant transferential and countertransferential issues emerged in his therapy.

The therapist found herself disliking Peter's behavior, and by extension, viewing Peter unfavorably and becoming tense in his presence. Yet his willingness to work—indeed his desperation at the onset of therapy—compelled her to want to assist him therapeutically. She sought supervision in an attempt to understand the strength of her reaction to Peter and explored issues in her past that might be contributing to her countertransference. She discovered that her tendency to tighten her body and physically pull away from Peter was identical to a pattern she had developed as a child in response to her own needy mother, who had expected care from her daughter. These insights gave her the information she needed to understand her countertransference rather than blindly react to it. When Peter came for his therapy session, she reminded herself that her mother and Peter were different people and consciously refrained from the physical actions of tensing and pulling back; instead, she breathed deeply and leaned forward slightly, relaxing her body.

Peter's positive transferential feelings developed as therapy progressed. Feelings of love, arousal, and sexual desire became evident, and his therapist noticed his increased flirtatious behavior in his open body posture, arms stretched across the sofa, head tilted to the side, maintaining eye contact longer than usual, and other seductive behavior. She gently brought these behaviors to Peter's awareness, and he acknowledged his attraction to her. Within a good therapeutic alliance, where safety, clear boundaries, and support were paramount, Peter's feelings were validated and accepted as positive at the same time that the therapist established clear professional boundaries and reminded/reassured him that his feelings would not be acted upon (Davies & Frawley, 1994).

Rather than providing traditional therapeutic interpretations of Peter's transference responses, the therapist asked him if he would be willing to explore his physical posture. He agreed, and the therapist asked him to become aware of his open body posture and the tilt of his head, mindfully noticing what occurred inside him. As Peter did so, he became sad, reporting a memory of his father's absence and his (Peter's) desire as a small child to be close to, and help, his mother, whom he adored. He remembered trying to cheer her up by bringing her gifts and entertaining her, trying to take his father's place. His flirtatious behavior in a situation where his love and help were not received in kind was similar in the therapy session to his memory of childhood. Peter spontaneously realized that his attraction to his therapist was reminiscent of his relationship with his mother. This awareness provided a jumping off point to explore Peter's childhood feelings of futility, which were still affecting him today and were reflected in his somatic tendencies and his persistence in dissatisfying, dead-end relationships.

The therapist's countertransference commonly interfaces with the client's transference. If a negative transference is present, a therapist may be immobilized by fear of anger or conflict. Positive transference may trigger the therapist's need to demonstrate competence, omniscience, or ability to rescue the client. "Enactments" of transference/countertransference dynamics may provide an opportunity for client and therapist to engage in an authentic relationship in which interpersonal difficulties are addressed; such an opportunity promotes a greater degree of healing for the client as these issues are resolved (Stark, 1999). However, both transference and countertransference responses often occur outside of awareness. If countertransference and their somatic tendencies go unrecognized, therapists are at risk of acting on these tendencies. It is the therapist's responsibility to address his or her countertransference through self-awareness and supervision, so that it can function as an asset rather than a liability in therapy. Transference responses are also expected and desired; the particular physical and mental action tendencies that accompany them provide an opportunity for both greater awareness about these dynamics and a corrective emotional and developmental experience for the client.

INTEGRATIVE CAPACITY AND THE BODY

Rather than defining traumatization in terms of the magnitude of the precipitating event, Janet defined it as a failure of integrative capacity (1889). Without adequate integrative capacity, clients cannot maintain regulated arousal, resolve their memories, or lead productive, satisfying lives. Thus the primary treatment goal is to expand the client's integrative capacity. Posture, movement, and gesture can serve to either support or detract from integrative capacity.

Integrative capacity requires both differentiating and linking the separate components of internal experience and external events in order to create meaningful connections among them (Van der Hart et al., 2006). As we become aware of internal experience and relate it to external sensory input, we engage in a process of making sense of the environment and how it pertains to us. If our interpretations and understandings are relatively accurate, adaptive action results. This accuracy requires the ability to recognize our internal experience: our thoughts, emotions, internal images, body sensation, and movement. In sensorimotor psychotherapy, great attention is given to developing this capacity.

Janet (1903) referred to the ability to differentiate one's own experience—body sensations, movements, thoughts, and emotions—as separate from that of others as "personification." Similarly, Schnarch (1991) refers to the capacity to distinguish one's own internal experience from that of others as "differentiation." This capacity facilitates the maintainence of an internal locus of control over one's body, emotions, and thoughts.

In therapy the organization of the body is used to foster the capacity for personification and differentiation. For example, Bill was married to a woman who periodically became depressed. When his wife had a depressive episode, Bill's body would droop, his breath would become shallow, and his gait would become plodding. Without knowing it, he mimicked his wife's physical tendencies, and consequently he also felt depressed. His integrative capacity was lowered by his inability to differentiate his own posture and movement from that of his wife. As he learned to become aware of this tendency and return to his "own" physical organization of uplifted spine and deeper breath, his integrative capacity, along with the ability to respond adaptively in his relationship, improved.

Along with differentiation, adequate integrative capacity requires (1) separation of current internal and external reality from past experiences, and (2) the accurate prediction of the impact of internal experience and external events on the future (Janet, 1928; Van der Hart & Steele, 1997). For example, the client who experiences panic symptoms when men get on an elevator with her must learn to discriminate her internal experience (racing heart, constricted breathing, feelings of fear) from current external reality (these men are her own colleagues, liked and well known to her; there are other people in the elevator; she is able to protest if approached inappropriately). Janet (1928) referred to this capacity as "presentification," defining it as being aware of the present moment while realizing its relevance to the past and its implications for the future.

Presentification gives a sense of continuity over time and contributes to a stable sense of self (Van der Hart et al., 2006). The ability to be present in the moment includes awareness of which postures and movements are appropriate to the current context and which ones reflect maladaptive somatic tendencies programmed by the past. For example, when Megan was given negative feedback in a supportive manner by a coworker, she instinctively cowered without realizing that this behavior was an artifact from her childhood abuse. She reported interpreting this incident as an angry attack, although she knew intellectually that this was not the case. Her integrative capacity was undermined as her cringing body posture rendered her unable to interpret or respond appropriately to the present moment, no matter how much she "told" herself she was not in danger. To overcome this distorted and inaccurate mixing of past and present, Megan had to learn how to orient away from the trauma-related stimulus (being given feedback) toward her sensorimotor experience and, instead of cringing, to practice literally "standing tall" in the face of criticism.

Integrative capacity thus requires a synthesis of the components in all three levels of information processing—cognitions, emotions, sensory perceptions, body sensations and movements, and the sense of self (Steele et al., in press). In the case of Megan, her body movement, sensation, and cognitions were not congruent. Although Megan "knew" she was not in danger, her body told her that she was. If sensorimotor habits are firmly entrenched, accurate cognitive interpretations may not exert much influence on changing bodily organization and arousal responses. Instead, the traumatized person may experience the reality of the body rather than that of the mind. To be most effective, the sensorimotor psychotherapist works on both the cognitive and sensorimotor levels. With Megan, a purely cognitive approach might foster some change in her integrative capacity, but the change would be only momentary if the cowering response were reactivated each time she received feedback at work. Her cowering posture would also adversely affect her self-image and her ability to accurately perceive power differentials in current relationships as different from those in previous traumatic relationships. However, if she is encouraged to remember to "stand tall" in the face of criticism, her body and her thoughts will be congruent with each other and with current reality.

The end result of therapy leads to a higher level of integrative capacity: "realization" (Janet, 1935b; Van der Hart, Steele, Boon, & Brown, 1993). The two overlapping actions of presentification and personification are involved in realization. When clients achieve realization, the past trauma is accepted as having occurred to them *in the past*; this perspective enables them to respond adaptively to current life challenges (Van der Hart et al., 2006). By most accounts, realization requires putting the traumatic experience into words (Van der Hart et al., 1993). However, when the person does not recall what happened, the realization is reflected in a body that is no longer taken over by defensive subsystems of fight, flight, freeze, or submit. Instead, the individual has developed new physical tendencies appropriate to current reality. Realization includes the reorganization of old tendencies and the development of new cognitive, emotional, and physical actions that support more adaptive responses to the arousal of all action systems (Janet, 1898).

PHASE-ORIENTED TREATMENT

A phase-oriented treatment approach was first conceptualized by Janet in 1898 and is systematically recommended in various guidelines on the treatment of trauma (Brown & Fromm, 1986; Brown, Schefflin, & Hammond, 1998; Cardeña, Van der Hart, & Spiegel, 2000; Chu, 2005; Cloitre et al., 2002; Courtois, 1988, 1991, 1999; Herman, 1992; National Collaborating Centre for Mental Health, 2005; Steele et al., 2005; van der Kolk, McFarlane, et al., 1996). Sensorimotor psychotherapy adheres to the guidelines of phase-oriented treatment, and interventions are evaluated in terms of the treatment goals of each phase. This treatment model has three phases, each with its own goals, interventions, and skill-building requirements. In Janet's (1898) original description, the first phase is devoted to symptom reduction and stabilization; the second phase to treatment of traumatic memory; and the third to personality integration and rehabilitation. Although the three phases are conceptualized sequentially, they tend to occur in a spiral fashion in their clinical application (Brown et al., 1998; Courtois, 1999; Herman, 1992; Janet, 1898, cited in Van der Kolk & Van der Hart, 1989; Steele & Van der Hart, 2001; Steele et al., 2005; Van der Kolk & Van der Hart, 1989). For example, clients who have become stabilized in phase 1 treatment often become destabilized during the challenging work of addressing traumatic memory in phase 2, necessitating a return to phase 1 interventions.

As we have discussed in previous chapters, trauma leaves in its wake action tendencies that were adaptive in the original context: profoundly dysregulated autonomic arousal, somatic patterns of tension and collapse, a limited affect tolerance, and a host of nonverbal memories often subjectively disconnected from the events that caused them. At the beginning phase of treatment, the focus on symptom reduction and stabilization requires attending to the dysregulated sensorimotor, affective, and cognitive remnants of the trauma with the goal of stabilizing the client. Although client and/or therapist may wish to focus on the event memories or creation of a narrative, that work is put aside until such time as the client has developed a sufficiently expansive window of tolerance to permit contacting those memories without causing further dysregulation, decompensation, or dissociation. Interventions are geared to restore the capacity for self-regulation and provide correction or challenge to trauma-related action tendencies that destabilize the client. The client's increased ability to self-regulate enables progression to the next phase of treatment: working with traumatic memory.

The work of phase 2 centers not on retrieving traumatic memory but on overcoming the phobic avoidance of it (Van der Kolk & Van der Hart, 1989) and addressing truncated or incomplete defensive actions incipient in the traumatic experience; the goal in this phase is to attain realization and integration of the traumatic memory (Van der Hart et al., 2006; Van der

Hart et al., 1993). Therapist and client draw on the phase 1 skills that foster mastery over dysregulated arousal, to address traumatic memory within a window of tolerance: to reexperience mindfully the traumatic activation, movement impulses, shaking, trembling, or numbing, and to find incipient empowering actions and execute them. Transforming of maladaptive defensive action tendencies while maintaining social engagement helps to expand the client's responsiveness to action systems of daily living and paves the way for the work of phase 3: integration and success in normal life.

In this final phase the work shifts to overcoming trauma-related blocks to full participation in life. Therapeutic goals include helping the client to (1) take up the tasks of adult development, (2) overcome fears of challenge and change, (3) participate fully in work and relationships (especially intimate ones), and (4) increase tolerance for positive affect. Clients' ability to respond to the arousal systems of daily living finally supersedes their defensive responses, and they learn to attend to areas of their life that they have heretofore neglected. They learn to use their body in new ways that challenge them to execute new actions, such as reaching out to others for connection.

The duration of therapy can be quite variable. Clients with greater integrative capacities will terminate sooner than those without such abilities (e.g., clients with a history of complex childhood traumatization). It is important to recognize that clients whose instability remains their most significant problem may never have the integrative capacity to attempt the challenges of phases 2 and 3; these clients gain the greatest benefit from the ongoing stabilizing resources of phase 1.

Use of the Body in the Three Phases of Treatment

The body is engaged in different ways in the three phases of treatment. In phase 1, clients learn to keep arousal within a window of tolerance by recognizing triggers, changing orienting tendencies, and limiting their access to overstimulating situations. The unnecessary activation of defensive responses that usurps the functioning of other action systems is mitigated through the use of somatic resources. Awareness of the body is emphasized so that clients can learn to recognize the beginning somatic signs of hyper- and hypoarousal and use somatic resources to return arousal to the window of tolerance. Clients learn about the core and periphery of the body and utilize autoregulatory resources that pertain chiefly to the core of the body, and interactive–regulatory resources that concern primarily the periphery of the body, to change the movement and sensation of their bodies to facilitate optimal arousal. Self-care skills that stabilize the energy regulation system, such as regular sleep and eating habits, are also established in phase 1.

In phase 2, unintegrated memory fragments—the physical sensations, sensory intrusions, emotions, and actions—are addressed. Clients identify and embody the resources that helped them cope with traumatic events and learn to use the body to discover actions that provide a sense of mastery even when remembering those past traumatic events. Through awareness of the physical impulses that emerge when the memory is evoked, clients find and complete the innate "acts of triumph," the mobilizing defenses that were ineffective at the time of the original trauma. Practicing these empowering defensive actions diminishes feelings of helplessness and shame. As mobilizing actions are exchanged for the immobilizing defenses and newly associated with the traumatic memory, a sense of mastery over the traumatic past ensues.

In phase 3, with the somatic skills to maintain arousal at a tolerable level, the embodied experience of empowering actions in relationship to traumatic memories, and a developing awareness of, and confidence in, the body as an ally instead of an enemy, clients are psychologically equipped and somatically reinforced to turn their attention to enriching their everyday lives. The resources learned in previous phases of treatment are used again in phase 3 to support healthy risk taking and more active engagement in the world. Clients learn about the dynamic relationship between the core and periphery of the body and discover how the integration of core and periphery supports adaptive action and new meaning. Cognitive distortions—and the ways in which the body sustains them—are explored to help clients change negative beliefs and engage in the action systems of daily life with increasing satisfaction.

CONCLUSION

The techniques and work of sensorimotor psychotherapy were described as they pertain to each phase of treatment in the ensuing chapters. Throughout, the principles of treatment prevail:

• Attending to the organization of present-moment experience;

• Integrating top-down and bottom-up interventions;

• Evoking action systems such as social engagement, exploration, and play;

• Expanding the window of tolerance and overall integrative capacity;

• Negotiating a change in orientation from past trauma to present experience;

• Allowing meaning making to emerge organically from the physical experience;

• Attending to somatic transference and countertransference; and

• Increasing integrative capacity.

Chapter 9

✖·✖·✖

The Organization of Experience: Skills for Working with the Body in Present Time[1]

THE CLINICAL PRACTICE OF SENSORIMOTOR PSYCHOTHERAPY blends techniques from both cognitive and psychodynamic therapies (such as attention to cognitive schemata and putting language to felt experience) with somatically based interventions (such as learning to track bodily sensations and working with movement). This combination is thought to foster the client's ability to engage the frontal lobes in mindful self-witnessing and in practicing new actions that promote empowerment and success. Interventions are implemented that help clients learn about and become aware of the interplay between cognitive, emotional, and sensorimotor levels of information processing. Mindfulness techniques that help clients notice how self-representations (e.g., "I'm a bad person") or trauma-related emotions (e.g., panic) affect physical organization. These types of interventions gradually increase integrative capacity by helping clients become capable of and facile at moving from one layer of experience (cognitive, emotional, or sensorimotor) to another, thereby laying the groundwork to unify both the physical and mental components of traumatic events. The body becomes an ally

---

[1] The concept of the organization of experience, and the skills of tracking, contact, mindfulness questions, and experiments are adapted from Ron Kurtz's Hakomi method of body-centered psychotherapy (1990).

in the task of overcoming of posttraumatic defeat, no longer experienced as the source of vulnerability and humiliation and no longer omitted from therapeutic attention (Levine, 1997; Ogden & Minton, 2000; Rothschild, 2000; van der Kolk, 2002).

TRACKING AND BODYREADING

The foundational skill of a sensorimotor psychotherapist is that of tracking present experience, especially as it is encoded in the body (Kurtz, 1990). *Tracking* refers to the therapist's ability to closely and unobtrusively observe the unfolding of nonverbal components of the client's immediate experience: movements and other physical signs of autonomic arousal or changes in body sensation. Somatic signs of emotions (e.g., moist eyes, changes in facial expression or voice tone) and how beliefs and cognitive distortions that emerge from the client's narrative and history affect the body (such as the thought "I'm bad" correlating with tense shoulders and downcast eyes) are also tracked.

Most therapists are skilled at tracking the client's affect, thoughts, and narrative. Sensorimotor psychotherapy also requires tracking, in precise detail, the moment-by-moment physical organization of experience in the client, both the subtle changes (e.g., flushing or paling of the skin, dilation of the nostrils or pupils, slight tension or trembling) and the more obvious gross changes (e.g., flexion or "collapse" through the spine, a turn in the neck, a lifting of the hand or push with the arm, or any other muscular movement). These changes may be fleeting, such as a momentary narrowing of the eyes or a sigh, or they may be more lasting, such as mobilizing defensive "fight" actions emerging in the clenching of the fists and arm muscles, or a continuing tension across the shoulders accompanying a recount of the trauma experience. The therapist especially tracks the physical changes that correspond to emotions, thoughts, and narrative. For example, Jennifer's body tensed as she talked about attachment relationships but then relaxed when she spoke of her job.

Whereas *tracking* is defined as the moment-by-moment observation of physical changes, *bodyreading* refers to the observation of persistent action tendencies, such as the habitual posture of lifted, tense shoulders. Bodyreading helps therapists become aware of the client's chronic patterns of physical structure, movement, and posture that remain consistent over time and are correlated with longstanding beliefs and emotional tendencies. For example, chronically hiked shoulders may correspond to the belief "I'm always in danger" and a perpetual feeling of fear.

When therapists learn to read the body for ever-present physical tendencies that indicate chronic beliefs and regulatory capacities, they glean the information needed to teach clients the movements necessary to change not only the body but also to influence cognitive and emotional levels of processing. In the words of Janet, "Does it not seem likely enough that a transformation of movements by means of a process of [somatic] education may have an effect upon the totality of the [client's] activities, and thus prove competent to prevent or remove the mental troubles?" (1925, p. 725). Different movements and postures are addressed in different phases of treatment, and therapists bodyread for the presence or absence of a variety of physical capacities depending on the phase of treatment. In phase 1, bodyreading is used to assess somatic abilities that foster stabilization (such as alignment in the spine, grounding in the legs, or breathing fully); the therapist thus notes which abilities are missing and need to be taught to the client. In phase 2, bodyreading is used to assess potential mobilizing defensive responses that were not executed at the time of the trauma, such as tension in the shoulders, arms, or hands (possibly indicating an incomplete "fight" response) or tension in the legs (possibly indicating a truncated "flight" response), thus providing information about actions that may need to be executed to meet the goals of phase 2. In phase 3, bodyreading is used to assess the physical manifestation of chronic beliefs that interfere with the client's ability to meet the goals of engaging more fully in normal life. For instance, the belief that "I have to be a high achiever to be loved" may be reflected in overall tension, quick, focused movements, and erect, rigid posture, all of which are physical tendencies that support working hard.

The sensorimotor-trained therapist is unobtrusively and consistently attuned to the communications of the body, and tracking and bodyreading take place throughout the session. Whether the client is standing, walking, sitting, talking, or gesturing, the therapist is noticing which movements are habitual, easy, and familiar, which movements are difficult to execute or apparently unfamiliar, and hypothesizing about what these tendencies might mean.

It is essential that the therapist note not only the bodily organization that reflects traumatic reactions (e.g., hyperarousal, held breath, constriction, collapsed chest and shoulders, trembling), but also the physical signs of competence and well-being (e.g., deep, regular breath, physical alignment or length in the spine, flexibility and relaxation) (Eckberg, 2000; Levine, 1997; Ogden & Minton, 2000). For example, when Jennifer described how her boss paid her a compliment, her spine lengthened and her chin lifted. But when she described her childhood, her shoulders slumped and her head turned down. The therapist may choose to spend a session working with the memory of the compliment so that Jennifer becomes aware of the length in her spine and learns to maintain that length in the face of challenging experiences.

CONTACT STATEMENTS

Through tracking and bodyreading, the therapist gathers information and then communicates relevant information to the client in the form of a "contact statement" (Kurtz, 1990). Physical experiences often remain unnoticed by the client until the therapist brings attention to them through a simple statement that describes what has been noticed; for example, "Seems like your body is tensing," or "As you say those words, your hand is beginning to curl up into a fist," or "It looks like your legs are starting to tremble." Most therapists are familiar and comfortable with reflecting the client's cognitions and emotional states: "Yes, it feels frightening, doesn't it?" or "It makes you feel worthless when people treat you that way." In sensorimotor psychotherapy, the therapist also pays particular attention to tracking the client's sensorimotor reactions and then verbally reflecting them.

To ensure that attention is paid to all levels of information processing, the therapist follows and mirrors emotional or cognitive aspects of the narrative while simultaneously noting how the narrative affects present body experience. In other words, the therapist must track and contact the physical process communicated by the body as well as the meaning making and emotion evoked by the content (Kurtz, 1990). For example, when Jennifer spoke about her boss complimenting her work, which challenged her belief that he did not value her, her spine lengthened. A contact statement about her body might be "You seem to be sitting taller"; a contact statement about her emotions might be "It feels good to remember that!"; a contact statement about her cognitions might be "You seem to realize that you have something to offer."

By tracking and describing changes that occur in the body as they unfold in the moment, the therapist redirects the client's orienting and attention to present bodily experience and engenders curiosity in how that experience is being organized in both mind and body (Kurtz, 1990). If a therapist only references the content of the story the client is telling, or the emotions accompanying it, then the client will attend to content or emotion, assuming that is what interests the therapist or what is most important in therapy. If a therapist also tracks and contacts the client's physical experience rather than only the emotions or story, the client will orient toward, and become interested in, his or her physical experience as well.

When therapists attend to both the traumatic reactions and the physical signs of mastery and well-being, clients' "phobia" (Steele et al., 2005) of internal experience diminishes and they become "friendlier" toward their inner landscape. The therapist's contact statements assist the "interactive regulation of the [client's] state [and] enables him or her to begin to verbally label the affective [and sensorimotor] experience" (Schore, 2001b, p. 76). As clients acquire the skills needed to track and name their own physical, emotional, and cognitive experiences, an internal locus of control is strengthened.

Contact statements are simple and short, intended to facilitate self-observation rather than analysis (Kurtz, 1990; Naranjo, 1993). Clients are not required to think about or translate a short, uncomplicated statement such as "Your hand seems to be tightening." Such precise and clear statements of obvious changes keep clients aware of present experience and minimize the effort required to think about the therapist's words. Because the focus is on the organization of present experience, the therapist does not try to interpret or make meaning of the client's physical phenomena (Gendlin, 1981), but rather simply observes and describes the sensorimotor elements in the simplest, most concrete terms possible.

Contact statements evoke and maintain social engagement. As Kurtz noted: "Contact statements are not mandatory. They are optional. Creating a connection is mandatory" (1990, p.77). Good contact statements may be few, but if they are precise and resonant for the client, social engagement and attunement are induced, maintained, and increased. For that reason, contact statements that demonstrate the therapist's attunement not only to the body but to emotion and cognition, as they emerge in the client in the present moment, cannot be overlooked: "Looks like a lot of emotion is coming up right now" or "Seems like these thoughts are confusing" are ways of contacting mental and emotional experience that demonstrate attunement without encouraging a *thinking about* action.

To preserve social engagement, attunement, and collaboration, the client is always provided with the opportunity to refute or refine the therapist's contact statements. Thus, contact statements should carry a sense of subtle questioning, a tone that implies an invitation for revision by the client. Adjunct clauses at the beginning of a statement (e.g., "sounds like," "seems as if," "looks like") leave contact statements appropriately open-ended, as do adjunct expressions at the end of a statement. For example, in the phrase "Starting to relax, huh(?)" the "huh" turns it into a rhetorical question. If a therapist observes "You seem to be pulling back," and the client's response is a furrowing of the brow or words such as "No, I'm not," the therapist does not dispute the client's experience. Rapport and social engagement would be sacrificed if identifying present experience were to turn into a struggle over who is "right." The therapist's statement may be accurate, but accepting and even encouraging the client's disagreement maintains social engagement by showing respect, patience, and a willingness to collaborate, as well as a validation that no one but the client can know his or her inner experience.

The opportunity to correct the therapist may also allow the client to attune more deeply to what is actually happening in his or her body and fine-tune the description of how he or she experiences sensations in the body. For instance, if the therapist says "Your shoulders are tensing, huh?" the client might respond by saying "No, it's more like they're pulling in . . . like I'm getting smaller." In this interaction the therapist was not rebuffed; on the contrary, the rapport may be enhanced after the client offers this "correction."

The invitation to the client to accept, refute, correct, or refine a contact statement places the authority and locus of control within the client, rather than the therapist, thereby reinforcing the sense of collaboration so necessary in sensorimotor work. In addition, the client's adjustment of the therapist's statements is usually an emotional risk, and taking it provides an opportunity for the client to differentiate him- or herself from the therapist.

MINDFULNESS

Tracking and contact statements set the stage for exploring present-moment experience by facilitating mindfulness in the client. Kabat-Zinn defines mindfulness as "paying attention in a particular way; on purpose to the present moment, and nonjudgmentally" (1994, p. 4). Linehan (1993) describes mindfulness as a combination of the "what" skills of observing, describing, and participating and the "how" skills of a nonjudgmental attitude, focusing on one thing at a time, and being effective. In a sensorimotor approach, mindfulness entails orienting and attending to the ebb and flow of present internal experience. Awareness and attention are directed toward the building blocks of present experience: thoughts, feelings, sensory perceptions, inner body sensations, muscular changes, and movement impulses as they occur in the here-and-now. In normal daily life, the beliefs and habits that exert their influence on our perceptions and actions usually remain just outside of conscious awareness. "One of the main goals of the therapeutic process is to bring this organizing material into consciousness, to study it and understand it. Mindfulness, as a state of consciousness, is the tool we use" (Kurtz, 1990, p. 27). In a discussion or conversation, we "talk about" rather than study our internal experience. In ordinary consciousness, we tell the story; in mindful awareness, we watch the experience of the story unfold in the present moment, through changes in body sensation, movement, sensory perception, emotion, and thought.

Through tracking and contact, the therapist redirects the client's orienting to present experience, and through mindfulness, the client's ability to attend to present experience is maintained and expanded. Although mindfulness does not exclude awareness of the external environment, it is directed internally to the effect of internal stimuli (e.g., remembering a traumatic event) and of external stimuli (e.g., a contact statement) on sensations, perceptions, movements, emotions, and thoughts.

The therapist teaches mindfulness by asking questions that require awareness of present-moment experience to answer. Such questions might include:

"What do you feel in your body right now?"

"Where exactly do you experience that tension?"

"How big is the area of the tension—the size of a golf ball or the size of an orange?"

"What sensation do you feel in your legs right now as you talk about your abuse?"

"What happens in your body when you feel angry?"

The more precise the question, the more deeply "tuned-in" and mindful of body experience the client will become.

The intention of mindfulness is to "'allow' difficult thoughts and feelings [and body sensations and movements] simply to be there, to bring to them a kindly awareness, to adopt toward them a more 'welcome' than a 'need to solve' stance (Segal, Williams, & Teasdale, 2002, p. 55). This nonjudgmental mindful observation has a positive effect on brain functioning (Davidson et al., 2003): It engages the prefrontal cortex in support of observing sensorimotor experiences, rather than allowing these bottom-up trauma-related processes to escalate and "hijack" higher-level information processing. As thoughts or emotions emerge, mindful observation leads not to interpretation but to curiosity and self-study: for example, the therapist might ask, "When that thought comes up, what happens to that tension in your shoulder?" or "When you have that feeling, what happens in your body?"

Mindfulness questions discourage discussion, ordinary conversation, and brooding about past or future experiences. When we have a "conversation," a discussion, or tell a "story," we are not necessarily mindful. We are not observing the *effects* of our speaking on internal experience: We are "talking about." To facilitate mindfulness when the client is talking *about* a significant event, recent or past, the therapist gently directs the client's orienting back to the internal experience evoked by that content: the feelings, thoughts, and body sensations and movement that occur as the client remembers the past or thinks about the future. In this way, mental and physical action tendencies that reveal the client's legacy of procedural learning become the objects of exploration, rather than the events that engendered that procedural learning (Grigsby & Stevens, 2000).

Because mindfulness questions require an "observing ego," clients are "forced" to step back from the chronic somatic or emotional experiences of trauma in order to formulate a mindful answer. In endeavoring to answer a question framed to deepen mindfulness, the client no longer "is" the traumatic experience. Instead, by observing and reporting on current experience with an observing ego, the client "has" an experience rather than "being" it (Ogden & Minton, 2000). Retraumatization is minimized because the prefrontal cortex remains "online" to observe inner experience, thus inhibiting escalation of subcortical activation.

Using questions to elicit present-moment attention to a symptom or behavior manifesting in the client in the here-and-now provides conscious access to underlying traumatic tendencies and resources (Eckberg, 2000; Kurtz, 1990; Levine, 1997; Ogden & Minton, 2000; Rothschild, 2000). For example, rather than sensing tension in the body and immediately trying to relax it, mindful attention would be used to observe the tension and discover more about it—how it is pulling, how strong is it, what its parameters are, what the sensation of the tension is like, if the tension is a precursor to a particular physical action, and perhaps what emotions or thoughts accompany it.

EXPERIMENTS AND EXPLORATION

In a state of mindfulness, action tendencies can be observed and studied and then transformed through the practice of new actions (Janet, 1925). The therapist adopts an "experimental attitude"—a mind-set of openness and receptivity that is characterized by curiosity and playfulness rather than effort or fear (Kurtz, 1990). The experimental attitude invites exploration of new experiences without investment in a specific outcome—an attitude that renders "right" and "wrong" answers irrelevant and is reflected in the phrasing of contact statements and mindfulness questions. Jennifer's therapist invoked an experimental attitude by reflecting back to her: "Isn't it interesting that today, you are having the feeling that I might hurt you? Let's find out more about that. Maybe first we can experiment: What would happen if you looked at me and just noticed what happens in your body?" This first experiment failed to help Jennifer feel safer. Instead, she reported feeling more frightened and tense. The therapist was surprised but remained nonjudgmentally curious about how Jennifer had responded to the experiment of looking at him. He then gently suggested another experiment: "I wonder if we could experiment with what would make you feel safer? How about exploring what would feel like a 'safe' or or 'right' distance between us is right now? What if I moved my chair back? Let's see what happens." As her transferential defensiveness was challenged by this experiment, and as she mindfully felt her fear diminish, she was able to recognize how dysregulated she had felt, and the therapy progressed to the practice of new, more adaptive actions.

Therapeutic experiments are always conducted to make discoveries about the organization of experience (Kurtz, 1990), to bring awareness to the effects of trauma and the ensuing action tendencies. These discoveries arise unprompted from mindful experiments; they are "unforced, automatic, and spontaneous, and therefore reflective of habits and core organizers" (Kurtz, 1990, p. 69). Often both therapist and client are surprised by the unantici- pated result of an experiment, as exemplified by Jennifer: She was amazed that, when she experimented by drawing a circle around herself to indicate "her space" (Rosenberg et al., 1986), she spontaneously relaxed and had the thought "I am worth something!"

Through conducting collaborative experiments, the curiosity of both ther- apist and client is engaged; the exploration action system is activated, in turn deactivating the defensive action system; and without the domination of the defensive action system, unpredictability is expected and welcomed. The client's experience of separation from the event and the ability to observe internal experience rather than merge with it leads to a deepening of dual awareness: "I am terrified" becomes "I experience a violent trembling in my extremities." Both client and therapist can then become interested in how the elements of experience change: "When you direct me [the therapist] to move across the room, what happens in your body? What thoughts emerge? What emotions or pictures are evoked spontaneously by the experiment?" The experimental attitude requires that the therapist remain unattached to any particular agendas or outcome and willing to work with whatever emerges from the client's organization of experience, while all the time providing interactive regulation to maintain arousal within a window of tolerance.

Experiments occur in the context of collaboration and social engagement. Clients are asked if they "would be willing" to participate in the described experiment in a tone that suggests that the answer "No" is just as welcome as the answer "Yes." The client's willingness and resistance are of equal interest to the therapist and equally merit further curiosity and study. If the client responds negatively, collaboration helps to determine the next step in the session. If the client responds positively, the question is then followed by the mindfulness-invoking phrase, "Let's notice what happens when . . ." (and then the particular experiment is stated; possible experiments are explored below). This clause instructs the client to observe the effect of the experiment on body and mind: how he or she organizes experience in response to the experiment.

The experimental attitude encourages thoughtful "trials" of new responses as an alternative to maladaptive tendencies and emphasizes nonbiased observation of their impact. As a challenge to the automatic action tenden- cies, small, precise experiments are conducted to gather new information and heighten curiosity. For example, clients might experiment with grounding exercises of softening and relaxing their feet against the floor and unlocking their knees, noticing what happens as they do so. An "experiment" is a "trial change": a change in words used, a change in posture, a movement or a still-ing of movement, a change in orientation, a change in sensory modality. Experiments can be either physical or verbal, as in the following illustrations (adapted from Kurtz, 1990):

1. In one type of experiment, therapist and client might study what hap-pens when the *client senses or performs something physical.* For example, as a client becomes aware of tingling in her arms, the therapist proposes an experiment by asking, "Notice what happens when you focus just on that tingling in your arms." Or, as the client makes a pushing gesture with the arms, the therapist asks, "Would it be okay if we studied what happens when you repeat that gesture with your arms? Let's see what happens when you repeat it again." Or the therapist might say, "Let's explore what hap-pens if you stand up and plant your feet and then make that same gesture?"

2. Another type of experiment involves the *client's verbalization of a par-ticular word, phrase, or sentence.* For example, a client with a tendency toward collapse and submission said, "I wish I could say 'No.' " The thera-pist then proposes that the two of them explore what happens when the client instead repeats the phrase "I *can* say 'No' *now.*" Or, a client might spontaneously say, "I know it was not my fault." The therapist might ask, "What happens in your body and emotions when you repeat that sentence?"

3. In yet another way of experimenting, therapist and client study what happens *when the therapist performs a physical action.* For example, the therapist notices, and asks the client to study, how she (the client) averts her eyes while simultaneously turning her body away. In one case, the client reported the belief that "it's not safe to be seen," accompanied by the phys-ical response of an accelerated heart rate and constricted breathing. To talk about that belief and its origins might provide some insight, but an experi-ment would offer an opportunity to challenge the belief in some way. The therapist might try a variety of experiments: "Could we study what happens inside you if I close my eyes and you keep your eyes open? How about if I pull my chair back a little—what happens? How about if I pull my chair back and turn my head slightly away from you?" Each experiment is stud-ied by client and therapist and its results evaluated: They notice that, as the therapist pulls her chair back and looks slightly away, the client's heart rate and breathing settle, and she reports a sense of greater control. This explo-ration of her bodily responses results in a kind of somatic insight, a felt change resulting in an understanding from the body up.

4. In yet another variation on experiments, the therapist and client observe the results when *the therapist says a certain statement or repeats a phrase.* For example, the client says, "I know I have the *right* to be angry, but I can't *let* myself get angry." The therapist offers him the opportunity

to study that predicament by proposing, "Let's study what happens in your body when I repeat your words, 'You have a right to be angry.' Let's notice what happens inside when I repeat those words again."

The variety of experiments and their potential uses are almost infinite. Experiments can be utilized when clients become hyper- or hypoaroused to help them regulate traumatic activation. When a client is numb and hypoaroused, active strategies are indicated (Courtois, 1991). The therapist might suggest an experiment in which the client stands and walks purposefully to the door. Or what happens if the client rotates her head and neck to orient to the environment around her? If, on the other hand, the client is hyperaroused and feeling overwhelmed, "containment" strategies may be useful (Courtois, 1991). The therapist might propose that they experiment with what happens inside when both of them stand up and ground themselves, sensing their legs and feet. With each experiment, the responses are carefully studied, and the next experiment reflects what has been learned from the last.

PUTTING SKILLS TOGETHER

At any given moment in a therapy session, there are numerous options for tracking, making contact statements, applying mindfulness, and experimenting. Through bodyreading and tracking, the therapist selects which elements of present-moment experience to identify with a contact statement. The therapist must discriminate thoughtfully among the myriad of sensorimotor, emotional, and cognitive phenomena occurring at any given moment and select elements that best support the overall therapeutic process and the aims of each session: for example, strengthening a resource, regulating arousal, executing truncated defensive responses, or other adaptive actions. Because contact statements bring attention to a particular aspect of experience, they influence the direction of the therapy session; the choice of mindfulness questions and experiments further enhances the focusing of attention on those aspects of the client's experience most likely to support a transformation of the habitual maladaptive responses.

Integrating Resources

Tracking the indicators of the client's resources—that is, his or her strengths, competencies and skills—is just as vital as working with traumatic material (Eckberg, 2000; Levine, 1997; Phillips, 1995; Rothschild, 2000). Indeed, care must be taken to balance interventions that address traumatic material with interventions that support the client's resources for integrating that material. Therapists look for signs of competence, integrative capacity, positive experiences, and empowering or playful actions. Potential or manifest resources can be noted at all three levels of information processing. Sensorimotor, or somatic, resources include muscular tone that is neither too relaxed nor too tense; a balanced, erect, relaxed posture; states of optimal arousal; and movements that are graceful and economical. The therapist might track emotional or cognitive resources that become available when a client expresses, even momentarily, positive affects (e.g., joy, calm, delight) or verbalizes new, more positive thoughts (e.g., "I have a right to say 'no.'"). In each and every moment, the therapist is monitoring the client's level of arousal to assess: Is it optimal? Too low? Too high? If arousal is outside the window of tolerance, working with resources may bring it back to within the window of tolerance.

Differentiating the Building Blocks
of Present Experience

For traumatized individuals, body awareness can be problematic in a variety of ways. First, becoming aware of the body may be disconcerting or even frightening, sometimes triggering feelings of being out of control, terrified, rageful, panicky, or weak and helpless. Second, traumatized clients often experience the body as numb or anesthetized. Rather than becoming overly activated by body awareness, these clients are challenged by a level of hypoarousal that lowers their sensitivity to the body. A third difficulty emerges when body awareness stimulates thoughts such as "My body is disgusting," "I hate my body," "My body let me down," "I don't have a body," or "My body is dead."

Clients are taught to distinguish between physical sensations or actions and trauma-based emotions or cognitions through cultivating deeper, more focused awareness of sensations and movement. One client experienced panic when he became aware of his body; he learned to "put aside" the panic and just follow his body sensations as they fluctuated in texture, quality, and intensity, until they settled. Another client who stated "I hate my body" was encouraged to differentiate this thought from the actual sensation of the accompanying physical action: curling up in a fetal position, which relaxed her muscles and felt comforting. Another who felt her body had betrayed her by not protecting her from abuse explored the sensation and movement of making a "stop" gesture with her arms and hands, putting aside her thoughts and emotions to notice only how this movement felt physically.

The therapist asks the client to limit the amount of information to integrate by focusing attention exclusively on body sensations and movement, experiencing them as distinct from emotions and thought (Ogden & Minton,

2000). In this way, clients gain an effective tool with which to address their disturbing body perceptions and sensations: learning to uncouple sensations and movements from trauma-related emotions and cognitive distortions.

Linking Building Blocks

As clients become increasingly able to track present-moment somatic experience, the therapist builds on that increased awareness by helping them study the interplay of their thoughts, feelings, movement impulses, sense perceptions (images, smells, sounds, tastes, and touch) and body sensations. The therapist directs the client's attention to how thoughts and emotions are affecting present-moment body experience by making contact statements such as "I notice that your jaw tightens as you talk about feeling angry," which links the tension with the emotion. Mindful questions are asked to further "stitch together" elements of experience: "What happens when you notice both the anger and the tightening?" or "What happens in your body or your feelings when you have the thought, 'I'm a loser?'" or "When you feel happy, how does your body respond? What images emerge?" The therapist pays close attention to how linking together these building blocks affects the client's arousal and sense of mastery. Generally speaking, therapists choose to facilitate the linking of experiential elements when doing so when does not take the client's arousal out of the window of tolerance, and when the client's integrative capacity is sufficient to be able to tolerate and utilize more information. These building blocks are also linked when exploring memories or experiences during which a client feels a sense of mastery, pleasure, or positive affect. This helps to reinforce and expand upon the sense of mastery or pleasure, and to offset clients' frequent experience of pain or lack of competence (discussed in Chapter 11).

TOUCH INTERVENTIONS IN PSYCHOTHERAPY PRACTICE

In traditional psychotherapy practice, the use of touch has generally been avoided out of concerns that it might be misinterpreted or misexperienced by the client as sexual, the effects on the transference would promote regression or gratification instead of insight, or the therapist would misuse it to further his or her own psychological or sexual needs. The same concerns exist in sensorimotor psychotherapy. Although touch can be therapeutic, there are potential pitfalls and it must be used cautiously and judiciously, if at all. If therapists choose to use touch in their clinical work, they should be well trained not only in the use of touch itself but also in combining touch with psychotherapy. The laws of their licensing body must condone the use of touch in clinical practice, and their liability insurance should cover the use of touch. Therapists are advised to use a written informed consent form that describes the use of touch and explicitly states that the client is always in control of the use of touch in the therapeutic setting. Conducting a "touch history" that includes inquiring about clients' past experience with being touched, touching, and witnessing touch can be a useful intervention to elucidate their past difficulties with touch (Caldwell, 1997b). Establishing the client's capacity to differentiate past from present and therapeutic from non-therapeutic uses of touch is also a necessary component of the therapeutic work preceding any consideration of incorporating touch into treatment.

Consideration of the therapist's own potential contertransferential reactions to, and beliefs and attitudes toward, touch and what effects the use of touch might have on the therapist, the client, and the power differential inherent in the therapeutic relationship is essential (Hunter & Struve, 1998). In order to utilize touch, the therapist must be capable of maintaining his or her own very clear psychological and sexual boundaries and be comfortable with the use of therapeutic touch in professional contexts. Therapists must assess the appropriateness of using touch on a case-by-case, session-by-session basis, evaluating the client's ego strength, sense of boundaries, diagnosis, and overall functioning, as well as assessing their own capacity to manage any transference responses, including sexual, that might ensue. Both the therapist and the client's motivations for the use of touch should be examined: For example, touch that is used to rescue either the client or therapist from uncomfortable emotions should be avoided (Caldwell, 1997b). Touch—even well-considered, boundaried, therapeutic touch—may evoke unworkable transference if the therapist is uncomfortable or unskilled, if the patient has poor ego strength, if the therapeutic alliance is weak, or if the connection resulting from touch exceeds the working intimacy in the therapeutic relationship.

It should also be noted that the use of direct touch between client and therapist is not necessary to accomplish the goals of sensorimotor psychotherapy. In the case where some type of physical contact might enhance therapeutic outcome, but direct touch is ill advised, objects such pillows or balls can be used to buffer physical contact between client and therapist. The client's use of his or her own touch can also be effective (e.g., wrapping arms around him- or herself).

Despite all of the cautions inherent in the use of touch as an intervention in psychotherapy, it can be an efficient, useful, effective intervention and there are specific clinical purposes for its judicious use (Caldwell, 1997a; Hunter & Struve, 1998). Physical touch activates nerve endings on the surface of the skin, thereby increasing sensation intensity, making touch particularly useful in restoring or increasing awareness of body sensation. If the client tends to lose connection with the body or has little awareness of body sensation, having him or her touch a particular area (e.g., neck, shoulder, stomach) can restore body awareness.

The efficacy of using touch in this way lies in helping the client become aware of the exact depth, placement, and type of touch (with palm of hand, fingertips, etc.) that would accentuate the sensations in a particular area. For example, a client who suffered from alexythymia reported numbness in her chest, especially around her heart. Her therapist suggested that she place her own hand on this area. At first, the client said she felt "nothing." However, when the therapist suggested that she try different kinds of touch until she discovered the exact form of touch that helped her feel this area of her body, the client found that a certain depth and movement of her own fingers indeed promoted sensations in her chest. The client remarked, "I can feel my heart—this is the first time my heart has felt supported by me."

Touch can also help build new somatic resources or support awareness of existing resources. If a client has difficulty staying grounded, touching his or her own legs and feet to increase sensation may facilitate the experience of feeling grounded. When a client is mindfully executing a defensive movement of pushing with the hands and arms against the therapist's hands, or against a pillow held by the therapist, he or she may experience a welcome feeling of strength and competence. The client is encouraged to find the exact kind of touch and pressure that is used with the pillow or hands that feels "right," such as pushing with one hand or both, pushing against firm resistance or against resistance that "gives way," or any number of other variations. A client who had been sexually abused reported that she was not allowed to refuse the advances from her father, and said she thought pushing would be frightening. With encouragement from her therapist, she first chose to stand and push against the wall, reporting that that would be "safer" than pushing against her therapist. Feeling confident in this act, she then decided to experiment with pushing against a pillow held by the therapist. With the help of her therapist, she discovered that by directing the pressure the therapist used (she requested that the therapist use strong pressure that then gave way as she pushed hard), she felt in control and her body felt strong and capable. This sense of competency contradicted the feelings of futility that she had previously associated with using her arms to defend herself.

The use of touch can facilitate the learning of new actions and postural patterns. For example, for a client who exhibited a collapsed or flexed chest and swayback, gentle pressure in the lower back with the instruction for him to press back against the hand of the therapist led to spontaneous straightening and alignment of the spine. In that squared stance, the client began to experience a more energized, less overwhelmed relationship to the environment.

Because touch is always used as a collaborative experiment, it is necessary to allow time for clients to observe and verbalize their inner experience prior to the touch (whether self touch or pressing against the therapist's hands, etc.) and then the resultant effects of the touch on the client's organization of experience after the experiment. Asking a client to become aware of his or her body prior to using touch increases mindfulness and enhances awareness of the effects of touch once it does happen. Such awareness may also prevent some of the pitfalls discussed previously, because the client may notice somatic signals that indicate the expectation of a boundary crossing before the touch occurs, as did one client who observed that her body was bracing prior to the use of touch. Awareness of the body as a client considers the possibility of touch may also clarify transference; the client who braced discovered she had placed her therapist in the role of perpetrator, for example.

When physical contact is made, a reaction happens: The client may feel an impulse to pull away, experience movement in the body, breathe a sigh of relief, have a particular thought, emotional response, or memory emerge. All of these reactions are grist for the mill, and provide jumping-off points for therapeutic inquiry: What about the touch helps you relax (or pull away)? Does it feel safe? Do you feel like you are in control of the kind of touch? What is the nonverbal message of the touch that made you relax (or pull away)? What does the touch tell you? The effect of the experiment with touch may be contrary to the therapist's intention or the client's expectation, so it is imperative that the therapist track the client's reaction and elicit reports on "what happens inside" as the touch is implemented.

Provided that the therapist's touch is attuned and professional, the client's reaction will tend to reflect his or her automatic translation of the sensation in the context of past experiences of touch. Experiencing a particular sensation in a part of the body that has been injured or abused may remind the client of past trauma (Janet, 1925). For example, a client who had been beaten in political torture requested gentle touch on his back, but when the therapist first touched his back, the client cringed and was reminded of the torture. Eventually, with skillful therapeutic intervention, he was able to experience the therapist's touch as different, and slowly the physical sensations changed to positive ones.

Mindful, collaborative experiments with touch may help the client become aware of how she or he might use touch outside of the session. Many clients have discovered types of touch (touching their legs to promote a sense of grounding, placing their own hands on their belly or heart, etc.) that they utilize in their daily lives. Numerous clients who have been sexually abused have explored self touch on their forearms and hands under the guidance of their therapist, and have been able to slowly appreciate their own sensual touch. They have often gone on to successfully enjoy touch with their partners, provided that they felt sufficient control and influence on the kinds, placements, timing, and contexts of the touch.

The meaning of the physical contact for the client may derive from a previous negative or traumatic experience. For example, one client wanted to push against the therapist's hands to experience a sense of boundary. However, she tensed her body and pulled away as the therapist began to put her hands in a position so that the client could push. Actual touch had not yet occurred, but the client already had a reaction of tensing. As the meaning was explored, the client said, "I know this is not true, but your hand looks menacing." Her previous abuse had biased her toward interpreting any kind of touch as hurtful. Other times the meaning is positive: Another client experienced relaxation and took a deep breath when touch was used. He reported that he could tell that this touch was different from the past, saying to the therapist, "These hands want to help me, not hurt me." When the therapist asks for the meaning or words of the touch, it is most effective to set up the process as an experiment in mindfulness. In this example, the therapist had the client feel the exact kind of touch that felt "right" to him. When they had negotiated the right touch, the therapist said in a slow, mindful voice, "Feel the quality of this touch. If my hands could speak in words instead of sensation, what would they be saying to you? Let the meaning come from my hands rather than your thoughts." As therapist and client mindfully explore clients' automatic reactions to touch, and the meaning of the reactions, a new experience can be facilitated and the habitual response transformed.

The client's physical and psychological state is constantly fluctuating, so, to be effective, touch must be adapted moment by moment to the client's process and boundary needs: more pressure or less, on the side of the shoulder or the back of the shoulder, experimenting with decreasing the touch or increasing it to determine how much is "enough." The therapist offers an experience of "boundaried" touch that is respectful, noninvasive, and consistently open to refinement by the client. Consequently, clients know that they are in complete control of the touch and can modify or terminate it at any time—an experience that can be a powerful new learning for those who were not in control of when and how they were touched in the context of past trauma. The effective use of touch in therapy can anchor the client to the here-and-now and to the relationship with the therapist, not catapult the client back into trauma-related implicit memory states.

CONCLUSION

The sensorimotor-trained therapist approaches the phase-oriented treatment of trauma with a repertoire of techniques that serve specific functions:

- Gathering information by tracking and bodyreading trauma-related action tendencies and regulatory abilities;

- Evoking the social engagement system via the use of attuned contact statements;
- Engaging the exploration system by heightening the client's mindfulness and self-study;
- Challenging habitual responses and promoting the acquisition of new patterns by using experiments.

Differentiating or linking the different levels of information processing, developing the client's resources, and judiciously using the therapist's touch or client's self touch all serve to meet the goals of each phase of treatment.

In different phases of treatment, as we describe in subsequent chapters, these techniques provide the substrate upon which a variety of therapeutic interventions can build. In phase 1 treatment, the techniques help the client develop his or her ability to regulate arousal by learning the resources needed to inhibit the overactivation of defensive responses. In phase 2 treatment, tracking, making contact statements, applying mindfulness, and experimenting support the resolution of traumatic memory by facilitating the client's ability to tolerate and track the sensations of traumatic arousal until the sensations themselves settle to a point of resolution in the body, and complete truncated mobilizing defensive responses. And, finally, in phase 3, these very same tools are put to use in the service of expanding the client's capacity to engage action systems of daily life, develop intimate relationships, create new meanings, and increase tolerance of positive affects.

Chapter 10

※·※·※

Phase 1 Treatment: Developing Somatic Resources for Stabilization

TRAUMATIZED CLIENTS TYPICALLY PRESENT for treatment with dysregulated arousal, unchecked defensive subsystems, compromised functioning, and the perceived or actual loss of psychological and/or physical safety. Past and present have become somatically, emotionally, and cognitively confused: reactivated traumatic memories in the form of intrusive affects and body sensations signal danger even in peaceful moments. Daily life is avoided while attention focuses narrowly on threat cues or on internal dysregulation.

If we attempt to treat symptoms by exploring memories of the events that caused them, we may destabilize our clients further. Instead, in the first phase of treatment, interventions must be chosen that facilitate both physiological and psychological homeostasis and that emphasize self-regulatory skills that maintain arousal within a window of tolerance and reduce or eradicate self-destructive tendencies. Phase 1 interventions are geared toward raising clients' integrative capacity so that adaptive functioning in daily life is increased. They must learn to experience the dysregulating emotion and arousal without reacting self-destructively (e.g., engaging in self-harm, dangerous activities, violence, suicidal ideation) or otherwise maladaptively (Steele et al., 2006).

As the therapy gets underway, the therapist becomes an interactive psychobiological regulator for the client's dysregulated nervous system. Tracking the body to assess the stimulation of defensive subsystems and excessive arousal, the therapist adjusts the pace and process of therapy to help clients develop resources needed to self-regulate. The therapist acts as an "auxiliary cortex" (Diamond et al., 1963) and "affect regulator of the patient's dys-regulated states in order to provide a growth-facilitating environment for the patient's immature affect-regulating structures" (Schore, 2001b, p. 264). Gradually, through the interactive regulation of the therapist combined with psychoeducation, recognition of their triggers, and mindful observation of their own arousal and defensive subsystems, clients learn to become aware of when their arousal exceeds the window of tolerance and to implement resources that help them stabilize at those times.

Phase 1 treatment for trauma must involve reinstating lost resources, learning new resources, and strengthening existing resources. By *resources* we mean all the personal skills, abilities, objects, relationships, and services that facilitate self-regulation and provide a sense of competence and resilience. For example, the resources necessary for the client to engage in treatment might include medications aimed at stabilization, sufficient money and skills to drive to therapy or pay for parking and gas, or sufficient interpersonal skills to negotiate time off work to attend therapy. Note that both internal resources (interpersonal skills, ability to drive) and external resources (med-ications, financial resources) are required in tandem to facilitate the client's visit to the therapist.

Developing resources begins with recognizing and acknowledging exist-ing resources: clients' abilities and current competencies as adults, as well as their "survival resources" that enabled them to cope with past traumatic challenges. From this basic orientation of validation, existing resources are acknowledged and expanded, and those resources that are undeveloped or absent are taught. Developing resources helps clients stabilize during phase 1, provides the support for facing and integrating the traumatic memories in phase 2, and fosters competence and creativity to meet life's ongoing chal-lenges during phase 3. With guidance, effort, practice, and time, clients can develop effective resources for all phases of treatment.

SOMATIC RESOURCES

Psychological capacities and beliefs are inextricably linked with the structure and movement of the body. Arms that hang limply by the side might reflect an inability to set boundaries or behave assertively; a gait that is always fast and purposeful might reflect attempts at self-regulation via "staying on the go," living a fast-paced life with no opportunity for reminders of the trauma to surface. Somatic resources comprise the category of abilities that emerge from physical experience yet influence psychological health. They include the physical functions and capacities that support self-regulation and provide a sense of somatic and psychological well-being and competence. For example, the action of pushing away with the arms combined with the felt experience of having a right to establish personal boundaries and defend oneself integrates empowering movement with an adaptive belief. Sensorimotor psychotherapy explores the interface between physical action and meaning; however, in contrast to top-down methods, the meaning making *follows* from the physical experience rather than precedes it. Cognitive reflections are stimulated by the experience of the action itself: Through the act of pushing, clients realize that they have the right to defend themselves; through the act of reaching out, they understand that they can ask for help.

Phase 1 treatment involves establishing a sense of safety and self-care, which "begins by focusing on control of the body" (Herman, 1992, p. 160). Resources that support this goal can involve top-down resources, such as coping or safety plans or using cognition to remind oneself that there is no current danger, as well as bottom-up somatic resources, such as the physical capacities and actions that promote a return to the zone of optimal arousal. Clients learn to use the movement, sensation, and posture of the body to stabilize themselves and increase the ease of their daily life functioning. Self-care resources that stabilize the energy regulation system, such as regular sleep and eating habits, are also established in phase 1.

Literally thousands of somatic resources exist, from basic physiological functions (e.g., digestion) to sensory capacities (e.g., the ability to see, hear, smell, and taste) to self-regulatory abilities (e.g., the ability to ground and center oneself). In this chapter we focus on physical capacities and actions that can be taught to clients to accomplish the goals of stabilization beginning in the very first session.

In the initial intake interview, clients learn how working with the body can help them stabilize without addressing the memory of the traumatic events. Some clients are relieved to learn that they are not required to talk about their memories, whereas others need to be assured that there will be ample time to work with those memories after stabilization has been achieved.

Although clients may feel that they have no resources, we have found that even the most dysregulated client has used survival resources that may go unnoticed until the therapist draws attention to them. Conveying to clients that they come to therapy with multiple somatic resources is itself stabilizing; it is also an encouraging surprise and a radically different way of thinking for the chronically traumatized client. Assessment of both existing and missing resources (through tracking, bodyreading, dialogue, questions, and history taking) is a priority as therapy gets underway.

During assessment, the therapist teaches clients how to evaluate their own somatic resources by directing awareness to body sensation, areas of tension and relaxation, movement, pain, discomfort, structure, and alignment. Clients thereby discover which physical capacities are resources and which need to be challenged and changed. The therapist also gathers information from the client (and at times from the client's friends or family members), asking questions about past and present experiences, patterns, competencies, and limitations. Questions are asked about existing resources: "What got you through that experience? How did you survive? What was of help to you?" In addition, inquiries are made about the connection between the body and psychological issues: "Do you remember when you first began feeling that tightness in your neck?" or "Were there any lasting physical effects after the rape, such as tension, pain, or numbness?" or "Can you remember a time when your body felt comfortable or good?"

The therapist tracks the client's body as past and present experiences are discussed as well as during therapist–client interactions as the therapeutic relationship is formed. Even the manner in which the client shakes hands yields information about his or her somatic resources. The handshake might be limp, overly strong, quick, or sustained, with eye contact or without, with full extension of the arm or not, with full hand contact or only the fingers. Each pattern holds important data about the presence or absence of resources.

The therapist bodyreads, unobtrusively noting the client's general physical tendencies, to assess existing somatic resources—for example, deep regular breathing, extension in the spine, flexible movement, sturdy legs, relaxed shoulders, ability to make eye contact—as well as the chronic signs of dys-regulated arousal and truncated defenses.

Amy's lifelong tendency toward hypoarousal, compliance, and submission effectively "collapsed" her posture so her head hung and her shoulders rounded, creating lasting physical tendencies that interfered with her ability to self-regulate. As an adult, these tendencies, coupled with cognitive distortions that lowered her self-esteem, produced serious consequences: Amy routinely submitted to physical abuse from her boyfriend. Although she expressed the desire to leave the relationship, she had been unsuccessful in doing so. In keeping with the phase 1 priority of restoring safety, the therapist focused on somatic resources that would first challenge and then reorganize her tendency toward hypoarousal and compliance.

Because clients usually experience immobilizing defenses of freezing or submission as personal defects, it is important to reframe them as survival resources that helped them live though inescapable trauma. When the therapist validates clients' defensive subsystems as coping strategies that they were forced to employ, clients are encouraged to view them as capacities rather than as weaknesses and then can work with them more effectively to dismantle their chronic engagement. As clients begin to appreciate these survival resources, their felt sense of powerlessness and identity as victims are challenged. For example, Amy recognized in therapy how trying to fight her perpetrator or run away as a child would have been ill advised and how her "survival resource" of automatic compliance and submission minimized the severity of the trauma at that time.

Clients can never have "too many" resources: The intention of building somatic resources must always be to expand the current movement and sensation repertoire, rather than take away existing coping strategies (even many maladaptive ones). The goal of resource work in phase 1 is to develop a sufficiently broad range of somatic resources to modulate arousal. Amy's therapist taught her how to set personal boundaries as an alternative to compliant and submissive behavior. Using her own body, the therapist offered to demonstrate a more assertive physical and psychological organization to counter Amy's submissive tendencies: the movement of extending her spine to stand more erect and nonverbally communicating "NO" in her posture and gesture. The therapist tactfully contrasted this movement with Amy's collapsed posture and asked her to try out both options so that she could experience for herself which one supported her personal boundaries. Amy then practiced the new alternative until it began to feel more comfortable, solid, and connected to the affects and cognitions that accompany "no!" Through the therapist's willingness to demonstrate different movements, the therapist normalized movement as a resource and helped Amy to mirror her actions.

CREATING SAFETY FOR SOMATIC EXPLORATION

Because clients with complex trauma can be easily triggered by interventions that access the body too quickly, attention is given to pacing, boundary maintenance, and safe, conscious, mindful, and gradual reconnection with the body. Many clients come to therapy with a negative sense of their bodies: frightened to experience sensation, feeling numb and disconnected, angry at their bodies for not working the way they want or for betraying them, or even feeling that the body is "fodder for the devil," as one client put it. The traumatized person often views the prospect of experiencing body sensation as scary, foreign, repulsive, uninteresting, tedious, or simply not possible. Because of the dysregulating effect of unassimilated traumatic experience, even the conscious awareness of ordinary sensations can trigger traumatic activation. For example, a heart rate raised in response to physical exercise can have the disconcerting effect of evoking helplessness or panic because it is experienced not as a normal body response to physical activity, but as an indication of the need to fight or flee from threat.

Clients vary widely in their awareness of body sensation and the connection between their body and self-regulation. Some clients are aware of sensation only in certain parts of the body but not in other parts. Other clients are unaware of tension in their body or unaware of physical sensations altogether. Some clients come to the first session aware of, and wanting to work with, the relationship between physical tendencies and psychological issues, whereas others are not aware that there might be such a connection. For example, a client who was extremely tense across his shoulders, arms, and back came to therapy to manage his anger, but did not realize that the tension corresponded with the anger until he experienced several sessions of somatic awareness interventions.

During the assessment phase, the therapist determines if connecting to the body feels comfortable for clients, noting if they are able to reflect on their subjective embodied experience and its influence on self-regulation. If this awareness is not present, the therapist tries to determine the reasons that block it. Is the client phobically avoidant of body awareness? Is the client numb and disconnected from bodily experience? Does connecting to the body trigger shame or alarm? Depending on the obstacle, the therapist can begin to find a way to work somatically that is comfortable for the client. Some clients are uncomfortable with the word *body* so avoiding the word at the beginning of therapy helps to increase comfort; for others, providing a menu of words with which to label body sensations, learning to self-observe in order to decrease the sense of being "looked at," and normalizing somatic experience through psychoeducation or a brief illustrative anecdote that describes difficulties similar to theirs establish comfort with sensorimotor approaches.

EXPERIENCES OF COMPETENCE AND PLEASURE

Finding the physical correlates to feelings of competence and positive affect creates a safe framework for becoming aware of the body. This focus may seem anomalous to some clients, but a sensitive therapist can usually help even the most highly traumatized person eventually find an island of physical neutrality, if not mastery. The therapist might question the client about what he or she does, or used to do, well and then track what happens to the client's body when he or she reports these strengths. For example, a client reported that he was good at football, and, as he described his football prowess, his spine straightened and his chin lifted very slightly. The therapist brought his attention to this bodily shift, mirrored it, and encouraged him to repeat describing his prowess several times, noticing his physical correlates. This unconscious straightening of the spine and lifting of the chin subsequently became his somatic anchor for feeling competent—an anchor that he learned to simulate voluntarily when feelings of inadequacy arose. Thus, once a somatic resource is identified, the therapist can ask the client to become aware of this resource, exaggerate it, and study it mindfully to sense the finer feelings and effects of the movement. The resource can then be used by choice, as needed in daily life.

Questions about positive experiences in the body are as important for the therapist to ask as questions about trauma-related somatic experience. When asked what she was experiencing in her body, one client, diagnosed with dissociative identity disorder, replied vehemently that her body was dirty while rubbing her arms and legs aggressively. Seeing that she was becoming hyperaroused by simply being asked about her body, the therapist asked her if she could remember a time, either past or present, when she felt good in her body. The client immediately reported a memory of being pushed on a swing by her grandfather. This memory provided the jumping off point for reclaiming a positive physical experience: The therapist asked her to "hang out" in the sensations connected to that memory—sensations of feeling giggly in her chest, the feeling of air "whooshing" against her skin, the feeling of strength in her legs—all sensations that competed with the posttraumatic sensation of dirtiness. The therapist next had her oscillate back and forth between the "dirty" feeling and the positive sensations in her chest, skin, and leg muscles from the memory of swinging. After the client did this for a few minutes, she exclaimed in surprise, "I'm not dirty!"

EXPERIMENTS TO BUILD SOMATIC RESOURCES

There is nothing more detrimental to building somatic resources than making the process of re-connecting with the body an effortful, painful, negative experience. Noticing and reinforcing how clients are already able to sense their body–rather than how disconnected from it they are–and capitalizing on existing strengths fortifies their confidence and stimulates enthusiasm for further somatic exploration. Positive reinforcement and praise for their efforts to contact the body (e.g., "It's wonderful that you can actually *feel* that tension—some people don't have that awareness.") can be encouraging for clients to hear.

From a position of acknowledging existing resources, the therapist collaborates with clients to create appropriate somatic experiments that challenge them to stretch beyond their current capacities but do not generate excessive frustration by being too difficult (Bundy, Lane, & Murray, 2002; Janet, 1925). Collaboration generates interest, curiosity, and, most of all, hope. Planning mutually agreeable somatic interventions with clear goals sets the stage for success. The therapist seeks "to learn specifically how the client would behave differently or what they would like to be able to do after an intervention that they cannot currently do" (Bundy, 2002, p. 212). Imagining alternatives to habitual responses assures that the particular somatic resource selected for development has meaning and value for the client.

When Amy was asked to imagine how, if she could wave a magic wand, she would like her internal experience to be different, she replied, "I would like to feel strong and not so numb so I could leave this relationship." This wish set the stage for persistent exploration of the somatic resources she needed to achieve her goal. Without the inspiration generated by her vision of a future different from her present and past, she might not have been able to maintain the focus and motivation necessary to build all the resources she needed to mitigate her longstanding tendencies of chronic hypoarousal, physical collapse, and compliance.

Many clients with somatic awareness deficits are unable to utilize feedback from their bodies to sense their posture or movement or what they have accomplished after a somatic intervention. To remedy this deficit, therapists can serve as a "mirror" or model for clients by demonstrating the missing somatic resource and contrasting it with the one that enables increased self-regulation (e.g., differentiating alignment from collapse).

Betty, who expressed the belief that "No one will ever support me" was helped to change the posture and orienting tendencies that contributed to this belief through a slow, titrated process. The therapist first made empathic contact with Betty's wish for support. Then he imitated Betty's posture of tightening and rounding her shoulders and looking down and avoiding eye contact, saying to Betty, "From this position, I can't tell if you are smiling or frowning at me." From the therapist's demonstration, Betty became aware of her own physical tendencies and their effect on her capacity to recognize and receive support.

The therapist also demonstrated a somatic resource and reported his own experience of it: "When I sit taller, instead of collapsing and looking away, I get a feeling of opening in my chest—it is a good feeling. And when I make eye contact with you, I can sense that we are more in contact." Betty was then invited to imitate the resource. She first experimented with raising her gaze a few inches upward so that she could see the legs of the therapist's coffee table, then taking time for her arousal to settle before going further. Next she was asked if she could raise the level of her eyes to the surface of the table so that she could see the objects on it. Over a series of attempts, she gradually brought her gaze and orientation upward, and her shoulders straightened. Not only was she now supported by visual contact with the therapist but also by her straight spine and squared shoulders. This physical shift was reflected in a more active, collaborative dialogue with the therapist, increasing Betty's awareness of his support and countering her trauma-related belief.

These demonstrations of a somatic resource may be particularly effective because "mirror neurons" fire in observers who are watching the movement, replicating the precise pattern that the observers would use if they were doing the movement themselves (Rizzolatti & Craighero, 2004; Rizzolatti,

Fadiga, Gallese, & Fogassi, 1996). The visual input of watching another person move even slightly "gets mapped onto the equivalent motor representation in our own brain by the activity of these mirror neurons" (Stern, 2004, p. 79). As clients observe their therapist demonstrating a somatic resource, they experience it in the brain as if they were executing the same action and experiencing the same emotional effect, essentially "rehearsing" the movement themselves.

Somatic resources are highly individual and must be tailor-made for the unique needs and therapeutic goals of each client. What serves as a resource for one person may be experienced as an obstacle for another: One client might need grounding in order to modulate activation, whereas another might find grounding dysregulating because it competes with flight responses, and instead need to work with movement.

Monitoring hyper- and hypoarousal responses becomes the barometer for evaluating the efficacy of any somatic resource explored during phase 1 treatment: If the resource promotes arousal that stays within a window of tolerance, then it is "resourcing"; if it stimulates hyper- or hypoarousal, it is "deresourcing." Similarly, a somatic resource may be useful at one particular point in therapy and not at another point. In phase 1 treatment, one client, overwhelmed by intrusive emotions that accompanied the belief "I don't have a right to say 'no,'" benefited from a pushing movement to create a boundary and settle his arousal. In phase 3 treatment, this same client learned to practice reaching out to develop his capacity for intimacy, using his capacity for boundary as a defense less often.

THERAPIST AS INTERACTIVE
PSYCHOBIOLOGICAL REGULATOR

Because most traumatized clients have an extensive history of interpersonal violations, they often experience a plethora of difficulties that interferes with the formation of a therapeutic relationship. As Courtois (1999) explained:

> The client may be beset by shame and anxiety and terrified by being judged and "seen" by the therapist. The therapist, in turn, may be perceived as a stand-in for other untrustworthy and abusive authority figures to be feared, mistrusted, challenged, tested, distanced from, raged against, sexualized, etc., or may be perceived as a stand-in for the longed-for good parent or rescuer to be clung to, deferred to, and nurtured by, or the two may alternate in unpredictable, kaleidoscopic shifts. (p. 190)

Steele et al. (2001; 2006) have conceptualized this traumatic legacy as a "phobia of contact," or phobia of therapy and the therapist. They argue that a central goal of phase 1 treatment is overcoming of the phobic avoidance of a therapeutic relationship. This process begins with normalizing, validating, and appreciating the phobia as a survival resource. Then the therapist teaches the client to observe how the over-activation of the defensive system undermines the formation of a therapeutic relationship between them, and challenges this pattern in small, incremental steps. This phobia is inevitably expressed somatically. As Betty revealed her yearning for support, her body and gaze were turned away; her body was rigid and armored; and the expectation of rejection and danger rendered her acutely sensitive to the therapist's tone and choice of words. The phobia was not interpreted but was instead addressed somatically by slowly transforming her orienting and physical tendencies so that she could integrate new information about the therapy from the environment. Without challenging Betty's beliefs that she had never been supported and without working with the narrative, the therapist challenged the phobia of contact in such a way that safe, supportive contact could then be experienced. If unchallenged, Betty and other clients end up reenacting the survival-oriented patterns of relatedness over and over again.

Chronic interpersonal trauma results in significant deficits in the ability to recognize internal signals indicating what is needed or not needed within a relationship, including the therapeutic relationship. The therapist watches closely for any evidence of distress from the client in response to the therapeutic techniques or relationship, noticing a client's impulse to cling (which may be a sign of the phobia of detachment from the therapist; Steele et al., 2001, Steele et al., in press), attack, or withdraw. The therapist's sensitivity to these impulses enables him or her to provide opportunities for choice and feedback in conjunction with attention to personal boundaries (Williamson & Anzalone, 2001).

In the initial stages of Rita's treatment, as her therapist leaned toward her, Rita tightened slightly. As the therapist noticed and named the tightening ("It looked like your body tightened up as I leaned forward"), Rita acknowledged that she felt it but quickly stated that his leaning forward was "fine" with her. The therapist noted the discrepancy between Rita's body statement and her verbal statement and suggested that they spend some time studying it, proposing that there might be an optimal distance for both her mind and her body. He asked Rita to identify the "right" distance between them, and she again said that where he sat was "fine." The therapist, remaining curious about the discrepancy between words and body response, continued to wonder out loud which position felt better. First he moved his chair away and then moved it closer, asking Rita if she noticed any difference in her reactions. Rita immediately recognized that it felt better when he moved away. As the therapist helped her to notice her body sensations, she reported that she felt a sensation of tightening in her stomach when he moved closer.

This sensation became their "warning" that she was beginning to feel a sense of threat, and they agreed that she would notice whenever this sensation emerged in the therapy session so that they could explore what was feeling threatening to her and, if necessary, readjust to her personal boundaries, physical or psychological.

Effective interactive psychobiological regulation requires paying more attention to how interventions affect autonomic arousal than to the content of the client's narrative. The therapist remains curious about the client's organization of experience and action tendencies, noticing and contacting the client's present experience rather than only the content of the conversation. The "story" or the event becomes less important than learning about arousal tendencies and how to return to levels within the window of tolerance. As psychobiological regulator, the therapist always endeavors to foster the client's curiosity to discover more about physical tendencies that maintain hypo/hyperarousal, and to develop needed somatic resources.

Experiments become the vehicle for discovering somatic resources for self-regulation. Client and therapist join together in curiosity about what happens when the client says the word "No"? What happens when he or she takes a breath? Makes a gesture? Changes orientation or proximity? Initially, working with sensation can be disruptive for a fragile client. Focusing internally requires being able to stay grounded and mindful, and the more dysregulated clients often are triggered by studying their own somatic responses. These clients must first learn actions based on somatic resources (e.g., grounding) before they can work with internal sensation.

WORKING EFFECTIVELY WITH HYPO- AND HYPERAROUSAL

When indicators of hyper- or hypoarousal are noted, the therapist endeavors to help the client find just the right physical action to facilitate regulation. If the therapist notices signs of hyperarousal (e.g., tension, shallow breath, rapid speech), he or she may gently interrupt the client's narrative before the arousal escalates further. As the therapist redirects the client's orienting away from the narrative account and toward current body resources or actions, the amount of information in the client's awareness is curtailed to the somatic experience—to awareness of the sensations and movements without interpretation. The therapist interrupts the client's trauma-related orienting tendencies before they cause further dysregulation. Allowing the client to repeat the traumatic reaction of fear, horror, and helplessness is of little therapeutic benefit and usually draws the client out of the window of tolerance. Instead, the therapist might notice that, as the client begins to speak about the trauma, her body tightens and her breath becomes shallow. The therapist can then interrupt the content of the story before the traumatic pattern is fully engaged and redirect the client's orienting away from her memories and toward her current body sensation or physical action. For example, as the therapist observes the client looking and sounding distressed and notes that arousal is nearing the upper limits of the window of tolerance, she might say, "I notice how hard this is and how much distress it's bringing up. So, for a moment, would it be all right to drop the narrative? Let's stop talking about the event, and let's just focus on what is going on in your body and find what movements could help you calm down. You can come back to telling me what happened in a minute." By interrupting the automatic and habitual response, the process is slowed down and made more available for observation, thereby creating opportunities to develop resources to transform it.

A first step when working with a hypoaroused client might be for the therapist to direct the client to orient only toward objects in the present environment rather than to those in the past. The therapist might ask such a client to "pause from thinking about the difficulties of your past and look around this room and find four objects that are red and name them for me." This technique evokes an active orienting response and helps both hyper- and hypoaroused clients return their arousal to within a window of tolerance. If dysregulated arousal continues, asking clients to stand up and walk around the therapy office, bringing awareness to the movement of the legs and sensing the capacity to move toward and away from objects or people (associated with a mobilizing flight response) usually brings arousal back into the window of tolerance. Standing and walking seem to help clients better sense their body in a "resourced" way, and movement in general appears to be helpful in working with both hyper- and hypoarousal.

OSCILLATION TECHNIQUES

Oscillation techniques involve directing the client to repeatedly and mindfully orient back and forth between calm or "resourced" body areas, experiences, or sensations and areas or experiences that are painful or uncomfortable. Such alternation is useful in helping clients in both hyper- and hypoaroused states to shift their focus from traumatic activation to more resourced or present-time experience. The client might be asked to shift back and forth between an image, sensation, or experience that evokes positive feelings, and one that evokes negative feelings. For example, as one client complained of hyperarousal accompanied by a terrible headache, the therapist asked him to imagine a visual picture that represented the pain in his head and a picture that represented the opposite. The client immediately had an image of the inside of a golf ball that represented the pain, whereas a marshmallow represented the opposite. As the therapist asked the client to oscillate between these two images and notice his body's response, the hyperarousal and the headache began to dissipate.

INTEROCEPTIVE AWARENESS: BODY SENSATION

Interoceptive awareness can become compromised after trauma. It is therefore important for the therapist to inquire, early on in therapy, about clients' responses to their body sensations, particularly to sensory stimulation and concurrent fluctuations in arousal. Many clients have a negative reaction to the sensation of their own movement, whereas others have an adverse reaction to the sensation of sitting still. Tracking these responses and helping clients understand them and accommodate to them are important elements in building somatic resources.

A college student who came to therapy because she was finding it increasingly difficult to study reported that when she sat down to study, she soon "blanked out" and could not focus. Observing this pattern during therapy, she realized that the bodily sensations she experienced when sitting still for long periods were similar to those of an immobilizing defensive response, a residue of childhood molestation. Understanding this correlation between her sensations and past trauma, as well as taking frequent "movement" breaks when studying, helped her arousal level stay within the window of tolerance so that she could study more effectively.

The association between specific bodily sensations, dysregulated arousal, and emotions may influence traumatized clients to think that current relationship tension is responsible for their discomfort. As van der Kolk noted, "Rather than understanding uncomfortable sensations as memories that are the result of having been triggered by some current event, they act as if restorative action in the present environment could alter the way they feel" (2002, p. 14). In therapy clients learn to recognize uncomfortable sensations that herald the beginning of dysregulated arousal, rather than numbing out, acting out, or avoiding these sensations. They learn to identify early somatic precursors to hyperaroused or hypoaroused states and discriminate between sensations triggered by reminders of the trauma and those relating to nontraumatic here-and-now experience.

Modulation of arousal and control over reflexive, self-destructive behavior are fostered through awareness of sensation and learning new physical actions. One client who came to therapy upset because he had struck his children in rage learned to identify the body sensations that preceded and heralded his aggression. When these sensations arose, he practiced centering himself through breathing and going for a walk. Learning how to sense and identify internal sensations such as feeling tense, cold, heavy, numb, or tingly can help clients recognize the precursors to traumatic arousal and plan alternative coping strategies.

Identifying and Verbalizing Body Sensation

The first phase of treatment includes the identification and verbalization of bodily states (Van der Kolk, McFarlane, et al., 1996). Therapists have struggled with the challenge of helping traumatized clients experience and find the words for body sensation for over a century. Many clients suffer from alexisomia, the inability to put words to sensation (Bakal, 1999). In the 1800s Paul Sollier was convinced that reestablishing body sensation was the most important part of treatment. He instructed his patients to "make movements while attending carefully to these movements and appreciating accurately what they are doing . . . [and to] pay attention to all their sensations, to practice feeling delicately in all parts of the body" (1897, as cited in Janet, 1925, p. 806). Sollier emphasized helping patients find the words for body sensations: "the tinglings, the sensations of pins and needles, the twitchings, the burning sensations . . . their feelings of torsion or relaxation, of enlargement or diminution of the limbs." In phase 1, if awareness of sensation is not destabilizing, providing a "menu" of sensation vocabulary may help clients learn how to refine or elaborate their description of sensation. Clients are taught a vocabulary for body sensation reminiscent of Sollier's, using words such as *clammy, electric, tight, numb, tingly, vibrating*, and so on. For example, a client in physical pain may simply say "It hurts," failing to distinguish this particular pain from the many different kinds of pain. The therapist may ask, "I wonder what kind of pain it is . . . maybe it's dull, sharp, achy, paralyzed, tingly. Or maybe it feels like a pressure pushing out or in." The therapist thus provides verbal options from which to choose and sparks the client's own acuity for the language of body sensation. Developing a precise vocabulary for sensation helps clients expand their perception and processing of physical feelings in much the same way that familiarity with a variety of words that describe emotion aids in the perception and processing of emotions (Ogden & Minton, 2000).

As clients turn their attention toward these sensations, they can begin to feel movement occurring in their bodies: from the micromovement of a slight tremble to the gross motor movement of lifting an arm. However, if the client is very destabilized, it may be more effective to work exclusively with movement rather than sensation, such as standing or pushing, and to encourage the client to find a way of moving that "feels good." Clients can also be instructed to attend purely to here-and-now sensory experience: what they smell, see, hear, and experience with their sense of touch (such as hands resting on the arms of the sofa) in the present moment.

Differentiating Body Sensation from
Emotions and Cognitions

Clients are taught to differentiate body sensations from emotions and to study the physical experience of emotion. Frequently, when clients are asked to describe sensation, they do so with words such as *sad* or *angry*, words that refer to their emotions rather than to their physical sensations. Clients can learn to describe sensations, and the correlation between emotions and the body, in language that is physical rather than emotional. One client was able to verbalize the somatic experience of her emotions this way: "I feel the sadness in a collapse in my chest that has an aching around my heart. There's tension in my left shoulder, and my arms feel limp and heavy. And I feel the pressure of tears behind my eyes." Such a description clearly describes the sensations that correspond to the emotion of sadness.

Just as sensation and affect are often undifferentiated by clients, sensation can also be confused with meaning, interpretation, or cognitive distortion. For example, a client with frequent traumatic activation in response to everyday stimuli might interpret the autonomic alarms as a belief that "The world is never safe," yet remain unaware of the physical sensations. Asking how this belief is experienced in the body allows the physical components of the belief to become known. The client is encouraged to study the somatic correlates of belief, which might be manifested in a hardening in the chest, trembling in the core of the body, fast heartbeat, constriction or numbness in the limbs, or a feeling of high energy throughout the body. Such descriptions clearly distinguish physical sensations from the belief with which they coincide.

Increasing Sensation

For clients who have difficulty understanding or being aware of body sensation, self-touch or movement can be used to increase sensation. Physical touch amplifies and localizes sensation by activating the nerve endings on the skin. Clients might be instructed to use their own touch to increase sensation in particular areas of the body. For example, a client who reports feeling numb can be encouraged to knead his or her arm with the hand of the other arm, up and down, generating sensation. Comparing the arm that is being squeezed with the one that has not been touched can increase sensitivity to the body (Bentzen, personal communication, June 14, 1992).

Movement also alters and increases sensation, and many clients find it easier to focus on and feel the body if they are moving (Segal et al., 2002). Clients can be asked to walk, raise their arms, or stretch the body in some way, and to notice the various sensations in the joints and muscles as they do so. The therapist also may model for the client by raising his or her own arm and reporting: "I can feel the general tension in my forearm and a sharper tight feeling in my shoulder; most of the sensation is on the top surface of my arm; I don't feel much on the lower surface. As my arm gets higher, I sense a different kind of tight feeling in my shoulder as it starts to engage. If I really stretch my arm, the sensations increase."

SOMATIC RESOURCE MAP

The relationship between personal psychology and the body's structure, posture, and movement is complex, and mapping this relationship to assess and develop somatic resources is challenging. An effective map needs to be sufficiently complex to reflect this relationship, yet simple enough that the therapist can understand primary somatic themes quickly. Schore's (1994) division of self-regulatory capacity into autoregulation and interactive regulation, as reflected through body structure, posture, and movement, provides an accessible framework within which to map somatic resources. As discussed in Chapter 2, autoregulation is the ability to self-regulate without the help of another, to calm down when arousal rises to the upper limits of the window of tolerance, and to self-stimulate when arousal drops too low. Interactive regulation involves the ability to calm down or to increase arousal by interactions with others. Both auto- and interactive regulatory capacities develop in the context of attachment relationships in infancy, prior to the acquisition of language. Thus the first resources that an infant develops are non-verbal, somatic resources.

Auto- and Interactive Regulation:
The Core and Periphery of the Body

In an oversimplification for the purpose of mapping somatic resources, we distinguish between resources related to the body's core and periphery (Melchior, personal communication, June 5, 1995; Bowen, personal communication, November 10, 2000) and consider their relationship to auto- and interactive regulation. The physical core of the body comprises the pelvis, spine, ribcage; the physical periphery, the arms, and legs. The core provides support and stability to the entire structure and is grounded securely through the inside of the legs. The periphery provides mobility and interaction with the environment. In this schema, the neck, head, and face are included in both the body's core and periphery. They are a part of—or an extension of—the spine, and thus pertain to the core. They also facilitate social engagement and interaction with the environment, and thus pertain to the periphery. The first movements of an infant start at the core of the body and radiate out to the periphery, then contract inward to the core (Aposhyan,

2004; Cohen, 1993). These movements of extension and flexion build tone in the core—the spine, including the neck—as well as in the periphery—the arms, legs, and neck. Movements that are initiated from, and connected with, the core tend to be stable, coordinated, and effortless (Aposhyan, 2004; Cohen, 1993; Kurtz & Prestera, 1976).

Kurtz and Prestera noted that the core also has a psychological meaning as the "place inside" to which we may "go for sustenance" (1976, p. 33). The spine provides an axis around which larger movements of the limbs and head can occur in interaction with the environment. The muscles of the head and limbs are involved with mobility, expression, and action. The tone of the periphery is built further as the infant uses the peripheral muscles to achieve developmental milestones such as reaching out, crawling, standing, walking, and running—movements that reciprocally contribute to core strength.

Generally speaking, somatic resources that involve awareness and movement of the core of the body (centering, grounding, breath, alignment) provide a sense of internal physical and psychological stability and therefore support autoregulation. Somatic resources that develop awareness and movement of the periphery (pushing away, reaching, locomotion) tend to facilitate social skills and interactions with the world at large and support the capacity for interactive regulation. In this oversimplified schema, the core is a "supporting pillar" for the movement of the extremities (Kurtz & Prestera, 1976); in turn, positive interactions with the environment support and develop the core and provide a sense of "having a core."

As a consequence of childhood neglect or abuse, the trauma survivor "may [either] seek to surround herself with people at all times, or she may isolate herself completely" Herman (1992, p. 162). The interactive regulatory pattern suggests a reliance more on the periphery for regulation and a lack of connection with the core of the body and the self. The autoregulatory strategy relies more on the core and is accompanied by corresponding deficits in the ability to use the arms effectively in reaching out to, and setting personal boundaries with, others; or the legs in moving toward and away from objects or people in the environment. Thus the core and periphery of the body can be conceptualized as having a reciprocal relationship with auto- and interactive regulatory capacities.

Consider Mary, whose posture was very good but whose body was constricted, particularly in the neck, arms, and shoulders. Her chin and chest were lifted, but she demonstrated little movement in her neck. She held her arms stiffly out to her sides when walking and had a habit of crossing her arms in front of her torso when sitting. Her legs were spindly, seeming out of proportion to her thick torso, and her knees were locked. As a consequence, her movements were heavy and undifferentiated, lacking grace and fluidity. As her limbs moved, her spine and torso remained rigid. Mary tended to stabilize herself through tension and rigidity rather than through a flexible, integrated body with good support through her legs. She complained of feeling as if she were "going through the motions of living," interspersed with sudden escalations of arousal from which she had difficulty recovering. She reported that she also experienced periods of depression during which she had trouble leaving her room.

Through somatic assessment, the therapist determined that Mary's primary somatic resources were core ones: an aligned structure and a lift in her chest and chin, all "easy" actions for her, which, she said, helped her feel a sense of identity, power, and determination. Her habit of crossing her arms in front of her torso was also a somatic resource involving the periphery of her body. Her arms in this position, she reported, helped her feel safe, a survival resource she had needed in her abusive childhood. However, Mary attempted to stabilize herself through tension and restrained movement that prevented spontaneous action of both core and periphery. Grounding, by sensing her legs and their support of her body, was difficult for her, as was the ability to use action in her arms and legs to experience an ability to protect herself.

At the beginning of treatment, the therapist acknowledged Mary's aligned posture and helped her sense it more fully to discover what it meant psychologically to her. She reported that it gave her a feeling of identity, determination and power. That intervention, concomitant with exploring the crossing of her arms as another somatic resource or competency, helped her experience a sense of confidence in her body, and set the stage to address resources that were missing. After these existing resources were acknowledged, the missing somatic resources were assessed and developed during the first phase of treatment: Mary's "difficult" actions, including the following: gaining a sense of "living" in her legs (the absence of which left her feeling ungrounded) and energizing her arms through pushing movements (without which she felt frozen and disempowered). Although these movements were initially unfamiliar to Mary, they gradually became resources. Practicing becoming aware of her legs gave her a sense of being grounded, and practicing pushing movements mitigated the frozen defensive subsystem, giving her a feeling of self-protection and an ability to take action to defend herself. Additionally, Mary began to experience a sense of movement in the core of her body, which helped her feel less rigid and more connected with herself.

Core Resources for Autoregulation

Autoregulatory resources primarily involve the core of the body and confer a sense of stability, connection with the self, and an internal locus of control. Establishing these capacities entails keeping awareness focused or "centered" on oneself and is facilitated by assessment and awareness of the spine. Is this physical core experienced as hard, soft, collapsed, mobilized, flexible, or rigid? The therapist helps clients develop a sense of their physical core as strong but flexible. If the spine is rigid, working with centering and movement of the spine can be useful; if the spine is bent forward, slumped, or flexed, working with vertical alignment can be useful.

Vertical alignment refers to an erect posture wherein the head sits centered over the shoulders, the chest rests over the lower half of the body, the pelvis supports the torso, and the legs and feet are under the body (Aposhyan, 2004; Kepner, 1987; Kurtz & Prestera, 1976). Observing a person standing from the side, plumb line through the top of the head, middle of the ear, shoulder, hip joint, knee joint and ankle can be imagined to assess alignment. When these points are in a straight line, each segment of the body supports the one above, and the body is in balance with gravity. Often this imaginary line is jagged as parts of the body are displaced from optimal alignment. Some bodies are bowed forward, others are bent backward, the head may jut forward, or the pelvis may be retracted. When the body is out of alignment, an increase in muscular tension and energy is required to hold the person upright. The more the body is in alignment, the less effort is needed.

Alignment can be explored by directing clients to stand and exaggerate their vertical deviations to experience the tendencies clearly and discover their psychological correlates. Possibilities for small changes to foster alignment then become apparent. It is important to encourage alignment without using muscular compensation, because compensation could lead to another set of postural distortions and effort (Kepner, 1987). A visualization, such as imagining being lifted upward by the crown of the head while the feet are planted firmly, can help the spine to straighten and the chest to lift, which in turn enhances breathing. This posture may feel awkward initially to people who are strongly out of alignment, but with practice it will become increasingly comfortable.

Simple exercises to increase awareness of the back of the body facilitate alignment and core resources, in general. One hyperaroused client discovered that she had no awareness of her back. She was instructed to experiment with pressing her back against the wall to bring sensation to that area; she also experimented with walking backward, "seeing" with her back. These exercises helped her "inhabit" the back of her body, providing her with a sense of "backbone" and helping to return her arousal to the window of tolerance.

Clients who struggle with irritable, aggressive impulses can especially benefit from centering exercises. Sinclair (2001), who works with violent male inmates, teaches these men to notice the sensations of arousal that are somatic precursors to violence. He then teaches them a very simple centering resource of putting one hand on the abdomen and one hand over the heart and then just paying attention to the shifts in sensation. This intervention gives the men a chance to slow down their responses and provides an alternative to violent action by offering a different action—a somatic resource that is potentially calming and centering.

Grounding affords a sense of self-support and integrity through the spine. As a core somatic resource, grounding is the physical process of being aware of the legs and feet, their weight, and their connection to the ground. Through focused grounding exercises, the support of the earth can be experienced, giving a feeling of both physical and psychological solidity and stability. Tension or flaccidity in the feet and legs, locked knees, the inability to sense the legs and feet or experience them as a base of support for the upper body all diminish the experience of feeling grounded.

Exercises to increase awareness of the feet and legs and help a client feel grounded include standing and shifting the weight of the body to the toes, heels, and sides of the feet and then balancing the weight on the entire surface of the feet, letting them soften on the floor; unlocking the knees; shifting the weight from leg to leg and then allowing the weight to balance between them. During these exercises, clients can be instructed to sense the weight of their body and the pull of gravity downward. Pressing the feet into the floor while sitting or mindfully attending to the weight balanced on the "sitz" bones of the pelvis and relaxing the pelvic floor supports grounding while sitting.

For clients who have difficulty even sensing their legs, stomping the feet on the ground or using their hands to squeeze and massage their legs and feet can increase sensation and help them gain a sense of their legs. Grounding is reinforced and supported by vertical alignment through the entire body. Each structural segment is supported by, and grounded on, that which is below it.

Breathing is directly related to the regulation of energy and arousal. We breathe faster and harder under exertion, slower and deeper during relaxation; under threat, we may hold our breath in an effort to stop movement (Conrad, 1997). In Western medicine, respiration exercises have been recognized as useful in the treatment of trauma since the 1800s (Janet, 1925), perhaps because autonomic arousal almost invariably results in respiratory changes. It is important to realize that there is no "correct" way to breathe; different ways of breathing are appropriate in different circumstances (Aposhyan, 1999). However, two primary breathing patterns that can be problematic tend to be observed in traumatized clients: overbreathing (tending toward hyperventilation) and underbreathing (tending toward hypoventilation) (Levine & MacNaughton, 2004). Clients can be taught to notice their breathing tendencies and the sensations generated from them, then alter their breathing to study the difference in sensation and arousal. They are asked to note whether their breathing is shallow or deep, centered more in the chest or belly, fast or slow, and so on. Instructing clients to place their hands on their ribcage while experimenting with breath can help them notice whether they are breathing from the chest or diaphragm.

Awareness of breathing tendencies and working with deepening the breath stimulate intrinsic core movements. Generally, clients observe that emphasizing the inhale increases arousal, whereas emphasizing the exhale decreases arousal and supports relaxation. This awareness can be useful for stabilizing both hyper- and hypoarousal states. Because breathing exercises are potent and can rapidly destabilize trauma clients, they should be used with caution and with an emphasis on awareness and integration of resulting sensations (Levine, 2004).

Peripheral Resources for Interactive Regulation

Interpersonal relationships can be somatically regulated through actions of the extremities. In addition to facial expression, gazing, and vocalization, reaching out and holding on are an infant's first resources for regulating proximity to caregivers, followed by crawling and then toddling to achieve proximity. Pushing away with the arms or putting the legs in motion can provide a sense of safety by creating distance between the self and others and can activate truncated mobilizing defensive responses of fight or flight.

Trauma is a violation of interpersonal boundaries. Both physical and psychological integrity are shattered, leaving the individual with a sense of having no protection and heightened vulnerability. The violation of boundary creates a subsequent sense of inadequate protection in interpersonal relationships. An important emphasis in phase 1 treatment is to help clients develop boundaries that are capable of assuring their safety (Kepner, 1987, 1995; Levine, 1997; MacNaughton, 2004; Rosenberg, Rand, & Asay, 1989; Rothschild, 2000; Scaer, 2001).

Traditional insight-oriented, process-oriented, and interpretive forms of treatment address boundaries primarily through either emotional or cognitive approaches, or both. Another element that is profoundly important in the treatment of boundary issues is the *somatic sense of boundary*. The somatic sense of a boundary is differentiated from cognitive and emotional understanding of boundaries by its feeling component: It is founded on the *felt sense* of boundary in the experience of safety, protection, and the ability to defend. Traditional therapists often query clients as to whether they *feel* safe, and based on cognitive processing, clients may say "yes," meaning that they believe this intellectually. However, if the therapist observes constriction, lack of full breathing or very high and rapid breathing, or other signs of hyper- or hypoarousal, then the client probably does not have an adequate somatic sense of safety or boundary.

Reinstating a sense of somatic boundaries is facilitated by exploring actions involving the extremities, such as pushing away with the arms, kicking away with the legs, or walking away. Interpersonal distance is set by these gross motor actions, as well as with more indirect and subtler movements, such as leaning back, tightening the body, or turning away. Through a variety of exercises, clients experience how the right personal distance can help them feel safe. The therapist might stand across the room and walk slowly toward the client until the client experiences a somatic sense that the therapist should stop, at which time the client gestures to indicate "stop" (lifts the hands, palms outward) and/or speaks the words to indicate that the therapist should stop. Studying somatic responses to proximity is especially important for clients who cannot use language or voice to set a boundary or to say "No." As one client said, "It feels safer when my body talks (by lifting the arms to indicate "stop") than when *I* talk." The identification of the "No" response in the body is a prerequisite for being able to set a boundary.

Experiments (moving toward and away from a client or moving an object such as a pillow toward and away) can be conducted to assess automatic responses to proximity, such as bracing, moving backward, holding the breath, or changes in orienting or attention. Actions such as using the arms to push away, adding words to set appropriate physical distance, or walking away can be practiced and evaluated. For many traumatized clients, negotiating physical distance between therapist and client becomes an initial element of each session. For clients for whom the above exercises are too provocative, introducing simpler exercises—such as rolling a therapy ball toward them or gently tossing a pillow toward them while they use their arms to push it away—can strengthen their capacity to push away and lay a foundation upon which other exercises can be introduced.

Traumatized individuals tend to be either too passive, failing to defend or protect themselves, or too aggressive, failing to regulate feelings of anger (Bloom, 1997). Clients with dysregulated arousal manifesting as explosive aggression may benefit from working with slow, integrated, mindful movements of the arms and hands that simulate aggression. Bob was in therapy to learn to regulate his emotional and physical aggression. The therapist worked with him to experience a sense of personal boundary by first walking toward him until Bob could sense his reaction somatically. Bob started to learn about the sensation that told him that his boundary was being threatened or crossed. This exercise was repeated several times while Bob practiced tracking his internal experience and saying "stop" both verbally and with his body. He held up both hands in front of his face, palms toward the therapist, instead of his usual fist-clenching response to perceived threat. Bob reported he immediately felt violated and aggressive when his personal boundary was crossed, and he practiced taking pillows and putting them in a circle around him so that he could sense his own space. The therapist and Bob co-created many practice exercises wherein his boundary was "breached" by the therapist; for example, the therapist would move an object into his space, and Bob would practice pushing it away in a slow, thoughtful, and contained manner rather than with an eruption of aggression. He also practiced pushing against a wall, feeling the energy of his aggression move slowly from his feet out through his hands. With many iterations of these exercises, Bob began to experience the ability to re-establish his boundary through contained, self-regulated action, and his aggressive outbursts diminished in his daily life.

Visual boundaries can be explored with clients who feel unsafe or threatened by eye contact or by being seen: Therapist and client can experiment with having either one look away, close the eyes, or sit at an angle to the other, noticing the somatic signs of what feels most comfortable to the client.

Locomotion, the activity of moving forward through space, can "contain within it repeated movement patterns that create an ongoing sense of identity" (Caldwell, 1995, p. 44). Exploring and changing the movement patterns of locomotion that participate in a client's trauma-related identity can support the client's improved interactions with the environment. For example, one client noticed that, with each step, her spine collapsed into flexion, causing a painful sensation in her lower back and evoking a feeling of helplessness. This pattern accompanied a submissive, defensive attitude. First she became aware of this pattern in locomotion and then she began to practice another, more adaptive way of walking: by pushing off from the soles of her feet with each step. She found that this small change enabled her to feel safer when out in public places and more comfortable in approaching others.

Clients who have been unable to get away from threatening stimuli may not experience the felt sense of their legs as capable of carrying them away from unwanted situations; in short, they may often feel trapped. Lisa, a survivor of child abuse from a series of foster parents, reported that she felt spacey and foggy when she tried to sense her body. During the first phase of therapy, the therapist suggested that she and Lisa stand up and walk around the therapy room together, noticing how Lisa's legs supported her body and attending to how her legs could carry her away from what she did not want and toward what she did want. Aware of Lisa's difficulty staying within the window of tolerance when she tried to sense her body, the therapist chose not to ask her to report on body sensation, nor was mention made at this time of Lisa's severe childhood trauma. As she and the therapist walked around the office, Lisa reported feeling more present and observed that it felt good to notice her legs. The experience of mobility was a simple resource that Lisa came back to again and again—it mitigated the pattern in her body of a frozen, trapped response, and it also helped to prevent the hypoarousal-related spaciness when she sat still in her chair.

Using Core and Periphery

As noted, the previous categories for auto- and interactive regulatory resources are primarily associated with either the core or the periphery of the body. However, some somatic resources pertain equally to both the spine and the limbs, thus requiring the core as well as the periphery for their execution.

CHANGING ORIENTING TENDENCIES

Orienting is a somatic resource that equally engages both the core and periphery and is relevant to both auto- and interactive regulation. Orienting is a core resource because it involves rotations of the core of the body and the spine, including the neck. It also involves movement of the periphery—the head and face—occurring in response to stimuli from the environment. Thus orienting is also an interactive-regulatory, peripheral resource. Building adaptive orienting capacities can assist clients to attain their goals of stabilization in challenging situations. Russell, a sophomore in college, decided he wanted to go home for Christmas vacation to visit his parents but became anxious and activated at the thought of seeing his father, who had beaten him repeatedly during his childhood. The therapist asked Russell to stand up and choose an object in the therapy office that could represent his father. Once Russell had chosen an object, the therapist asked him to experiment with first turning away from the object and then slowly orienting toward it, noticing what happened in his body. Russell's movement became disjointed: His spine sagged, and his upper body twisted away even as he was turning toward and facing his "father." His movement exemplified a helpless and defeated position. In collaboration with the therapist, Russell next began to work on somatic resources that supported the ability to orient toward his father from a position of strength rather than defeat. With practice and instruction, he learned to orient toward his father with his spine erect and his legs grounded, maintaining core integrity. In his first post-vacation session, Russell reported that, for the first time, he did not "lose himself" in the presence of his father, which he attributed to standing tall, to not allowing his spine to sag in a submissive posture.

THE "CONTAINER" OF THE BODY

Because traumatic experiences and their reactivation cause intense, uncomfortable, and disturbing physical sensations of emotional and physiological arousal, often leading to dysregulating behavioral catharsis or discharge, learning to "contain" these sensations and their trauma-related emotions becomes an important resource in phase 1 treatment. Some clients are unwilling to contain their emotions because of the short-term relief obtained through discharge, but can benefit from the long-term advantages of learn-ing containment. Others who are plagued by intrusive reliving symptoms need containment interventions (Courtois, 1991, 1992).

Clients learn containment as a somatic resource by mindfully experienc-ing the "container" of their physical body: the skin and superficial muscu-lature (Kepner, 1987; Rothschild, 2000). Sensing the skin as a literal body boundary can be experienced by asking a client to touch or rub the surface of the body. If clients become dysregulated when touching their body, it may be less destabilizing for them to sense their skin in contact with objects in the environment, such as the chair arm, the floor, or a wall.

Containment can also be explored through tightening the large muscles of the body (Kepner, 1987; Rothschild, 2000). This contraction literally hard-ens the superficial extrinsic muscles around the body, giving a feeling of less permeability and strengthening awareness of the ability to both "keep things in" and "keep things out." Asking clients to say "no" with the body (as the therapist says "No" concomitantly with his or her body to model and col-laborate) teaches clients about containment, because extrinsic muscles are typically tightened in order to say "no" somatically. Conversely, clients can explore softening their superficial musculature, making the body more avail-able and open to the environment (saying "yes"), and becoming aware of the difference between the "yes" and the "no."

SELF-SOOTHING

Somatic resources for self-soothing are autoregulatory resources that can involve either the core or the periphery of the body, or both. These resources are often discovered as the therapist tracks clients' spontaneous attempts to soothe themselves through physical action when arousal is heading out of the window of tolerance. These actions can then be brought to awareness, acknowledged, and developed. One client rocked from side to side; a war veteran automatically placed his hand over his stomach; a young girl who was molested rubbed her hands on her thighs; a sexual abuse survivor stroked her cheek; yet another pressed her back into her chair. All these movements occurred spontaneously and unconsciously for the client but were closely tracked by the therapist and acknowledged by both as the auto-matic ways in which the client instinctively knows how to self-soothe.

In sensorimotor psychotherapy the therapist has the client explore the experience of self-soothing resources at length by repeating the action, observing what happens in the present moment, and practicing self-soothing resources outside of the therapy hour. The therapist can also ask what movement or body position feels soothing and then help clients practice that movement. One client, Ann, discovered that she felt soothed when she hugged herself by wrapping her arms gently around her body. As she executed this motion, the therapist asked her to notice the effect on her internal experience. Ann reported that it calmed her down and that she felt comforted; hugging herself evoked memories of being with her aunt, to whom she was close as a child and who often held her when she was small. Exploring this motion helped Ann recognize and appreciate that she had internalized the comforting feeling of being with her aunt, and also paved the way for her to consciously use this action when she needed self-soothing.

External self-soothing somatic resources can also be introduced: warm baths, gently brushing or touching the skin, deep pressure massage, pleasant scents, favorite foods, the touch of soft fabrics. Designing a "sensory diet," a plan for what sensory stimulation can be reduced or increased so that the client can feel soothed, such as sitting in a darkened room, wearing earplugs to reduce auditory stimulation, or listening to enlivening music to mitigate hypoarousal, is an important phase 1 activity (Aubrey Lande, personal communication, June 25, 2003; Wilbarger & Wilbarger, 2002).

DEVELOPING HIGHER INTEGRATIVE CAPACITY

Somatic resources are built gradually and consecutively over time. Steele et al. assert that trauma treatment should follow "a specific order such that [clients] experience a gradually developing *capacity to engage in purposeful and high-quality adaptive action*, both mental and physical" (2005b, p. 14). First, existing resources are acknowledged and experienced, along with the sense of mastery they evoke. The client is then challenged to learn a new resource: one that addresses either hyper- or hypoarousal and that is practiced until it is no longer difficult. Over the course of phase 1 treatment, the client is encouraged to attempt increasingly more complex resourcing actions that require higher degrees of integrative capacity.

Kim illustrates this process of gradually learning increasingly more complex actions that challenged her integrative capacity over many sessions. A sexual abuse survivor, Kim felt unable to protect herself. In therapy she became markedly uncomfortable when executing physical gestures of pushing away, which felt "awkward" and "unfamiliar." When she attempted such motions as pushing with her arms, she would become dissociated ("not be there"). Her neck and spine contracted, with limited range of motion, and her knees, which were already locked, became tenser. Her arms collapsed limply at her sides after her first attempt at pushing, and she said, "I give up." Her first physical task was to experiment with unlocking her knees, which allowed her to feel more grounded and provided an autoregulatory resource that reduced her feelings of being overwhelmed. This simple action was practiced over several sessions until it became familiar.

She then learned a centering resource of focusing on sensations in the core of her body. Following the accomplishment of these somatic resources of grounding and centering, a higher-level task was explored. Kim was encouraged to focus on the actions of moving away and running. Attention to these physical actions and their accompanying sensations awakened a flight response in Kim that had been suppressed and unavailable at the time of her childhood abuse. As she mindfully walked around the therapy office, and in a later session, ran in place, she was instructed to sense how her legs could now carry her away from unwanted or threatening situations—a capacity she could not utilize as a child. The physical and accompanying psychological possibility of fleeing served to strengthen an interactive regulatory resource. She began to feel that she was more in the "here-and-now."

After several weeks of treatment Kim was able to successfully execute the action of pushing away with her arms without hypoarousal interfering with this assertive gesture. By that time, she was aware of the support of her lower body and spine, and she and her therapist had worked to track and focus on her ability to stay present in the therapy session, grounded and oriented to the here-and-now. She was able to consider how her previous belief of "I don't deserve to have any rights" had developed into a sense of "I have a right to protect myself," and she was able to recognize how angry she felt at having been violated. As the new physical and mental actions were practiced in therapy, Kim also showed more focus and greater capacity to stay within her window of tolerance in interpersonal relationships.

PRACTICING SOMATIC RESOURCES

As new somatic resources are taught and practiced in therapy, clients gradually learn the mechanics of each action and how to tolerate the uncomfortable sensations, emotions, and cognitions that inevitably accompany the new learning. Clients find that, over time, somatic reprogramming helps them to separate the past from the present and become less disrupted by their arousal states and dysregulated defensive responses. With a body that is more resourced, traumatized clients experience a fuller capacity to stabilize and self-regulate. Janet (1925) summed up both the initial difficulty of learning somatic resources and the necessity of the therapist's function as an "auxiliary cortex":

> At first these operations demand intense conscious effort, but through repetition, in virtue of the mechanism of habit, they are performed with increasing ease and quickness, so that, at long last, they can be executed correctly without attention and almost unawares. Education thus consists of the production and repetition of a new action performed in the presence of a competent witness, who supervises it, corrects it, and has it repeated until the action becomes, not merely correct, but automatic. (p. 736)

Somatic resourcing begins with the therapist's ability to recognize the client's health, rather than only the pathology, acknowledging that despite significant traumatic experience, each client already has a rich variety of resources intact. From this basic orientation, the client's existing strengths can be validated and elaborated, and those resources that are absent or immature can be taught. The client is assigned incremental homework tasks to practice the action in his or her environment and report on the experience in the next therapy session. The use of suitable props (e.g., a pillow or a wall or a door frame to push against) can be used both in therapy sessions and at home, between sessions. A variety of objects can be used creatively for practicing actions in nonthreatening contexts: therapy balls to push against, ankle weights or weighted vests to enhance grounding exercises; doing push-ups or lifting weights or even pushing against one's own arm or thigh can be useful in providing resistance. Journaling can promote motivation and provide a framework for studying the automatic thoughts or reactions that may accompany both old somatic tendencies and new actions.

Finally, the client can deepen acquired somatic resources or develop a broader range of resources by utilizing "future templates": that is, rehearsing future challenges by calling up images of anticipated real-life situations. As the client brings up the image of a challenging situation, it will frequently evoke the old tendency, creating a context for practicing the use of the whole repertoire of somatic resources until ones are discovered that answer the challenge. These rehearsals can be quite potent exercises and represent the final stages of successfully incorporating new somatic resources.

CONCLUSION

Therapy that focuses on negative experiences, memories, and current life situations that are problematic for clients but omits exploration of positive ones can be destabilizing in and of itself. Clients have difficulty separating past experience from present and feeling good about themselves partly because they are habituated to the dysregulated states that are triggered by traumatic reminders. Unchecked defensive systems undermine their ability to function in daily life and respond adaptively to action systems. Through learning somatic resources in the context of therapy, dysregulated arousal can be addressed in a manner that clients experience as personally empowering and engendering of a new, more positive way of relating to the body. Careful monitoring allows the client to remain within a window of tolerance and learn to inhibit dysregulated defensive systems while mindfully validating old resources and learning new ones. Practicing those somatic resources serves to stabilize arousal and reduce symptoms, enabling fuller engagement with daily life and preparing the way to address traumatic memories.

Chapter 11

※※※

Phase 2 Treatment: Processing Traumatic Memory and Restoring Acts of Triumph

TRAUMATIZED CLIENTS OFTEN PRESENT with symptoms rather than with coherent verbal stories placed in time. Because traumatic "memory" consists largely of reactivated, nonverbal memories, sometimes combined with incomplete narrative accounts, Janet (1919, 1925; Van der Kolk & Van der Hart, 1989) suggested long ago that these memories are split off from conscious awareness and stored as sensory perceptions, obsessive thoughts, and behavioral reenactments. The individual apparently "remembers" what happened through reliving these nonverbal iterations of the historical traumatic event or through mysterious physical symptoms that seem to have no organic basis. These nonverbal traumatic memories are "self-contained form[s] of memory that [do] not necessarily interact with general autobiographical knowledge" Brewin (2001, p. 376). Inaccessible to verbal recall, they typically remain unintegrated and unaltered by the course of time (Van der Kolk & Van der Hart, 1991).

The lack of integration allows reminders of the trauma to trigger somatosensory fragments, causing detrimental effects on the client's ability to modulate arousal and function in daily life. Because the trauma is not fully recollected as a coherent, autobiographical narrative, clients are unable to deal with the effects and implications of their memories by reflecting upon, discussing, or thinking about them. The memories remain unintegrated, and clients often become phobic of their contents (Steele et al., 2005b). As a result, phase 2 work with traumatic memories is daunting for many clients and unnerving for their therapists, who fear that their clients will become overwhelmed and mired still further in their past.

Successful memory work results in recall of, and reflection on, the traumatic event(s) and their implications (Claridge, 1992; Courtois, 1999; Van der Hart et al., 1993). Clients generally come to therapy with the hope of resolving the past by using the more familiar avenues of cognitive and emotional processing. The assumption of therapists and clients alike is that if dissociated fragments of the trauma are integrated into flexible, linguistic autobiographical memory, reduction or cessation of symptoms will result. Yet their best efforts to resolve their memories through these avenues can fail. Clients frequently continue to feel out of control as everyday stimuli continue to ignite bottom-up hijacking. And even after clients have created a relatively coherent narrative of the trauma, physiological symptoms may remain and occasionally worsen. Moreover, because the memories that need to be associated are unavailable through language, a verbal account of past trauma is not always possible.

What *is* available, no matter how much or how little narrative memory is intact, are the visual images, olfactory and auditory intrusions, intense emotions, sensations, and maladaptive physical actions. It is not the events themselves but these nonverbal fragments from the past and their unresolved maladaptive action tendencies that wreak havoc on the client's experience and ability to function in daily life. Accordingly, successful treatment of traumatic memory might be conceptualized as the resolution of the effects of the traumatic past on the client's current organization of experience, rather than as the formulation of a narrative.

Sensorimotor processing of traumatic memory is organized to target these repetitive sensory and physical tendencies until they no longer disrupt self-regulation and cognitive–emotional processing of current as well as past experience. Clients are helped to "overcome the traumatic imprints that dominate their lives, which are the sensations, emotions, and actions that are not relevant to the demands of the present but are triggered by current events that keep reactivating old, trauma-based states of mind" (Van der Kolk, 2002, p. 59). By identifying these imprints as they emerge in clients' organization of experience and helping them study, rather than react with trauma-related tendencies (dissociation, dysregulated arousal, and maladaptive defensive responses), the nonverbal traumatic residue can be resolved.

Traumatic Memory

Memory is not a unitary process but a network of interconnecting systems that contributes to the storage and retrieval of information (Cordon, Pipe,

Mayfan, Melinder, & Goodman, 2004). A careful clinical recognition of, and ability to distinguish between and work with, memory that is declarative or explicitly held in a conscious, narrative verbal format and nonverbal, implicit memory that is evoked by traumatic reminders is vital to the work of sensorimotor psychotherapy.

Explicit memory is generally described as containing both episodic representation as well as semantic or factual memory (Siegel, 2003). When we recall a past experience with a subjective sense that we are remembering something, we are retrieving explicit memory. This type of memory is verbally accessible and "supports ordinary autobiographical memories that can be retrieved either automatically or using deliberate, strategic processes (Brewin, 2001, p. 375). Explicit memory retrieval is often a kind of "memory modification" rather than an exact recall of events (Siegel, 2003). Thus recall is not necessarily "factually" accurate; rather, it is an "active and constructive" process, subject to distortions and revisions based on the emotional state of the person at the time of recall and associations with both previous and subsequent experiences (Van der Kolk, 1996b). Schachtel explained that explicit memory "can be understood as a capacity for the organization and reconstruction of past experiences and impressions in the service of present needs, fears, and interests" (1947, p. 3). Like all narratives, explicit memories become elaborated in the service of "telling the story": Those details essential to the story's main points are elaborated, whereas other details may be discarded or become part of the subtext (Janet, 1928; Van der Kolk & Van der Hart, 1989). The elements of traumatic memory that are verbally accessible can be revised, edited, and placed in relationship to the individual's autobiographical knowledge so that the trauma is "represented within a complete personal context comprising past, present, and future" (Brewin, 2001, p. 375).

In contrast, implicit memory is memory for the nonverbal aspects of experience: the smell of your grandmother's attic, the tensing of your body at the sound of a siren, an opening in your chest when you remember seeing the dawn break over the ocean, and so on. Implicit memories are best thought of as somatic and affective memory *states* that are not accompanied by an internal sense that something from the past is being remembered (Siegel, 1999, 2001). The implicit memories are often "situationally accessible," activated in the client's present life by both internal and external stimuli reminiscent of the trauma: They "[contain] information that has been obtained from more extensive, lower level perceptual processing of the traumatic scene (e.g. visuospatial information that has received little conscious processing) and of the person's bodily (e.g. autonomic, motor) response to it" (Brewin, 2001, p. 375) This form of memory includes the reactivated sensorimotor components of memory that emerge in response to traumatic reminders and are not usually integrated with verbally accessible, explicit components.

A century ago Janet (1909; quoted in Van der Kolk & Van der Hart, 1989, pp. 1532–1533) wrote that the vehement emotions—the intense arousal evoked in trauma—prevent adaptive information processing and thus impair efforts to formulate the traumatic event into an explicit narrative. One hundred years later research corroborates Janet's observations, identifying significant alterations of frontal lobe functioning and Broca's area (the part of the brain responsible for language) as a result of high arousal states associated with remembering traumatic experience (Van der Kolk, 2002). When memories cannot be organized through language, they are organized on a more primitive level of information processing (Piaget, 1962) that comprise three forms of implicit memory: procedural, perceptual, and emotional (Siegel, 2003). The traumatized person "remembers" via all three avenues: through somatic action tendencies (procedural), sensory intrusions and sensations (perceptual), and emotional storms (emotional).

Of particular importance in a sensorimotor approach to traumatic memory is procedural memory, which is "expressed in behavioral acts independent of cognitive representational storage" (Sokolov et al., 2002, p. 338). The unconscious nature of procedural memory is efficient. As noted in Chapter 1, it enables us to automatically perform many tasks, and accounts for many of the behavioral tendencies that help us cope with trauma as well as defensive tendencies that persevere long after the danger is past.

"Body" memory is another term that has been used clinically to identify implicit somatic memory (Siegel, 2003). *Body memory* refers to recollections of trauma that emerge through somatic experience: muscle tension, movements, sensations, autonomic arousal, and so on. In 1907 Janet described body memories and their contribution to trauma symptoms:

> The different regions of our body participate in all the events of our life and in all our sentiments. Let us consider two individuals, both of them wounded in the shoulder, one by an elevator, the other by an omnibus. These wounds have long been cured, but you can easily understand that the remembrance of a sensation in the shoulder, that even the idea of the shoulder, is a part of the remembrance of the accident; it is enough that you touch one of these patients on the shoulder for this peculiar sensation to remind him of his accident and determine the crisis. (p. 99)

Thus tactile sensations, internal sensations (such as trembling), kinesthetic responses (such as muscular tension), vestibular responses (such as feelings of dizziness that occur in response to trauma stimuli), and the somatic components of a defensive subsystem (such as the constriction associated with freezing) are all examples of ways in which the trauma is remembered through implicit body memories.

These nonverbal memories are difficult for most traumatized individuals to understand, let alone revise or change. They manifest in somatosensory intrusions and confusing emotional outbursts, as Raine eloquently described: "I could not connect the intense feelings that overpowered me that day . . . with the rape. They did not 'come with a story,' a linear narrative, the way non-traumatic memories do. They had no verbal context, and seemed to occupy another dimension, parallel to, but never intersecting with, language" (1998, p. 185). Without verbal representation, these memories may remain dissociated, with detrimental consequences. The failure to integrate traumatic memories is described as "the pathogenic agent leading to the development of complex biobehavioral changes, of which PTSD is the clinical manifestation" (Van der Kolk, 1996b, p. 286).

In phase 2 work with the traumatic memory, the primary goal is the integration of all dissociated components of the memory. Achieving this goal reduces symptoms, as Janet explained: "The memory was morbific because it was dissociated. It existed in isolation, apart from the totality of the sensations and the ideas which comprised the subject's personality; it developed in isolation, without control and without counterpoise; the morbid symptoms disappeared when the memory again became part of the synthesis that makes up individuality" (1925, p. 674). The unassimilated fragments that have remained separate or incoherent must be explored, metabolized, completed, and integrated in phase 2 treatment. Successful integration enables clients to think about the past when they want or need to, and although doing so may cause them to feel sad or troubled, it no longer hijacks their thoughts, emotions, and body to cause involuntary reexperiencing. Reminders of the trauma are manageable and do not disrupt daily functioning. The memory of the trauma has become one of many memories—some good, some bad, and some neutral—that constitute any individual's life.

Disrupting Procedural Memory

Grigsby and Stevens suggested that disrupting what has been implicitly, procedurally learned is more effective in changing dysfunctional patterns than talking about what initially happened to cause them: "Talking about old events (i.e., episodic memories), or discussing ideas and information with a patient (the semantic memory system), may at best be indirect means of perturbing those behaviors in which people routinely engage" (2000, p. 306). For change to occur, the procedural learning—especially the body's tendencies—must be "disrupted." It may not be enough to gain insight: the tendency to enact the old pattern somatically must be changed. New actions must replace the old. (Here, cognitions are useful in motivating engagement in new actions.) Grigsby and Stevens described two ways that procedural learning can be addressed in therapy: "The first is ... to observe, rather than interpret, what takes place, and repeatedly call attention to it. This in itself tends to disrupt the automaticity with which procedural learning ordinarily is expressed. The second therapeutic tactic is to engage in activities that directly disrupt what has been procedurally learned" (2000, p. 325).

Rather than focusing primarily on the development of a narrative, sensorimotor psychotherapy facilitates a gradual exposure to the situationally accessible, implicit components of the memory, with a primary focus on sensorimotor processing. Where appropriate, the memory narrative is utilized to stimulate implicitly held recollection, as when clients are asked what happens in their internal experience and body movement when they talk about the trauma. As the thoughts, emotions, sensations, perceptions, and actions associated with the memory are brought to consciousness and studied both separately and together, what has been procedurally learned is disrupted.

Speculation on Memory and the Brain

The intention of memory work is not just to disrupt procedural learning or to effect a verbal account of previously nonverbal memory, but also to bring nonverbal memory into a domain that is regulated by a different part of the brain (Siegel, 1999, 1995). Brewin (2001) proposed that the elements of the trauma that are encoded in amygdala-dominated situationally accessible memory need to be exposed gradually to the hippocampally mediated verbally accessible memory system. In this way the memory fragments acquire a verbally accessible component that gives them a particular context:

> This in turn will assist the process whereby reminders of the trauma are inhibited by cortical influences from activating the person's panoply of fear responses. Instead of reminders being processed by a memory system that does not discriminate between present and past time, the more sophisticated processing afforded by the hippocampus, with its access to the whole of autobiographical memory, will enable the event to be located in its appropriate context. (Brewin, 2001, p. 381)

In this process the situationally accessible memory system, with its procedural, sensory, and autonomic components, "gradually acquires" verbal representation, and the client's experience of the memory changes. At an explicit memory level, the client may have long *known* that the traumatic events are over. The work of phase 2 facilitates the *felt experience* that the danger is past by helping clients engage in new, empowering actions and experience sensorimotor remembering without dysregulation. The verbal representation then emerges out of this new, empowering experience, not the other way around.

FUNDAMENTAL CONCEPTS FOR MEMORY WORK

Memory work is inherently destabilizing and often terrifying to the client. As Remarque wrote, "It's too dangerous for me to put these things [combat trauma] into words. I am afraid they might become gigantic and I will be no longer able to master them" (1929/1982, p. 165). Working with traumatic memory necessitates careful planning, psychoeducation, and good collaboration between therapist and client. As with any exposure intervention, caution and pacing are imperative in order to assure the client's continuing stability and to maximize therapeutic success.

At the beginning of work with traumatic memory, arousal often escalates. However, through emphasis on the resolution and prevention of bottom-up hijacking by attending to somatic sensations and movements rather than to the emotional and cognitive dimensions, arousal is brought back into a window of tolerance. Frequently, this restabilization process necessitates a temporary return to phase 1 resources. If phase 1 work has been carefully and thoughtfully accomplished, the client will be familiar with the importance of maintaining arousal within a window of tolerance and will have access to both top-down and bottom-up strategies as well as increased integrative capacity to accomplish this goal.

A major therapeutic error is to prioritize memory retrieval at the expense of the "less glamorous" aspects of good therapy. Some clients may strongly believe that the only way to effect real therapeutic change is to "get to the memories" and to get there quickly—which can lead to rapid destabilization if clients lack the capacity to integrate the material. Instead, clients are encouraged to commit to the "slower we go, the faster we get there" approach (Kluft, 1996), which minimizes the tendency to abreact and helps ensure that arousal remains manageable.

Therapist and client often need to negotiate the purpose of memory work. Some clients come to therapy with the hope that it will help them to learn "what really happened." The therapist emphasizes that sensorimotor psychotherapy is not a memory retrieval technique; rather, it is intended for resolution, not recollection of the traumatic event. Therapy is not about judging the accuracy of the past in a fact-finding endeavor, although once recalled, the memories may provide insight, relevance, and meaning to the client. The therapist must refrain from verifying the memory as fact and, at the same time, avoid "[questioning] the credibility of a story, or [implying] that a memory is imagination, fantasy, or magical thinking [which] may make clients feel as misunderstood and discounted as they have in other relationships" (Sable, 2000, p. 339). Therapists should follow good judgment in working with memories: Avoid leading questions, refrain from making recollection a goal of therapy, and decline to confirm or disconfirm memories that might emerge from somatic interventions, while providing appropriate empathic validation of the client's experience.

The overarching intention in working with traumatic memory is integration. Abreaction and regression are not encouraged because both involve a loss of mindfulness that impedes integration. Further, "abreaction or uncontrolled catharsis of overwhelming traumatic affects leads to states of hyperarousal and, at times, to complete psychological decompensation" (Van der Hart et al., 1993, p 165). Abreactive reexperiencing is not only potentially retraumatizing but also unlikely to resolve the trauma unless accompanied by integrative techniques, cognitive awareness, and nonchaotic emotional expression (Braun, 1986; Brown & Fromm, 1986; Horowitz, 1986; Maldonado & Butler, 2002; Maldonado & Spiegel, 2002; Spiegel, 1981, 2003; Van der Hart & Brown, 1992; Van der Hart, Nijenhuis, & Steele, 2006b). Because sensorimotor psychotherapy works at a slow pace to study the organization of present experience in response to memory, prioritizes keeping the client within the window of tolerance, and facilitates a return to the window when it is breached, abreaction is almost impossible.

The risks of addressing traumatic memory are many: further dissociation, retraumatization, reliving of traumatic tendencies, intensification of triggers, and loss of ability to function well in normal life. To minimize these risks, phase 2 treatment is embarked upon only after an adequate therapeutic alliance has formed, phase 1 goals are completed, and the client is able to self-regulate sufficiently to return arousal to within the window of tolerance when necessary. In preparation for memory work, the therapist and client consciously review and practice resourcing skills by working with the activation that is stimulated by "thinking about thinking about" working with memory. The client's capacity for mindfulness, utilization of resources, staying in the here-and-now, and ability to self-reflect with the therapist are all considered in determining readiness to move into phase 2.

Maintaining Social Engagement and Optimal Arousal

The client's ability to rely on the therapeutic relationship as a "safe base" reflects his or her utilization of the social engagement system for interactive regulation. However, as clients begin to recount the trauma, they tend to lose contact with their social engagement system. For example, as Mary, a middle-aged, successful businesswoman who was raped repeatedly by her uncle from age 4–10, began to talk about her history, she spoke rapidly with few pauses that would provide opportunity for verbal interaction with the therapist. Her social engagement system was markedly diminished; it was almost as though she were talking to herself. As she spoke, Mary appeared increasingly isolated and alone. At times she experienced panic and hyperarousal, and she repeatedly spoke in judgment of herself for having "allowed" the abuse: "Why did I ever change clothes in front of him? Why didn't I tell my mother what was happening?" She also condemned herself for her inability to defend herself against the abuse, interpreting her dissociation and freezing as a personal weakness—a common response among trauma survivors (Steele et al., 2005b).

When social engagement between client and therapist is diminished or lost, reestablishment through interactive regulation by the therapist and use of the somatic resources learned in phase 1 is essential. In Mary's case, the therapist facilitated interactive regulation by tracking changes and movements in her body, making contact statements, demonstrating an ability to understand Mary's distress and tolerating the description of her traumatic experience without withdrawing or becoming hyperaroused himself. He also encouraged Mary to look around the therapy room and name objects and colors of objects, thus reestablishing her orientation to the here-and-now, asked her to press her feet into the floor to facilitate grounding, and also experimented with her making eye contact with him as she spoke. Gradually, Mary began to soften slightly in her body, slow her speech, and engage in reciprocal interaction with the therapist.

Limiting the Amount of Information

Stabilization needs to be reinstated after any challenging therapeutic task or personal crisis experienced by the client. The therapist must track the client's capacity to regulate him- or herself psychologically, somatically, and socially in every session. Clients are helped to understand that stabilization always takes precedence over memory work, and that as exposure to the memory takes place, stabilization achieved by deliberately limiting the amount of information available to the client facilitates integration. For example, when Martin began speaking about his Viet Nam experience, his hyperarousal, shaking, panic, and terror began to escalate. Martin was instructed to "drop the content" of the memory, focus exclusively on his body, and concentrate on the sensations in the soles of his feet until he felt his arousal coming back into the window of tolerance. Only then did he resume talking about the memory, which was now accompanied by a level of activation that he could tolerate.

Limiting the amount of information the client must process and integrate at any given moment entails focusing selectively on the body and excluding awareness of emotions, cognitions, and the "story." This focus makes the process more manageable and enables arousal to return to the window of tolerance. Directing the client to attend exclusively to sensorimotor experience usually entails a fair amount of therapeutic direction. The therapist must ask specific mindfulness questions that bring the client's attention to precise details of sensorimotor experience in the body. For example:

> "Let's put the content and the emotions aside for now. Focus on your feet touching the floor—what do you notice? Do you experience tension? Shaking? Numbness? What impulses do you notice? Maybe there is a movement your body wants to make. Let's just stay with your body and observe any movements that want to happen, until your arousal settles down."

The client is taught to direct mindful, focused attention on body sensation and movement until the arousal settles. As therapy progresses and the client's window of tolerance expands, cognitive and emotional elements of the memory can be carefully reintroduced, one at a time, into the therapy process.

Working at the Edge of the Window of Tolerance

To integrate traumatic memory, a piece or sliver of the memory itself must be reactivated. This reactivation may send arousal to the limits of the window of tolerance or over it, into the hyper- or hypoaroused zones. If this arousal dramatically exceeds the client's window of tolerance, then the traumatic material cannot be integrated. Instead, "arousal levels must be carefully managed during [work with traumatic memory]. If arousal becomes too high, frontal and hippocampal activity will again become impaired and the person will reexperience the trauma without transferring information from the [situationally accessible memory system] to the [verbally accessible memory] system" (Brewin, 2001, p. 386). On the other hand, if arousal does not approach the limits but remains within the middle of the window of tolerance (e.g., levels of arousal typical of low fear and anxiety states), integration can be hindered because the nonverbal traumatic memory fragments have not been adequately evoked. The therapist needs to elicit, carefully and slowly, fragments of the memory at a pace that enables the client to approach the edges of the window of tolerance but not remain in a hyper- or hypoaroused zone. The challenge is to process the past without retraumatizing the client, to facilitate a steady integration of fragments and increase in the "transfer" of memory from situationally accessible memory to verbally accessible memory. The work must take place at the upper and lower edges of the window of tolerance, accessing enough of the traumatic material to work with, but not so much that the client becomes dysregulated, dissociated, and retraumatized.

To accomplish this task, it is necessary, first and foremost, to induce mindfulness to help the client describe his or her experience without "going back there." In phase 1 treatment, clients become capable of "dual processing" by learning to use mindful observation to stay in the here-and-now. They have learned to sense when arousal is reaching the limits of their window of tolerance. Therapist and client agree to track arousal and signal when it is beginning to exceed the window on either end, and then to turn the focus exclusively to body sensation and movement until the arousal settles. Accessing more traumatic material or content at such moments is discouraged. As a result of their phase 1 work on developing integrative capacity to achieve mastery over the dysregulation, clients understand that, at these times, they must cease talking about the trauma, inhibit any thoughts about it, put the emotions aside, and instead focus solely on the somatic sensations and movements—or, if that is not possible, on utilizing stabilizing resources to reregulate their physiology.

WORKING WITH RESOURCES

Memory work in phase 2 occurs in the context of resources: to reiterate, those skills, competencies, mental and physical actions, images, things, relationships, and memories that give people a sense of mastery and internal cohesion. When people feel "resourced," they feel safer and more competent and subsequently tend to experience positive affect and pleasurable physical sensations—which, in turn, lead to other memories and experiences in which they felt similar pleasurable sensations. Identifying, acknowledging, and developing resources increase the availability of feelings of well-being and the corresponding pleasurable body sensations.

Identifying Peritraumatic Resources

Working with memory and working with resources thus go hand in hand. As the memories are addressed, new resources are cultivated and the resources used long ago to cope with the traumatic event are discovered and strengthened. The pleasurable body elements or those that heighten feelings of mastery are emphasized. Although it may seem counterintuitive, no matter how sudden or unexpected the traumatic event was, peritraumatic resources were utilized by the client and subsequently can be brought to awareness in therapy.

For example, as Joyce began to work with a memory of a home invasion and sexual assault, she recalled an image of allowing the assailant to force her to dance with him, which first evoked a sense of helplessness and shame. As she discussed this incident with her therapist, tracking her body sensation and movement, Joyce noted that she began to breathe more deeply and felt less terrified. She then remembered that his body relaxed as they danced and she sensed that he became less angry. Immediately, she felt a bodily shift from powerlessness to mastery: "I didn't do it just because he forced me: I did it to save my life!" The client's discovery of the resources that were present before, during, and after the event thus challenged her feelings of powerlessness.

Associating the past trauma with other nontraumatic elements might prove to be integrative and healing for the client (Breuer & Freud, 1895/1955; Janet, 1889, 1925). By identifying and experiencing existing peritraumatic resources, clients learn to associate trauma with nontraumatic, even positive, experiences. Acknowledging and "reliving" the memory of the resource and experiencing it somatically often help clients feel more competent, capable, and even proud of the resources they used, despite being "unsuccessful" in preventing the traumatic experience.

As a child Adanich had accidentally fallen through a glass door and nearly died from the injuries. She suffered from intrusive images of blood and hospital equipment for years following the event. Her therapist discussed with her doing a slow-paced recall of the events before, during, and after the accident, with the purpose of searching for, and remembering, the resources that were available and utilized during the time of her accident. The therapist asked Adanich to remember the "good things" that were occurring prior to the trauma. She reported that she had been roughhousing playfully with her brother in the living room and that it was "a wonderful feeling." The therapist guided her to simply remember the play, to "hang out" in this moment in the memory and experience the pleasurable physical sensations as she remembered this resource of roughhousing with her brother. By making that moment the whole focus of her attention, Adanich started to find the building blocks of that "resourced" experience: the sounds of their childish laughter, the image of herself playing, the joyful and alive feeling in her body.

After this resource was identified and experienced, Adanich was encouraged to remember the accident itself—not to relive it but to discover what had supported her and how she coped during the event. She remembered that immediately her father rushed to pick her up in his arms with a tender, worried expression on his face. This was a particularly important recollection to Adanich because, prior to this therapy session, she could not recall even one time when her father had held her. The therapist, noting a change in Anadich as she mentioned her father's expression, asked her to "pause right there: See his face in your mind's eye . . . what happens when you remember the way he looked at you?" Anadich replied, "I take a breath . . . and my heart gets warm." The therapist said, "There is something very important about this moment for you—just see his face . . . maybe the way he is looking at you communicates something . . . what might this special look tell you?" Anadich continued to focus on the image of her father's face, enjoying the memory of his concern and tenderness. Finally, she realized, "His eyes tell me that he loves me," and she began to softly cry. The somatic component of "warmth in my heart" and the meaning of "I am loved" were a revelation to her—the only time when she could remember this feeling with her father. It is important to emphasize that neither of these resourced experiences was recalled until the therapist guided Adanich to remember what had supported her and to feel the effects of that support on her body sensation.

Through "resourcing," the nontraumatic elements of a traumatic experience are remembered, and clients learn to orient toward, and maintain attention to, these positive experiences—which in turn helps them learn that they can make more conscious choices about what they orient toward. Allocating attention to resources, rather than exclusively to traumatic elements of the memory, mitigates both the phobic avoidance of the memory and the continual replaying of it in a fixed form. As Adanich said after that session, "The memory will never be the same—now I will also remember how much I loved playing with my brother and my father's love and the warmth in my heart."

Helping the client uncover peritraumatic resources requires a particular kind of therapeutic artistry. The felt sense of having had any access to resources at that time of trauma may be overshadowed by strong negative feelings of fear and helplessness. For instance, as Bob recalled a difficult moment of a motor vehicle accident in which he suffered extensive injuries, he reported feeling that he had no resources. Without intruding too much on this vulnerable moment, the therapist said gently, "Somehow you came out alive; you could so easily have died." Bob nodded in agreement, and the therapist softly asked, "What did you do that helped you at that terrible time?" After a pause, Bob replied, "I stayed very still." In the midst of experiencing his utter helplessness, he had found the resource. The therapist responded by trying to help him deepen the experience, saying, "Somehow you knew that would help you—someone else might not have had the intuition to do that." As Bob explored this spontaneously remembered capacity to remain physically still, he could experience in his body how the stillness helped him feel less helpless. As he and his therapist continued to experience the memory of his staying so still, he reported feelings of greater confidence in himself and his body. What allowed him to come to an appreciation of the resource on his own terms was his therapist's slow pace and careful attunement, trying to find just the right words to bring his appreciation to that moment so that he could make the discovery himself. Prematurely positive or flattering comments would have taken him out of the resourced experience rather than deepening it.

Validating and experiencing resources help to bring balance to the traumatic memory, so that strength and competence are remembered along with the helplessness and overwhelming feelings (Levine, 1997). Assisting clients to oscillate between the two conditions of competence and traumatic reactions appears to help integrate trauma responses, prevent the reactions from escalating, and deepen feelings of confidence and mastery.

Installing New Resources While Working with a Memory

Sometimes the client cannot spontaneously locate peritraumatic or survival resources in the context of working through a memory. In this instance, it is the therapist's job to help the client install new resources, which then become part of the transformation of the memory. For instance, while working with a memory of her childhood sexual abuse, Sally began to "fog out," feeling hypoaroused and depersonalized and losing contact with current reality. The therapist asked Sally to drop the content of the memory and work with grounding, centering, and pushing to help regulate her arousal and stimulate a mobilizing defense. Sally felt powerful and forceful as her muscles engaged in pushing against the pillow held up by her therapist. After the session, she reported feeling fully present in her body and finally having a way to come out of the "fog" and be in the here-and-now.

Uncovering, strengthening, or installing resources, particularly their somatic components, in the context of the traumatic memory may change the way that memory is encoded by making the newly encoded memory "highly distinctive." Clients tend to remember their feelings of mastery, competence, or pleasure. Taking the time in a therapeutic context to expand upon the resourced memories by facilitating the client's awareness of the building blocks of present experience that correspond with this recollection—the somatic components, images, smells, sounds, thoughts, and emotions—strongly encodes these "unusual, distinctive attributes" of the memory, rendering them more available to recall (Brewin, 2001, p. 387). These distinctive memories—such as remembering the compassion on a father's face or experiencing the capacity to move during recall of a traumatic event that previously evoked immobility—"compete" with nondistinctive, nonverbal, situationally accessible memories. These recollections of competence become more available to clients as they continue to access associations connected with a specific event.

ACTS OF TRIUMPH: MOBILIZING DEFENSES

Janet eloquently wrote: "The patients who are affected by traumatic memories have not been able to perform any of the actions characteristic of the stage of triumph. . . . They are continually seeking this joy in action . . . which flees before them as they follow" (1925, p. 669). More recently,

Van der Kolk suggested that "performing the actions that would have over-come one's sense of helplessness at the time of the experience that became traumatic and expressing the sensations associated with the memory of trauma effectively helps people overcome their traumas" (2002, p. 62).

Failed mobilizing defensive responses can perpetuate action tendencies, delay resolution of the trauma, and fuel distressing trauma-related symp-toms (Ogden & Minton, 2000). It is as if time stopped at the moment of threat, and the body is continuing to reenact the sequence of events: The threat is perceived, mobilizing defenses are stimulated, then suddenly halted, followed by persistent dysregulated arousal and immobilizing defenses of freezing, collapse, and numbing. Each time the traumatic memory is acti-vated, the client may experience somatic initiation of a mobilizing defen-sive response followed by its truncation.

Janet (1919, 1925) referred to a variety of mental and physical actions that remain incomplete for people with trauma-related disorders. A senso-rimotor approach to traumatic memory addresses the incomplete defensive responses, which, when completed, foster a sense of mastery and "triumph" that then facilitates the execution of more adaptive mental actions and the formation of autobiographical memory. As Levine wrote, "When the implicit (procedural) memory is activated and completed somatically, an explicit narrative can be constructed; not the other way around" (2005).

The therapist helps the client to "complete" failed defensive actions—to execute "acts of triumph"—through reactivating a "sliver" of memory, just enough to evoke the mental and sensorimotor tendencies. Then the physi-cal actions that "wanted to happen" are discovered through awareness of the body. These actions, when executed, mitigate feelings of helplessness and shame and give rise to moments of joy, confidence, and satisfaction. A help-less response is exchanged for an active, empowering response (Levine, 1997). Through state-specific processing, the traumatic responses are acti-vated but then processed in such a way that new reactions are evoked, and the traumatic memory becomes associated with empowering actions and their corresponding emotions and cognitions. These actions are usually dra-matically different from those evoked by the original event.

Sexually assaulted during a home invasion when she was in her early 20s, Jenny had not been able to sleep through the night on the anniversary of the trauma in the ensuing 25 years. She and her therapist carefully scheduled an appointment on that date to work with the action tendencies evoked by the anniversary. As Jenny observed her internal experience in reaction to the decision to work on this memory, she noticed that trembling and shaking had already begun, along with a retraction of her field of consciousness to images of the assault. She felt a clenching in her jaw and "electricity" in her legs and arms. Her shoulders and head bent inward and she felt a pull to curl up into a ball. Instead, she and her therapist concentrated on the "electrical surges" she experienced in her limbs, and Jenny was invited to notice any action her body wanted to make. She reported that she could feel how she had wanted to push away her assailant, and she wanted to stand and push against the wall during the session. It is important to note that the impulse to push emerged from Jenny's awareness of her body as she remembered the assault, and not as an idea or concept. As she mobilized not only her arms but her whole body in pushing, she began to feel a new sense of her own strength and power. Her anger, usually experienced with a sense of impotence, felt pleasurable and exciting. Jenny left the office with the words, "It's over—I am done being scared." And that night, she slept peacefully through the hours when the assault had occurred years ago.

Executing Voluntary Acts of Triumph

To uncover latent acts of triumph, it is necessary to reevoke a sliver of the nonverbal memory, slowly and mindfully in a step-by-step manner, with meticulous attention to the body's responses. Often the somatic components of implicit memory emerge even when talking about working with the memory, as in the case of Jenny. They also can be stimulated by deliberately thinking about the memory or discussing reminders of the trauma. It is worth emphasizing again that the sensorimotor psychotherapist is not primarily interested in the client's trauma narrative. The narrative in sensorimotor psychotherapy is a means to an end; its importance lies in its ability to bring the unassimilated nonverbal components of traumatic memory into present-moment conscious experience.

As the nonverbal components of the memory are activated, clients are helped to observe, rather than relive, the "state-specific" processing—that is, what happens inside. The therapist must cultivate the client's acute awareness of body sensations and movement, first via tracking and making contact statements about the client's sensorimotor experience, and second, as the client begins to become mindful, by encouraging the client to notice sensations and movement without prompting by the therapist. The evoked physical re-enactments of orienting, defense, and arousal are slowly and consciously observed. Mindfulness questions are asked, such as: "What sensation do you feel in your body as you remember this incident? What happens inside as your hand makes a fist?" Because these questions compel the client to observe and report internal organization of experience, they maintain dual awareness and prevent reliving.

When clients remember the trauma, immobilizing defenses of freeze or submission/collapse are usually aroused. The somatic indicators of these defenses are noted by the therapist, who is also looking for indicators of orienting and mobilizing defensive responses that were not fully executed or were unsuccessful during the original trauma. These are often first seen in a barely perceptible movement, such as the client's hand just starting to make a fist, or the client's report of a precursor to movement, such as tightening in the jaw or arms. These are the involuntary and anticipatory movement adjustments that occur before a voluntary movement, such as hitting, and they are dependent upon the planned or voluntary movement for the form they take (Bouisset, 1991).

The therapist carefully tracks, and teaches the client to track, the body, looking for these small preparatory movements that might indicate that a more overt motor action is available. Once the therapist catches a glimpse of such a movement, or the client reports feeling a defensive impulse, the therapist helps the client drop the narrative and voluntarily execute the action "that wants to happen" slowly and mindfully.

In phase 1 treatment, a client might work with executing voluntary defensive movements such as pushing in order to experience the felt sense of having the capacity to resist or push away thus regulating arousal. In phase 2 treatment, the mobilizing defense that was originally truncated is elicited via state-specific processing, so that the client executes the active movement as it emerges spontaneously from the somatic experience of the memory that previously evoked only immobilizing defenses.

For example, as Martin began to talk about his war experience, his hands were resting quietly on his knees. Then the therapist noticed his fingers moving slightly upward, suggesting a larger movement of protection. This movement had occurred just as Martin recalled having had the sense that someone was aiming at him, although he could not see the enemy. The therapist requested that Martin cease his narration—momentarily "drop" the content—in order to focus his attention exclusively on his hands to look for what "wants to happen" somatically. Martin described feeling that his arms wanted to lift upward. As the therapist encouraged him to allow the movement, Martin reported that his arms wanted to move upward in a protective gesture. In staying with this movement, Martin started to notice a slight change. Instead of covering his head with his arms and freezing in a habitual immobilizing defense, he said that he had a feeling in his arms of wanting to push away. The therapist encouraged the slow enactment of this mobilizing defense, which had not been possible at the time of the trauma, holding a pillow for Martin to push against. The therapist asked Martin to temporarily disregard all memory and simply focus on his body in order to find a way to push that felt comfortable and "right." Martin's internal locus of control was increased as he was encouraged to guide this physical exploration by telling the therapist how much pressure to use in resisting his pushing with the pillow, what position to be in, and so on.

DISTINGUISHING TRAUMA-BASED EMOTIONS FROM SENSATION

At one point when Martin was pushing, he described feeling panicky. The therapist asked him to focus on only the physical elements of the panic, which Martin reported as increased heart rate and tingling, rather than the emotion. This was an important directive whose intention was to separate trauma-based emotions from sensation so that sensorimotor processing could occur without interference from emotional processes—and without overloading Martin with more information than he could integrate effectively. As Martin focused only on his body sensation, and continued to experience the pushing along with the increased his heart rate and tingling, the therapist tracked his body responses and made contact statements about the somatic experience, such as, "The strength of the pushing is increasing," and "You seem to be settling down now." Martin's panic, experienced not as emotion but as rapid heart rate, began to quiet, and he was again instructed to be mindful of the details of his sensations: "What happens as your heart quiets and you continue to push? What do you feel in your back and spine?" Slowly and mindfully, Martin was able to experience a full sequence of active defensive responses: lifting the arms, pushing tentatively at first, then increasing the pressure and engaging the muscles of his back, pelvis, and legs. As the therapist continued to use contact statements and mindfulness questions to ensure Martin's mindful focus on the sensation, he began to experience the physical pleasure of pushing, reporting, "This feels great!" He was encouraged to push as long as he liked, until the exercise felt complete to him. When the defensive sequence had been thoroughly explored and completed, Martin was calmer, his arousal had returned to the window of tolerance, and he resumed the telling of the story—until somatic components were again stimulated, and sensorimotor processing began anew.

FINDING OTHER INCOMPLETE ACTIONS

This defensive pushing movement is one among many common "incomplete actions." The therapist helps clients discover the action that is naturally emerging from their awareness of body sensation and impulses. One client experienced the urge to kick as she remembered sexual abuse; the therapist held a large therapy ball so that she could mindfully explore the motions of kicking with her legs and feet. Another client, who had suffered a terrible fall, experienced a twisting impulse in her body just before she struck the ground. Gently executing that impulse slowly and mindfully led to the awareness of how her body had tried to protect her by twisting away from the danger. Still another, who had suffered a motor vehicle accident, was able to reexperience and complete the impulse to push with his legs.

Rather than inadvertently facilitating the reenactment of immobilizing defenses, therapists must be diligent in their search for mobilizing, empowering defensive actions so that mobilizing (active) and immobilizing (passive) defensive subsystems can be integrated, rather than remain dissociated. The therapist's meticulous search for empowering action is illustrated in Ashley's therapy. Ashley was working on the memories of a date rape. Her therapist had expected that the hand movements elicited by her trauma story were precursors to a mobilizing defense of pushing, as in Martin's case. However, as the therapist and Ashley focused on her arms moving very slowly up and over her head, Ashley suddenly said that she was so ashamed that her whole body wanted to curl up into a fetal position and hide. In allowing this movement of curling up, Ashley expressed sadness and shame, thus executing a "mental" action of expressing her emotion in the context of a supportive therapeutic relationship. However, in doing so, Ashley was moving away from mobilizing defenses into immobilizing defenses and their concomitant emotions of shame and sadness. Continuing to explore this posture after the emotions were expressed, even in the context of a supportive therapeutic relationship, would reenact the currently maladaptive fixed action tendency and most likely augment her feelings of helplessness and failure.

Therefore, after Ashley's emotional arousal settled, the therapist asked her to go back to the moment in her memory when her date was beginning to make sexual advances and explore her somatic experience *right then*, as if she could extend the moment, making it last several minutes without moving forward in the memory. As Ashley came out of her curled up position, sat up slowly and explored that moment just before the rape occurred, she reported slight tension in her hand, which proved to be the nascent mobilizing defense that she had not been able to execute. What helped it emerge was taking one moment in Ashley's memory where it was likely that mobilizing defenses were experienced but not executed, and drawing out that one moment so that she might notice all the subtle body sensations and impulses inherent in that one "sliver" of memory. As this moment was experienced, Ashley reported the tension in her hand, and said she wanted to make a fist. Following that tension and allowing it to develop into a movement, that is, of becoming a fist and pushing hard against a pillow, provided her, finally, with the possibility of a new action. In that moment she recognized that she was no longer doomed to the repetition of that disempowering, immobilizing response.

THE STORY AS A MEANS TO AN END

Although the narrative of the date rape was the starting point for the work with Ashley, the story is only the means to an end. It is a way to activate the nonverbal implicitly held memories and action tendencies, and with them, the mobilizing defensive movements that were truncated or interrupted so that they can be completed in current time. Executing these actions after so many years of reenacted failures to take action promotes a sense of mastery, giving rise to moments of joy, confidence, and satisfaction. Martin noted that after executing these mobilizing defensive reactions in therapy, a habitual cringing response was absent in his day-to-day life. He had progressed in his therapy from awareness of his implicit memories in the form of immobilizing tendencies, to the verbally encoded recognition of his past fear and helplessness, to the execution of a mobilizing defensive action, and finally to the verbal expression of power and mastery. Subsequently, Martin became more comfortable with asserting himself appropriately in his daily life. The years of therapeutic work he had previously spent retelling the events of his war experience had not succeeded in providing the bodily *experience* that action and self-assertion were now safe and empowering options. It was his *in vivo* somatic experience of being able to access his mobilizing defenses in their entirety that allowed this powerful transformation to take place.

Executing "Involuntary" Acts of Triumph: Sensorimotor Sequencing

Trauma-related involuntary movements and sensations tend to persist long after the danger has passed. *Sensorimotor sequencing* is a therapeutic technique that facilitates the completion of these involuntary bodily actions that are associated with traumatic memory. Instead of executing actions wilfully and voluntarily, sensorimotor sequencing entails slowly and mindfully tracking, detail by detail, the involuntary physical movements and sensations that pertain primarily to unresolved autonomic arousal, orienting, and defensive reactions. Clients are initially taught to cultivate awareness of sensations (e.g., tingling, buzzing, heaviness, temperature changes) and micromovements (e.g., trembling and miniscule changes in muscular tension) as they fluctuate in texture, quality, and intensity. Next, they are asked to mindfully track (a top-down cognitive process) the sequence of physical sensations and small movements (a sensorimotor process) as they progress through the body. These sensations and movements are experienced by clients as at least partially involuntary—that is, out of conscious control—and are typically perceived as threatening when they occur unbidden. To prevent dysregulation, it is essential to teach clients how to "uncouple" trauma-related emotions and traumatic content from these sensations and impulses in order to limit the amount of information to a manageable amount. Clients are directed to temporarily disregard the emotions and thoughts that arise, until the bodily sensations and movements resolve to a point of rest and stabilization. While the sequencing is unfolding, the therapist encourages the client to allow these involuntary impulses to happen and to "follow them." This unique orientation emphasizes allowing the movements and refraining from voluntarily directing them through conscious control.

Using mindfulness, the client is able to witness and support the progression of sensations and impulses in the body, but not to control it. In the original trauma, the person's awareness was embedded in the experience, and information-processing mechanisms were overwhelmed and out of conscious control. In sensorimotor sequencing, the client's attention hovers over the experience, observing it, parsing it, and reporting it to the therapist. The slowness of this microprocessing and the maintenance of social engagement with the therapist keep the experience safe and manageable, thereby challenging the habitual reexperiencing. Clients often state that these movements seem to "happen by themselves," without conscious intention or control, and generate feelings of well-being when they come to completion.

When working with traumatic memory, clients frequently experience involuntary trembling and shaking, which may be considered to be a discharge of "the tremendous energy generated by our survival preparations" (Levine, 2005). The immense arousal mediated by the sympathetic nervous system that is stimulated under threat serves to mobilize vigorous defensive actions. When those actions do not take place, as is so often the case in trauma, a similar heightened energy may emerge in therapy. "What is significant in the resolution of trauma is the completion of incomplete responses to threat and the ensuing discharge of the energy that was mobilized for survival" (Levine, 2005). Through sensorimotor sequencing, clients learn to stay with these involuntary sensations and movements until they are "discharged" and settle by themselves.

The therapist tracks closely for incipient signs that offer the possibility of sensorimotor sequencing: slight trembling or vibrating, or a movement that "wants to happen," or the client's report of sensations such as tingling or buzzing. At these moments, the client may be encouraged to track these sensations and involuntary movements until they resolve and the body is calm.

SENSORIMOTOR SEQUENCING OF MOBILIZING DEFENSES

To illustrate involuntary sensorimotor sequencing of defenses, we will use the example of Mary, the client who was repeatedly raped by her uncle throughout her childhood. As Mary talked about this long-lasting trauma, her jaw began to tighten, her right shoulder and arm began to constrict, and her breath became labored—all possible signs of defensive responses emerging spontaneously. After bringing her attention to these physical observations, saying, "Your jaw and arm seem to be tightening up and your breathing is changing," the therapist directed Mary to be mindful of her bodily sensations, suggesting that Mary drop the content of the memory ("Let's take a few moments to sense what's happening in your body before we go on with the content"). Mary was aware of physical impulses that seemed involuntary, as if they were happening "by themselves." At this point, Mary was no longer describing the past but was attentive only to present bodily experience. Her body seemed to take on a life of its own as she was encouraged to be mindful of her sensations and movements. Mary reported that "my hand wants to become a fist," and the therapist encouraged her to "feel the impulse and allow that to happen" but without doing it voluntarily. Very slowly, as client and therapist tracked her micromovements, Mary's hand now began to curl into a fist.

Next, Mary reported that her arm wanted to "hit out." The mobilizing defensive movement sequence was now emerging without conscious top-down direction from either the client or the therapist. The therapist said, "Feel that impulse to hit out and just notice what happens next in your body." Mary was encouraged to simply track and allow the involuntary micromovements and gestures, rather than "do" them voluntarily. Sensorimotor sequencing was occurring spontaneously in response to the mindful attention given to body sensation and impulses, and through a harnessing of cognitive direction by suspending content and emotion.

As the therapist directed Mary to track her sensations and involuntary movements, her right hand formed a fist, her forearm also tightened, and her arm slowly rose off her lap apparently without conscious intention on her part. Gradually, Mary's right arm progressed through an extremely slow rising and hitting motion accompanied by shaking, quite possibly the "discharge" described above. This experience of shaking is similar to that of shudders passing through the body when one is cold. After several minutes of sensorimotor sequencing, during which both Mary and the therapist followed the slow and unintended progression of movements, accompanied by shaking and trembling, Mary's arm finally came to rest in her lap. She continued to shudder for a bit longer and was instructed to stay with the shudders and sensations as long as she was comfortable doing so, until they stopped spontaneously.

All the while, Mary was encouraged to trust her body by allowing the movements and the shudders to occur without trying to direct them or change them in any way. She was also encouraged to self-regulate—to stop if the feelings became too intense or if she felt too much discomfort to go on. Because physical sensations from the gradual "exposure" to the traumatic memory can be extremely intense before they begin to unwind and soften, clients need the therapist's help in following the sensorimotor process. Eventually the shudders ceased, and Mary said she felt relief and a sensation of tingling throughout her body. The therapist instructed her to savor her bodily feeling and sense of relief and to describe these new sensations in detail. Reporting a softening in her musculature, a slowed heart rate, and a good feeling of heaviness throughout her body, Mary stated that she felt peaceful for the first time in weeks.

Involuntary movement indicative of mobilizing defensive responses can often be experienced in the legs as well. During the step-by-step exposure of Martin to his Viet Nam experience, he reported being in the jungle and having the thought "This is the wrong place to be." Realizing that the moment of threat recognition is a potential indicator of a mobilizing flight response, the therapist encouraged Martin to focus on what happened in his body when he said those words, "This is the wrong place to be." Martin reported a tension in his thighs and some small restless leg movements and then realized that he "wanted to flee." Note that Martin's verbalization of a flight response emerged from his awareness of his body as he remembered the trauma. Encouraged to track these movements, Martin's legs began to vibrate; he remained aware of these micromovements until they discharged and settled on their own, at which point he reported feeling calmer. It must be noted that the therapist has no specific agenda for how the sequencing occurs: In Mary's case, it led spontaneously to the execution of a mobilizing defense; in Martin's case, the same approach led to a resolution of the autonomic dysregulation and vibratory energy in his legs.

SENSORIMOTOR SEQUENCING OF ORIENTING RESPONSES

A traumatic memory can also be explored for incomplete acts of orienting, so that orienting actions can be reestablished and executed during state-specific processing of the memory. Incipient orienting actions are often evident in slight movements of the neck indicative of the "scanning" stage of the orienting response. Truncated orienting responses sometimes manifest as neck tension. For example, Amelie came to therapy complaining of nightmares and chronic neck tension and pain following a skiing accident. As she began to describe the accident, she and the therapist noticed that her neck was becoming tenser and stiffer. As she became aware of the stiffness, Amelie spontaneously remembered being at the top of a very steep mountain with her father, who was encouraging her to ski down a slope that she felt was beyond her capabilities. She reported wanting to please her father and being pulled internally to acquiesce to his wishes. When the therapist asked Amelie what happened in her body as she remembered this moment, Amelie described an increase in neck tension on the left side. The therapist and Amelie took their time to explore the sensations and tension in her neck, and

Amelie slowly felt her head turning, following the pull of the tension. Amelie's experience of her neck turning had a strangely nonvolitional aspect to it. She found her neck moving to the left, as if "by itself," saying, "I'm not trying to move it; I'm just following it." As she did so, Amelie realized that the slope she had wanted to ski down—a much more gradual and safer route—was to the left of the mountain where she had stood with her father. Instead of orienting forward and following her own desire to ski down the gentle slope, she had complied with her father's request, resulting in the accident. In the treatment session, Amelie took several minutes to follow the turn of her head and experienced a relaxation of the tension in her neck as this orienting action, truncated during the actual event, was executed. By following the movement of turning to the left, she realized that she had wanted to ski down the easier slope; this realization created a new verbal representation of the accident that challenged her previously held self-blame. The completion of the orienting movement left her feeling a somatic, emotional, and cognitive sense of resolution.

INDICATORS OF AROUSAL, ORIENTING,
AND DEFENSIVE RESPONSES

Orienting, arousal, and defensive responses manifest themselves in any of the building blocks of present experience: thoughts, emotions, sensations, sensory perceptions, or movement. As noted in the above examples, tracking the client's body reveals moments when preparatory or intentional movements herald the beginning of an orienting or defensive response. The thoughts, emotions, and perceptual experiences that accompany memory recall also indicate the availability of mobilizing defenses. For example, the statements "I feel like running away" or "I wish I could have hit him back" suggest that fight and/or flight responses may be activated. If the client reports a feeling that "Something's not right," an orienting response may be evoked. When the verbal indicators of an orienting or defensive action are expressed, the therapist may call attention to them by asking the client to repeat those words and notice what happens in the body. Almost always, the client will sense an impulse that accompanies the words and seems to fit with them. Other examples of thoughts that signal the presence of defensive impulses include:

"My jaw is getting tight."
"My neck wants to turn."
"My hands are clenched."
"I can feel my heels pushing into the floor."
"My eyes get narrow when I hear that sound."

Similarly, clients' expressions of feeling scared, nervous, angry, or guarded often indicate incipient mobilizing defenses or arousal. The therapist may again ask the client to focus on those emotions and notice what the body is doing—"what wants to happen in the body"—or what sensations the client notices when these feelings emerge.

THE SPONTANEOUS EMERGENCE OF RESPONSES

An important element of sequencing involuntary defensive impulses is to let them emerge involuntarily and refrain from making them bigger, smaller, or faster than they already are. Characteristically, involuntary defensive and orienting movements emerge in a slow pattern of unfolding. As they manifest, the client is directed to "just stay with" the sensation of the micromovements that prepare for the defensive response. This movement often reflects what *didn't* get to happen at the time of the traumatic event, but what wanted to happen in the body—the action potential. It may have been cut off due to fear of being physically overpowered, or because of lack of time (e.g., in a high-speed car accident). If the memory of the traumatic event is being used to access the defensive and orienting responses, the client is instructed to remember the events to evoke body movement, but then follow the movement impulses in the body that want to happen *now*. The movements that happen in the body now may be precisely what did not happen at the time of the trauma.

This is not a somatic rewriting of history: It is a completion as the body is allowed to execute, and thereby restore, the defensive responses that were disabled. Sequencing involuntary movement may permit the body to unwind or unpack the stifled impulse that still "wants" to happen as the memory is recalled—allowing the long-delayed moment of triumph to occur spontaneously. These involuntary responses appear not only to provide a powerful sense of relief and mastery, but also seem to bring calmness and peace in place of depletion and exhaustion.

Working with Hyper- and Hypoarousal

Clients often report being intimidated by the prospect of reexperiencing traumatic hyperarousal and, as a result, feel revictimized by exposure to their own memories. As noted, voluntary resources can be utilized to regulate arousal. In addition, sensorimotor sequencing of these hyperaroused states can restore a sense of distance and control over the excessive activation and possibly discharge, and consequently lower, the arousal by allowing the accompanying involuntary trembling. When hyperarousal is noted, the client learns to orient away from the narrative and become mindful of body sensations and movement. These sensations may vary from tingling to the micromovement of a slight tremble or even to strong tremors, if unchecked. At these moments clients are encouraged to follow the progression of the spontaneous sensations, movements, and impulses through the body until the arousal has subsided. To press for additional traumatic material when clients are already activated can promote an escalation of arousal and dissociation. Because clients are being asked to attend solely to body sensation and movement, excluding emotions, cognitions, and content, the amount and intensity of information available to be processed in the moment become tolerable.

Because of the dysregulating nature of hyperarousal, the therapist endeavors to work slowly through one arousal cycle at a time. When arousal is noted, the client is instructed to become mindful of that sensation until the nervous system begins to settle down. That is one cycle of arousal, starting with a sensation or micromovement, processing through discharge or involuntary movement, and then the autonomic settling and resolution that brings arousal back into the window of tolerance. The arousal is metabolized, either through bodily discharge (e.g., tingling, trembling, shaking) or mobilization and demobilization of defensive responses. As the cycle comes to completion, another sliver of traumatic material is accessed if time allows in the therapy session, and the cycle is repeated.

By processing one arousal cycle at a time, clients begin to trust that working with arousal is manageable. They learn that even if the arousal becomes quite high, it will not escalate beyond control if they attend exclusively to the body. By uncoupling the arousal from trauma-related emotions, images, and repetitive thoughts, sensorimotor sequencing minimizes the risk of the escalation that occurs when emotions, meaning making, and interpretations drive arousal out of control. As clients learn to track the sequence of the sensation of arousal, they often experience a new freedom and a sense of mastery. As one client said, "Following the sensation lowers the fear." No longer is the sensation of arousal experienced as trauma; now it is just sensation.

During many years of therapy, Cate worked with her teenage experience of identifying her sister's murdered body, reexperiencing the terror and grief. Her symptoms of panic and hyperarousal, which alternated with depression, did not abate. With the help of a new therapist who practiced sensorimotor psychotherapy, Cate was asked to refrain from orienting to the emotions as she described the memory and to orient exclusively toward her body sensation. Rather than cathartically discharging the energy associated with the traumatic memory in sobs and continued recollection, or suppressing it by contraction of the body or "spacing out," she was encouraged to stay mindful of her inner somatic experience without interpreting or interfering with it. Her body began to tremble slightly, but the emotions did not escalate. Cate focused all her attention on body sensation and the trembling, describing to her therapist how the sensation changed and moved through her body. After several minutes, the sensation settled, the trembling stopped, and Cate's arousal was once again within the window of tolerance. Gradually, Cate learned to inhibit her internal orienting tendencies toward the emotions and memories and instead orient toward body sensations and movements, without wilfully interfering with her internal somatic process. Only when her sensations had settled was additional content described and emotional and cognitive processing included. Eventually, through this fractionated, mindful reexperiencing, the arousal was discharged, her emotions and memories were integrated, and her symptoms abated. Cate reported that up to now, she had not been able to talk with her adult daughter about her sister because she became too dysregulated. After the session she was able, for the first time, to tell her daughter the full story of what had happened.

Clients frequently become hypoaroused during phase 2 treatment, which often indicates the emergence of a submissive defensive response, an increase in dorsal vagal tone, and a decrease in sympathetic tone. At this point, clients' social engagement and ability to feel their bodies and maintain awareness of present reality can be lost quickly. They are "there" instead of "here," reexperiencing the helplessness and numbing responses that accompanied the original event. At such times the focus of the work becomes finding some type of active defensive response—an action "that wanted to happen"—within the memory recall. Often clients discover these actions by exploring a point in the memory when mobilizing defenses were available as preparatory movements. If that fails, the therapist might propose experimenting to find a somatic resource in the session, such as standing and moving the legs. Often after helping the client become somatically resourced, a mobilizing defense emerges spontaneously.

As Victoria began to talk about her early sexual abuse, she stopped being aware of her therapist's face and voice, and her social engagement system became disabled. Orientation to present reality was lost. The therapist tried to help her resource herself while she was still sitting down by having her look around the therapy office, but that experiment was unsuccessful: She still felt numb and in a "fog." Eventually, Victoria was asked to notice what happened if she stood up. Immediately, she felt more resourced because this movement enabled her to sense her legs firmly on the ground. She then spontaneously experienced the urge to push out with her arms, an impulse that the therapist encouraged in order to capitalize on the emerging mobilizing defense. As she and the therapist allowed the active movement to unfold, the fog lifted; Victoria's vision cleared, and her contact with the therapist was reestablished.

COGNITIVE AND EMOTIONAL PROCESSING

Breuer and Freud wrote, "Recollection without affect almost invariably produces no results" (1895/1955, p. 6). Just as sensorimotor reactions need to be expressed to a point of resolution, so do emotions. However, the therapist must be careful to assess whether the focus on emotional responses will prove useful, deciding when to put affect aside and focus on sensorimotor processing and when to focus on emotional processing. Brewin (2001) cautioned that if the client is overly activated, the situationally accessible memory system will be sparked off and instead of reorganizing the memory through the hippocampally mediated and verbally accessible memory system, these fragments will simply be retriggered. Therefore, the nonverbal memory fragments must be evoked with caution, preventing abreaction to keep the verbal memory system and its attendant hippocampal machinery online.

When adequate sensorimotor processing has occurred so that arousal can remain within a window of tolerance, emotional and cognitive work with traumatic experiences can resume. Dysregulated sensorimotor tendencies no longer usurp these upper levels of information processing. For example, after Martin's work with truncated mobilizing defenses and hyperarousal, he reported, "I feel really easy in my body—more connected there, an easier overall feeling. I'm able to go back and think about that event and not really get activated. I've done a lot of emotional work around it [in previous therapy] but there was still that inner body stuff going on when I would think about it." At this point in his therapy, he was able to work with the profound despair and suicidal tendencies while remaining anchored in the body. During work with emotions, his processing occurred at the upper limits of the window of tolerance, not far out of the optimal arousal zone. Afterward he reported, "There were no negative repercussions from this work, not like the last time" (when he did emotional processing in his previous therapy).

The therapist and client must assess whether the client can remain within or at the edge of the window of tolerance during work with trauma-related emotions. Cate had completed years of therapy in which she expressed her panic, anger, and grief at her sister's murder, but her therapy had not been completely successful because the work took place as Cate was hyperaroused, outside of her window of tolerance: She would talk about her sister's murder while she was highly anxious and emotional. In hyper- and hypoaroused zones, clients are dissociated and cannot integrate the emotions or other fragments of the traumatic memory. When Cate came to a sensorimotor psychotherapist and spoke of the memory, it was clear that sensorimotor processing was needed: Her arousal escalated immediately, her body began to tremble, and her automatic emotional tendency was to cry profusely. Such emotional catharsis was incapable of changing her tendency, because the root of the hyperarousal was physiological activation—that is, her sensorimotor, rather than emotional, experience of the trauma. Whereas "talk" therapies often return to stabilization at this point in order to regulate the arousal, sensorimotor psychotherapy offers an alternative: to focus on sensorimotor processing of the arousal. Cate's therapist did just that by asking her to put her emotion aside and just sense, describe, and track what was going on in her body.

When emotion emerges, the therapist and client can assess together what is contributing to the emotional arousal: physiological activation; a lack of mobilizing defenses; a trauma-based, habitual emotional response; or an emotional response that reflects the true weight of emotional meaning for the client. In the latter case, the emotion has a genuine, fresh quality, rather than a habitual, repetitive quality, and although arousal will likely be at the edge of the window of tolerance, it usually does not escalate to hyperarousal. For example, after several rounds of sensorimotor processing, Cate expressed a deep grief at her "loss of innocence." Because her arousal was right at the edge of the window of tolerance, but not far over, her therapist encouraged Cate to mindfully experience this deep emotion. However, if the emotion is accompanied by strong physiological responses, such as shaking, or if the emotion brings arousal excessively over the window of tolerance, it may be associated primarily with physiological arousal, a lack of mobilizing defenses, or trauma-based emotions. In these cases, the sensorimotor processing techniques described above can be used.

Trauma-based emotions—what Janet called "vehement emotions"—involve powerful feelings of fear, terror, anger, shame, horror, and helplessness that emerge when an individual cannot respond adaptively to an inescapable threatening situation (Van der Hart et al., 2006). These traumatically driven emotions manifest as repetitive and reactive: Neither their intensity nor their expression changes over time, nor do they change when they are vented. This emotional tendency is evident in clients who habitually interpret the experience of arousal as anger. Even when the authentic feeling might be more accurately recognized as fear or sadness, the client feels and expresses it as anger. This was the case with Martin, who reported that "I get angry at the drop of a hat—it feels like that's the only emotion I ever feel!" The expression or discharge of these repetitive emotions often reinforces maladaptive tendencies that do not resolve, despite best efforts of client and therapist, as was the case for Cate in the years of cathartic therapy. As Janet wrote: "The subjects, who seem so emotional . . . are indifferent to all new feelings and confine themselves to reproducing with an automatic exaggeration a few old feelings, always the same. Their emotions, which seem so violent, are not just; that is to say, they are not *en rapport* with the event that seems to call them up" (1907, p. 314). Trauma-based emotions feel familiar, circular, endless, and without resolution. They may appear dramatic, but they do not have the quality of emerging from an authentic contact with oneself. The therapist often finds it difficult to resonate with them. These trauma-based emotions are usually best addressed on the sensorimotor, rather than emotional, level of information processing.

Not only do traumatized individuals demonstrate emotional tendencies fueled by traumatic activation and immobilizing defensive tendencies, but also repetitive and habitual cognitive tendencies that do not resolve no matter how much they are confronted or interpreted. Janet (1945) used the term *substitute beliefs* to describe the habitual cognitions or mental actions that resulted from low integrative capacity, such as "It was all my own fault" or "I am bad and that is why these things happened to me." Although these cognitive distortions may provide the client with a sense of internal locus of control and mitigate severe helplessness, they also prevent adaptive functioning in current life (Steele et al., 2005b). These beliefs, along with dysregulated arousal and immobilizing defenses, form the underpinning of trauma-based emotions.

Although direct work with cognitive distortions is primarily the purview of phase 3 treatment, often beliefs change on their own in phases 1 and 2 as the client's body reorganizes and becomes more "resourced" for example, more aligned or grounded. These physical changes alone help to mitigate substitute beliefs and their emotional counterparts; the "meaning" and somatic sense of self is naturally different when the body is more resourced. After her sensorimotor psychotherapy sessions, Cate reported that, contrary to her previous belief of "It's not okay to feel good," it was possible for her to feel sensations in her body that were actually pleasurable. These sensations came about not as a result of cognitive work but in the aftermath of a shift in sensorimotor experience from hyperarousal and overwhelm to calmness, aliveness, and pleasure. After she experienced the power of previously lost mobilizing defenses, Victoria reported, "I can reach out; I can say no; I feel empowered in my body!"—statements that were in sharp contrast to her belief "It's not safe to reach out to others or to set a boundary." Martin, after years of feeling powerless in the face of debilitating, overwhelming experiences related to his Viet Nam memories, had come to believe that he would never be free from the energy-sapping and humiliating hold of these memories. After his sessions, he reported:

"Since [the sessions,] something's really shifted. I'm so much more attentive to my body and aware of any reactions. . . . Sometimes I feel challenged, but it is so different for me . . . more comfortable, easy. I'm not as excitable. It's much more manageable. I was just sharing some of my experience [in Viet Nam] and it was not charged at all. Before, there was always some charge. And with world events [specifically, the war in Iraq] I just take a breath and move on. It's not as triggering. The despair is not so much present—I sense it a little bit, but I'm much more willing to be with it and let it move through, which it does. That's different. . . . I feel good about myself. It brings tears [of relief] to my eyes . . . I've done such long and hard work."

Somatic reorganization provides the resource to work on these "pathogenic kernels" and prevent the reexperiencing the trauma-based emotions (Van der Hart & Op den Velde, 2003, p. 89). Many deep emotions were often denied in the past, especially when there was no support for them. Martin described how, in Viet Nam, the despair and grief were never addressed; Mary reported that she put aside her hurt and grief because no one believed her. Grief, especially, is an important emotional response to trauma that emerges, not only during the work of traumatic memory, but when the client completes actions and achieves a higher level of mastery. At these moments, the grief for what was lost and for "all the years spent so miserable" is especially salient. Van der Hart et al. wrote: "Grief is an important part of the emotional pain which must be worked through. With the passage of time, episodes of grief gradually increase in intensity and duration. Survivors come to understand and accept that loss is an inevitable part of trauma, and that it is ultimately a lifelong task to assimilate the ebb and flow of re-experienced grief with equanimity" (1993, p. 175).

This view is illustrated in Mary's case, wherein the grief emerged with each therapeutic gain. As she developed the skill of tracking her body sensation and executing mobilizing defenses, she stated that she felt more "in" her body. She was able to feel her legs as more grounded, supporting her, and with this support she expressed grief for "all the years when I was out of my body." Mary eventually confronted the memory of the moment she first watched from the ceiling and saw what "he [her uncle] was doing to another little girl," while another part of her submitted to the abuse. She was again instructed to be mindful of her body, and as she remembered the trauma, she became aware of the physical reactions she had experienced as a child. She experienced the physical components of submitting and "leaving" her body (numbness, muscle flaccidity, the feeling of paralysis) *along with the impulse to fight back* (tension in her jaw and arms). Awareness of sensation became the unifying force in resolving this "dissociative split," as Mary realized that "This disintegration is not real—I'm two bodies in the same body, doing two different things." As Mary experienced this dissocia-

tive compartmentalization somatically and processed the physical components of it (such as the impulse to fight her uncle), she experienced a deeper
sense of grief associated with the abuse while remaining within her window
of tolerance.

After working with her somatic tendencies, and then her emotions, Mary
was better able to process her cognitive distortions about herself and eventually replace them with a sense of accomplishment in the realization of how
she had actually been able to defend herself through the trauma-induced dissociation that occurred because she was unable to defend herself physically.
As a result, she experienced several compartmentalized parts of herself: parts
that first fought, but then submitted and froze. Realizing the risk it would
have been to continue to engage mobilizing defenses that would have
angered her uncle and increased the abuse, she was able to acknowledge
how effective her immobilizing defenses had been in that particular situation. At one point in the session, Mary proudly stated: "There is nothing
wrong with me—look what I did!" Her cognitive distortion ("There's something wrong with me") had finally been replaced by a sense of confidence
and mastery. Again, this realization was also accompanied by grief, as Mary
said, "It only took me 50 years to find out there is nothing wrong with me."

In speaking about the abuse, Mary became less judgmental toward herself
and also able to express her anger that her mother had turned a blind eye
to her uncle's behavior, saying: "No 4-year-old girl should have to endure
such abuse!" Although she had not worked directly with the self-judgments,
beliefs, or emotions associated with the traumatic experience, sensorimotor
processing had had a positive effect on both her emotional and thinking
processes. Mary gave full expression to her sadness and grief and arrived at
new meanings, all in the process of becoming fully conscious of her sensorimotor reactions. Ultimately, she experienced a new integration and reorganization of the physical, emotional, and cognitive levels of her experience as these levels were addressed simultaneously. Six months after Mary's
therapy was terminated, she wrote:

> I am aware that there has been a lasting and profound change in both
> my body (the way I hold it) and my sense of integration and ability to
> stay present with fearful situations, memories and sensations that
> would previously have been so overwhelming that they would be sup-
> pressed. . . . I also feel emotionally integrated in a new way. It's as
> though the part of me that had been the victim of . . . abuse is not
> alone any more but has other stronger, more whole and resistant parts
> mixed up with it. I no longer so desperately need the contact [with the
> therapist]. It's as though I can be there for myself.

CONCLUSION

Because traumatic "memory" is composed largely of nonverbal, situationally accessible memories, techniques for resolving trauma must elicit, process, and aid in the digestion of all its components: procedural, perceptual, autonomic, motor, emotional, and cognitive. When the traumatic event remains a nonverbal situationally accessible memory, unavailable to verbal recall or processing, the client continues to reexperience its activation without resolution and often without even the conscious awareness that the sensations and emotions are traumatically driven.

In phase 2 work using sensorimotor psychotherapy, titrated amounts of the memory of the event are carefully evoked to activate its somatic and autonomic components at a pace that does not unduly dysregulate the client. By slowly and mindfully observing the bodily expression of the nonverbal memory, clients are helped to have a new experience in relationship to the trauma: Rather than becoming needlessly dysregulated, clients feel the mastery inherent in their ability to use somatic resources to maintain a window of tolerance. Instead of reliving habitual frozen or collapsed, submissive tendencies, clients experience the emergence and completion of actions "that wanted to happen" at the time of the trauma—which leaves them feeling alive and triumphant instead of numb and defeated.

Rather than becoming overwhelmed by the emotions or cognitive distortions connected to the trauma, clients discover that that these can be contained and reworked from the bottom-up, that it is possible to feel grief and stay present or to laugh with pleasure as new empowering actions are experienced, where before there were feelings of helplessness and worthlessness. As clients slowly integrate these new experiences of old events, they are able to formulate a narrative that makes sense of the past.

The final result of phase 2 work is what Janet called a process of "realization": "the formulation of a belief about what happened (the trauma), when it happened (in the past), and to whom it happened (to self). The trauma becomes personalized, relegated to the past, and takes on symbolic, rather than sensorimotor properties" (as cited in Van der Hart et al., 1993, p. 171). Janet (1919, 1925) emphasized that realization requires a change in both physical actions—movement, arousal, and sensation—and mental action—the way the person thinks and talks about the trauma. It is important to note that realization is a process, evolving over time as more information from the traumatic events is discovered, processed, and integrated (Van der Hart et al., 1993).

Clients often complain that their responses to the traumatic events "just don't make sense. I know that I'm okay now, but I react in my body as if the trauma were still happening." This description captures the experience of nonverbal memory fragments, retriggered by traumatic reminders, that have not been assimilated in the process of working with narrative memory, cognition, or emotion. Successful integration of these fragments is optimized when therapist and client work somatically with the nonverbal memory. A new realization emerges—a sense of "Yes, this did happen, and it greatly affected me for many years. But now I have experienced it in my body without being overwhelmed by it and, in fact, I feel empowered in relation to it. It is in the past now, and I can finally move on."

Chapter 12

※·※·※

Phase 3 Treatment: Integration and Success in Normal Life

THE GOAL OF THERAPY IS NOT ONLY TO FACILITATE symptom reduction and memory processing but also to empower clients to develop a life after trauma—a life no longer dominated by the shadow of traumatic events or their intrusions into ordinary or pleasurable experience. In phase 3 the therapeutic focus shifts to themes of self-development, adaptation to normal life, and relationships (Brown et al., 1998; Chu, 1998; Courtois, 1999; Herman, 1992; Steele et al., 2005b), addressing the profound developmental neglect endured by so many clients whose attempts to engage in normal life activities, particularly intimate relationships, bring up unresolved developmental deficits (Steele et al., 2005b). Although phases 1 and 2 treatment reduce symptoms and resolve traumatic memories, full engagement in life is often not achieved without completion of phase 3 work (Steele et al., 2005b). In this final phase of treatment, the abilities and skills gained in phases 1 and 2 are applied to enable flexible, adaptive responses to the arousal of action systems governing normal life: sociability, attachment, exploration, caretaking, play, energy regulation, and sexuality. With increased integrative capacity and a window of tolerance wide enough to better tolerate arousal, clients are now ready to expand their social connections, overcome their fears of daily life, evaluate and take appropriate risks, and explore change and intimacy. They also begin to develop other neglected areas of their lives, such as occupational and professional needs and goals, recreational activities, and spiritual interests (Brown et al., 1998; Courtois, 1988).

Discovering and changing cognitive distortions and corresponding physical tendencies that hinder clients in meeting these goals becomes a major focus of phase 3. In this last phase of treatment, clients are more able to sustain participation in activities they find meaningful and pleasurable, increasing their tolerance for positive affect. Eventually, their increased capabilities for integration and meaning making imbue past and current experience with new import and significance (Herman, 1992).

Although the phases of treatment are presented in a linear fashion, therapy is not a linear process. Frequently new memories or previously unknown fragments of memories arise in phase 3, perhaps partially due to the client's increased integrative capacity that enables tolerance for previously dissociated memories (Steele et al., 2005b). For example, working with relationship problems inevitably evokes formative memories of interactions with attachment figures who shaped the cognitive distortions and behaviors that prevent satisfying current relationships. Additionally, life changes such as birth, death, marriage, loss of employment, retirement, or illness, as well as the imminent termination of therapy, frequently stimulate unresolved traumatic memories and feelings of grief and loss (Herman, 1992). These memories, as well as healthy risk taking, may temporarily destabilize the client, requiring the use of phase 1 resources or a return to phase 2 work with traumatic memories. Thus the therapist incorporates interventions for each of the three phases of treatment as the need arises. This flexibility permits the client to retain emotional, somatic, and cognitive stability (phase 1), process and integrate memories as they emerge (phase 2), and apply the skills learned in these two phases to new challenges and satisfaction in daily life (phase 3). Helping clients develop an ever more integrated self entails a balance between providing support, facilitating resourcing, guiding trauma processing, challenging maladaptive action tendencies, and practicing alternatives in "real" life, always proceeding at a pace that allows them to stay resourced and maintain or expand their window of tolerance.

MAKING MEANING: CHANGING COGNITIVE DISTORTIONS

Trauma "shatters" basic core beliefs about self, others, and the world, and the resulting posttraumatic cognitive distortions may persist long after symptoms have subsided and memories have been processed (Janoff-Bulman, Timko, & Carli, 1985). Kurtz noted that "the goal of therapy is not any particular experience; it is a change which organizes all experiences differently, a change in the way of experiencing. To make that kind of change, we must deal with meanings" (1990, p. 139). The importance of even small shifts in meaning, made in the first phases of treatment and developed further in phase 3, cannot be underestimated. Individuals who are able to construct more realistic or positive meanings in the wake of trauma are more successful in overcoming the impact of traumatic experience than those whose interpretations remain distorted or negative (Janoff-Bulman, 1992). Although, as noted, some shifts in belief occur in the first two phases, effecting successful and enduring change in beliefs early in treatment is unlikely (Brown et al., 1998). The tendency to revert to the old beliefs under stress typically continues.

These remaining trauma-related beliefs, as well as cognitive distortions not directly related to trauma, are both addressed in phase 3 (Brown et al., 1998). Sue, who suffered ongoing sexual abuse in childhood from a non-family member, had developed two trauma-related beliefs: "I'm damaged goods" and "All men are dangerous." These beliefs prevented her from engaging in sexual relations. Her body mirrored these beliefs in rounded shoulders that Sue said "hid" her breasts so that men would not notice her, a tendency to keep her head down, which echoed her sense of being damaged, and chronic hyperarousal. Sue also had formed the non-trauma-related belief, "I have to be a high achiever to be loved," which grew out of being raised by extremely accomplished parents who insisted upon excellence in all endeavors. Sue's body was mobilized for action by an overall tension, her breath was high and shallow, and her movements were quick and incessant. Even when she was sitting, some part of her body was in motion: Her leg jiggled, and she squirmed in her chair. These physical tendencies supported her need to stay active and achieve at all costs, which combined with her trauma-related beliefs, drove her to workaholism and an inability to relax. In therapy Sue learned about the interplay between her trauma and non-trauma-related cognitive distortions. She discovered that the trauma-related hyperarousal she so often experienced propelled her into constant activity, and that her unrelenting professional obligations distracted her from her sorrow at feeling too damaged to be attractive to a man.

In phase 3, cognitive distortions are evoked by attempts to increase participation in daily life. When faced with even minor challenges, mental and physical action tendencies will reflexively engage, leading clients down well-worn pathways that include these cognitive distortions. As Janet stated long ago, "Older [actions] are the most fixed and the easiest; the more recent ones, which are still in the process of formation [such as the ability to reflectively separate past from present], are variable and difficult" (1937b, p. 69). Becoming aware of cognitive distortions is a reflective process as well as an emotional one because these beliefs "come with conviction and all the emotional charge that created them" (Kurtz, 1990, p. 117). By the time of phase 3 treatment, clients have developed the integrative capacity to tolerate and process the strong emotions that accompany these beliefs. Major goals of phase 3 are to help clients (1) identify reflexive beliefs, (2) explore how they interface with physical tendencies, (3) endure the associated affects, (4) consider the inaccuracies of the beliefs, and (5) further develop their integrative capacity to challenge and restructure these beliefs and their somatic counterparts.

THE DYNAMIC RELATIONSHIP OF CORE AND PERIPHERY

Physical tendencies are "a statement of . . . psychobiological history and current psychobiological functioning" (Smith, 1985, p. 70). When trauma has induced a negative belief about oneself, others, or the world, the harmonious interaction between core and peripheral areas of the body is typically sacrificed. A belief such as "I'm bad" may set off physical tendencies of constriction, hunched shoulders, held breath, shortened neck muscles, and restricted movement. The corresponding emotions of shame, anxiety, or hopelessness further exacerbate the physical tendencies. These physical tendencies support cognitive distortions and trauma-based emotions, and, in turn, cognitive distortions and concomitant emotions manifest in physical tendencies that hinder the integration of core stability and peripheral movement.

In phase 1, clients learn resources for both auto- and interactive regulation, resources that loosely correspond, respectively, with the core and periphery of the body. In phase 3, the relationship and dynamic balance between the core and periphery are explored, with an emphasis on achieving integration between core and periphery and exploring how this integration supports new meaning and adaptive action.

Clients are encouraged to define their inner desires and goals and to develop the initiative to fulfill them. Such fulfillment requires "courage to move out of the constricted stance of the victim to . . . dare to define [one's] wishes" (Herman, 1992, p. 202). Becoming aware of the core—the symbolic and physical center of the body that represents the core sense of self—helps clients accomplish this task. In a "core state," which in sensorimotor psychotherapy includes connection to the core of the body, clients are "deeply in touch with essential aspects of [their] own experience" (Fosha, 2000, p. 20). From this awareness, clients learn to execute actions that are balanced and integrated between core and periphery, moving in a more self-possessed manner that is consistent with their desires and goals.

To review, the core involves the intrinsic muscles of the thorax, the pelvis, and the small muscles that join the segments of the spine and are responsible for holding the body upright. A strong and balanced core provides a stable axis around which peripheral movements, involving the large, gross muscles of the limbs and torso, are made—locomotion, actions of the arms, turning of the head and trunk. Core support allows extrinsic peripheral movement of the arms, legs, and head to be made with less effort and energy. A strong core provides an internal physical and psychological sense of stability, helping a person feel "centered," and strengthening an internal locus of control.

Actions that are adaptive in response to action systems require sufficient strength, flexible movement, and integration between core and periphery of the body. Whether they occur in the form of peripheral gross motor movement, such as walking, running, or reaching, the inner movements of the deep, core intrinsic muscles, or the fine movements of facial expression, all actions involve movement. However, "if movement is restrained, structurally limited in range, or painful, or one's muscular strength and capacity are not adequate to the task, then the actions taken will be limited or inadequate" (Kepner, 1987, p. 146). For example, when the pelvic muscles constrict and the body recoils at the mere thought of sexual intimacy, sexual difficulties are likely to ensue even if the individual expresses the desire for a sexual relationship.

Janet (1925) wrote about the inability of traumatized clients to complete actions and the necessity of facilitating the completion of actions in treatment. During phase 2, truncated mobilizing defenses incipient in traumatic memories are completed. In phase 3, clients become increasingly aware of their physical and psychological center and learn to execute actions that stem from the core of the body, completing them through peripheral movements such as walking, running, reaching, grasping, holding on, and letting go. When actions are integrated and used to both initiate and respond to contact with the environment and with other people, a stronger somatic sense of self is facilitated—a felt sense of a connected, embodied self, rather than an abstract concept or image of the self. In Kurtz's words: "As the core becomes vitalized . . . emotional dependency and the constrictions of defensive attitudes yield to a sense of self, and open flexible interchange with others. [The client] finds he no longer needs the external support or extrinsic rigidity to hold himself up. He can surrender these, and begin to feel the pleasure of . . . an integrated self" (Kurtz & Prestera, 1976, p. 35).

The intrinsic muscles of the core are sometimes considered the "being" muscles, whereas the extrinsic muscles of the periphery are thought of as the "doing" muscles. The extrinsic muscles of the periphery mediate mobility, enabling movement through space and thus interaction with the environment. Included in the periphery are the movements of the legs, feet, shoulder girdle, arms, and hands. The head and muscles of the face communicate emotions and social engagement and include both core and periphery. Facial expression reflects core experience and also facilitates interaction with others. Whereas the intrinsic skeletal muscles of the core are deeper in the body, moving more slowly and precisely, the extrinsic muscles are closer to the surface and tend generally to move more quickly but with less precision (with the exceptions of some movements, such as the precise movements of the hand required for handwriting). Phase 3 treatment endeavors to integrate core and periphery, being and doing, so that clients learn to execute ever more adaptive actions that stem from a core sense of self.

Peripheral movements that are integrated with a stable core lead to well-coordinated action and engender a sense of integrity, harmony, and satisfaction. The person can move with precision as well as with strength and speed, as needed. Conversely, "without the internal balance given by the core, the actions carried out by the limbs lack flow, grace and harmony" (Kurtz & Prestera, 1976, p. 33). When the core muscles are weak, rigid, or unstable, peripheral movements of the arms, legs, neck, and head lack coordination and poise (Laban, 1975). When the core is unstable, movements are also unstable; when the core is rigid, movements lack grace and flow; when the core is weak, movements may be initiated from the large muscle groups rather than from the center.

These physical tendencies usually feel "normal" to the individual, who may only be aware of them when they are so extreme as to cause pain, but they look unbalanced to the trained observer. This lack of balance between core and periphery reflects cognitive distortions. For example, the tension of the periphery (e.g., the pulling in of one client's shoulders toward the spine) combined with a weak core (e.g., an exaggerated spinal curve) reflected the belief "I'm worthless, I must hide." Even if the person is unaware of these maladaptive tendencies when the core and periphery of the body are not well-integrated, he or she may unconsciously experience a corresponding lack of integration psychologically.

Without a strong and stable core, the spine may flex and sag, resulting in a physical structure that is slumped and an appearance of "not being able to hold yourself up." This physical tendency may correspond to the propensity to feel "spineless," needy, helpless, incompetent, and dependent. In this case, both the core and the extensor muscles are underutilized and lack tone. An impulse to take action in the world may be felt, but the person does not possess sufficient psychological motivation, will, or peripheral strength to carry the action through to completion—as was true for the client who said that she felt "weak" and that it was too "hard" to reach out to others or apply for a job: "It makes me tired."

A person may utilize tension in the extrinsic peripheral musculature to compensate for a weak or unstable core (Kurtz & Prestera, 1976). The body is held upright by a heightened tonicity in the extrinsic muscles, rather than by a strong core. Subsequently, this increased superficial tension inhibits movement from the core outward and may contribute to beliefs such as, "I can't express myself" and "It's not okay to connect with others—I'll get hurt." Concomitant physical manifestations may include tightness in the throat, immobility in facial muscles, resulting in an inability to express emotions associated with impulses for interpersonal connection and affiliation. Yet the needs for attachment and affiliative relationships remain because they stem from psychobiological action systems that engender hard-wired "core" needs. The movements related to seeking connection, such as reaching out, may be experienced or initiated from the core of the body—the spine or pelvis, for example—but when they meet rigidity and tension from the periphery and in the extrinsic musculature, they remain incomplete. When clients with this physical tendency are approached by another, they are likely to pull back and stiffen.

Both the core and periphery can be overly tense, in which case the person may be excessively rigid, lack flexibility and mobility, and report that that he or she feels "stuck" or "unable to move." Such an individual may not have much awareness of his or her core. Executing movements that originate in the core and extend smoothly out into peripheral action may be problematic. If movements are initiated, they are met with peripheral tension. With diminished internal awareness and self-expression, this person may feel stuck, sluggish, and disconnected, and expend effort in attempt to take action, with little satisfaction or sense of progress.

The consecutive or simultaneous approach-and-avoidance/defensive movements of clients with unresolved disorganized-disoriented attachment patterns form a focus for treatment in phase 3. These movements clearly reflect a lack of integrated movement between core and periphery. The concurrent impulses of approach and avoidance result in a body that is "going in different directions," as when proximity-seeking actions are combined with simultaneous avoidance or defensive actions. One client could not reach out without simultaneously pulling back in the core of his body; another could not sustain a movement away from an unwanted encounter; she would quickly shift back to approach movements when she attempted to move away. Other clients exhibit uncoordinated, jerky movements such that the parts of the body do not move together in an integrated fashion, such as the client whose pelvis was thrust forward as he walked, while his chest was pulled back. The concomitant beliefs accompanying these discordant actions were also conflicted: "I want to be close, but it is dangerous; others will take advantage of me if I get close; I will be hurt if I honor my own boundary."

Assessment of Incomplete Actions
in Core and Periphery

Assessment of which actions remain incomplete or unexpressed is accomplished by noting the relationship between the spine, neck, head, arms, and legs. Is the core stable yet flexible and able to support peripheral movement? Or is it weak and slumped, so that peripheral movement cannot be supported? Is movement, such as reaching out, restrained by peripheral tension, or does the movement progress gracefully from core to periphery? Is the extrinsic, surface musculature flexible so that movement emanating from the core is unrestrained? Is there grace and integrity in the movement as it progresses from core to periphery, or is the movement jerky and disjointed?

In working to help the client achieve greater integration and more adaptive action tendencies, the therapist is careful not to convey the notion that there is a "right" way to move. Rather, the objective is to facilitate a client's mindfulness, so that he or she develops an ever-increasing ability to be aware of body sensation and physical action. With awareness, clients begin to identify their own maladaptive actions, choose to inhibit them, and decide to initiate and sustain actions that bring them more satisfaction. As Juhan noted: "The goal . . . should not be to impose universalized standards of posture and movement upon an individual, but rather to help the individual to cultivate the mental awareness and the physical flexibility to continually adapt to the changing needs of the moment" (1987, p. 142). Thus *control* and *choice* always remain with the client whose movement, with practice, becomes self-correcting.

ACTIONS IN PHASE 3 TREATMENT

Insistent engagement with certain action systems, such as caregiving or professional endeavors (exploration), to avoid the expected disappointment and pain that occurred in past attachment relationships is common for traumatized individuals (Sable, 2000). In phase 3, clients are encouraged to balance their responsiveness to the arousal of all action systems and are challenged to integrate and respond adaptively to complex situations that evoke several action systems simultaneously. Relationships may include the complex interactions of several action systems related to daily living: attachment, sexuality, caregiving, friendship (sociability), exploration, energy management (e.g., eating together), and play. Clients learn to distinguish between various kinds of relationships correlating with different actions systems and to differentiate among kinds of intimacy: emotional, physical, sexual, intellectual, spiritual.

Clients are especially challenged in intimate partnerships, where cognitive distortions and physical tendencies learned in the context of their early attachment relationships interfere with the ability to form a constructive intimate relationship in adulthood. A variety of attachment disturbances are explored in phase 3: repetition of traumatic attachments, attachment to the perpetrator, isolation (a denial of attachment needs), insecure attachment patterns, and unresolved disorganized-disoriented attachment. For mature intimacy to occur when intimacy was formerly accompanied by abuse or loss (which is the "pinnacle of successful treatment"), integrative capacity must be high enough to allow the person to tolerate frustration, resolve conflict, and separate the present from the past (Steele et al., 2005b).

The phobia of intimacy (Steele et al., 2005b) is articulated through the body's communication. Because the phobic response is a precognitive sensorimotor/emotional one, it is crucial to treat it on a sensorimotor level as well as on the level of cognitive processing. Relational connection includes expression and movement of the arms: reaching, grasping, letting go, holding on, embracing, and so on. Physical experiments with action of the arms, such as asking a client to reach out, are revealing in the assessment of relational disturbances. As Kepner stated, "If you want to reach out to others but restrain your arms at your side, you will have difficulty completing your need. If you wish to express your joy in movement but are structurally bound up and muscularly inflexible in your movements, you cannot fully express your internal feeling" (1987, p. 146). If a client has difficulty initiating, sustaining, or responding to relational contact, experimenting with reaching out can be a useful somatic intervention. Some clients reach out with the elbow bent, some reach from the shoulder, some keep their upper arms pinned to their torso. Clients may reach with the whole body, leaning forward, eyes intensely focused on the therapist, whereas others pull back and look away even as their arm is reaching forward. For some, the gesture is weak, lacking tone and energy; for others, the gesture is strong but stiff. Each pattern holds significant psychological information. When people cannot initiate this impulse from the core and carry through the act of connection with their arms in an integrated fashion, communication in relationship is typically limited.

Expanding Intimacy through Integrated Action

Goaded into therapy by a wife who threatened divorce if he did not work on his "intimacy issues," Sam grudgingly agreed to explore his aversion to emotional intimacy. Sam's posture and arm movements were tense; his spine was stiff, reflecting tension in both core and periphery, and he had a habitual gesture of putting his bent arms out in front of him with palms facing outward. Furthermore, he had an abrasive manner that his wife described as intimidating. Raised by a father who was physically abusive and alcoholic, Sam was left to his own devices throughout his childhood. He learned at an early age that he could depend on no one but himself. Although Sam was able to autoregulate, his ability to interactively regulate and engage fully in relationships was compromised.

During therapy sessions Sam unconsciously made movements of defense, including putting his hands up in front of his body, backing away from the therapist when standing, and bracing and pulling back while seated. These peripheral movements became stronger and more frequent when discussing his relationship with his wife, despite Sam's stated conviction that he wanted to deepen his intimacy with her. Although his conscious response to the arousal of the attachment action system in relation to his wife was to seek proximity, his movements expressed the opposite.

Within the context of an attuned relationship, the therapist gently pointed out these movements, drawing them to Sam's attention, and he agreed to explore them. When Sam made the defensive movements voluntarily and mindfully, he realized that from this posture he did not feel connected to his desire for intimacy with his wife; in fact, he did not desire a connection with anyone. As he explored further, executing various defensive movements as an experiment, he reported a childhood memory of approaching his father and became aware that, as a child, he never knew if his father would receive him or turn violent. Sam reexperienced the fear and unpredictability that he had endured during childhood, which led to the spontaneous realization that these defensive arm movements were telling others to keep away: "It's not safe to be close. People might turn on me."

During therapy, Sam was encouraged to experience his need to connect with others and to become more fully aware of the core of his body—his spine and pelvis—as he did so. Sam felt the rigidity of his spine and experimented with gentle movements and breathing that softened the core of his body. He reported feeling less defensive and more vulnerable as his spine softened, and then said he could also feel the desire for connection with others "deep in my belly." Sam's therapist suggested that he experiment with making the gesture of reaching out with his arms, sensing the desire in his belly, and initiating the movement from the core of his body. In these initial experiences, only the physical action was practiced, devoid of thoughts about reaching out to another person, thus reducing the risk of reaching. Nevertheless, Sam first said the mere thought of reaching out made him uncomfortable. When he did, his arm was stiff, the movement was mechanical, and his spine became rigid again. Sam said that the gesture felt unfamiliar and that he felt more vulnerable because he didn't expect a response to his reaching—no one had ever responded to him supportively. He became sad and said, "What's the use of reaching out? Others will only hurt me." Verbalizing these abuse- and abandonment-related beliefs with increasing anger and hurt in the context of a relationally attuned therapy served to soften Sam's aversion to intimacy and as well as to relax his spine and his extrinsic musculature.

Sam's therapist then encouraged him to explore various kinds of actions related to reaching out, maintaining the softening in his spine and always initiating the action from his core: stepping forward, softening his chest, and so on. The therapist observed the movements and helped Sam to perform the action efficiently and without undue physical tension, such as first sensing and softening his core, then relaxing his arm and leaning slightly forward instead of pulling back. Executing these movements that reflected greater integration between core and periphery brought more insight and affect about the impact of his early attachment history on his current relational capacity. Sam realized that his feelings of vulnerability increased as he executed these relational movements from a more relaxed physical core—but that it also felt "good."

Appropriate Challenges: Graduated Actions

Assessing the degree of difficulty of a particular challenge offered to the client and evaluating its impact are key to successful integration of a new skill. The specific action requested of clients should be appropriately challenging: that is, at a level that facilitates the likelihood of success and evokes the highest integrative capacity possible, while avoiding discouragement or failure (Janet, 1925). Practicing new actions of incremental complexity builds clients' integrative capacity and confidence over time. With graduated or step-by-step instruction for executing the actions integrating core and periphery, the client "will then make correct and automatic reactions which will spare him the loss that would be caused by failure" (Janet, 1925, p. 737).

Sam first practiced actions of reaching out merely as a physical exercise, attending only to integrating core and periphery, with no focus on psychological content, until that task was accomplished. He then practiced reaching out to the therapist, which brought up long forgotten childhood longing for his mother, and Sam wept with grief. Eventually, he practiced reaching out while imagining his wife standing before him. The therapist addressed Sam's fear that reaching out to his wife would make him too vulnerable and that he would get hurt; his impulse was again to pull away and disconnect from his core. After processing these erroneous beliefs, formed in the context of an abusive childhood, Sam was able to reach out while imagining his wife standing before him, but he said he felt ungrounded. The therapist suggested the use of grounding resources Sam had learned in phase 1: sensing his legs under him and the support of his upper body by his legs. Eventually Sam was able to carry through the reaching movement from core to periphery while imagining reaching out to his wife.

Sam gradually became able to execute actions of connection with relative ease and comfort, sensing his need to reach out in a particular sensation in his belly, executing the movement in a fashion that integrated the core and periphery of the body, and staying grounded. Naturally, these new motor actions were accompanied by new meanings: He began to express the conviction that perhaps it would be safe to reach out in his current life, that he knew everyone was not like his father. He reported that the intimacy and satisfaction in his relationship with his wife correspondingly improved. Sam found himself spontaneously reaching out to others instead of remaining isolated, which had been his tendency for so long. He reported a difficult visit to his childhood home to reconnect with his best childhood friend, who unbeknownst to Sam had become a rageful alcoholic like his father. After this visit, he wrote:

> The reaching out in therapy had a profound effect in terms of recognizing how I don't reach out and doing something different. When I was back home, I realized I don't have to just pull in and endure; I can find something different. I stayed connected to my core, and did a lot of reaching out to people when I was there, and I would attribute it to the practice in therapy. Talking about it doesn't touch it—I have talked about how I have difficulty acknowledging my needs and connecting with others, but it didn't change anything. On that trip I talked to my wife and to friends, and even cried a little. I would never do that before.

Janet (1925) wrote that previously incomplete or undeveloped actions, both mental and physical, when practiced and completed, are the starting points of more sophisticated, creative, and complex tendencies. Therapists often find that unexpressed grief must be experienced and completed. Sam expressed grief for his childhood and his loss of relational intimacy during all the years he had "pulled in and endured" in solitude. This, along with his completion of the action of reaching out in a somatically integrated way, incipient in his childhood longing for contact but never satisfactorily executed, diminished his isolation and freed him for increasing intimacy with his wife and with friends. Ultimately, it altered the cognitive distortion that he always had to "do it alone."

Exploring New Actions to Meet
Daily Life Challenges

In the final phase of treatment, clients are encouraged to consider which of their daily activities are meaningful to them (Brown et al., 1998; Janet, 1925) and to rediscover old dreams and desires (Herman, 1992). Phase 3 can be a time of discovery and self-fulfillment as

> the therapist helps the patient identify a range of new interests and aspirations, explore new possibilities, discover previously unrecognized talents and human potentials, and playfully experiments by engaging in a variety of new activities, until the patient can better discern which

activities, talents, potentials, interests, and activities seem most identified with core aspects of the self and which do not. (Brown et al., 1998,
p. 494)

This is not an easy process. When nondefensive action systems are enlivened
and their interaction with other systems fostered, traumatic reactivation
inevitably occurs. Negative cognitions, maladaptive somatic tendencies, and
trauma-related phobias fuel clients' conviction that they are not ready to navigate the world when, in fact, they may be capable of doing so. Clients may
misread unfamiliarity with an ordinary experience as a warning of its danger.

The everyday life challenges that clients face are used to create opportunities to explore, develop, and practice new, more adaptive actions. Mindfulness and curiosity are used to track what happens in both the core and
periphery of the client's body as he or she thinks about or remembers a challenging situation, such as making a phone call, leaving the house, going on a
date. Client and therapist together notice the building blocks of present experience: thoughts, emotions, sensations, movements, and sensory perceptions,
and assess these tendencies. Is the tendency a familiar, habitual traumatic
response associated with past trauma? Is it an orienting response to novelty,
in which excitement and arousal naturally increase? Does this tendency contribute to a new sense of self, creating a more adaptive relationship with the
world, or does it reenact a tendency from the past? Does it feel empowering? Does the response further the development of a neglected action system, such as that of play or sexuality?

Paying special attention to what happens in the core and periphery of
the client's body is essential to detect actions that are not adequately completed or satisfying and work on changing them. For example, when one
client thought about picking up the phone to schedule a job interview, a risk
he wanted to take, the therapist observed that his arm tightened by his side.
Another client considered accepting a date, and the therapist and client both
noticed that her jaw tensed. The therapist helps the client become curious
about the meaning of these maladaptive actions. For example, what is the
meaning of tightening the arm when considering reaching for the phone? Is
it: "I will open myself to danger? Failure? Loss? Shame? Criticism?" Does
the client expect to be rejected or abused when she thinks of dating?

Together, therapist and client explore these reactions by considering their
cost–benefit ratio: whether the defensive action tendency is serving the client
(as it would in a truly dangerous or undesirable situation), whether it is an
accurate perception of danger that could benefit from a more active response
(flight instead of freeze, or social engagement and dialogue instead of fight),
or whether it is an archaic response to an old situation imposed upon current reality.

For example, when Sally thought of asking her boss for a raise, her newly found sense of extension in the spine (developed in phase 1) suddenly collapsed into the familiar tendency of caving in her chest and a "weakness" in her arms and legs (her periphery). To work with this issue, the therapist placed a pillow in the corner of the room to represent the boss and observed Sally's reactions as she began to covertly orient toward "him." As Sally sensed "his" presence in the room, she had thoughts that "I don't deserve a raise" and "I'm not good enough." As she slowly oriented toward the pillow, turning her body to face her "boss," she noticed that her breathing became shallow, her shoulders began to draw up, followed by a gradual downward movement of her chin, which tucked down toward her chest. She reported: "I lose my arms and legs—they feel like they're not there." Sally remembered the feelings of submission and low self-esteem she felt as a child with her physically abusive father. She began to realize that this maladaptive pattern was outdated, no longer appropriate for her current life. With this realization, she found herself able to lengthen her spine, and her cognitive distortions of disempowerment began to shift ("I am powerful; I am okay just as I am; I did not deserve to be abused"). She reported "feeling my legs under me" and "energy in my arms." Sally described a different relationship to her boss when she was able to maintain elongation in her spine and connection to the strength in her limbs while facing his pillow representative.

The next step for Sally was to deliberately change her maladaptive tendency of collapsing in the core and losing tone in her limbs in her daily life. She began to purposely maintain extension in her spine and awareness of her arms and legs when talking with her boss. As this posture became comfortable, she was better able to separate past and present, her father and her boss. To prepare to ask her boss for the raise, Sally and her therapist used a variety of experiments to promote her ability to sustain feelings of competence and to keep her spine lengthened and connected to her center. At this stage of treatment, the change in alignment and connection with her core served phase 1 goals of modulating arousal within a window of tolerance and supported Sally's healthy risk taking by carrying her new impulse out through her extrinsic musculature. Eventually Sally asked her boss for a raise, with positive results.

As new physical actions are evoked, memories, emotions, and new insights emerge and are addressed. The therapist then supports the client to embody the needed resources (e.g., grounding, eye contact, centering) and inhibit certain actions (e.g., tightening the arm, collapsing the core) that interfere with completing the movement. The therapist encourages slow, mindful motion and helps the client become meticulously aware of the moment-by-moment changes in the body and in feelings and thoughts as he or she executes a new, risky movement. Through this process, the new movement is guided by the therapist, who

> is carefully generating a flow of sensory [and motor] information to
> the mind of the client, information that is not being generated by the
> client's own limited repertoire of movements—new information that
> the mind can use to fill in the gaps and missing links in its appraisal
> of the body's tissues and physiological processes. It is then the mind
> of the client that does the "fixing"—the appropriate adjustment of
> postures . . . the fuller and more flexible relationship between neural
> and muscular responses. (Juhan, 1987, p. xxix)

With sufficient mindfulness, resources, time, interactive support of the therapist, and iterations of the movement, the client begins to manifest more adaptive movements that emanate from the core, or center, of the body and are carried out by gross motor movements, expanding the client's capacity to fulfill his or her desires.

Mindful Arm Movements: Paths to Change

In addition to reaching out, exploring a variety of other arm movements can be vehicles for change. Grasping motions, holding on, letting go, boundary motions of pushing, hitting, circular motions that define one's personal boundary, expressive movements of opening the arms widely in gestures of embrace or expansion, movements of self-touch, such as hugging oneself—all are significant and the manner in which they are executed reflects beliefs about oneself, others, and the world.

Meg complained of always being worried about money. As she spoke about her desire to earn more money, she spontaneously made motions of reaching out and then bringing her arms toward her torso as if drawing something in toward her chest. Her therapist asked her to repeat that motion mindfully, exploring it for meaning and memories. Meg said that the movement felt connected to "taking in" and "receiving for myself." Memories emerged of being raised by a single mother: Money was tight and Meg remembered feeling ashamed when she wanted a new dress. Through exploring this gesture, the belief of "I don't deserve good things" emerged, accompanied by sadness and grief. After these emotions were expressed, the cognitive distortions of their veracity were challenged.

In a follow-up session, Meg and her therapist worked with reaching, grasping, and pulling movements. Meg chose a pillow to represent "good things" and then experimented with the movements of reaching, grasping, and pulling the pillow to her as it was held by her therapist. At first, her grasping and pulling movements were feeble. The core of her body weakened, and her arms had little strength or endurance. She gave up quickly. Again, emotions, beliefs, and memories emerged, this time involving her "right" to assertively reach for and take what she wanted. Meg worked to sustain support from her core and strength and persistence in her arm movements, especially when pulling the pillow—the "good things"—toward her. Feelings of guilt and selfishness for "going for what I want" and concomitant beliefs were again challenged. Through this process, those movements gradually became easier for Meg, and she chose the homework of practicing them daily until they felt effortless and natural.

Whereas reaching out, grasping, and pulling movements can be a challenge for many traumatized clients, holding on and being unable to let go can be equally challenging. Kay habitually did not want to end her therapy sessions. When the therapy session neared completion, she would express an intense need to tell her therapist something "really important." Her therapist discussed this tendency with her at the end of a session, and they decided to explore it further at the next session. At the end of therapy sessions, Kay and her therapist normally shook hands, and her therapist suggested that they mindfully study this gesture as if it were the end of the session, noticing what happened when it was time to "let go." Kay's reaction was to tighten her grip rather than let go. As this tendency was explored, Kay noticed that she leaned forward, reaching toward her therapist with her body and her eyes. Instead of letting go and saying goodbye, Kay was holding on. Her therapist asked her to sense these "holding on" movements and to see what her body was saying: "If your body could talk instead of hold on, what would it say?" Softly, Kay began to cry and whispered: "Don't leave me; I'm all alone . . . only you understand me."

Her underlying beliefs seemed to replay an old script in which the separation would be permanent and she would be abandoned. Reminding Kay that she had her regular appointment for the following week, the therapist encouraged her to experience and study the body sensations that were evoked. Even as Kay heard these words, she felt a physical sense that she could not bear the pain of separation; these physical sensations became even more intense just as it was time for her to let go. Memories emerged of being left alone in a hospital for surgery when she was very young. Her therapist helped Kay process these painful memories and then focused on developing a tolerance for normal separation, assisting Kay to sense the physical support of her spine, the feeling of her feet firmly on the ground, the calming effect of taking deep, regular breaths, and the difference between her experience as a dependent child and her experience as an adult. Kay's therapist asked her to notice her reactions to a verbal experiment in which the therapist repeated, "I will be here next week." At first, Kay reported images of her parents leaving her and from the "little girl place" within, said that she did not believe that her therapist would remember her next appointment. She also realized that from this "child place," she lost connection with her center, the core of her body. Eventually, Kay felt she could endure the grief and sadness triggered as she let go of her therapist's hand. Gradually, as this and other experiments were practiced week after week, Kay was able to sense her therapist as different from her parents, stay connected with her center, and eventually endure feelings that the separation evoked. She slowly became more familiar with managing separation, which led to the new meaning that perhaps separation was normal and tolerable—and often temporary.

The Ability to Mentalize:
Attuned Actions in Relationships

Early childhood experiences replete with cognitive distortions, faulty belief systems, and maladaptive defensive tendencies result in less than optimal adult interpersonal interactions (McCann & Pearlman, 1990). Moreover, clients who are insensitive to social cues are not able to respond appropriately in social situations.

The ability to "mentalize" is the ability to be aware of our own internal experience as differentiated from that of others (personification), combined with the ability to "resonate" with others in such a way that we can speculate about their motivations and intentions (Fonagy, Gergely, Jurist, & Target, 2002). If we can mentalize, we can "put ourselves in someone else's shoes" and make guesses about his or her motivations. Mentalizing helps us predict not only the possible results of our own actions with regards to others, but also the intentions and actions of others in a way that is somewhat accurate and based on present reality.

The capacity to mentalize also includes identifying, distinguishing, and predicting another person's actions at visceral and motor levels. A lack of awareness or misinterpretation of these sensorimotor cues disrupts accurate mentalizating and can lead to distortions of communication. People without the capacity to mentalize cannot successfully read the emotional intention or social cues of others. This inability reflects low integrative capacity. Mentalization is especially central in making adaptive responses to relational action systems of sociability, attachment, sexuality, and caregiving; this capacity is strengthened in phase 3 treatment. Fonagy and Target (1997) have suggested that the capacity to mentalize is not an all-or-none phenomenon and is, to some extent, context dependent, as is illustrated by the following example.

Susan came to therapy with her husband Jim because Jim complained that there was "no room for him" in the relationship and that Susan didn't "connect." Susan's movements were the opposite of Jim's: Susan leaned forward, talking animatedly, her eyes were bright, her face was very expressive, and frequent gestures punctuated her speech. She was dynamic, funny, loud, and entertaining. Although her movements appeared integrated and fluid, she seemed wrapped up in her own expression rather than engaged in a genuine connection. She appeared oblivious to social cues, such as her husband's slight shrinking back as she spoke. When the therapist pointed out her husband's response, Susan was shocked; she said she was "just being herself" and was surprised that she apparently had a negative effect on her husband. This exploration led to memories of "performing" for her father: She reported that he was often absent, and she had to work hard for his attention: "I had to be really cute and funny or my father just ignored me." Susan had formed the cognitive distortion that she must "work" at relationship; otherwise men would ignore her.

Susan's therapist encouraged her to become mindful of the sensations in her spine and pelvis and to practice centering exercises (explained in Chapter 9). As she developed the capacity to stay connected to herself and the core of her body, Susan gradually learned to sense the changes in her body when she was interacting with Jim. She learned to orient and attend to social cues, specifically tracking her husband's reaction to her, moment by moment. Gradually, as Susan became aware of Jim's reactions and sensed the effect of *his* reactions on the sensations in the core of her body (her feelings of being centered), her interactions began to be slightly less animated and more spacious. She hesitated when she saw her husband pull back and learned to ask him about his feelings and his response to what she had said. This shift in Susan gave her husband room to come forward in approach movements instead of withdrawing repeatedly. Gradually, as Susan became familiar with the sensation of feeling centered and recognized the impact of her interactions on Jim and others in her life, she was able to allow room and space for more reciprocal interactions. Correspondingly, she also addressed and changed the belief that she had to entertain to get attention.

In summary, the directional flow between core and periphery is a two-way street. Not only do actions emanate from the core outward, but the impact of environmental stimuli upon the person must progress from the periphery inward to the core in ever-changing dynamics of interaction. As clients are encouraged to pay attention to both sensorimotor directional responses, their capacity to mentalize increases. And correcting distorted interpersonal difficulties and cognitive distortions also supports an environment within which mentalizing can develop (Green, 2003).

INTIMACY AND BOUNDARIES: A DELICATE BALANCE

Good boundaries are critical for healthy intimacy, but survivors of trauma are susceptible to engaging in relationships that repeat past boundary violations (Briere, 1992; Chu, 1988, 1998; Harper & Steadman, 2003) and often come to therapy with little understanding of adaptive boundaries. Steele et al. explained (2005b):

> Patients generally have to learn the importance of personal boundaries, how and when to apply them, and how to respond effectively to others' boundaries without feeling rejected by recognizing that "good fences make good neighbors." Effective boundaries reduce fear of intimacy, giving some sense of personal control, and equalize the balance of power in relationships.

In phase 1 clients acquire somatic boundary resources to assure safety and regulate arousal, and in phase 2 they reestablish the ability to mobilize self-protective defenses. In phase 3 the focus shifts to developing boundaries that are flexible, resilient, and ever-changing, depending upon the client's internal state and relational interactions. With safety assured and arousal within the window of tolerance, the subtler effects of inadequate boundaries, related more to rights and preferences than safety, can be addressed.

In the wake of trauma, some people become "underboundaried"—that is, unable to set adaptive boundaries, and thus are vulnerable to submissive behaviors such as acquiescing, complying, always being "nice," and rarely making appropriate demands in relationship. Others, such as Sam, above, become "overboundaried"—that is, they have difficulty allowing people to come close and are likely to avoid contact with others or remain physically and/or psychologically distant when in relationships. Both boundary styles are defensive in nature and therefore compete with adaptive responses to relational action systems.

The somatic sense of boundary is based on the felt sense of one's preferences, wishes, and rights, as well as on the felt sense of safety. This somatic sense is differentiated from a cognitive understanding of boundaries. For example, Sue said that she wanted to take a vacation from work—something she had not done for years. However, as she stated her verbal preference was incongruent with her physical expression. The therapist observed muscular tightening, slightly held breath, and pulling back of her body. As Sue learned to listen to and translate the language of her body (her body was saying, "I can't tell my boss I want a vacation; I don't deserve a vacation"), her beliefs about her right to set her own boundaries were brought to awareness and challenged. In this way, trauma-related sensorimotor schemata can be changed, so that clients then begin to experience, often for the first time, a felt sense of personal boundary, rights, and ability to discern appropriate preferences. This felt sense is palpable, and its barometer is the body.

When clients' sense of self is relatively undifferentiated, their internal locus of control, connection with the core, and capacity for intimacy are all diminished. Working with boundary exercises helps to restore a sense of self that is differentiated and capable of intimacy. Tanya suffered early childhood abuse and neglect. In phases 1 and 2 Tanya worked with mobilizing defensive actions of pushing and flight and establishing a somatic sense of her ability to defend herself and escape danger. In phase 3, however, as she sat in the therapist's office, her body was tense and still, her movements restricted. She showed decreased emotion, expression, relational connection, and shallow breathing. As she explored her responses to significant others in her life, she eventually said, "I feel like a Geiger counter or a radar. My whole body is constantly gauging what is happening with everyone and everything else. I'm always trying to please them." When asked about her internal sense of herself and her connection with her core, she made statements about how others in her world respond to her. Here Tanya demonstrates a boundary style based on the perceived needs of others.

In phase 3 treatment the therapist first worked to develop her awareness of internal somatic barometers to the environment by helping Tanya observe her core and peripheral movements. For instance, the therapist asked Tanya to notice what happened as she moved closer to, or further away from, him—particularly if she noticed any change in her muscular tension, quality of movement, or breath (Heckler, 1984; Rosenberg et al., 1989). To her surprise, Tanya found that her body relaxed more when she was a little further away from her therapist. Before she began the exercise, Tanya had thought that she was "fine" with a closer proximity, but this thought was based on cognitive and emotional appraisals, not felt somatic responses. Tanya continued the experiment until she experienced what she called the *klunk*, the distance from her therapist at which her body felt most comfortable. The *klunk* was palpable: her muscular tension began to release, her breathing deepened, and her activation began to settle. Over phase 3 treatment, this *klunk* became the indicator that, as Tanya said, "tells me what is right for *me*." In this way, the therapist helps clients find a word or phrase, to develop a lexicon of their own with which they can describe their sensorimotor/somatic experience of a boundary. For Tanya, the word *klunk* expressed her experience of an adequate boundary. The client's word or phrase can be used intermittently throughout treatment to help bring the somatic sense of boundary to conscious awareness. As Tanya reported real-life problems, she and her therapist noted what solutions elicited the *klunk* that indicated an appropriate choice for Tanya.

Next the therapist asked Tanya to construct a symbolic boundary around her body, using a piece of string as an outline and adding pillows to form a little buffer between her body and the world. At first Tanya made a cognitive judgment that this experiment was "silly and childish," but she soon found that her body responded to the construction of a tangible boundary and that she felt more "centered." The relationship between core and periphery kept changing as this exercise continued; her breath deepened, eye contact increased, the *klunk* felt stronger, movement became more integrated, and Tanya began to experience a sense of self-referential awareness. She began to feel her body respond to environmental stimuli, and as time progressed, she was able to identify her own needs and wants. She no longer felt that she needed to monitor every move that another person made or adapt her actions to suit him or her. She began instead to experience her own internal world; her core, her breath, the *klunk* that informed her about her preferences in relationship.

Tanya challenged this process by asking what good it is to construct a boundary in the therapy session because she cannot go through life with pillows around her, nor can she ask everyone to take a step back from her body. The therapist explained that the exercise functions to assist her in discovering an internal locus of control, a new way of feeling "boundaried." The *klunk* signaled Tanya's somatic sense of boundary. By experiencing a physical sense of boundary and preference in the therapist's office, Tanya began to acquire a somatic barometer attuned to her inner experience of nondefensive self-awareness, security, well-being, groundedness, and openness in her body, which slowly began to carry through to relationships. Gradually, Tanya began to move from the phobia of intimacy toward the experience of knowing what it would be like to tolerate and even enjoy intimacy, and not have to worry all the time about pleasing others. It had not been possible previously to entertain the idea of intimacy without a stronger sense of her own preferences and desires. Tanya subsequently began to work in therapy with peripheral movements of reaching out, walking nearer to the therapist, able to tolerate less distance.

Conflicting movements and sensations frequently accompany boundary-setting, resulting in physical actions that are not synchronous or mobilized in a unified direction. When clients attempt to execute a previously conflicted, ineffective, impeded, or disabled action, they may use the body inefficiently, often at odds with their conscious intent. The core and periphery are not working together. A client who is conflicted about her right to turn away from an unpleasant stimulus will execute that action in an unintegrated fashion; a person whose survival strategy was characterized by collapse and submission will encounter difficulty lifting her chest or breathing deeply and stating preferences without tightening elsewhere in her body.

The body holds past traumatic experiences, whether or not the details of these traumas are remembered, and these past traumas contribute to disorganized actions and inadequate boundaries. Karen, a victim of chronic childhood sexual and physical abuse by her father, struggled with establishing appropriate boundaries that reflected her preferences. The first goal in phase 3 treatment was for Karen to develop a healthy dating pattern in the wake of pervasive childhood violation. She had experienced increasing satisfaction from her success as a college sophomore, had a strong social support system, but reported that sometimes she acquiesced to the sexual overtures of men she dated and later had the feeling that her dates were "taking advantage" of her sexually. Karen and her therapist decided that boundary work was needed. Karen first explored setting a boundary by pushing against a pillow held by the therapist, in a symbolic gesture of saying "no" to an interpersonal overture she did not want. Both noticed that her body pulled backward while her arms pushed forward and her spine curved backward and down. Her head was bent forward, her gaze averted. She appeared to be moving backward while simultaneously trying to push. This conflicted physical action was the physical counterpart of the "mixed message" she gave to others, particularly to the men she dated.

As she studied the conflict in her movements, Karen expressed a loss of connection with her core and reported the thought that pushing away meant that she would be alone—the very same conflict inherent in her childhood relationship with her father. If she had tried to push him away or move away from him, the price would have been loss of connection. It should be noted that many clients prefer inappropriately close proximity when they have learned in childhood that saying "no" or verbalizing their preferences results in a loss of a needed attachment relationship.

Teaching Adaptive Boundary Actions:
The Role of the Therapist

In sensorimotor psychotherapy it is the therapist's objective to teach the client how to study habitual patterns and then to organize and carry out unfamiliar actions, thus helping him or her move from reflexive to reflective movement. Even a century ago, Janet noted how necessary the therapist is to this process: "The [client] . . . is not familiar with the mechanism of the action which he is trying to learn. He would not know how to decompose it into its elements; he would not be able to repeat the useful elements of the movement one by one or to eliminate the futile elements, and he would not be able to perform the action" (1925, p. 758). Because the way in which Karen moved was habitual and felt "right" to her, she could not sense that there was a way to move that integrated both the core and periphery of her body: The therapist had to help her become aware of how the familiarity of her habitual way of moving made it "invisible" to her (Gelb, 1981).

The therapeutic objectives, coformulated by the therapist and Karen, included teaching Karen to execute an integrated and coordinated movement of pushing away with her arms, with this extrinsic movement emanating from her core. First, the therapist modeled the action so that Karen could visually see it. The therapist also demonstrated Karen's own unintegrated action to help her see her habitual movement in contrast to an integrated movement. When Karen observed the therapist's demonstration of her disorganized action, she was astonished, saying, "I didn't know if you were trying to tell me to stop or not!" Karen then experimented with exercises to increase her awareness of her spine and pelvis, mindfully pushing against a pillow held by the therapist, initiating the movement from the base of her spine. The therapist encouraged Karen to lengthen her spine so that her core was aligned, and to lift her head to make eye contact. These movements were executed while pushing not only with her arms but also with her back and legs, thus involving her entire body—the core and periphery—in one coordinated, intentional, and directional movement.

After performing this movement several times, with progressively more integration and efficiency, Karen noted the unfamiliarity of this economical, well-organized, and integrated action, reporting that the movement was "entirely new—it makes me wonder what's been going on all this time." She realized that although she had said "no" on those dates, her body had said both "yes" and "no"—an artifact of her conflict between her own needs and desires, reminiscent of her earlier fear of loss of contact with her father if she refused his advances. Through this exploration, Karen gradually began to experience integration of boundaries with relationships, as well as integration between her core and peripheral movement. After practicing this more integrated movement of pushing away while working simultaneously with the trauma-related belief "I will always be alone," Karen reported being able to maintain clearer sexual boundaries with men, as well as risk verbalizing her preferences in other relationships.

REFLEXIVE ACTION TENDENCIES AND SOCIABILITY

As a result of the work in phases 1 and 2, phase 3 relationships are less intense, more harmonious. Crises and disruptions in the therapeutic relationship are rare, signaling a readiness to challenge other less dramatic but more pervasive patterns of relating (Herman, 1992). Characteristic ways of coping in social situations, such as submitting, acquiescing, becoming aggressive, or withdrawing, are explored and changed (Brown et al., 1998; Herman, 1992; Van der Hart, Nijenhuis, & Steele, 2006). Clients develop the skills that allow them to remain relatively autonomous, connected to their core, while in relationship with others.

In phase 3 the client's integrative capacity must be raised to expand the range and improve the quality of actions to include increasingly more complex, diverse, sophisticated, and integrated actions. Many clients have reflexively avoided responding to certain action systems, and thereby avoided certain actions, or if they have tried to execute those actions, they have been less integrated and less successful.

Therapists can encourage clients to address the mental actions that impede and accompany the physical actions. Mental actions of perception, planning, initiation, execution, and completion are required for every physical action. When their integrative capacity is low, traumatized individuals are likely to engage in mental actions of low quality, such as avoidance, compliance, and cognitive distortions (Van der Hart et al., 2006). Therapy helps clients raise their integrative capacity to the level at which they can discover, initiate, execute, and complete these mental and physical actions that require reflection, inhibition of defensive tendencies, self-awareness, affect regulation, thinking "on your feet," and separating the past from the present.

After completing phases 1 and 2, Marika, age 46, was ready to work on her tendencies to avoid relationships. She had never experienced a sexual relationship, had few friends, and felt that she wanted to find out more about these patterns, after having discovered that she had a terminal illness. Her body reflected chronic peripheral tension in a hunch of her shoulders and constriction in her breathing. Her spine was stiff with very little flexibility. These patterns suggested an "overbounded" boundary style, and when talking about her childhood, Marika's tense body tightened even more.

Marika expressed a desire to expand her capacity for social relationships. To reveal Marika's tendencies as she sought proximity, her therapist suggested an experiment in which she asked Marika to walk slowly toward her from across the office. This experiment caused Marika to tighten from her spine out to her extrinsic musculature, and her movements were uncoordinated and jerky. She reported feeling uncomfortable, feeling the "familiar" tightening of her body when in social relationships. Her physical tendency was accompanied by the thought that she needed "space" along with irritability toward others. Underpinning these actions was a belief that proximity leads to being forced to submit to more contact than she wanted. These physical and mental actions conspired to produce a tendency that persisted even in the absence of abuse.

Although Marika maintained a high level of functioning in her profession as a lawyer, she had difficulty suspending reflexive distancing tendencies in nonprofessional relationships and could not reflect thoughtfully on the appropriateness of her reflexive behavior. The complex mental actions of mindfulness, the ability to observe the internal organization of experience (thought, emotion, body sensation, and movement), and the reflective ability to give careful thought and consideration to observations, actions, present demands, and goals are difficult for traumatized clients, particularly when their reflexive tendencies are active. Mindfulness and reflection are sophisticated actions that require much more integrative capacity—observation, reflection, delayed gratification, planning, reasoning, and critical thinking—than longstanding reflexive action tendencies possess (Janet, 1925; Van der Hart et al., 2006).

In phase 3 clients are encouraged to become increasingly aware of the sequence of mental and physical actions that comprises maladaptive tendencies. Over the course of therapy, Marika learned that her first action when exposed to social contact, prior to actually physically withdrawing, was holding her breath, followed by a sensation of tightening in her spine and viscera. She then noticed that the thought "Now they want something from me, and I will have to give it to them" came up repeatedly. She felt "stuck" in an emotional numbing and a physical preparedness to move away from proximity with others. Through reflection on these experiences, Marika became aware that they recapitulated being forced to submit to abuse during her childhood, a realization that was accompanied by the pain and despair that she had felt as a child.

Through mindfulness of mental and physical actions, insight into the origin of these reflexes is achieved, typically accompanied by increased affect and adaptive emotional expression. In Marika's case, her mindful awareness of her somatic responses allowed her to gradually refrain from tightening the core of her body and to remain more relaxed when in social situations. Marika reminded herself to take a breath, sense her spine, and soften her extrinsic musculature. She also tried new mental actions, such as repeating to herself that she was no longer a child and that she did not have to do anything she did no want to do. In order to execute these complex actions, she had to inhibit her longstanding reflexive physical and mental tendencies.

Complex physical actions that integrate core and periphery require practice, time, and the development of integrative capacity. Marika achieved a new baseline after repeated practice and hard work in therapy, until the benefits of reflection and practicing new actions were literally incorporated. Marika's response to social situations gradually and reliably became more adaptive to her present reality. She developed a responsive quality of restful alertness, connection with her core, ergonomic efficiency in the sequencing of movement from core to periphery, and increased capacity to orient to social cues, sense her response to them, and engage in adaptive actions. This progress was attributed to her capacity to reflect upon the reflexive tendencies and practice new, more complex actions that involved relaxation of both core and periphery, as well as engage in movements that promoted social contact. A new tendency had been established that brought Marika more satisfaction in response to the arousal of her sociability system. Even while Marika battled her terminal illness, she was able to form more deeply rewarding relationships with her friends and family and engage in satisfying interactions with medical personnel.

PLEASURE AND POSITIVE AFFECT TOLERANCE

As Janet noted, a vital characteristic of successful treatment is the client's increased capacity for pleasure, "which we must do our utmost to obtain however difficult it may be" (1925, p. 988). Helping clients increase their capacity for pleasure may engender "substantial gains in resiliency" (Migdow, 2003, p. 5) and provide an antidote to trauma-related ills. (Resnik, 1997). However, achieving this goal is complicated. Individuals with trauma-related disorders demonstrate significant impairments in their capacity to experience pleasure (Migdow, 2003). Many traumatized people are chronically depressed, anhedonic, or even hedonophobic. Both posttraumatic depression and fear are associated with the lack of a capacity for pleasure, and there is some evidence that disruptions in the dopaminergic system may underlie this difficulty (Cabib & Puglisi-Allegra, 1996; Depue, Luciana, Arbisi, Collins, & Leon, 1994; Watson, 2000).

After years of reliving and/or fending off traumatic memories and being consumed by cognitive distortions and traumatic preoccupations, traumatized individuals may have little experience with, or room for, pleasure (Luxenberg, Spinazzola, Hidalgo, et al., 2001; Luxenberg, Spinazzola, & Van der Kolk, 2001; van der Kolk et al., 1996). Their capacity for positive affect is also markedly reduced. They have come to associate positive affect with vulnerability to danger, especially if relaxing, laughing, playfulness, and pride and pleasure in accomplishment rendered them at risk for humiliation or exploitation. In addition, although elevated sympathetic arousal is associated with "intense elation" (Schore, 2003a, p. 10) in infants the same arousal may evoke defensive subsystems in the traumatized person. The fine line between pleasurable excitement and traumatic arousal may be hard to differentiate for individuals whose most common experiences of physiological activation have been trauma-related (Migdow, 2003). Although many of the pleasurable activities of life are paired with excitement, excitation itself may become something to avoid. This avoidance response interferes with adaptive responses to action systems of exploration, play, and sexuality, whose arousal includes varying degrees of excitement. Moreover, the cognitive distortions formed out of traumatic experiences further limit the positive affect that clients are able to experience (Kurtz, 1990; Migdow, 2003).

During some forms of trauma, clients may have experienced a complex mixture of sensations of pain and pleasure, as in cases of sexual abuse that was coupled with sexual arousal and orgasm. They may thereafter feel guilty or bad for the pleasure they felt during the abuse, or fear that pain and shame will come with pleasure, or even habitually seek the coupling of pain and pleasure, as seen in some clients who engage in harmful, sadomasochistic encounters.

Generally, traumatized individuals have become more accustomed to actions and goals that involve avoiding pain and fear rather than seeking out positive affect associated with pleasure. Preoccupied with the possibility of danger, they have not learned to attend to activities that might bring them pleasure. Such clients report that they do not know their own preferences—what activities would bring them pleasure, satisfaction, joy, or other feelings of well-being, what they are curious about or interested in, or what sensory stimuli feel good or meaningful to them (Migdow, 2003; Resnik, 1997).

Pleasure and Action Systems

The experience of pleasure is intimately related to action systems. The amplification of pleasure in infancy (and in adulthood) creates a "positively charged curiosity that fuels the burgeoning self's exploration of novel socioemotional and physical environments" (Schore, 2003a, p. 78), facilitating risk taking and fuller engagement in the action systems of daily living. Pleasant movements and sensations "are pleasant *because* they are recognized by the organism as fit to trigger and steer the behavior systems" (Frijda, 1986, p. 368). Panksepp (1998) expanded upon this point:

> A general scientific definition of the ineffable concept we call pleasure can start with the supposition that pleasure indicates something is biologically useful. . . . Useful stimuli are those that inform the brain of their potential to restore the body toward homeostatic equilibrium when it has deviated from its biologically dictated "set-point" level. (p. 182)

Pleasure ensues when we take action to restore balance or mitigate disequilibrium (Damasio, 1999; Panksepp, 1998). The internal motivation, emanating from the core, to accomplish the goals of psychobiological action systems also fuels desire for the pleasure of that completion. Thus pleasure can be seen as the stimulation of an action system and the fulfillment of its goals (Frijda, 1986).

Stimuli that are useful to survival are appealing and pleasurable as long as the action system is aroused but not when it is dormant or sated. Once the goals of an action system have been met, we no longer seek the stimuli that would fulfill those goals: After a full meal, food is no longer appealing, and the sight or smell of it may even be unpleasant. When satiation is accomplished, the capacity of the action-system-related stimuli to bring pleasure is markedly diminished.

Damasio stated that "pain is aligned with punishment and is associated with behaviors such as withdrawal or freezing [and other defensive subsystems]. Pleasure, on the other hand, is aligned with reward and is associated with behaviors such as seeking and approaching" (1999, p. 78). Pleasure is experienced when one anticipates reward, finds solutions to unfulfilled goals of a particular action system, and fulfills those goals. The need to restore equilibrium, and the accompanying expectation of pleasure, "cause[s] organisms to open themselves up and out toward their environment, approaching it, searching it, and by so doing increasing both their opportunity of survival and their vulnerability" (Damasio, 1999, p. 78). Thus, the search for the pleasure of meeting the goals of action systems is coupled with increased risk-taking, often frightening to traumatized individuals.

All too often, the traumatized person's attempts to seek pleasure through actions of approach and expansion, even when initiated from the core, are met by a collapse and loss of energy or by a contraction, either of which hinders and dampens the experience of pleasure (Lowen, 1970). The movements reflect a lack of integration between core and periphery and may be tense, jerky, uncoordinated, or weak. In contrast, pleasure is felt in "quiet and harmonious movements" or, when accompanied by excitement, intense and lively movements (Lowen, 1970) that are executed smoothly, from the core out to the periphery.

The Pleasure of Completing Actions

For the traumatized individual in phase 3 treatment, a primary goal is to discover the physical and mental tendencies that encourage the completion of seeking and approaching actions. Janet (1925) noted that traumatized patients seek the joy that emerges when challenges are met and actions are satisfactorily completed. The "stage of triumph" thus includes not only completing truncated mobilizing defensive actions but also completing a variety of mental and behavioral actions: physical actions such as reaching, mental actions such as changing cognitive distortions, and expressing emotions. "This joy and this triumph are . . . present after every action that has been well completed" (Janet, 1925, p. 666).

In this final phase clients learn to sense the core of their body, which helps them reestablish an internal locus of control and define their true desires and impulses. From an increased connection, clients begin to initiate, implement, and complete actions in a manner that increases satisfaction and joy. For example, Marika learned to form rewarding relationships by practicing sensing the core of her body, relaxing her habitual core tension in social situations, and eventually reaching out to significant friends—all actions that brought her deep satisfaction. As Janet (1925) wrote:

> When an action is being functionally restored, and when improvement is taking place, we almost always notice at a certain moment that satisfaction reappears in one form or another, a sort of joy which gives interest to the action, and replaces the feelings of useless absurdity, and futility which had formerly troubled the patient in connection with the action. (pp. 988–989)

Helping clients experience the pleasure of completed actions by asking them to find ways of executing actions that feel "good" and "right" assists them in learning to distinguish pleasurable actions from unpleasurable ones.

Interventions for Pleasure

In phase 3 clients are challenged to expand their ability to experience and tolerate increasing levels of pleasure and excitement without triggering the fear, anxiety, or numbing that accompany defensive tendencies (Brown et al., 1998). Pleasure is experienced on a continuum, and it is intimately related to, as well as a trigger for, certain emotions such as happiness or joy (Damasio, 1999, p. 78). Migdow wrote: "The first developmental task in the evolution of the capacity for pleasure is awareness of sensation" (2003, p. 19). Clients are encouraged to risk becoming aware of pleasurable sensations, feelings of aliveness and increased energy, challenging their perceptions that body sensations, or even the actual awareness of having a body, will lead to pain rather than pleasure. They are taught new skills of discerning what they are curious about, what sensory experiences feel good to them, even what clothes, foods, and activities they enjoy or prefer (Migdow, 2003). Clients are also encouraged to learn new things and discover the internal joy and satisfaction in mastering difficult tasks (Brown et al., 1998). They might acquire new skills and competencies such as increasing their prowess at sports, playing a musical instrument, or becoming comfortable in large groups. In these endeavors they learn to tolerate frustration *and* the pleasurable experience of achievement and success.

Therapists should be aware that an increase in positive affect may be anxiety producing to the client who has little or no history in relation to the new experience. Often such clients are unable to tolerate the unfamiliar pleasurable experience and quickly return to their old tendencies, seeking refuge in the familiarity of longstanding numbing and avoidance strategies. "By moving [from pleasurable states] back to the accustomed dysphoria, the separation anxiety from that familiar experience-identity is quelled" (Krueger, 2002, p. 173). They need the support and encouragement of the therapist to resist the pull of trauma-related tendencies and persevere in tolerating positive affect.

The sensitive and judicious use of touch can be a means of reintroducing clients to, and reeducating them on, the experience of pleasure. With a torture survivor, for example, gentle touch was used to reestablish the pleasure of body sensation and counteract the torture experience. For a client who experienced childhood beatings, the therapist gently touched his back and asked him to compare that somatic sensation to the memory of the beatings. This comparison began to enable the client to attend to and feel neutral and pleasurable sensations in his back, which had previously been "screened out" in favor of the more vividly remembered experience of the beatings. A childlike quality of wonder and amazement may accompany the reconnection with pleasurable sensations of the body, a phenomenon observed in the late 1800s:

> When the restoration of [sensation] is complete, when the patient has been fully reawakened, he usually gives utterance to feeling of astonishment and joy, in such terms as . . . "It is strange how large everything is here; the furniture and the other objects in the room seem brighter, I can feel my heart beating. . . ." These feelings of well-being make the patient laugh, and give him a general aspect of gaiety and health. (Sollier, 1897, in Janet, 1925, p. 808)

Teaching patients to find pleasure in bodily sensation and actions during therapy sessions paves the way for their finding pleasure, on their own, in other activities such as eating, touch, warm baths, and other sensual pursuits. Focusing on becoming acutely aware of present-moment sensory perceptions—colors, smells, sounds, sensations on the skin from textures, air currents, and temperature—can also be helpful ways for clients to learn about, and tolerate, pleasurable sensations.

As with all challenges given to the client, enjoyment is highest when the goal is met but lowest when it is beyond his or her capabilities (Frijda, 1986) and a sense of failure ensues, the opposite of enjoyment (Janet, 1925). Phase 3 interventions must be designed to maximize chances for success so that clients learn to tolerate and enjoy incrementally greater experiences of pleasure, thereby counteracting past traumatic experiences. When goals are achieved and actions are completed, clients experience the pleasurable sense of accomplishment and are encouraged to continue to expand their capacity for pleasure. As Herman pointed out: "The best indices of resolution are the survivor's restored capacity to take pleasure in her life and to engage fully in relationship with others. She has become more interested in the present and the future than in the past, more apt to approach the world with praise and awe than with fear" (1992, p. 212). The pleasure and satisfaction gleaned from these interactions with others and the world are augmented by integration between the core and periphery of the body, resulting in movements that are graceful and aligned and that, in turn, increase the somatic sense of pleasure.

The therapist can track when a present experience is pleasurable by noting a slight smile, a deep breath, an integrated movement, increased energy, and so on. These moments can be acknowledged and expanded through awareness of the body and associated memories, thoughts, affective tone, and words. It is also important to help clients find movements and postures that they experience as pleasurable or, at least, as *not* uncomfortable. One client, for instance, felt an absence of disturbing sensations when she curled up on the therapist's couch, wrapped in a blanket. She was encouraged to identify these sensations and savor the absence of discomfort.

For some clients, even the mere presence of the therapist in the room, attentive to their pain, is pleasurable. One client tearfully said to her therapist, "I'm here because you're here—I couldn't hold this on my own." Her therapist gently helped this client sense the pleasurable feelings in her body in this tender and powerful moment—feelings that the client described as "solid" and "substantial" through her tears of old pain mixed with the new pleasurable feeling of no longer being alone.

Joan grew up under very stressful conditions as the oldest of eight children with abusive, poor, and drug-addicted parents. Joan adapted to this dysfunctional environment by learning to "hunker down," a mental tendency that was mirrored in tension across her shoulders, a compression in her spine, a lack of movement and freedom in her upper body, and a plodding quality to her gait. Joan felt she could endure nearly any hardship, but this ability "to bear up under difficult conditions" left her with "little sense of joy and lightness" (Kurtz, 1990, p. 40). When Joan first became aware of her body, she discovered that her core felt compressed and her extrinsic muscles were tight. She felt weighted downward, with little spontaneous movement or "aliveness" in her body. Exploring different styles or habits of walking (tentative steps, heavy, plodding steps, quick, rigid movements, or slow, "sloppy" movements) assisted her in studying how she literally "moved" in the world. In becoming aware of her heavy, plodding, slow gait, Joan discovered the words that correlated with her movements: "I have to work hard; I can never have any fun." A primary focus of Joan's final phase of therapy then became to change these limiting beliefs and to increase her capacity for positive affect and pleasure. Alignment of posture and integrated movement were practiced to correspond with and support changes in her cognitive schemas. Joan practiced bringing more movement into her upper body and being "lighter" on her feet to mitigate the belief "I can never have any fun." Practicing reaching out with a relaxed arm supported her desire to take action to connect with others. As healthy beliefs about attachment, intimacy, and the other action systems were developed, she was encouraged to discover new physical actions compatible with these new orientations, and to savor the pleasurable sensations when she achieved the goals of these action systems.

Conclusion: Integration of a New Sense of Self

By the conclusion of phase 3, the skills learned in previous stages have become automatic, and previously underutilized action systems now can emerge without intrusions from defensive subsystems. A new capacity for positive states allows integration of a new somatic and linguistic sense of self. The systems of defense that served the client in the past become integrated with the other action systems that foster a normal life environment. The ability to self-regulate and self-soothe makes possible the risk of attempting social reconnection and engaging in all the action systems of daily life, including the cultivation of an expanded sense of pleasure. As successful mastery of skills learned in phase 3 transmutes clients' earlier experience of themselves, they discover a new sense of self that is more flexible, adaptive, and capable of pleasure and positive affect (Siegel, 2006).

Epilogue: From Tragedy to Triumph

Although words are indispensable in the treatment of trauma, they cannot substitute for the meticulous observation of how clients attempt to defend themselves in the present or how such defenses were thwarted during the original traumatic event. Nor can words replace the empowering therapeutic facilitation of the physical defensive actions that were impossible to implement during the actual traumatic event, or the satisfying actions that serve the goals of action systems related to daily life. As we have described over the course of this book, bodily experience becomes a primary avenue for intervention in sensorimotor psychotherapy, and emotional expression and meaning making arise out of the subsequent somatic reorganization of habitual trauma-related responses. Sensorimotor approaches synthesize top-down and bottom-up interventions, attending to the body directly, so that it becomes possible to address the more primitive, automatic, and involuntary tendencies that underlie traumatic and posttraumatic responses.

Since the time of Freud, most psychotherapeutic approaches have focused on cognitive and emotional processing over sensorimotor processing, and many of those approaches have been successfully utilized to relieve trauma symptoms. However, because somatoform symptoms are particularly significant in traumatized individuals, treatment efficacy may be increased by the addition of interventions that facilitate sensorimotor processing. Regardless of the nature of the trauma's origin, we find that confronting somatic issues by directly addressing sensorimotor processing can be useful in restoring normal healthy functioning for victims of trauma. A hierarchical information-processing model emphasizes that integration must always entail all three levels of experience. No experience that we encounter, including traumatic events, affects only a single level of information processing. Thus sensorimotor processing alone is insufficient; the integration of all three levels of processing—sensorimotor, emotional, and cognitive—is essential for trauma recovery.

Physical interventions can provide clients with the somatic resources and skills to deal with disturbing bodily reactions. As they begin to learn how to limit the amount of information they must process at any given moment by focusing attention solely on their sensations and tracking physical responses and arousal, clients frequently report increasing feelings of calm. Similarly, as they experience the potential to physically protect and defend themselves through executing empowering actions, feelings of safety in the world begin to develop. The events they endured have not changed, but the negative effects on mind and body have been transformed. Rather than feeling helpless, alone, and vulnerable in a threatening world, they begin to feel a sense of solidness and solidarity—an ability to protect themselves and a sense that others are there for help and support—thereby achieving mastery over arousal coupled with the feeling that they are not alone.

Moreover, the satisfaction and pleasure experienced when a client is finally able to execute direct physical actions related to defense or other action systems alter the somatic sense of self in a way that talking alone does not. Knowing, feeling, and doing—and thus experiencing—these physical actions help to transform the way in which clients consciously and unconsciously hold and organize past traumas in their bodies and minds, the way they respond (cognitively, emotionally, and physically) in their current lives, and the way they envision the future. Synthesizing these bottom-up interventions with top-down approaches combines the best of both worlds and enables chronically traumatized clients to find resolution by finally being able to integrate past and present, emotion and meaning, belief and body. As one traumatized client wrote months after termination:

Working with my body has helped me work with the beliefs that were doing so much damage—that I don't deserve to have a good life, I don't deserve anything from others, that I deserve to be hurt, that it's better to just disappear and be hurt now than to wait for it to happen. But now I can bring the strong resourced adult that I am to these feelings and not have to blindly act them out. . . . I can now feel and experience my past from a strong place that knows I survived and am so much bigger and more compassionate as a result. This is a big shift from feeling that I have no substance and must be some sort of awful abhorrent low-life to have deserved these experiences.

Out of the transformations in her physical experience, this client emerged finally with compassion for herself and a felt sense of worth. Our hope for all our clients is that they too can take up their lives as people who survived terrible experiences but were ultimately strengthened, not destroyed, by them. These hard-won achievements are the definitive mark of the successful completion of treatment. In the words of Victor Frankl, "Even the helpless victim of a hopeless situation, facing a fate he cannot change, may rise above himself, may grow beyond himself, and by so doing, change himself. He may turn a personal tragedy into a triumph" (1959/1984, p. 170).

References

Ainsworth, M. (1963). The development of infant–mother interaction among the Ganda. In B. Foss (Ed.), *Determinants of infant behavior* (pp. 67–104). New York: Wiley.

Ainsworth, M., Belhar, M., Waters, E., & Wall, S. (1978). *Patterns of attachment: A psychological study of the strange situation.* Hillsdale, NJ: Erlbaum.

Ainsworth, M., Bell, S., & Stayton, D. (1971). Individual differences in strange-situation behavior of one-year-olds. In H. Schaffer (Ed.), *The origins of human social relations* (pp. 17–25). New York: Academic Press.

Ainsworth, M., & Wittig, B. (1969). Attachment and the exploratory behaviour of one-year-olds in a strange situation. In B. Foss (Ed.), *Determinants of infant behaviour* (pp. 113–136). London: Methuen.

Allen, J. (2001). *Traumatic relationships and serious mental disorders.* England: John Wiley & Sons.

American Psychiatric Association. (2000). *Diagnostic and statistical manual of mental disorders* (4th ed.). Washington, DC: Author.

Aposhyan, S. (1999). *Natural intelligence: Body–mind integration and human development.* Baltimore, MD: Williams & Wilkins.

Aposhyan, S. (2004). *Body–mind psychotherapy: Principles, techniques, and practical applications.* New York: Norton.

Appelfeld, A. (1994). *Beyond despair.* New York: Fromm.

Arnold, M. (1968). *The nature of emotion.* Baltimore, MD: Penguin Books.

Austin, J. (1998). *Zen and the brain.* Cambridge, MA: MIT Press.

Ayres, A. (1989). *Sensory integration and the child.* Los Angeles: Western Psychological Services.

Babkin, B. (1949). *Pavlov: A biography.* Chicago, IL: University of Chicago Press.

Bakal, D. (1999). *Minding the body: Clinical uses of somatic awareness.* New York: Guilford Press.

Barach, P. (1991). Multiple personality disorder as an attachment disorder. *Dissociation, 4,* 117–123.

Bargh, A., & Chartrand, T. (1999). The unbearable automaticity of being. *American Psychologist, 54,* 462–479.

Barkes, J., Cosmides, L., & Tooby, J. (1992). The adapted mind: Evolutionary psychology and the generation of culture. New York: Oxford University Press.

Barlow, W. (1973). *The Alexander principle.* London: Victor Gollancz.

Beckoff, M., & Allen, C. (1998). Intentional communication and social play: How and why animals negotiate and agree to play. In M. Bekoff & J. Byers (Eds.), *Animal play: Evolutionary, comparative, and ecological perspectives* (pp. 97–114). New York: Cambridge University Press.

Beckoff, M., & Byers, J. (1998). *Animal play: Evolutionary, comparative, and ecological perspectives.* New York: Cambridge University Press.

Beebe, B., & Lachmann, F. (1994). Representations and internalization in infancy: Three principles of salience. *Psychoanalytic Psychology, 11,* 165.

Belsky, J. (1999). Modern evolutionary theory and patterns of attachment. In J. Cassidy & P. Shaver (Eds.), *Handbook of attachment: Theory, research, and clinical applications* (pp. 141–146). New York: Guilford Press.

Belsky, J., Rosenberg, K., & Crnic, K. (1995). The origins of attachment security: "Classical" and contextual determinants. In S. Goldberg, R. Muir, & J. Kerr (Eds.), *Attachment theory: Social, developmental, and clinical perspectives* (pp. 153–183). Hillsdale, NJ: Analytic Press.

Bergman, N. J., Linley, L. L., & Fawcus, S. R. (2004). Randomized controlled trial of skin-to-skin contact from birth versus conventional incubator for physiological stabilization in 1200 to 2199 gram newborns. *Acta Paediatrica, 93,* 779–785.

Berlyne, D. (1960). *Conflict, arousal and curiosity.* New York: McGraw-Hill.

Bion, W. (1962). *Learning from experience.* London: Karnac Books.

Bloom, S. (1997). *Creating sanctuary: Toward an evolution of sane societies.* New York: Routledge.

Bouisset, S. (1991). [Relationship between postural support and intentional movement: Biomechanical approach]. *International Archives of Physiology, Biochemistry, and Biophysics, 99,* A77–A92.

Bowlby, J. (1973). *Attachment and loss: Vol. 2. Separation: anxiety and anger.* Middlesex, UK: Penguin.

Bowlby, J. (1980). *Loss, sadness and depression.* New York: Basic Books.

Bowlby, J. (1982). *Attachment.* (2 ed.) (vols. 1) New York: Basic Books. (Original work published 1969).

Bowlby, J. (1988). *A secure base: Parent–child attachment and healthy human development.* New York: Basic Books.

Bradley, R., Greene, J., Russ, E., Dutra, L., & Westen, D. (2005). A multidimensional meta-analysis of psychotherapy for PTSD. *American Journal of Psychiatry, 162,* 214–227.

Bradley, S. (2000). *Affect regulation and the development of psychopathology.* Guilford Press: New York.

Braun, B. (1986). Issues in the psychotherapy of multiple personality disorder. In B. Braun (Ed.), *Treatment of multiple personality disorder* (pp. 1–28). Washington, DC: American Psychiatric Association.

Brazelton, T. (1989). *The earliest relationship.* Reading, MA: Addison-Wesley.

Bremner, J. D. (2002). Neuroimaging studies in post-traumatic stress disorder. *Current Psychiatry Reports, 4,* 254–263.

Bremner, J. D., & Brett, E. (1997). Trauma-related dissociative states and long-term psychopathology in posttraumatic stress disorder. *Journal of Traumatic Stress,* *10,* 37–49.

Bremner, J. D., Narayan, M., Staib, L. H., Southwick, S. M., McGlashan, T., & Charney, D. S. (1999). Neural correlates of memories of childhood sexual abuse in women with and without posttraumatic stress disorder. *American Journal of Psychiatry, 156,* 1787–1795.

Bremner, J. D., Staib, L. H., Kaloupek, D., Southwick, S. M., Soufer, R., & Charney, D. S. (1999). Neural correlates of exposure to traumatic pictures and sound in Vietnam combat veterans with and without posttraumatic stress disorder: A positron emission tomography study. *Biological Psychiatry, 45,* 806–816.

Bremner, J. D., Vermetten, E., Afzal, N., & Vythilingam, M. (2004). Deficits in verbal declarative memory function in women with childhood sexual abuse-related posttraumatic stress disorder. *Journal of Nervous and Mental Disease, 192,* 643–649.

Brennan, K., & Shaver, P. (1995). Dimensions of adult attachment, affect regulation, and romantic relationship functioning. *Personality and Social Psychology Bulletin, 21,* 267–283.

Breuer, J., & Freud, S. (1955). *Studies in hysteria (1893–1895).* London: Hogarth Press. (Original work published 1895).

Brewin, C. R. (2001). A cognitive neuroscience account of posttraumatic stress disorder and its treatment. *Behavioral Research and Therapy, 39,* 373–393.

Brewin, C. R., Dalgleish, T., & Joseph, S. (1996). A dual representation theory of posttraumatic stress disorder. *Psychological Review, 103,* 670–686.

Briere, J. (1992). Methodological issues in the study of sexual abuse effects. *Journal of Consulting and Clinical Psychology, 60,* 196–203.

Britton, J. C., Phan, K. L., Taylor, S. F., Fig, L. M., & Liberzon, I. (2005). Corticolimbic blood flow in posttraumatic stress disorder during script-driven imagery. *Biological Psychiatry, 57,* 832–840.

Bronson, G. W. (1972). Infants' reactions to unfamiliar persons and novel objects. *Monographs of the Society for Research in Child Development, 37,* 1–46.

Brown, D., & Fromm, E. (1986). *Hypnotherapy and hypnoanalysis.* Hillsdale, NJ: Erlbaum.

Brown, D., Schefflin, A., & Hammond, D. (1998). *Memory, trauma, treatment, and the law: An essential reference on memory for clinicians, researchers, attorneys, and judges.* New York: Norton.

Brown, S. (1995). Through the lens of play. *Revision, 17,* 4–14.

Bruner, J. (1951). Personality dynamics and the process of perceiving. In R. Blake & G. Ramsey (Eds.), *Perception: An approach to personality* (pp. 121–147). New York: Ronald.

Bundy, A. C. (2002). The process of planning and implementing intervention. In A. C. Bundy, S. J. Lane, & W. E. A. Murray (Eds.), *Sensory integration: Theory and practice* (pp. 211–228). Philadelphia: F. A. Davis Company.

Bundy, A., Lane, S., & Murray, E. (2002). *Sensory integration: Theory and practice.* Philadelphia: F. A. Davis Company.

Burnstein, M. I., Ellis, B. I., Teitge, R. A., Gross, M. L., & Shier, C. K. (1986). Radiographic features of anterior cruciate ligament reconstruction. *Henry Ford Hospital Medical Journal, 34,* 270–274.

Cabeza, R., & Nyberg, L. (2000). Imaging cognition II: An empirical review of 275 PET and fMRI studies. *Journal of Cognitive Neuroscience, 12,* 1–47.

Cabeza, R., & Nyberg, L. (2003). Functional neuroimaging of memory. *Neuropsychologia, 41,* 241–244.

Cabib, S., & Puglisi-Allegra, S. (1996). Stress, depression and the mesolimbic dopamine system. *Psychopharmacology (Berlin), 128,* 331–342.

Caldwell, C. (1997a). *Getting in touch: The guide to new body-centered therapies.* Wheaton, IL: Theosophical Publishing House.

Caldwell, C. (2003). Adult group play therapy. In C. Schaefer (Ed.), *Play therapy with adults* (pp. 301–316). Hoboken, NJ: Wiley.

Caldwell, C. (1995). Life dancing itself: The role of movement and play in evolution. *Revision magazine, 17,* 43–47.

Caldwell, C. (1996). *Getting our bodies back: Recovery, healing, and transformation through body-centered psychotherapy.* Boston and London: Shambahala.

Caldwell, C. (1997b). Ethics and techniques for touch in somatic psychotherapy. In C. Caldwell (Ed.), *Getting in touch: The guide to new body-centered therapies.* Wheaton, IL: Quest Books.

Cameron, O. G. (2001). Interoception: The inside story—a model for psychosomatic processes. *Psychosomatic Medicine, xx,* 697–710. www.psychosomaticmedicine.org

Cannon, W. B. (in press). Authenticity, the spirit of play and the practice of psychotherapy. *Review of existential psychology and psychiatry.* Seattle, Washington:

Cannon, W. B. (1928). The mechanism of emotional disturbance of bodily functions. *New England Journal of Medicine, 198,* 877–884.

Cannon, W. B. (1929). *Bodily changes in pain, hunger, fear and rage* (2nd ed.). New York: Appleton.

Cannon, W. B. (1953). *Bodily changes in pain, hunger, fear and rage: An account of recent researches into the function of emotional excitement.* Boston: Charles T. Branford.

Cardeña, E., Maldonado, J., Van der Hart, O., & Spiegel, D. (2000). Hypnosis. In E. Foa, T. Keane, & M. Friedman (Eds.), *Effective treatments for PTSD* (pp. 407–440). New York: Guildford Press.

Carlson, E., Armstrong, J., Lowenstein, R., & Roth, D. (1998). Relationships between traumatic experiences and symptoms of posttraumatic stress, dissociation, and amnesic. In J. D. Bremner & C. Marmar (Eds.), *Trauma, memory, and dissociation* (pp. 205–227). Washington, DC: American Psychiatric Press.

Carlson, V., Cicchetti, D., Barnett, D., & Braunwald, K. (1998). Finding order in disorganization: Lessons from research on maltreated infants' attachments to their caregivers. In C. Cicchetti & G. Carlson (Eds.), *Child maltreatment: Theory and research on the causes and consequences of child abuse and neglect* (pp. 494–528). New York: Cambridge University Press.

Carter, R. (1998). *Mapping the mind.* Berkeley, CA: University of California Press.

Cassidy, J. (1999). The nature of the Child's Ties. In J. Cassidy & P. Shaver (Eds.), *Handbook of attachment: Theory, research, and clinical applications* (pp. 3–20). New York: Guilford Press.

Cassidy, J., & Shaver, P. (1999). *Handbook of attachment: Theory, research, and clinical applications.* New York: Guilford Press.

Charney, D. S., Deutch, A. Y., Krystal, J. H., Southwick, S. M., & Davis, M. (1993). Psychobiologic mechanisms of posttraumatic stress disorder. *Archives of General Psychiatry, 50,* 295–305.

Chefetz, R. A. (2000). Affect dysregulation as a way of life. *Journal of the American Academy of Psychoanalysis, 28,* 289–303.

Chu, J. (1988). Ten traps for therapists in the treatment of trauma survivors. *Dissociation, 1,* 25–32.

Chu, J. (1998). *Rebuilding shattered lives: The responsible treatment of complex post-traumatic and dissociative disorders.* New York: Wiley.

Chu, J. (2005). *Guidelines for treating dissociative identity disorder in adults.* Retrieved August 20, 2005, xxxx, from www.ISSD.org.indexpage/treatguides.com

Chugani, H. T., Behen, M. E., Muzik, O., Juhasz, C., Nagy, F., & Chugani, D. C. (2001). Local brain functional activity following early deprivation: A study of post-institutionalized Romanian orphans. *Neuroimage, 14,* 1290–1301.

Ciccetti, D., & Toth, S. (1995). A developmental psychopathology perspective on child abuse and neglect. *Journal of the American Academy of Child and Adolescent Psychiatry, 14,* 541–565.

Cioffi, D. (1991). Beyond attentional strategies: A cognitive–perceptual model of somatic interpretation. *Psychological Bulletin, 109,* 25–41.

Claridge, K. (1992). Reconstructing memories of abuse: A theory-based approach. *Psychotherapy, 29,* 243–252.

Cloete, S. (1972). *A Victorian son: An autobiography 1897–1922.* London: Collins.

Cloitre, M., Koenen, K. C., Cohen, L. R., & Han, H. (2002). Skills training in affective and interpersonal regulation followed by exposure: A phase-based treatment for PTSD related to childhood abuse. *Journal of Consulting and Clinical Psychology, 70,* 1067–1074.

Cohen, B. (1993). *Sensing, feeling and action.* Northampton, MA: Contact.

Cole, P. M., & Putnam, F. W. (1992). Effect of incest on self and social functioning: A developmental psychopathology perspective. *Journal of Consulting and Clinical Psychology, 60,* 174–184.

Conrad, E. (1997). *Movement.* Retrieved August 9, 2001 from www.continuum movement.com/article3.html

Cordon, I., Pipe, M., Mayfan, L., Melinder, A., & Goodman, G. (2004). Memory for traumatic experiences in early childhood. *Developmental Review, 24,* 101–132.

Courtois, C. A. (1988). *Healing the incest wound: Adult survivors in therapy.* New York: Norton.

Courtois, C. A. (1991). Theory, sequencing, and strategy in treating adult survivors. *New Directions for Mental Health Services, 51,* 47–60.

Courtois, C. A. (1992). The memory retrieval process in incest survivor therapy. *Journal of Child Sexual Abuse, 1,* 15–31.

Courtois, C. A. (1999). *Recollections of sexual abuse: Treatment principles and guidelines.* New York: Norton.

Cowan, N. (1988). Evolving conceptions of memory storage, selective attention, and their mutual constraints within the human information-processing system. *Psychological Bulletin, 104,* 163–191.

Cozolino, L. (2002). *The neuroscience of psychotherapy: Building and rebuilding the human brain.* New York: Norton.

Craig, A. D. (2003). Interoception: The sense of the physiological condition of the body. *Current Opinions in Neurobiology, 13,* 500–505.

Crittenden, P. (1995). *Attachment and psychopathology.* In S. Goldberg, R. Muir, & J. Kerr (Eds.), *Attachment theory: Social, developmental, and clinical perspectives* (pp. 367–406). Hillsdale, NJ: Analytic Press.

Czeisler, C. A., Ede, M. C., Regestein, Q. R., Kisch, E. S., Fang, V. S., & Ehrlich, E. N. (1976). Episodic 24-hour cortisol secretory patterns in patients awaiting elective cardiac surgery. *Journal of Clinical and Endocrinological Metabolism, 42,* 273–283.

Damasio, A. (1994). *Decartes' error: Emotion, reason, and the human brain.* New York: Putnam.

Damasio, A. (1999). *The feeling of what happens.* New York: Harcourt, Brace.

Damasio, A., Grabowski, T. J., Bechara, A., Damasio, H., Ponto, L. L., Parvizi, J., et al. (2000). Subcortical and cortical brain activity during the feeling of self-generated emotions. *Nature Neuroscience, 3,* 1049–1056.

Darwin, C. (1872). *The expression of the emotions in man and animals.* London: John Murray.

Davidson, R. J., Kabat-Zinn, J., Schumacher, J., Rosenkranz, M., Muller, D., Santorelli, S. F., et al. (2003). Alterations in brain and immune function produced by mindfulness meditation. *Psychosomatic Medicine, 65,* 564–570.

Davies, J., & Frawley, M. (1994). *Treating the adult survivor of childhood sexual abuse.* New York: Basic Books.

Deese, J. (1958). *The psychology of learning.* New York: McGraw-Hill.

Depue, R. A., Luciana, M., Arbisi, P., Collins, P., & Leon, A. (1994). Dopamine and the structure of personality: Relation of agonist-induced dopamine activity to positive emotionality. *Journal of Personality and Social Psychology, 67,* 485–498.

Devilly, G. J., & Foa, E. B. (2001). The investigation of exposure and cognitive therapy: Comment on Tarrier et al. (1999). *Journal of Consulting Clinical Psychology, 69,* 114–116.

Diamond, S., Balvin, R., & Diamond, F. (1963). *Inhibition and choice.* New York: Harper & Row.

Donaldson, F. (1993). *Playing by heart: The vision and practice of belonging.* Deerfield Beach, FL: Health Communications.

Eckberg, M. (2000). *Victims of cruelty: Somatic psychotherapy in the treatment of posttraumatic stress disorder.* Berkeley, CA: North Atlantic Books.

Ellenberger, H. F. (1970). *The discovery of the unconscious.* New York: Basic Books.

Emde, R. (1989). The infant's relationship experience: Developmental and affective aspects. In A. Sameroff & R. Emde (Eds.), *Relationship disturbances in early childhood: A developmental approach* (pp. 35–51). New York: Basic Books.

Eysenck, M. (1979). Depth, elaboration, and distinctiveness. In L. Cermak & F. Craik (Eds.), *Levels of processing in human memory* (pp. 89–118). Hillsdale, NJ: Erlbaum.

Fanselow, M., & Lester, L. (1988). A functional behavioristic approach to aversively motivated behavior: Predatory imminence as a determinant of the topography of defensive behavior. In R. Bolles & M. Beecher (Eds.), *Evolution and learning* (pp. 185–212). Hillsdale, NJ: Erlbaum.

Fanselow, M., & Sigmundi, R. A. (1982). The enhancement and reduction of defensive fighting by naloxone pretreatment. *Physiological Psychology, 10,* 313–316.

Figley, C. (1995). Compassion fatigue as secondary traumatic stress disorder: An overview. In C. Figley (Ed.), *Compassion fatigue: Coping with secondary traumatic stress disorder in those who treat the traumatized* (pp. 1–20). Philadelphia: Brunner/Mazel.

Fisher, A., Murray, E., & Bundy, A. (1991). *Sensory integration: Theory and practice.* Philadelphia: Davis.

Foa, E. B., Dancu, C. V., Hembree, E. A., Jaycox, L. H., Meadows, E. A., & Street, G. P. (1999). A comparison of exposure therapy, stress inoculation training, and their combination for reducing posttraumatic stress disorder in female assault victims. *Journal of Consulting and Clinical Psychology, 67,* 194–200.

Fonagy, P., Steele, M., Steele, H., Leigh, T., Kennedy, R., Mattoon, G., & Target, M. (1995). Attachment, the reflective self, and borderline states: The predictive specificity of the adult attachment interview and pathological emotional development. In S. Goldberg, R. Muir, J. Kerr (Eds.), *Attachment theory: Social developmental and clinical perspectives.* Hillsdale, NJ: The Analytic Press.

Fonagy, P. (1999a). Memory and therapeutic action. *International Journal of Psychoanalysis, 80*(Pt. 2), 215–223.

Fonagy, P. (1999b). Psychoanalytic theory from the viewpoint of attachment theory and research. In J. Cassidy & P. R. Shaver (Eds.), *Handbook of attachment: Theory, research, and clinical applications* (pp. 595–625). New York: Guilford Press.

Fonagy, P., Gergely, G., Jurist, E., & Target, M. (2002). *Affect regulation, mentalization, and the development of self.* New York: Other Press.

Fonagy, P., & Target, M. (1997). Attachment and reflective function: Their role in self-organization. *Developmental and Psychopathology, 9,* 679–700.

Fosha, D. (2000). *The transforming power of affect: A model for accelerated change.* New York: Basic Books.

Fox, N., & Card, J. (1999). Psychophysiological measures in the study of attachment. In J. Cassidy & P. Shaver (Eds.), *Handbook of attachment: Theory, research, and clinical applications* (pp. 226–245). New York: Guilford Press.

Frankl, V. (1984). *Man's search for meaning.* New York: Pocket Books. (Original work published 1959)

Fraser, S. (1987). *In my father's house: A memoir of incest and of healing.* Toronto, Canada: Doubleday.

Frijda, N. (1986). *The emotions.* Cambridge, UK: Cambridge University Press.

Gaensbaur, T., & Hiatt, S. (1984). Facial communication of emotions in early infancy. In N. Fox & R. Davidson (Eds.), *The psychobiology of affective development* (pp. 207–230). Hillsdale, NJ: Erlbaum.

Gallup, G. G., Jr. (1974). Animal hypnosis: Factual status of a fictional concept. *Psychological Bulletin, 81,* 836–853.

Gazzaniga, M. S., Holtzman, J. D., & Smylie, C. S. (1987). Speech without conscious awareness. *Neurology, 37,* 682–685.

Gelb, M. (1981). *Body learning: How to achieve better health through the world famous method of mind–body unity.* New York: Aurum Press.

Gendlin, E. (1981). *Focusing.* New York: Bantam Books.

Genze, E., Vermetten, E., & Bremner, J. D. (2005). MR-based in vivo hippocampal volumetrics: 2 findings in neuropsychiatric disorders. *Molecular Psychiatry, 10*(2): 160–184.

George, C., & Solomon, J. (1999). Attachment and caregiving: The caregiving behavioral system. In J. Cassidy & P. Shaver (Eds.), *Handbook of attachment: Theory, research, and clinical applications* (pp. 649–670). New York: Guilford Press.

Gergely, G., & Watson, J. (1999). Early social–emotional development: Contingency perception and the social biofeedback model. In P. Rochat (Ed.), *Early social cognition: Understanding others in the first months of life* (pp. 101–137). Hillsdale, NJ: Erlbaum.

Gergely, G., & Watson, J. S. (1996). The social biofeedback theory of parental affect-mirroring: The development of emotional self-awareness and self-control in infancy. *International Journal of Psychoanalysis, 77*(Pt. 6), 1181–1212.

Geuze, E., Vermetten, E., & Bremner, J. D. (2005). MRI-based in vivo hippocampal volumetrics: 1. Review of methodologies currently employed. *Molecular Psychiatry, 10,* 147–159.

Gold, S. (1998). Training professional psychologists to treat survivors of childhood sexual abuse. *Psychotherapy, 34,* 365–374.

Goleman, D. (1995). *Emotional intelligence: Why it can matter more than IQ.* New York: Bantam Books.

Goodall, J. (1995). Chimpanzees and others at play. *Revision, 17,* 14–20.

Gottlieb, R. (2005). The psychophysiology of nearsightedness. Retrieved October 5, 2005, from www.iblindness.org/articles/gottlieb-psych/ch2.html

Gould, J. (1982). *Ethology: The mechanisms and evolution of behavior.* New York: Norton.

Graham, F. (1979). Distinguishing among orienting, defense, and startle reflexes. In H. Kimmel, E. Van Olst, & J. Orlebeke (Eds.), *The orienting reflex in humans* (pp. 137–167). Hillsdaly, NJ: Erlbaum.

Green, V. (2003). Emotional development: Biological and clinical approaches— towards an integration. In V. Green (Ed.), *Emotional development, psychoanalysis, attachment theory, and neuroscience: Creating connections.* New York: Brunner-Routledge Hove.

Greenough, W., & Black, J. (1992). Induction of brain structure by experience: Substrates for cognitive development. In C. Nelson (Ed.), *Minnesota symposium on child development* (pp. 155–200). Hillsdale, NJ: Erlbaum.

Grigsby, J., & Stevens, D. (2000). *Neurodynamics of personality.* New York: Guilford Press.

Grinker, R., & Spiegel, J. (1945). *Men under stress.* Philidelphia: Blakiston.

Grossman, K., Grossmann, K., & Zimmermann, P. (1999). A wider view of attachment and exploration: Stability and change during the years of immaturity. In J. Cassidy & P. Shaver (Eds.), *Handbook of attachment: Theory, research, and clinical applications* (pp. 760–786). New York: Guilford Press.

Hannaford, C. (1995). *Smart moves: Why learning is not all in your head.* Arlington, VA: Great Ocean Publishers.

Harper, K., & Steadman, J. (2003). Therapeutic boundary issues in working with childhood sexual-abuse survivors. *American Journal of Psychotherapy, 57,* 64–79.

Hazan, C., & Shaver, P. (1990). Love and work: An attachment theoretical perspective. *Journal of Personality and Social Psychology, 59,* 270–280.

Hazan, C., & Zeifman, D. (1999). Pair bonds as attachments: Evaluating the evidence. In J. Cassidy & P. Shaver (Eds.), *Handbook of attachment: Theory, research, and clinical applications* (pp. 336–354). New York: Guilford Press.

Heckler, R. (1984). *The anatomy of change: East/West approaches to bodymind therapy.* Boulder, CO: Shambhala.

Heckler, R. (1993). *The anatomy of change: A way to move through life's transitions.* Berkeley, CA: First North Atlantic Books.

Hedges, L. (1997). Surviving the transference psychosis. In L. Hedges, R. Hilton, V. Hilton, & O. J. Caudill (Eds.), *Therapists at risk: Perils of the intimacy of the therapeutic relationship* (pp. 109–145). Northvale, NJ: Jason Aronson.

Herman, J. (1992). *Trauma and recovery.* New York: Basic Books.

Hobson, J. (1994). *The chemistry of conscious states.* New York: Back Bay Books.

Hofer, M. A. (1970). Cardiac and respiratory function during sudden prolonged immobility in wild rodents. *Psychosomatic Medicine, 32,* 633–647.

Hofer, M. A. (1984). Relationships as regulators: A Psychobiologic perspective on bereavement. *Psychosomatic Medicine, 46:* 183–197.

Horel, J. A., Keating, E. G., & Misantone, L. J. (1975). Partial Kluver–Bucy syndrome produced by destroying temporal neocortex or amygdala. *Brain Research, 94,* 347–359.

Horowitz, M. (1986). *Stress response syndromes* (2 ed.). Northvale, NJ: Jason Aronson.

Hull, A. M. (2002). Neuroimaging findings in post-traumatic stress disorder: Systematic review. *British Journal of Psychiatry, 181,* 102–110.

Hunt, A. R., & Kingstone, A. (2003). Covert and overt voluntary attention: Linked or independent? *Brain Research Cognitive Brain Research, 18,* 102–105.

Hunter, M., & Struve, J. (1998). *The ethical use of touch in psychotherapy.* Thousand Oaks, CA: Sage.

Ikemi, Y., & Ikemi, A. (1986). An Oriental point of view in psychosomatic medicine. *Psychotherapy and Psychosomatics, 45*(3), 118–126.

Internet Encyclopedia of Philosophy: Embodied Cognition. Retrieved September 3, 2005, from www.iep.utm.edu/e/embodcog.htm.

Jaffe, J., Beebe, B., Feldstein, S., Crown, C. L., & Jasnow, M. D. (2001). Rhythms of dialogue in infancy: Coordinated timing in development. *Monograms Society of Research on Child Development, 66,* 1–132.

James, W. (1962). *Talks to teachers on psychology and to students on some of life's ideals.* New York: Henry Holt. (Original work published 1889.)

Janet, P. (1889). *L'automatisme psychologique* [Psychological automatisms]. Paris: Felix Alcan.

Janet, P. (1898). *Névroses et idées fixes* [*Neuroses and fixations*]. Paris: Felix Alcan.

Janet, P. (1898). Le traitement psychologique de l'hystérie [Psychological treatment of hysteria]. In A. Robin (Ed.), *Traité de thérapeutique appliquée.* Paris: Rueff.

Janet, P. (1903). *Les obsessions et la psychasthénie* [*Obsessions and psychasthenia*] (vols. 1). Paris: Félix Alcan.

Janet, P. (1907). *The major symptoms of hysteria.* New York: Macmillan.

Janet, P. (1909). *Les névroses.* [*The neuroses*] Paris: E. Flammarion.

Janet, P. (1909). Problèmes psychologiques de l'émotion [Psychological problems of emotion]. *Revue Neurologique, 17,* 1551–1687.

Janet, P. (1919). *Psychological healing.* New York: Macmillan.

Janet, P. (1925). *Principles of psychotherapy.* London: Allen & Unwin. (Originally published in Paris, 1919).

Janet, P. (1926). *Psychologie experimentale: Les stades d l'évolution psychologique* [*The stages of psychological evolution*]. Paris: Chahine.

Janet, P. (1928). *L'evolution de la mémoire et de la notion du temps* [*The evolution of memory and the notion of time*]. Paris: Chahine.

Janet, P. (1929). *L'évolution de la personnalité (New Société Pierre Janet Pris 1984 ed.)* [*The evolution of the personality*]. Paris: Chahine.

Janet, P. (1935a). *Les débuts de l'intelligence* [*The beginnings of intelligence*]. Paris: Flammarion.

Janet, P. (1935b). Réalisation et interprétation [Realization and interpretation]. *Annales Médico-Psychologiques, 93,* 329–366.

Janet, P. (1937a). Les troubles de la personnalité [Troubles of the personality]. *Annales Medico-Psychologiques, 95,* 421–468.

Janet, P. (1937b). Psychological strength and weakness in mental diseases. In R. Merton (Ed.), *Factors determining human behavior* (pp. 64–106). Cambridge, MA: Harvard University Press.

Janet, P. (1945). La croyance délirante [Delerious belief]. *Schweizerische Zeitschrift für Psychologie, 4,* 173–187.

Janet, P. (1998). *The mental state of hystericals.* (Reprinted from *The mental state of hystericals,* by P. Janet, 1901, New York: Putnam.) Washington, DC: University Publications of America.

Janoff-Bulman, R. (1992). *Shattered assumptions: Towards a new psychology of trauma.* New York: Free Press.

Janoff-Bulman, R., Timko, C., & Carli, L. (1985). Cognitive biases in blaming the victim. *Journal of Experimental Social Psychology, 21,* 161–177.

Jensen, E. (1998). *Teaching with the brain in mind.* Alexandria VA: American Association of Counseling and Development.

Joliot, M., Ribary, U., & Llinas, R. (1994). Human oscillatory brain activity near 40 Hz coexists with cognitive temporal binding. *Proceedings of the National Academy of Science U.S.A., 91,* 11748–11751.

Johnson, S. C., Baxter, L. C., Wilder, L. S., Pipe, J. G., Heiserman, J. E., Prigatano, G. P. (2002). Neural correlates of self reflection. *Brain, 125,* 1808–1814.

Juhan, D. (1987). *Job's body: A handbook for bodywork.* Barrytown, NY: Station Hill Press.

Kabat-Zinn, J. (1994). *Wherever you go, there you are: Mindfulness meditation in everyday life.* New York: Hyperion.

Keleman, S. (1985). *Emotional anatomy.* Berkeley, CA: Center Press.

Kepner, J. (1987). *Body process: A gestalt approach to working with the body in psychotherapy.* New York: Gardner Press.

Kepner, J. (1995). *Healing tasks: Psychotherapy with adult survivors of childhood abuse.* San Francisco: Jossey-Bass.

Kimmel, H., Van Olst, E., & Orlebeke, J. (1979). *The orienting reflex in humans.* Hillsdale, NJ: Erlbaum.

Kirsch, I., & Lynn, S. J. (1999). Automaticity in clinical psychology. *The American Psychologist, 54,* 504–515.

Kluft, R. P. (1996). Treating the traumatic memories of patients with dissociative identity disorder. *American Journal of Psychiatry, 153,* 103–110.

Krueger, D. (2002). *Integrating body self and psychological self: Creating A new story in psychoanalysis and psychotherapy.* New York: Brunner-Routledge.

Krystal, H. (1978). Trauma and affects. *Psychoanalytic Study of the Child, 33,* 81–116.

Krystal, H. (1988). *Integration and self-healing: Affect, trauma, alexithymia.* Hillsdale, NJ: Analytic Press.

Krystal, J., Bremner, J. D., Southwick, S. M., & Charney, D. S. (1998). The emerging neurobiology of dissociation: Implications for treatment of posttraumatic stress disorder. In J. D. Bremner & C. Marmar (Eds.), *Trauma, memory, and dissociation* (pp. 321–363). Washington, DC: American Psychiatric Association.

Kudler, H., Blank, A., & Krupnick, J. (2000). Psychodynamic therapy. In E. Foa, T. Keane, & M. Friedman (Eds.), *Effective treatments for PTSD: Practice guidelines from the international society for traumatic stress studies* (pp. 176–198). New York: Guilford Press.

Kuiken, D., Busink, R., Dukewich, T., & Gendlin, E. (1996). Individual differences in orienting activity mediate feeling realization in dreams: II. Evidence from concurrent reports of movement inhibition. *Dreaming, 6*(4). Retrieved June 18, 2005, from www.asdreams.org/journal/articles/6-4kuiken.com

Kurtz, R. (1990). *Body-centered psychotherapy: The Hakomi method.* Mendicino, CA: LifeRhythm.

Kurtz, R. (2004). Hakomi method of mindfulness-based body psychotherapy. Retrieved September 11, 2005, from www.ronkurtz.com/writing/Readings.Aug.2004.pdf

Kurtz, R., & Prestera, H. (1976). *The body reveals: An illustrated guide to the psychology of the body.* New York: Holt, Rinehart & Winston.

Laban, R. (1975). *A life for dance: Reminiscences.* New York: Theater Arts Books.

Lakoff, G., & Johnson, N. (1999). *Philosophy in the flesh: The embodied mind and its challenge to Western thought.* New York: Perseus Book Group.

Lane, R. D., Fink, G. R., Chau, P. M., & Dolan, R. J. (1997). Neural activation during selective attention to subjective emotional responses. *Neuroreport, 8,* 3969–3972.

Lane, R. D., & McRae, K. (2004). Neural substrates of conscious emotional experience: A cognitive-neuroscientific perspective. In M. Beauregard (Ed.), *Consciousness, emotional self-regulation, and the brain* (pp. 87–122). Philadelphia: Benjamins.

Lanius, R. A., Blum, R., Lanius, U., & Pain, C. (2006). A review of neuroimaging studies of hyperarousal and dissociation in PTSD: Heterogeneity of response to symptom provocation. *Journal of Psychiatric Research.*

Lanius, R. A., Hopper, J. W., & Menon, R. S. (2003). Individual differences in a husband and wife who developed PTSD after a motor vehicle accident: A functional MRI case study. *American Journal of Psychiatry, 160,* 667–669.

Lanius, R. A., Williamson, P. C., Bluhm, R. L., Densmore, M., Boksman, K., Neufeld, R. W., et al. (2005). Functional connectivity of dissociative responses in posttraumatic stress disorder: A functional magnetic resonance imaging investigation. *Biological Psychiatry, 57,* 873–884.

Lanius, R. A., Williamson, P. C., Boksman, K., Densmore, M., Gupta, M., Neufeld, R. W., et al. (2002). Brain activation during script-driven imagery induced dissociative responses in PTSD: A functional magnetic resonance imaging investigation. *Biological Psychiatry, 52,* 305–311.

Lanius, R. A., Williamson, P. C., Densmore, M., Boksman, K., Neufeld, R. W., Gati, J. S., et al. (2004). The nature of traumatic memories: A 4-T fMRI functional connectivity analysis. *American Journal of Psychiatry, 161,* 36–44.

Lanyado, M. (2001). The symbolism of the story of Lot and his wife: The function of the "present relationship" and the non-interpretative aspects of the therapeutic relationship facilitating change. *Journal of Child Psychotherapy, 27,* 19–33.

Laplanche, J., & Pontalis, J. (1998). *The language of psychoanalysis.* London: Karnac Books.

Lazarus, R. S. (1966). Psychological stress and the coping process. New York: McGraw-Hill.

LeDoux, J. (1994). Emotion, memory and the brain. *Scientific American, 270*(6) 50–57.

LeDoux, J. (1996). *The emotional brain: The mysterious underpinnings of emotional life.* New York: Simon & Schuster.

LeDoux, J. (2002). *Synaptic self: How our brains become who we are.* New York: Penguin Group.

LeDoux, J., Romanski, L. M., & Xagoraris, A. (1991). Indelibility of subcortical emotional memories. *Journal of Cognitive Neuroscience, 1,* 238–243.

Leitenberg, H., Greenwald, E., & Cado, S. (1992). A retrospective study of long-term methods of coping with having been sexually abused during childhood. *Child Abuse and Neglect, 16,* 399–407.

Levine, P. with Frederick, A. (1997). *Waking the tiger: Healing trauma.* Berkeley, CA: North Atlantic Books.

Levine, P. (2004). Panic, biology, and reason: Giving the body its due. In I. MacNaughton (Ed.), *Body, breath, and consciousness* (pp. 267–286). Berkeley, CA: North Atlantic Books.

Levine, P. (2005). Memory, trauma and healing: Foundation for human enrichment. Retrieved July 16, 2005, from www.traumahealing.com/art_memory.html

Levine, P., & MacNaughton, I. (2004). Breath and consciousness: Reconsidering the viability of breathwork in psychological and spiritual interventions in human development. In I. MacNaughton (Ed.), *Body, breath, and consciousness: A somatics anthology* (pp. 267–293). Berkeley, CA: North Atlantic Books.

Levy, J. (1978). *Play behavior.* New York: Wiley.

Lewis, L., Kelly, K., & Allen, J. (2004). *Restoring hope and trust: An illustrated guide to mastering trauma.* Baltimore: Sidran Institute Press.

Liberzon, I., & Phan, K. L. (2003). Brain-imaging studies of posttraumatic stress disorder. *CNS.Spectrums, 8,* 641–650.

Liberzon, I., Taylor, S. F., Fig, L. M., & Koeppe, R. A. (1996). Alteration of corticothalamic perfusion ratios during a PTSD flashback. *Depression and Anxiety, 4,* 146–150.

Lichtenberg, J. D. (1990). On motivational systems. *Journal of the American Psychoanalytic Association, 38*(2), 517–518.

Lichtenberg, J. D., & Kindler, A. R. (1994). A motivational systems approach to the clinical experience. *Journal of the American Psychoanalytic Association, 42,* 405–420.

Lichtenberg, J. D., Lachmann, F., & Fosshage, J. (1992). *Self and motivational systems: Toward a theory of psychoanalytic technique.* Hillsdale, NJ: Analytic Press.

Linehan, M. M. (1993). *Skills training manual for treating borderline personality disorder.* New York: Guilford Press.

Liotti, G. (1992). Disorganized/disoriented attachment in the etiology of the dissociative disorders. *Dissociation, 4,* 196–204.

Liotti, G. (1999a). Disorganization of attachment as a model for understanding dissociative psychopathology. In J. Solomon & C. George (Eds.), *Attachment disorganization* (pp. 297–317). New York: Guilford Press.

Liotti, G. (1995). Disorganized/disoriented attachment in the psychotherapy of dissociative disorders. In S. Goldberg, R. Muir, & J. Kerr (Eds.), *Attachment theory: Social, developmental, and clinical perspectives* (pp. 343–363). Hillsdale, NJ: Analytic Press.

Llinas, R. (2001). *I of the vortex: From neurons to self.* Cambridge, MA: MIT Press.

Llinas, R., Ribary, U., Contreras, D., & Pedroarena, C. (1998). The neuronal basis for consciousness. *Philosophical Transactions of the Royal Society of London, Series B, Biological Sciences, 353,* 1841–1849.

Lockhart, S., Craik, F., & Jacoby, L. (1976). Depth of processing, recognition and recall. In L. Brown (Ed.), *Recall and recognition* (pp. 75–102). New York: Wiley.

Lowen, A. (1970). *Pleasure: A creative approach to life.* Baltimore: Penquin Books.

Lowen, A. (1975). *Bioenergetics.* New York: Penquin Books.

Luria, A. (1980). *Higher cortical functions in man* (Rev. ed.). New York: Basic Books.

Luxenberg, T., Spinazzola, J., Hidalgo, J., Hunt, C., & van der Kolk, B. A. (2001). Complex trauma and disorders of extreme stress (DESNOS), part two: Treatment. *Directions in Psychiatry, 21,* 395–414.

Luxenberg, T., Spinazzola, J., & van der Kolk, B. A. (2001). Complex trauma and disorders of extreme stress (DESNOS) diagnosis, part one: Assessment. *Directions in Psychiatry, 21,* 363–392.

Lyons-Ruth, K. (2001). The two-person construction of defense: Disorganized attachment strategies, unintegrated mental states, and hostile/helpless relationsal processes. *Psychologist Psychoanalyst, 21,* 40–45.

Lyons-Ruth, K., & Jacobvitz, D. (1999). Attachment disorganization: Unresolved loss, relational violence, and lapses in behavioral and attentional strategies. In J. Cassidy & P. Shaver (Eds.), *Handbook of attachment: Theory, research, and clinical applications* (pp. 520–554). New York: Guilford Press.

MacLean, P. D. (1985). Brain evolution relating to family, play, and the separation call. *Archives of General Psychiatry, 42*(4), 405–417.

MacLean, P. D. (1990). *The triune brain in evolution.* New York: Plenum Press.

Mahler, M. S., & M. Furer (1968). *On human symbiosis and the vicissitudes of individualtion.* New York: International Universities Press.

Main, M. (1995). Recent studies in attachment: Overview, with selected implications for clinical work. In S. Goldberg, R. Muir, & J. Kerr (Eds.), *Attachment theory: Social, developmental, and clinical perspectives* (pp. 407–474). Hillsdale, NJ: Analytic Press.

Main, M., & Hesse, E. (1990). Parents' unresolved traumatic experiences are related to infant disorganized attachment status: Is frightened and/or frightening parental behavior the linking mechanism? In M. Greenberg, D. Cicchetti, & E. Cummings (Eds.), *Attachment in the preschool years: Theory, research, and intervention* (pp. 161–182). Chicago: University of Chicago Press.

Main, M., & Morgan, H. (1996). Disorganization and disorientation in infant strange situation behavior: Phenotypic resemblance to dissociative states? In L. Michelson & W. Ray (Eds.), *Handbook of dissociation* (pp. 107–138). New York: Plenum Press.

Main, M., & Solomon, J. (1986). Discovery of a new, insecure-disorganized/disoriented attachment pattern. In T. Brazelton & M. Yogman (Eds.), *Affective development in infancy* (pp. 95–124). Norwood, NJ: Ablex.

Main, M., & Solomon, J. (1990). Procedures for identifying infants as disorganized/disorientated during the Ainsworth Strange Situation. In M.Greenberg, D. Cicchetti, & E. Cummings (Eds.), *Attachment in the preschool years: Theory, research, and intervention* (pp. 121–160). Chicago: University of Chicago Press.

Maldonado, J. R., & Spiegel, D. (2002). Dissociative disorders. In T. J. Talbot & S. Yudosky (Eds.), *Textbook of psychiatry, fourth edition* (pp. 709–742). Washington, DC: American Psychiatric Association.

Maldonado, J., Butler, L., & Spiegel, D. (2002). Treatments for dissociative disorders. In P. Nathan & J. Gorman (Eds.), *A guide to treatments that work* (pp. 463–496). New York: Oxford University Press.

Markowitsch, H. J., Kessler, J., Weber-Luxenburger, G., Van Der Ven, C., Albers, M., & Heiss, W. D. (2000). Neuroimaging and behavioral correlates of recovery from amnestic block syndrome and other cognitive deteriorations. *Neuropsychiatry, Neuropsychology, and Behavioral Neurology, 13*, 60–66.

Marks, I., Lovell, K., Noshirvani, H., Livanou, M., & Thrasher, S. (1998). Treatment of posttraumatic stress disorder by exposure and/or cognitive restructuring: A controlled study. *Archives of General Psychiatry, 55*, 317–325.

Martin, L. J., Spicer, D. M., Lewis, M. H., Gluck, J. P., & Cork, L. C. (1991). Social deprivation of infant rhesus monkeys alters the chemoarchitecture of the brain: I. Subcortical regions. *Journal of Neuroscience, 11*, 3344–3358.

Marvin, R., & Britner, P. (1999). Normative development: The ontogeny of attachment. In J. Cassidy & P. Shaver (Eds.), *Handbood of attachment: Theory, research, and clinical applications* (pp. 44–67). New York: Guilford Press.

Maslow, A. (1970). *Motivation and personality* (Rev. ed.). New York: Harper & Row.

Maturana, H., & Varela, F. (1987). *The tree of knowledge: The biological roots of human understanding.* Boston: Shambhala.

McCann, I., & Pearlman, L. (1990). *Psychological trauma and the adult survivor: Theory, therapy, and transformation* (vol. 21). New York: Brunner/Mazel.

McDonagh-Coyle, A., Friedman, M., McHugo, G., Ford, J. D., Mueser, K., Descamps, M., Demment, C., & Fournier, D. (2001). Psychometric outcomes of a randomized clinical trial of psychotherapies for PTSD-SA. *Proceedings of the Annual Convention of the International Society for Traumatic Stress Studies, 17,* 45.

McEwan, B. (1995). Adrenal steroid actions of brain: Dissecting the fine line between protection and damage. In D. Friedman, D. S. Charney, & A. Y. Deutch (Eds.), *Neurobiological and clinical consequences of stress: From normal adaptation to posttraumatic stress disorder* (pp. 135–147). New York: Lipponcott-Raven.

McFarlane, A. C., Weber, D. L., & Clark, C. R. (1993). Abnormal stimulus processing in posttraumatic stress disorder. *Biological Psychiatry, 34,* 311–320.

MacNaughton, I. (2004). *Body, breath, and consciousness: A somatic anthology.* Berkeley, CA: North Atlantic Press.

Migdow, J. (2003). The problem with pleasure. *Journal of Trauma and Dissociation, 4,* 5–25.

Misslin, R. (2003). The defense system of fear: Behavior and neurocircuitry. *Clinical Neurophysiology, 33*(2), 55–66.

Morgan, M. A., Romanski, L. M., & LeDoux, J. E. (1993). Extinction of emotional learning: Contribution of medial prefrontal cortex. *Neuroscience Letters, 163*(1), 109–113.

Moscovitch, M., & Winocur, G. (2002). The frontal cortex and working with memory. In D. Stuss & R. Knight (Eds.), *Principles of frontal lobe function* (pp. 188–209). New York: Oxford University Press.

Mujica-Parodi, L., Greenberg, T., & Kilpatrick, J. (2004). *A multi-modal study of cognitive processing under negative emotional arousal.* Cognitive Science Society. Retrieved August 29, 2005, from www.cogsci.northwestern.edu/cogsci2004/papers/papers416.pdf

Murray, H. (1999). Explorations in personality. In J. Cassidy & P. Shaver (Eds.), *Handbook of attachment: Theory, research, and clinical applications* (pp. 3–20). New York: Guilford Press.

Myers, C. (1940). *Shell shock in France 1914–1918.* Cambridge, UK: Cambridge University Press.

Naranjo, C. (1993). *Gestalt therapy: The attitude and practice of a theoretical experientialism.* Nevada City, CA: Gateways.

National Collaborating Centre for Mental Health (2005). *Post-traumatic stress disorder (PTSD): The management of PTSD in adults and children in primary and secondary care.* National Institute for Clinical Excellence. Retrieved July 4, 2004, from www.nice.org.uk/pdf/c.G026niceguideline.pdf

Nijenhuis, E., & Van der Hart, O. (1999a). Somatoform dissociative phenomena: A Janetian perspective. In J. Goodwin & R. Attias (Eds.), *Splintered reflections: Images of the body in trauma* (pp. 89–127). New York: Basic Books.

Nijenhuis, E., & Van der Hart, O. (1999b). Forgetting and reexperiencing trauma: From anesthesia to pain. In J. Goodwin & R. Attias (Eds.), *Splintered reflections: Images of the body in trauma* (pp. 33–65). New York: Basic Books.

Nijenhuis, E., Van der Hart, O., & Steele, K. (2002). The emerging psychobiology of trauma-related dissociation and dissociative disorders. In H. D'Haenen,

J. DenBoer, & P. Willner (Eds.), *Biological psychiatry* (pp. 1079–1098). London: Wiley.

Nijenhuis, E., Van der Hart, O., & Steele, K. (2004). *Trauma-related structural dissociation of the personality.* Retrieved June 8, 2005, from www.trauma-pages .com/nijenhuis-2004.htm

Nijenhuis, E., Vanderlinden, J., & Spinhoven, P. (1998). Animal defensive reactions as a model for trauma-induced dissociative reactions. *Journal of Traumatic Stress, 11,* 243–260.

Nijenhuis, E., Van Dyck, R., Spinhoven, P., Van der Hart, O., Chatrou, M., Vanderlinden, J., et al. (1999). Somatoform dissociation discriminates among diagnostic categories over and above general psychopathology. *Australian and New Zealand Journal of Psychiatry, 33,* 511–520.

Ogawa, J. R., Sroufe, L. A., Weinfield, N. S., Carlson, E. A., & Egeland, B. (1997). Development and the fragmented self: Longitudinal study of dissociative symptomatology in a nonclinical sample. *Developmental Psychopathology, 9,* 855–879.

Ogden, P., & Minton, K. (2000). Sensorimotor psychotherapy: One method for processing traumatic memory. *Traumatology, 6*(3), 1–20.

Panksepp, J. (1998). *Affective neuroscience: The foundations of human and animal emotions.* New York: Oxford University Press.

Pavlov, I. (1927). *Conditioned reflexes: An investigation of the physiological activity of the cerebral cortex.* London: Oxford University Press.

Pearlman, L., & Saakvitne, K. (1995). *Trauma and the therapist: Countertransference and vicarious traumatization in psychotherapy with incest survivors.* New York: Norton.

Perls, F., Hefferline, R., & Goodman, P. (1951). *Gestalt therapy: Excitement and growth in the human personality.* New York: Dell.

Perry, B., Pollard, R., Blakely, T., Baker, W., & Vigilante, D. (1995). Childhood trauma, the neurobiology of adaptation, and "use dependent" development of the brain: How "states" become "traits." *Infant Mental Health Journal, 16,* 271–291.

Phillips, M. (1995). *Healing the divided self: Clinical and Ericksonian hypnotherapy for post-traumatic and dissociative conditions.* New York: Norton.

Piaget, J. (1962). *Play, dreams, and imitation in childhood.* New York: Norton.

Pissiota, A., Frans, O., Fernandez, M., von Knorring, L., Fischer, H., & Fredrikson, M. (2002). Neurofunctional correlates of posttraumatic stress disorder: A PET symptom provocation study. *European Archives of Psychiatry and Clinical Neuroscience, 252,* 68–75.

Pitman, R. K., Altman, B., Greenwald, E., Longpre, R. E., Macklin, M. L., Poire, R. E., et al. (1991). Psychiatric complications during flooding therapy for posttraumatic stress disorder. *Journal of Clinical Psychiatry, 52,* 17–20.

Pitman, R. K., Orr, S. P., Lowenhagen, M. J., Macklin, M. L., & Altman, B. (1991). Pre-Vietnam contents of posttraumatic stress disorder veterans' service medical and personnel records. *Comprehensive Psychiatry, 32,* 416–422.

Pitman, R. K., Orr, S. P., & Shalev, A. Y. (1993). Once bitten, twice shy: Beyond the conditioning model of PTSD. *Biological Psychiatry, 33,* 145–146.

Pitman, R. K., Shin, L. M., & Rauch, S. L. (2001). Investigating the pathogenesis of posttraumatic stress disorder with neuroimaging. *Journal of Clinical Psychiatry, 62*(Suppl. 17), 47–54.

Porges, S. W. (1995). Orienting in a defensive world: Mammalian modifications of our. *Psychophysiology, 32*(4), 301–318.

Porges, S. W. (2001a). The polyvagal theory: Phylogenetic substrates of a social nervous system. *International Journal of Psychophysiology, 42*(2), 123–146.

Porges, S. W. (2001b). Is there a major stress system at the periphery other than the adrenals? In D. M. Broom (Ed.), *Report of the 87th Dahlem Workshop on Coping with Challenge: Welfare in Animals Including Humans* (pp. 135–149). Berlin, November 12–17, 2000. Dahlem University Press: Berlin.

Porges, S. W. (2003a). The Polyvagal theory: Phylogenetic contributions to social behavior. *Physiology & Behavior, 79,* 503–513.

Porges, S. W. (2003b). Social engagement and attachment: A phylogenetic perspective. *Annals of the New York Academy of Sciences, 1008,* 31–47.

Porges, S. W. (2004). Neuroception: A subconscious system for detecting threats and safety. *Zero to Three.* Retrieved August 8, 2005, from bbc.psych.uic.edu/pdf/Neuroception.pdf

Porges, S. W. (2005). The role of social engagement in attachment and bonding: A phylogenetic perspective. In C. S. Carter, L. Ahnert, K. E. Grossmann, S. B. Hardy, M. E. Lamb, S. W. Porges, & N. Sachser (Eds.), *Attachment and bonding: A new synthesis* (pp. 33–54). Cambridge, MA: The MIT Press.

Portas, C. M., Rees, G., Howseman, A. M., Josephs, O., Turner, R., & Frith, C. D. (1998). A specific role for the thalamus in mediating the interaction of attention and arousal in humans. *Journal of Neuroscience, 18,* 8979–8989.

Posner, M. I. (1980). Orienting of attention. *Quarterly Journal of Experimental Psychology, 32*(1) 3–25.

Posner, M. I., DiGirolamo, G. J., & Fernandez-Duque, D. (1997). Brain mechanisms of cognitive skills. *Consciousness and Cognition, 6,* 267–290.

Posner, M. I., & Petersen, S. E. (1990). The attention system of the human brain. *Annual Review of Neuroscience, 13,* 25–42.

Posner, M. I., & Raichle, M. (1994). *Images of mind.* New York: Scientific American Library.

Posner, M. I., Walker, J. A., Friedrich, F. J., & Rafal, R. D. (1984). Effects of parietal injury on covert orienting of attention. *Journal of Neuroscience, 4,* 1863–1874.

Post, R., Weiss, S., Smith, M., Li, H., & McCann, U. (1997). Kindling versus quenching: Implications for the evolution and treatment of posttraumatic stress disorder. In R.Yehuda & A. C. McFarlane (Eds.), *Psychobiology of posttraumatic stress disorder* (pp. 285–295). New York: New York Acadamy of Sciences.

Putnam, F. (2000, March). Developmental pathways following sexual abuse in girls. Presentation at the conference, "Psychological Trauma: Maturational Processes and Therapeutic Interventions." Boston, MA.

Raine, N. (1998). *After silence: Rape and my journey back.* New York: Crown.

Ratey, J. (2002). *A user's guide to the brain: Perception, attention, and the four theaters of the brain.* New York: Vintage Books.

Rauch, S. L., van der Kolk, B. A., Fisler, R. E., Alpert, N. M., Orr, S. P., Savage, C. R., et al. (1996). A symptom provocation study of posttraumatic stress disorder using positron emission tomography and script-driven imagery. *Archives of General Psychiatry, 53,* 380–387.

Reich, W. (1972). *Character analysis.* New York: Farrar, Straus & Giroux. (Original work published 1945)

Reiman, E., Lane, R. D., Ahern, G., Schwartz, G., & Davidson, R. (2000). Positron emission tomography in the study of emotion, anxiety, and anxiety disorders. In R. D. Lane & L. Nadel (Eds.), *Cognitive neuroscience of emotion* (pp. 389–406). New York: Oxford University Press.

Remarque, E. (1982). *All quiet on the Western front* (A. W. Ween, Trans.). New York: Ballantine Books. (Original work published 1929).

Resnick, S. (1997). *The pleasure zone: Why we resist good feelings and how to let go and be happy.* Berkeley, CA: Conari Press.

Rieker, P. P., & Carmen, E. H. (1986). The victim-to-patient process: The disconfirmation and transformation of abuse. *American Journal of Orthopsychiatry, 56,* 360–370.

Rivers, W. (1920). *Instinct and the unconscious: A contribution to a biological theory of the psycho-neuroses.* Cambridge: Cambridge University Press.

Rizzolatti, G. & Craighero, L. (2004). The mirror-neuron system. *Annual Review of Neuroscience, 27,* 169–192.

Rizzolatti, G., Fadiga, L., Gallese, V., & Fogassi, L. (1996). Premotor cortex and the recognition of motor actions. *Cognitive Brain Research, 3,* 131–141.

Rosenberg, J., Rand, M., & Asay, D. (1989). *Body, self, and soul: Sustaining integration.* Atlanta, GA: Humanics Limited.

Rossi, E. (1993). *The psychobiology of mind-body healing: New concepts of therapeutic hypnosis* (2nd ed.). New York: Norton.

Rothschild, B. (2000). *The body remembers: The psychophysiology of trauma and trauma treatment.* New York: Norton.

Sable, P. (2000). *Attachment and adult psychotherapy.* Northville, NJ: Jason Aronson.

Sahar, T., Shalev, A. Y., & Porges, S. W. (2001). Vagal modulation of responses to mental challenge in posttraumatic stress disorder. *Biological Psychiatry, 49,* 637–643.

Sapolsky, R. (1994). Why zebras don't get ulcers: A guide to stress, stress-related diseases, and coping. New York: Freeman.

Scaer, R. C. (2001). The neurophysiology of dissociation and chronic disease. *Applied Psychophysiology and Biofeedback, 26*(1), 73–91.

Schachtel, E. (1947). On memory and childhood amnesia. *Psychiatry, 10,* 1–26.

Schacter, D. L. (1996). *Searching for memory: The brain, the mind, and the past.* New York: Basic Books.

Schiffer, F., Teicher, M. H., & Papanicolaou, A. C. (1995). Evoked potential evidence for right brain activity during the recall of traumatic memories. *Journal of Neuropsychiatry and Clinical Neuroscience, 7,* 169–175.

Schnarch, D. (1991). *Constructing the sexual crucible: An integration of sexual and marital therapy.* New York: Norton.

Schnider, A., Ptak, R., von Daniken, C., & Remonda, L. (2000). Recovery from spontaneous confabulations parallels recovery of temporal confusion in memory. *Neurology, 55,* 74–83.

Schore, A. (1994). *Affect regulation and the origin of the self: The neurobiology of emotional development.* Hillsdale: Erlbaum.

Schore, A. (2001a). The effects of early relational trauma on right brain development, affect regulation, and infant mental health. *Infant Mental Health Journal, 22,* 201–269.

Schore, A. (2001b). The right brain as the neurobiological substratum of Freud's dynamic unconscious. In D. Scharff & J. Scharff (Eds.), *Freud at the millennium: The evolution and application of psychoanalysis.* pp. 61–88. New York: Other Press.

Schore, A. (2003a). *Affect dysregulation and disorders of the self.* New York: Norton.

Schore, A. (2003b). *Affect regulation and the repair of the self.* New York: Norton.

Schore, A. (submitted). Attachment trauma and the developing right brain: Origins of pathological dissociation. In P. Dell (Ed.), *Dissociation and the dissociative disorders: DSM-V and Beyond.* Manuscript submitted for publication.

Schwartz, H. (1994). From dissociation to negotiation: A relational psychoanalytic perspective on multiple personality disorder. *Psychoanalytic Psychology, 11,* 189–231.

Scott, M. J., & Stradling, S. G. (1997). Client compliance with exposure treatments for posttraumatic stress disorder. *Journal of Traumatic Stress, 10,* 523–526.

Segal, Z. V., Williams, J. G. G., & Teasdale, J. D. (2002). *Mindfulness-based cognitive therapy for depression: A new approach to preventing relapse.* New York: Guilford Press.

Seligman, M. E. P. (1975). *Helplessness: On depression, development, and death.* San Francisco: Freeman.

Sereno, A. (2005). *Neural substrates of attention and orienting.* Retrieved May 8, 2005, from research.uth.tmc.edu/nih/Sereno2.htm

Servan-Schreiber, D. (2003). *The instinct to heal: Curing depression, anxiety, and stress without drugs and without talk therapy.* New York: Rodale.

Shalev, A. Y. (2001). *Biological responses to disasters.* American Psychiatric Association. Retrieved May 17, 2005, from www.psych.org/disasterpsych/sl/biological responses.cfm

Shalev, A. Y. (2005). *Biological responses to disasters.* American Psychiatric Association. Retrieved August 10, 2005, from www.psych.org/disasterpsych/sl/biologicalresponses.cfm

Shalev, A. Y., Orr, S. P., Peri, T., Schreiber, S., & Pitman, R. K. (1992). Physiologic responses to loud tones in Israeli patients with posttraumatic stress disorder. *Archives of General Psychiatry, 49,* 870–875.

Shalev, A. Y., & Rogel-Fuchs, Y. (1993). Psychophysiology of the posttraumatic stress disorder: From sulfur fumes to behavioral genetics. *Psychosomatic Medicine, 55,* 413–423.

Shin, L. M., Shin, P. S., Heckers, S., Krangel, T. S., Macklin, M. L., Orr, S. P., et al. (2004). Hippocampal function in posttraumatic stress disorder. *Hippocampus, 14,* 292–300.

Siegel, D. (1995). Memory, trauma, and psychotherapy: A cognitive science view. *Journal of Psychotherapy Practice & Research, 4*(2), 93–122.

Siegel, D. (1996). Memory, trauma, and psychotherapy: A cognitive science view. *Journal of Psychotherapy Practice and Research, 4*(2), 93–122.

Siegel, D. (1999). *The developing mind.* New York: Guilford Press.

Siegel, D. (2001). Toward an interpersonal neurobiology of the developing mind: Attachment relationships, "mindsight," and neural integration. *Infant Mental Health Journal, 22*(1), 67–94.

Siegel, D. (2003). An interpersonal neurobiology of psychotherapy: The developing mind and the resolution of trauma. In M. Solomon & D. Siegel (Eds.), *Healing trauma: Attachment, mind, body, and brain* (pp. 1–5). New York: Norton.

Siegel, D. (2006). An interpersonal neurobiology approach to psychotherapy: Awareness, mirror neurons, and well-being. *Psychiatric Annals, 36*(4), 248–256.

Siegel, D. (2007). *The mindful brain in human development.* New York: Norton.

Sifneos, P. (1973). The prevalence of "alexithymic" characteristics in psychosomatic patients. *Psychotherapy and Psychomatics, 22,* 255–262.

Sifneos, P. (1996). Alexithymia: Past and present. *American Journal of Psychiatry, 153,* 137–142.

Simpson, J. (1999). Attachment theory in modern evolutionary perspective. In

J. Cassidy & P. Shaver (Eds.), *Handbook of attachment: Theory, research, and clinical applications* (pp. 115–140). New York: Guilford Press.

Sinclair, H. (2001). Movement and action transform trauma. Paper presented at "Psychological Trauma: Maturational Process and Therapeutic Intervention." Boston, MA.

Siviy, S. (1998). Neurobiological substrates of play behavior: Glimpses into the structure and function of mammalian playfulness. In M. Beckoff & J. Byers (Eds.), *Animal play: Evolutionary, comparative, and ecological perspectives* (pp. 221–242). Cambridge, UK: Cambridge University Press.

Slade, A. (1999). Attachment theory and research. In J. Cassidy & P. R. Shaver (Eds.), *Handbook of attachment: Theory, research, and clinical applications* (pp. 575–594). New York: Guilford Press.

Smith, E. (1985). *The body in psychotherapy*. Jefferson, NC: McFarland.

Sokolov, E. (1960). Neuronal models and orienting reflex. In M. Brazier (Ed.), *The central nervous system and behavior* (pp. 87–276). Madison, NJ: Madison Printing.

Sokolov, E. (1969). The modeling properties of the nervous system. In M. Cole & I. Maltzman (Eds.), *A handbook of contemporary Soviet psychology* (pp. 671–704). New York: Basis Books.

Sokolov, E., Spinks, J., Naatanen, R., & Heikki, L. (2002). *The orienting response in information processing*. Mahwah, NJ: Erlbaum.

Sokolov, Y. (1963). *Perception and the conditioned reflex*. Oxford, UK: Pergammon Press.

Sollier, P. (1897). *Genèse et nature de l'hystérie, recherches cliniques et expérimentales de psycho-physiologie* [*Clinical and experimental studies in psychophysiology*]. Paris: F. Alcan.

Sperry, R. W. (1952). Neurobiology and the mind-brain problem. *American Scientist, 40*(2), 291–312.

Sperry, R. W., Zaidel, E., & Zaidel, D. (1979). Self recognition and social awareness in the deconnected minor hemisphere. *Neuropsychologia, 17*, 153–166.

Spiegel, D. (1981). Man as timekeeper. *American Journal of Psychoanalysis, 41*, 5–14.

Spiegel, D. (1990). Trauma, dissociation, and hypnosis. In R. Kluft (Ed.), *Incest-related syndromes of adult psychopathology* (pp. 247–261). Washington, DC: American Psychiatric Association.

Spiegel, D. (1997). Trauma, dissociation, and memory. *Annals of the New York Academy of Sciences, 821*, 225–237.

Spiegel, D. (2003). Hypnosis and traumatic dissociation: Therapeutic opportunities. *Journal of Traumatic Dissociation, 4*(3), 73–90.

Spiegel, D., & Cardena, E. (1991). Disintegrated experience: The dissociative disorders revisited. *Journal of Abnormal Psychology, 100*, 366–378.

Spitz, R. A. (1946). Anaclitic depression. *Psychoanalytic Study of the Child, 2*, 313–342.

Sroufe, L. A. (1997). Psychopathology as an outcome of development. *Developmental Psychopathology, 9*, 251–268.

Stark, M. (1999). *Modes of therapeutic action: Enhancement of knowledge, provision of experience, and engagement in relationship*. United States: Inson Aronson Inc.

Steele, K., Dorahy, M., Van der Hart, O., & Nijenhuis, E. (submitted). *Dissociation versus alterations in consciousness: Related but different concepts*. Manuscript submitted for publication.

Steele, K., & Van der Hart, O. (2001). The integration of traumatic memories versus abreaction: Clarification of terminology. *Newsletter of the International Society for the Study of Dissociation.* Retrieved Mar 9, 2002, from www.atlantapsychotherapy.com/articles/vanderhart.htm

Steele, K., Van der Hart, O., & Nijenhuis, E. (2001). Dependency in the treatment of complex posttraumatic stress disorder and dissociative disorders. *Journal of Trauma and Dissociation, 2,* 79–116.

Steele, K., Van der Hart, O., & Nijenhuis, E. (2005b). Phase-oriented treatment of structural dissociation in complex traumatization: Overcoming trauma-related phobias. *Journal of Trauma and Dissociation, 6*(3), 11–53.

Steele, K., Van der Hart, O., & Nijenhuis, E. (2004). [Phase oriented treatment of complex dissociative disorders: Overcoming trauma-related phobias]. In A.Eckhart-Henn & S. Hoffman (Eds.), [*Dissociative disorders of consciousness: Theory, symptoms, therapy*] (pp. 357–394). Stuttgard/New York: Schattauer.

Steele, M. (2003). Attachment, actual experience, and mental representation. In V. Green (Ed.) *Emotional development in psychoanalysis attachment theory and neuroscience: Creating connections* (pp. 87–107). New York: Brunner-Routledge Hove.

Stern, D. (1985). *The interpersonal world of the infant: A view from psychoanalysis and developmental psychology.* New York: Basic Books.

Stern, D. (1998). The process of therapeutic change involving implicit knowledge: Some implications of developmental observations for adult psychotherapy. *Infant Mental Health Journal, 19,* 300–308.

Stern, D. (2004). *The present moment in psychotherapy and everyday life.* New York: Norton.

Stien, P., & Kendall, J. (2004). *Psychological trauma and the developing brain: Neurologically based interventions for troubled children.* New York: Hawthorn Maltreatment and Trauma Press.

Sumova, A., & Jakoubek, B. (1989). Analgesia and impact induced by anticipation stress: Involvement of the endogenous opioid peptide system. *Brain Research, 503,* 273–280.

Tanev, K. (2003). Neuroimaging and neurocircuitry in post-traumatic stress disorder: What is currently known? *Current Psychiatry Reports, 5,* 369–383.

Tarrier, N. (2001). What can be learned from clinical trials? *Journal of Consulting and Clinical Psychology, 69,* 117–118.

Tarrier, N., Sommerfield, C., Pilgrim, H., & Humphreys, L. (1999). Cognitive therapy or imaginal exposure in the treatment of post-traumatic stress disorder: Twelve-month follow-up. *British Journal of Psychiatry, 175,* 571–575.

Taylor, G., Bagby, R., & Parker, J. (1997). *Disorders of affect regulation: Alexithymia in medical and psychiatric illness.* Cambridge, UK: Cambridge University Press.

Taylor, S., Koch, K., & McNally, R. (1992). How does anxiety sensitivity vary across the anxiety disorders? *Journal of Anxiety Disorders, 6,* 249–259.

Teicher, M. H., Ito, Y., Glod, C., Anderson, N., & Ackerman, E. (1997). Preliminary evidence for abnormal cortical development in physically and sexually abused children using EEG coherence and MRI. In R. Yehuda & A. McFarlane (Eds.), *Psychobiology of posttraumatic stress disorder* (pp. 160–175). New York: New York Academy of Sciences.

Thakkar, R. R., & McCanne, T. R. (2000). The effects of daily stressors on physical health in women with and without a childhood history of sexual abuse. *Child Abuse and Neglect, 24,* 209–221.

Timko, C., & Janoff-Bulman, R. (1985). Attributions, vulnerability, and psychological adjustment: The case of breast cancer. *Health Psychology, 4,* 521–544.

Todd, M. (1959). *The thinking body.* Brooklyn, NY: Dance Horizons.

Tortora, G., & Anagnostakos, N. (1990). *Principles of anatomy and physiology.* New York: Harper Collins.

Trevarthen, C. (1979). Communication and cooperation in early infancy: A discription of primary intersubjectivity. In M. M. Bullowa (Ed.), *Before speech: The beginning of interpersonal communication.* New York: Cambridge University Press.

Tronick, E. Z. (1989). Emotions and emotional communication in infants. *American Psychologist, 44*: 112–119.

Tronick, E. Z. (1998). Dyadically expanded states of consciousness and the process of therapeutic change. *Infant Mental Health Journal, 19*, 290–299.

Tulving, E., Kapur, S., Craik, F. I., Moscovitch, M., & Houle, S. (1994). Hemispheric encoding/retrieval asymmetry in episodic memory: Positron emission tomography findings. *Proceedings of the National Academy of Sciences U.S.A., 91*, 2016–2020.

Ursano, R. J., Bell, C., Eth, S., Friedman, M., Norwood, A., Pfefferbaum, B., et al. (2004). Practice guidelines for the treatment of patients with acute stress disorder and posttraumatic stress disorder. *American Journal of Psychiatry, 161*, 3–31.

Van der Hart, O., & Brown, P. (1992). Abreaction re-evaluated. *Dissociation, 3(5)*, 127–140.

Van der Hart, O., Nijenhuis, E., & Steele, K. (2006). *The haunted self: Structural dissociation and the treatment of chronic traumatization.* New York: Norton.

Van der Hart, O., Nijenhuis, E., & Steele, K. (2005a). Dissociation: An insufficiently recognized major feature of complex PTSD. *Journal of Traumatic Stress, 18*, 413–424.

Van der Hart, O., & Op den Velde, W. (2003). Traumatische herinneringen [Traumatic memories]. In O. Van der Hart (Ed.), *Trauma, dissociatie en hypnose* [Trauma, dissociation, and hypnosis] (pp. 83–105). Lisse, The Netherlands: Swets & Zeitlinger.

Van der Hart, O., Nijenhuis, E. R. S., Steele, K., & Brown, D. (2004). Trauma-related dissociation: Conceptual clarity lost and found. *Australian and New Zealand Journal of Psychiatry, 38*, 906–914.

Van der Hart, O., & Steele, K. (1997). Time distortions in dissociative identity disorder: Janetian concepts and treatment. *Dissociation, 10*, 91–103.

Van der Hart, O., Steele, K., Boon, S., & Brown, P. (1993). The treatment of traumatic memories: Synthesis, realization, and integration. *Dissociation, 2(6)*, 162–180.

Van der Hart, O., Van Dijke, A., Van Son, M., & Steele, K. (2000). Somatoform dissociation in traumatized World War I combat soldiers: A neglected clinical heritage. *Journal of Trauma and Dissociation, 1(4)*, 33–66.

Van der Kolk, B. A. (1987). *Psychological trauma.* Washington, DC: American Psychiatric Association.

Van der Kolk, B. A. (1994). The body keeps the score: Memory and the evolving psychobiology of posttraumatic stress. *Harvard Review of Psychiatry, 1*, 253–265.

Van der Kolk, B. A. (1996a). The complexity of adaptation to trauma: Self-regulation, stimulus discrimination, and characterological development. In B. A. van der Kolk, A. C. MacFarlane, & L. Weisaeth (Eds.), *Traumatic stress: The effects of overwhelming experience on mind, body, and society* (pp. 182–213). New York: Guilford Press.

Van der Kolk, B. A. (1996b). Trauma and memory. In B. A. van der Kolk, A. C. MacFarlane, & L. Weisaeth (Eds.), *Traumatic stress: The effects of overwhelming experience on mind, body, and society* (pp. 279–302). New York: Guilford Press.

Van der Kolk, B. A. (2002). *Beyond the talking cure: Somatic experience and sub-*

cortical imprints in the treatment of trauma in Francine Shapiro's EMDR: Promises for a paradigm shift. Washington, DC: American Psychological Association.

Van der Kolk, B. A., & Ducey, C. (1989). The psychological processing of traumatic experience: Rorschach patterns in PTSD. *Journal of Traumatic Stress, 2,* 259–274.

Van der Kolk, B. A., & Fisler, R. (1995). Dissociation and the fragmentary nature of traumatic memories: Overview and exploratory study. *Journal of Traumatic Stress, 8,* 505–525.

Van der Kolk, B. A., Greenburg, M., Boyd, H., & Krystal, J. (1985). Inescapable shock, neurotransmitters, and addiction to trauma: Toward a psychobiology of posttraumatic stress. *Biological Psychiatry, 20,* 314–325.

Van der Kolk, B. A., McFarlane, A. C., & Van der Hart, O. (1996). A general approach to treatment of posttraumatic stress disorder. In B. A. van der Kolk, A. C. McFarlane, & L. Weisaeth (Eds.), *Traumatic stress: The effects of overwhelming stress on mind, body, and society* (pp. 417–440). New York: Guilford Press.

Van der Kolk, B. A., McFarlane, A. C., & Weisaeth, L. (1996). *Traumatic stress: The effects of overwhelming experience on mind, body, and society.* New York: Guilford Press.

Van der Kolk, B. A., & Van der Hart, O. (1989). Pierre Janet and the breakdown of adaptation in psychological trauma. *American Journal of Psychiatry, 146,* 1530–1540.

Van der Kolk, B. A., & Van der Hart, O. (1991). The intrusive past: The flexibility of memory and the engraving of trauma. *American Imago, 48,* 425–445.

Van der Kolk, B., Van der Hart, O., & Marmar, C. (1996). Dissociation and information processing in posttraumatic stress disorder. In B. A. van der Kolk, A. C. McFarlane, & L. Weisaeth (Eds.), *Traumatic stress: The effects of overwhelming experience on mind, body, and society* (pp. 303–327). New York: Guilford Press.

Van Ijzendoorn, M., Schuengel, C., & Bakermans-Kranenburg, M. (1999). Disorganized attachment in early childhood: Meta-analysis of precursors, concomitants, and sequelae. *Development and Psychopathology, 11,* 225–249.

Van Olst, E. (1971). *The orienting reflex.* Paris: Mouton & Company.

Veronin, L., Luria, A., Sokolov, E., & Vinogradova, O. (1965). *Orienting reflex and exploratory behavior.* Baltimore: Caramond/Pridemark Press.

Vogt, B. A. (2005). Pain and emotion interactions in subregions of the cingulated gyrus. *National Review of Neuroscience 7,* 533–544.

Vogt, B., & Gabriel, M. (1993). *Neurobiology of cingulate cortex and limbic thalamus: A comprehensive handbook.* Boston: Birkhauser.

Watson, D. (2000). *Mood and temperament.* New York: Guilford Press.

Weinfield, N. S., Stroufe, L., Egeland, B., & Carlson, E. (1999). The nature of individual differences in infant–caregiver attachment. In J. Cassidy & P. Shaver (Eds.), *Handbook of attachment: Theory, research, and clinical application* (pp. 68–88). New York: Guilford Press.

Wenger, M., & Cullen, T. (1958). ANS response patterns to fourteen stimuli. *American Psychologist, 13,* 413–414.

Wilbarger, P., & Wilbarger, J. (1997). *Sensory defensiveness and related social/ emotional and neurological problems.* Van Nuys, CA: Wilbarger.

Wilbarger, J., & Wilbarger, P. (2002). The Wilbarger approach to treating sensory defensiveness. In A. Bundy, S. Lane, & E. Murray (Eds.), *Sensory integration: Theory and practice* (pp. 235–238). Philadelphia: F. A. Davis Company.

Wilber, K. (1996). *A brief history of everything.* Boston: Shambhala.

Williamson, G., & Anzalone, M. (2001). *Sensory integration and self-regulation in infants and toddlers: Helping young children to interact with their environments.* Washington, DC: Zero to Three.

Winnicott, D. W. (1945). Primitive emotional development. In D. W. Winnicott (Ed.), *Collected papers: Through paediatrics to psycho-analysis* (pp. 145–156). London: Hogarth Press.

Winnicott, D. W. (1971/2005). *Playing and reality* (new revised edition). London and New York: Tavistock Publications.

Winnicott, D. W. (1990). The theory of the parent-child relationship (1960). In *Maturational Processes and the Facilitating Environment* (pp. 37–55). London: Karnac Books.

Yehuda, R. (1997). Sensitizatation of the hypothalamic–pituitary–adrenal axis in posttraumatic stress disorder. In R. Yehuda & A. C. McFarlane (Eds.), *Psychobiology of posttraumatic stress disorder* (pp. 57–75). New York: New York Academy of Sciences.

Yehuda, R. (1998). Neuroendocrinology of trauma and posttraumatic stress disorder. In R. Yehuda (Ed.), *Psychological trauma* (pp. 97–131). Washington, DC: American Psychiatric Association.

Subject Index

Page numbers in *italics* refer to illustrations

abreaction, 240, 241, 261
abuse, xxiii, 32, 96, 99, 175, 184, 222, 281, 292; by caregivers, 36–38, 51–52, 53, 57, 112, 154, 177, 228, 229, 276, 287, 298; domestic violence, xxiii, 157; political torture, 203, 297; psychological, 144–45; in recuperative stage, 102; sexual, 20–21, 39, 62–64, 68, 87, 97, 100–102, 105, 121, 136, 202, 203, 231–32, 241, 254–56, 260, 264–65, 270, 289, 294; *see also* immobilizing defensive strategies
accident victims, 20, 38–39, 67, 158–60, 176, 245–46, 256–57
action potential, 258
action systems, 106, 108–38, 186; body and, 129–31; combinations of, 110; dissociation and, 133–38; emotions associated with, 110, 116, 129–30; goals of, 109–10, 111, 129–30; hierarchical interaction among, 122–25; insistent engagement with, 275; integrative capacity and, 110, 131–33, 137, 138; in Phase 3 treatment, 268, 272, 275, 284, 293, 294–95, 299; physical actions of, 129–31; physical sensations linked to, 129; pleasure and, 294–95; terms for, 109; *see also* defensive action systems and responses; *specific action systems*

action tendencies, xxvi, 21–23, 26, 37, 38, 39, 40, 62, 108, 126–38, 146, 189, 248, 252, 275; approach vs. avoidance behavior in, 130–31; of attachment patterns, 47; body and, 129–31; brain and, 22; defensive, 85–87, 106–7, 112, 113, 115, 170–72, 208, 284, 296; definition of, xix, 21, 22; emotions associated with, xix–xx; hypoarousal and, 35; and information processing, 19, 20, 21–23; learned, 92; levels of, 131–33; maladaptive, xxvi, 22–23, 167, 235, 269; prediction of outcome in, 127–29, 131; reflexive, 270, 290–93; in treatment, 132–33, 137–38, 157, 166, 168, 173, 185, 194, 195, 196–97, 204, 216
acts of triumph, 187, 247–60, 266, 272; distinguishing trauma-based emotions from sensation in, 251, 253–54; executing involuntary, 253–60; *see also* sensorimotor sequencing; executing voluntary, 249–50, 258; story as means to an end in, 252–53
adaptation, 108–38; *see also* action systems; action tendencies
affect synchrony, 45
Ainsworth, M., 114

327

Author Index

Ellis, B. I., 4
Emde, R., 45
Eth, S., xxix

Fadiga, L., 213–14
Fang, V. S., 87
Fanselow, M., 88, 89, 91, 93, 94, 98, 101,
    102, 109, 111
Fawcus, S. R., 57, 97
Feldstein, S., 44, 53
Fernandez, M., 155
Fernandez-Duque, D., 73
Fig, L. M., 141, 147
Figley, C., 180
Fink, G. R., 149–50
Fischer, H., 155
Fisher, A., 6, 15, 66, 173
Fisher, J., xxxi–xxxii, 139–61
Fisler, R., 143
Fisler, R. E., 145
Foa, E. B., xxix, 4
Fogassi, L., 213–14
Fonagy, P., 22–23, 41, 44, 47, 284
Ford, J. D., 4
Fosha, D., 271
Fosshage, J., 109
Fournier, D., 4
Fox, N., 49
Frankl, V., 301
Frans, O., 155
Fraser, S., 136
Frawley, M., 178, 181
Fredrikson, M., 155
Freud, S., 245, 261
Friedman, M., xxix, 4
Friedrich, F. J., 66
Frijda, N., 12, 20, 22, 31, 35, 79, 80, 82,
    91, 128, 130, 294, 298
Frith, C. D., 141
Fromm, E., 185, 241
Furer, M., 42

Gabriel, M., 149
Gaensbaur, T., 57
Gallese, V., 213–14
Gallup, G. G., Jr., 94
Gati, J. S., 34, 142, 143
Gazzaniga, M. S., 146
Gelb, M., 290
Gendlin, E., 78, 192
Genze, E., 151–52
George, C., 109, 116, 123
Gergely, G., 41, 42, 44, 284
Glod, C., 144–45
Gluck, J. P., 154

Gold, S., 165
Goleman, D., 21, 118
Goodall, J., 118, 119
Goodman, G., 235–36
Goodman, P., 176
Gottlieb, R., 70
Gould, J., 109, 111
Grabowski, T. J., 152, 154–55
Graham, F., 70
Green, V., 285
Greenberg, T., 99
Greenburg, M., xxi
Greene, J., xxix
Greenough, W., 154
Greenwald, E., 12
Grigsby, J., 22, 76, 194, 238–39
Grinker, R., 29
Gross, M. L., 4
Grossman, K., 114, 170
Grossmann, K., 114, 170
Gupta, M., 34, 157

Hammond, D., 185, 268–69, 270, 279, 290,
    296
Han, H., 165, 185
Hannaford, C., 14
Harper, K., 286
Hazan, C., 46, 120, 121
Heckler, R., 3, 287
Hedges, L., 60
Hefferline, R., 176
Heikki, L., 65, 66, 69–70, 71, 72, 74–75,
    77, 78, 237
Heiserman, J. E., 149
Heiss, W. D., 149
Hembree, E. A., xxix
Herman, J., 21, 60, 87, 96, 103, 104, 177,
    178, 185, 208, 222, 268, 269, 271, 279,
    290, 298
Hesse, E., 51
Hiatt, S., 57
Hidalgo, J., 126, 293
Hobson, J., 20, 70, 71, 72, 73, 78, 91, 99
Hofer, M. A., 41, 93
Holtzman, J. D., 146
Hopper, J. W., 158
Horel, J. A., 148
Horowitz, M., 241
Houle, C., 149
Howseman, A. M., 141
Hull, A. M., 147
Humphreys, L., xxix, 4
Hunt, A. R., 72
Hunt, C., 126, 293
Hunter, M., 178, 201